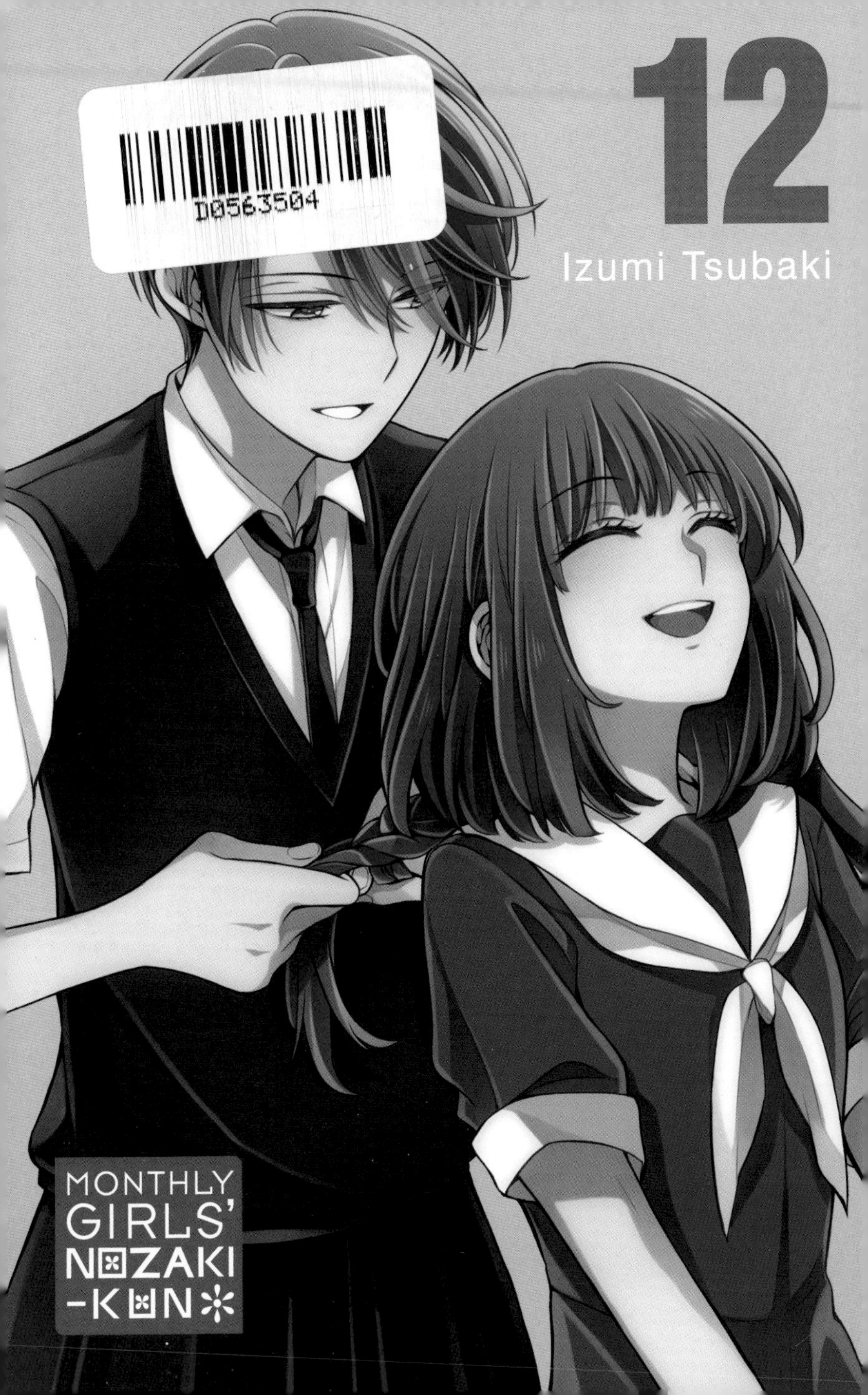

12

Izumi Tsubaki

MONTHLY GIRLS' NOZAKI-KUN

MONTHLY GIRLS' NOZAKI-KUN **12**

contents
✖ ✖ ✖

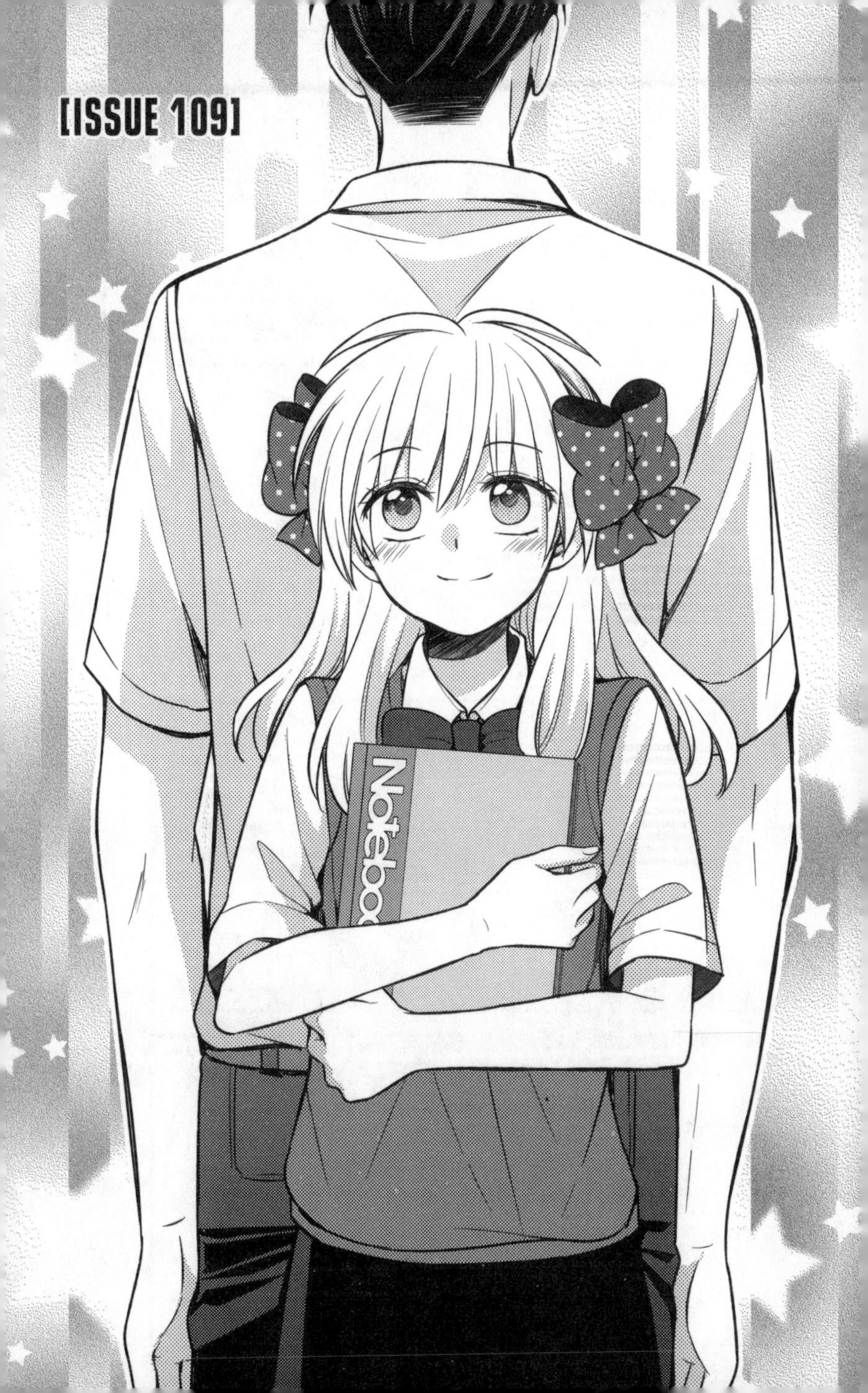
[ISSUE 109]
Noteboo

UNCHANGING OPINION

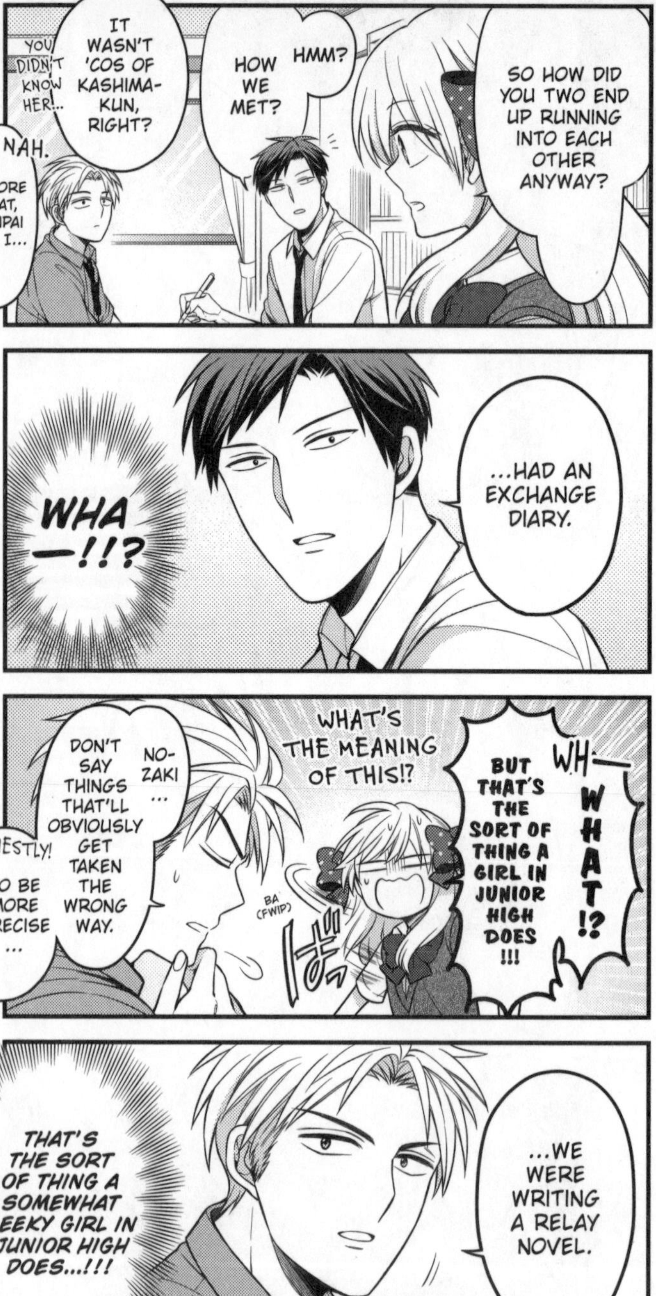
SO HOW DID YOU TWO END UP RUNNING INTO EACH OTHER ANYWAY?
HMM?
HOW WE MET?
IT WASN'T 'COS OF KASHIMA-KUN, RIGHT?
YOU DIDN'T KNOW HER...
NAH.
BEFORE THAT, SENPAI AND I...
...HAD AN EXCHANGE DIARY.
WHA—!!?
WH— WHAT!?
BUT THAT'S THE SORT OF THING A GIRL IN JUNIOR HIGH DOES!!!
WHAT'S THE MEANING OF THIS!?
BA (FWIP)
NO-ZAKI...
DON'T SAY THINGS THAT'LL OBVIOUSLY GET TAKEN THE WRONG WAY.
HONESTLY!
TO BE MORE PRECISE...
...WE WERE WRITING A RELAY NOVEL.
THAT'S THE SORT OF THING A SOMEWHAT GEEKY GIRL IN JUNIOR HIGH DOES...!!!

YOU'RE BOTH WEIRD

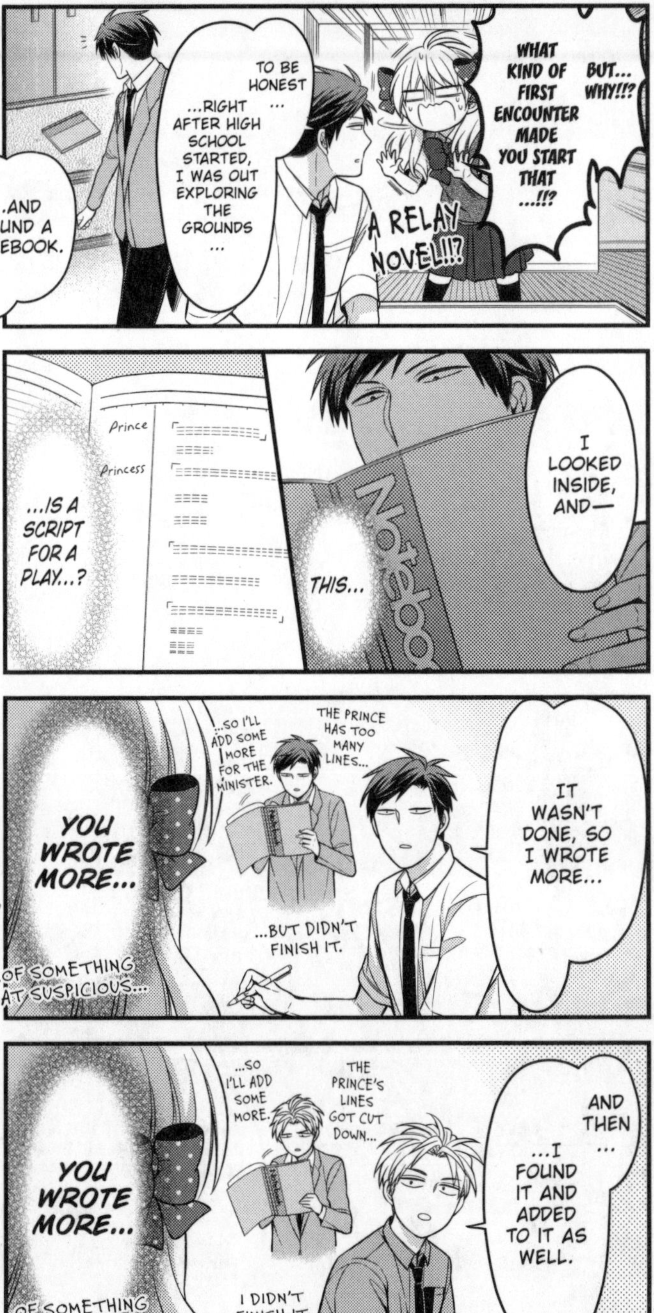
BUT... WHY!!?
WHAT KIND OF FIRST ENCOUNTER MADE YOU START THAT ...!!?
A RELAY NOVEL!!?
TO BE HONEST ...
...RIGHT AFTER HIGH SCHOOL STARTED, I WAS OUT EXPLORING THE GROUNDS ...
...AND FOUND A NOTEBOOK.
I LOOKED INSIDE, AND—
Notebook
THIS...
Prince
Princess
...IS A SCRIPT FOR A PLAY...?
IT WASN'T DONE, SO I WROTE MORE...
THE PRINCE HAS TOO MANY LINES...
...SO I'LL ADD SOME MORE FOR THE MINISTER.
...BUT DIDN'T FINISH IT.
YOU WROTE MORE...
...OF SOMETHING THAT SUSPICIOUS...
AND THEN ...
...I FOUND IT AND ADDED TO IT AS WELL.
THE PRINCE'S LINES GOT CUT DOWN...
...SO I'LL ADD SOME MORE.
I DIDN'T FINISH IT, THOUGH.
YOU WROTE MORE...
...OF SOMETHING THAT SUSPICIOUS...

THEIR EXCHANGE

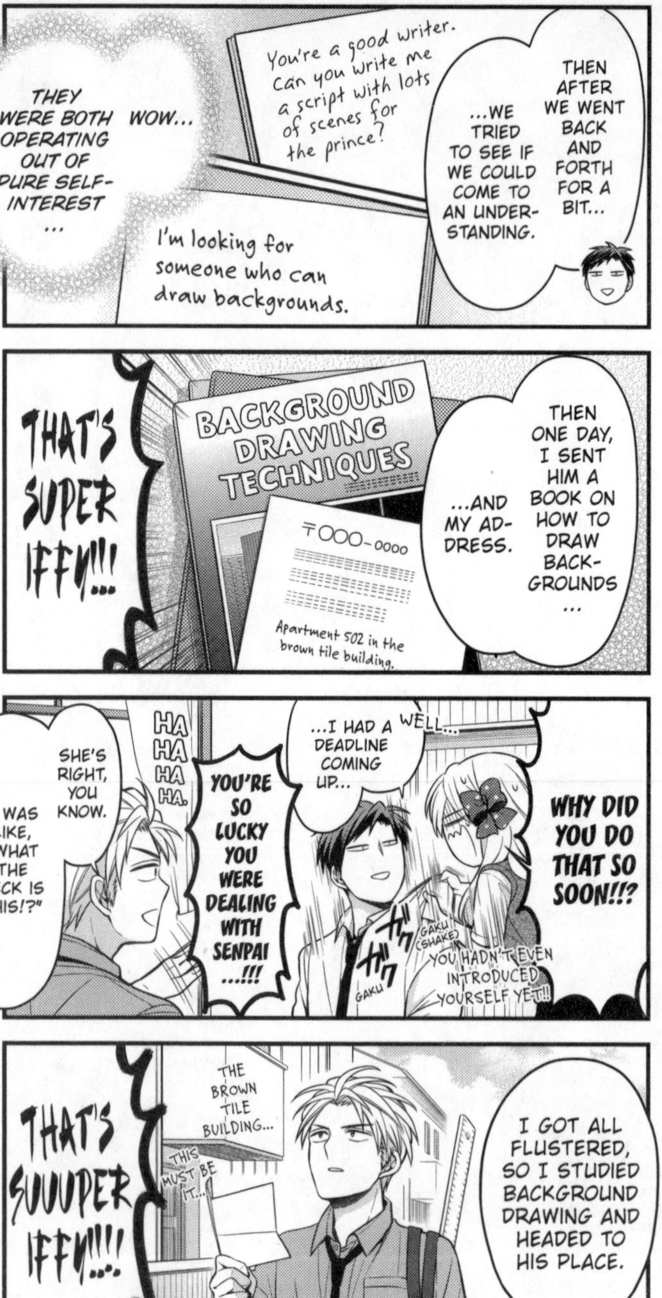
THEN AFTER WE WENT BACK AND FORTH FOR A BIT...
...WE TRIED TO SEE IF WE COULD COME TO AN UNDERSTANDING.
You're a good writer. Can you write me a script with lots of scenes for the prince?
I'm looking for someone who can draw backgrounds.
WOW...
THEY WERE BOTH OPERATING OUT OF PURE SELF-INTEREST...
THEN ONE DAY, I SENT HIM A BOOK ON HOW TO DRAW BACKGROUNDS...
...AND MY ADDRESS.
BACKGROUND DRAWING TECHNIQUES
〒OOO-OOOO
Apartment 502 in the brown tile building.
THAT'S SUPER IFFY!!!...
WHY DID YOU DO THAT SO SOON!!?
GAKU (SHAKE)
YOU HADN'T EVEN INTRODUCED YOURSELF YET!!
WELL...
...I HAD A DEADLINE COMING UP...
GAKU
YOU'RE SO LUCKY YOU WERE DEALING WITH SENPAI...!!!
HA HA HA HA.
SHE'S RIGHT, YOU KNOW.
I WAS LIKE, "WHAT THE HECK IS THIS!?"
I GOT ALL FLUSTERED, SO I STUDIED BACKGROUND DRAWING AND HEADED TO HIS PLACE.
THE BROWN TILE BUILDING...
THIS MUST BE IT...
THAT'S SUUUPER IFFY!!!...

THE ODD MAN OUT

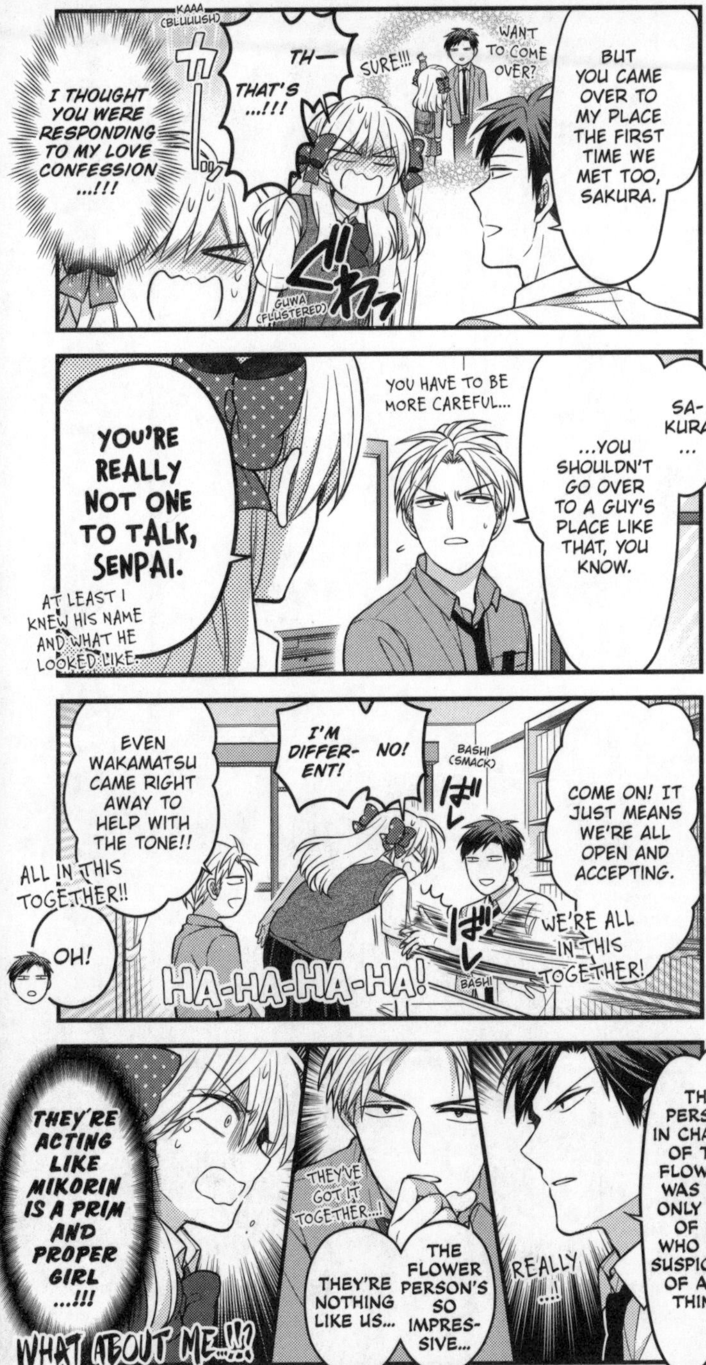
BUT YOU CAME OVER TO MY PLACE THE FIRST TIME WE MET TOO, SAKURA.
WANT TO COME OVER?
SURE!!!
TH— THAT'S ...!!!
KAAA (BLUUUSH)
I THOUGHT YOU WERE RESPONDING TO MY LOVE CONFESSION ...!!!
GUWA (FLUSTERED)
SA-KURA ...
...YOU SHOULDN'T GO OVER TO A GUY'S PLACE LIKE THAT, YOU KNOW.
YOU HAVE TO BE MORE CAREFUL...
YOU'RE REALLY NOT ONE TO TALK, SENPAI.
AT LEAST I KNEW HIS NAME AND WHAT HE LOOKED LIKE.
COME ON! IT JUST MEANS WE'RE ALL OPEN AND ACCEPTING.
BASHI (SMACK)
NO!
I'M DIFFERENT!
WE'RE ALL IN THIS TOGETHER!
BASH!
EVEN WAKAMATSU CAME RIGHT AWAY TO HELP WITH THE TONE!!
ALL IN THIS TOGETHER!!
HA-HA-HA-HA!
OH!
THE PERSON IN CHARGE OF THE FLOWERS WAS THE ONLY ONE OF US WHO WAS SUSPICIOUS OF ANY-THING.
REALLY ...!
THE FLOWER PERSON'S SO IMPRESSIVE...
THEY'RE NOTHING LIKE US...
THEY'VE GOT IT TOGETHER...!
THEY'RE ACTING LIKE MIKORIN IS A PRIM AND PROPER GIRL ...!!!
WHAT ABOUT ME...!!?

THEIR KOUHAI'S COMPREHENSION

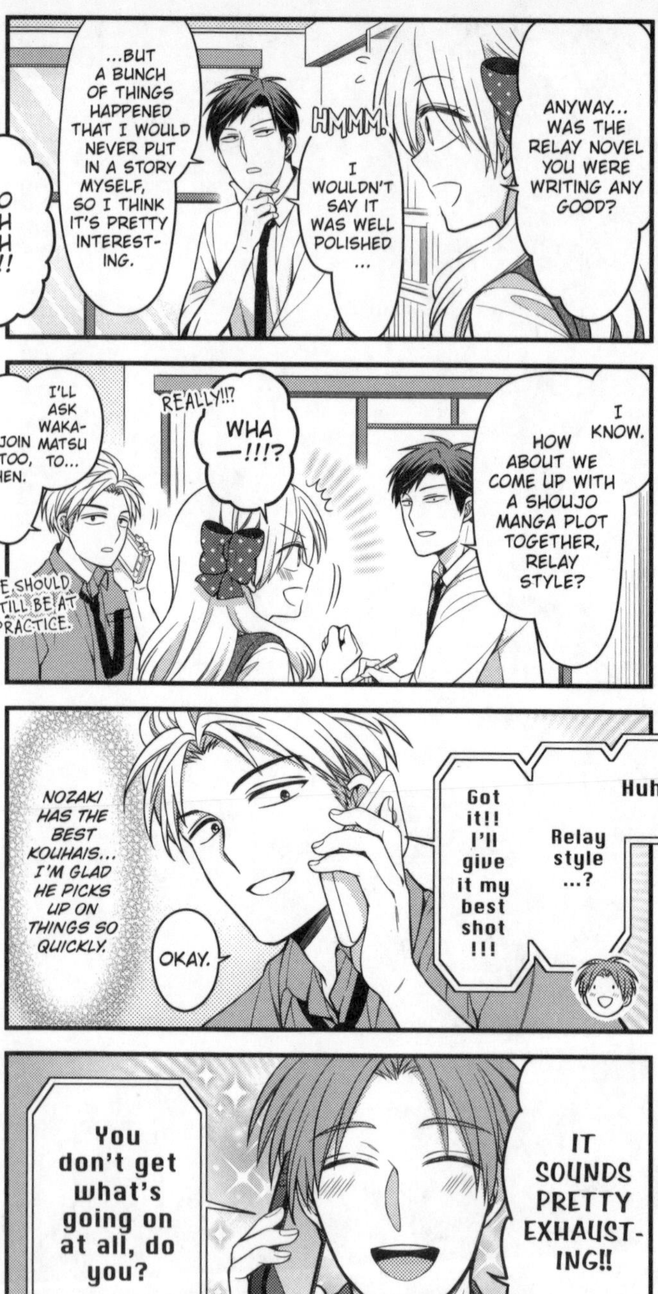

ANYWAY... WAS THE RELAY NOVEL YOU WERE WRITING ANY GOOD?
HMMM.
I WOULDN'T SAY IT WAS WELL POLISHED ...
...BUT A BUNCH OF THINGS HAPPENED THAT I WOULD NEVER PUT IN A STORY MYSELF, SO I THINK IT'S PRETTY INTEREST-ING.
OHH!!
I KNOW. HOW ABOUT WE COME UP WITH A SHOUJO MANGA PLOT TOGETHER, RELAY STYLE?
REALLY!!?
WHA—!!!?
I'LL ASK WAKA-MATSU TO... ...JOIN IN TOO, THEN.
HE SHOULD STILL BE AT PRACTICE.
Huh? Relay style ...?
Got it!! I'll give it my best shot !!!
OKAY.
NOZAKI HAS THE BEST KOUHAIS... I'M GLAD HE PICKS UP ON THINGS SO QUICKLY.
IT SOUNDS PRETTY EXHAUST-ING!!
You don't get what's going on at all, do you?
BUT IT'S A RELAY, SO WE'LL WIN THIS!!

PASS FROM NOZAKI-KUN

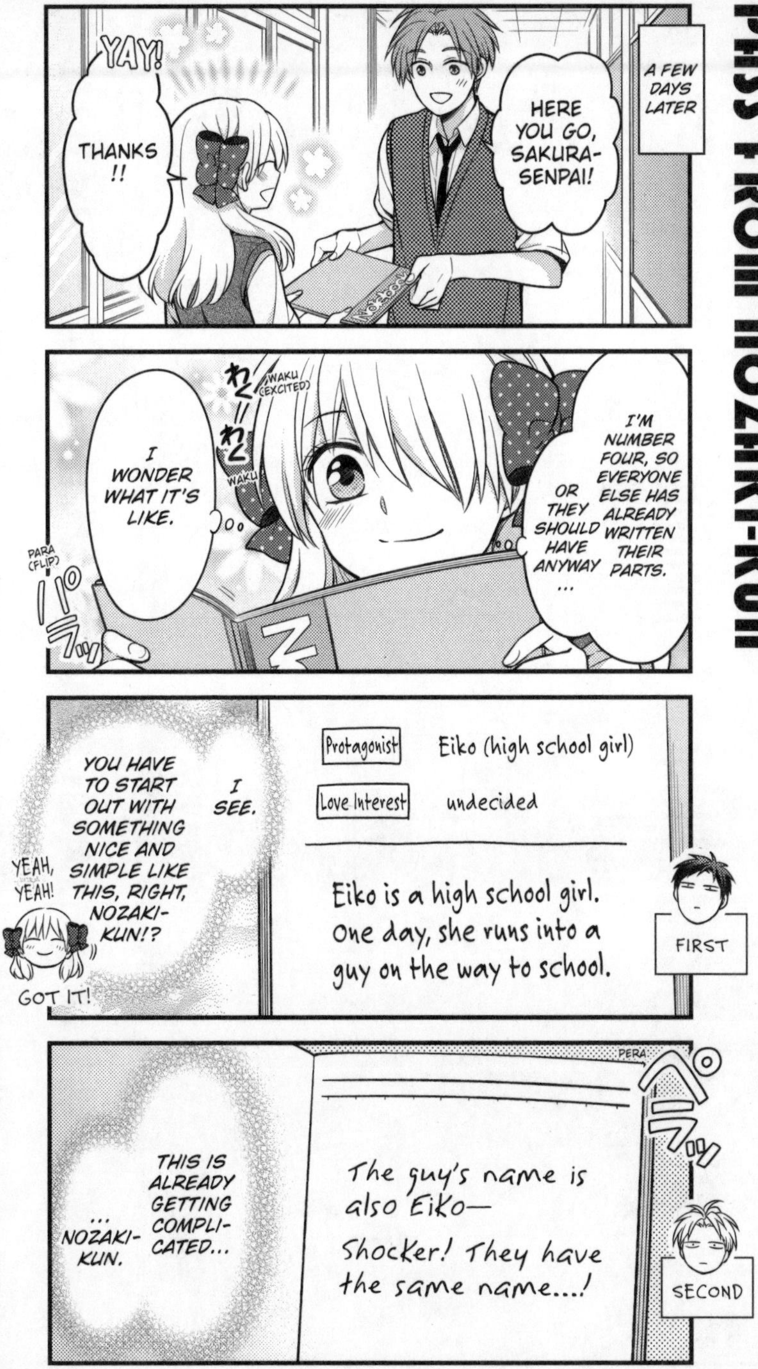
A FEW DAYS LATER
HERE YOU GO, SAKURA-SENPAI!
YAY!
THANKS!!
I'M NUMBER FOUR, SO EVERYONE ELSE HAS ALREADY WRITTEN THEIR PARTS.
OR THEY SHOULD HAVE ANYWAY...
WAKU (EXCITED) WAKU
I WONDER WHAT IT'S LIKE.
PARA (FLIP)
Protagonist Eiko (high school girl)
Love Interest undecided
Eiko is a high school girl. One day, she runs into a guy on the way to school.
FIRST
I SEE.
YOU HAVE TO START OUT WITH SOMETHING NICE AND SIMPLE LIKE THIS, RIGHT, NOZAKI-KUN!?
YEAH, YEAH!
GOT IT!
PERA
The guy's name is also Eiko—
Shocker! They have the same name...!
SECOND
THIS IS ALREADY GETTING COMPLICATED...
...NOZAKI-KUN.

DESPERATELY TRYING TO TIE IT TOGETHER

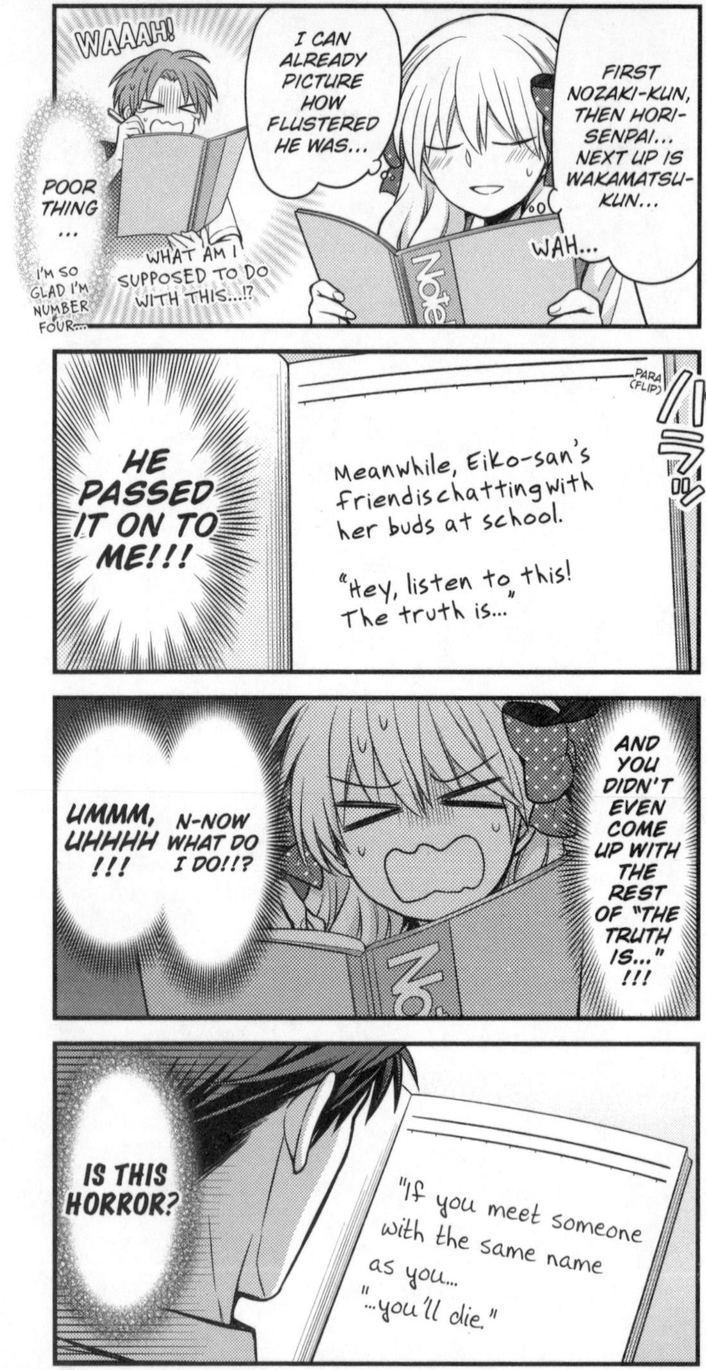
FIRST NOZAKI-KUN, THEN HORI-SENPAI... NEXT UP IS WAKAMATSU-KUN...
WAH...
I CAN ALREADY PICTURE HOW FLUSTERED HE WAS...
WAAAH!
WHAT AM I SUPPOSED TO DO WITH THIS...!?
POOR THING ...
I'M SO GLAD I'M NUMBER FOUR...
PARA (FLIP)
パラッ
Meanwhile, Eiko-san's friendischattingwith her buds at school.
"Hey, listen to this! The truth is..."
HE PASSED IT ON TO ME!!!
AND YOU DIDN'T EVEN COME UP WITH THE REST OF "THE TRUTH IS..." !!!
N-NOW WHAT DO I DO!!?
UMMM, UHHHH !!!
"If you meet someone with the same name as you... "...you'll die."
IS THIS HORROR?

ONCE MORE!

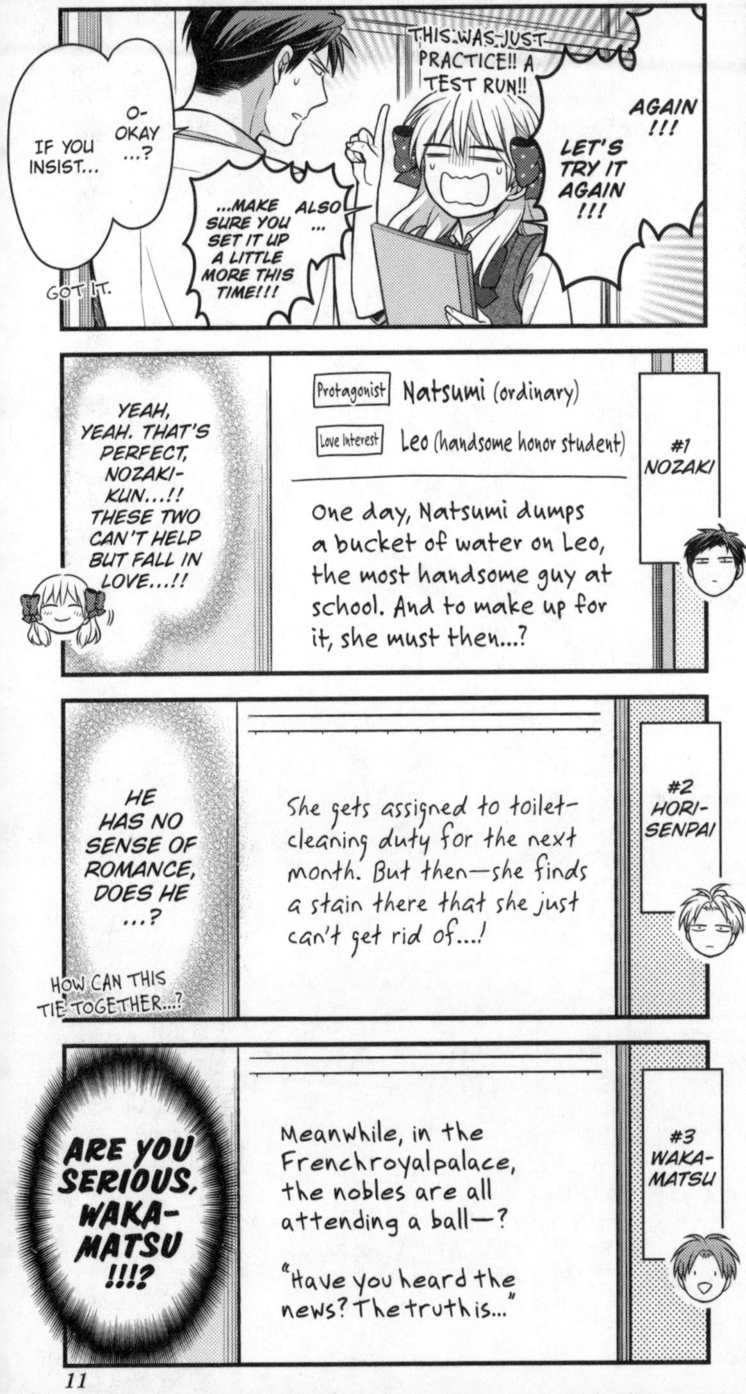

THIS WAS JUST PRACTICE!! A TEST RUN!!
AGAIN!!!
LET'S TRY IT AGAIN!!!
ALSO...
...MAKE SURE YOU SET IT UP A LITTLE MORE THIS TIME!!!
O-OKAY...?
IF YOU INSIST...
GOT IT.
#1 NOZAKI
Protagonist Natsumi (ordinary)
Love Interest Leo (handsome honor student)
One day, Natsumi dumps a bucket of water on Leo, the most handsome guy at school. And to make up for it, she must then...?
YEAH, YEAH. THAT'S PERFECT, NOZAKI-KUN...!! THESE TWO CAN'T HELP BUT FALL IN LOVE...!!
#2 HORI-SENPAI
She gets assigned to toilet-cleaning duty for the next month. But then—she finds a stain there that she just can't get rid of...!
HE HAS NO SENSE OF ROMANCE, DOES HE ...?
HOW CAN THIS TIE TOGETHER...?
#3 WAKA-MATSU
Meanwhile, in the Frenchroyalpalace, the nobles are all attending a ball—?
"Have you heard the news? The truth is..."
ARE YOU SERIOUS, WAKA-MATSU !!!?

IT'S SUPER EFFECTIVE!

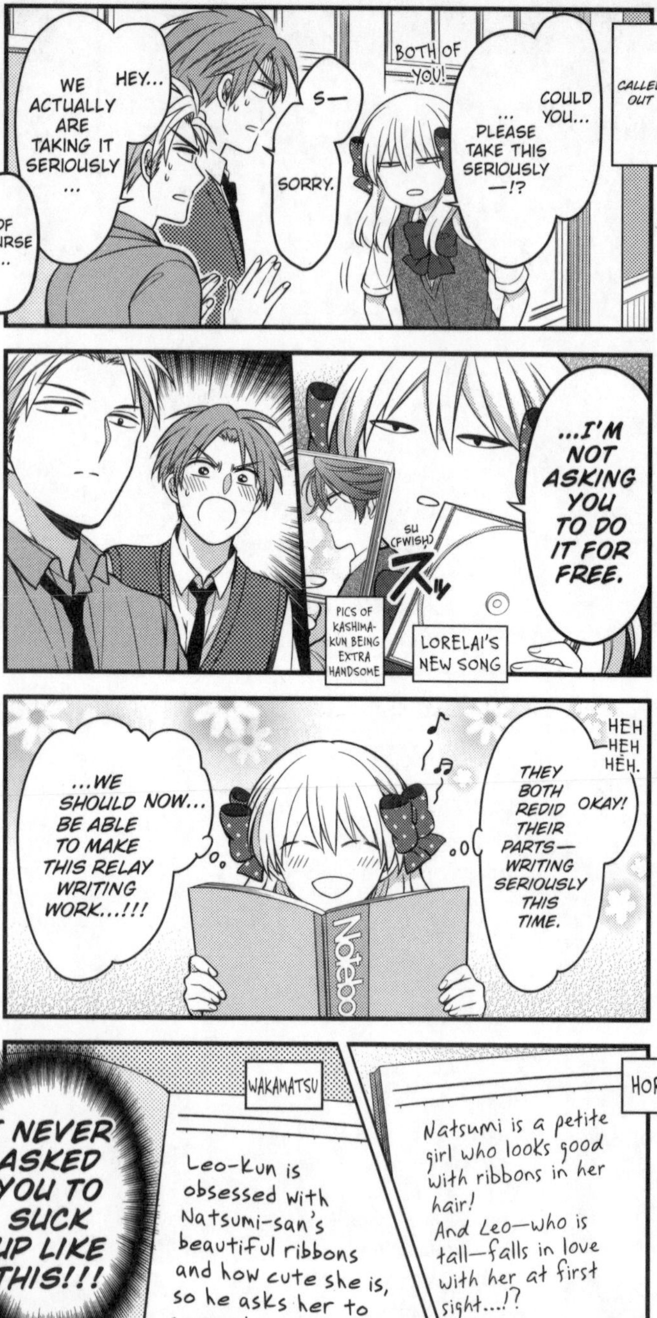
CALLED OUT
COULD YOU... ... PLEASE TAKE THIS SERIOUSLY—!?
BOTH OF YOU!
S— SORRY.
HEY... WE ACTUALLY ARE TAKING IT SERIOUSLY...
OF COURSE...
...I'M NOT ASKING YOU TO DO IT FOR FREE.
SU (FWISH)
LORELAI'S NEW SONG
PICS OF KASHIMA-KUN BEING EXTRA HANDSOME
HEH HEH HEH.
OKAY! THEY BOTH REDID THEIR PARTS—WRITING SERIOUSLY THIS TIME.
NOW... ...WE SHOULD BE ABLE TO MAKE THIS RELAY WRITING WORK...!!!
Notebo
HORI
Natsumi is a petite girl who looks good with ribbons in her hair! And Leo—who is tall—falls in love with her at first sight...!?
WAKAMATSU
Leo-kun is obsessed with Natsumi-san's beautiful ribbons and how cute she is, so he asks her to marry him.
I NEVER ASKED YOU TO SUCK UP LIKE THIS!!!

THE RELAY SHE HOPED FOR!!

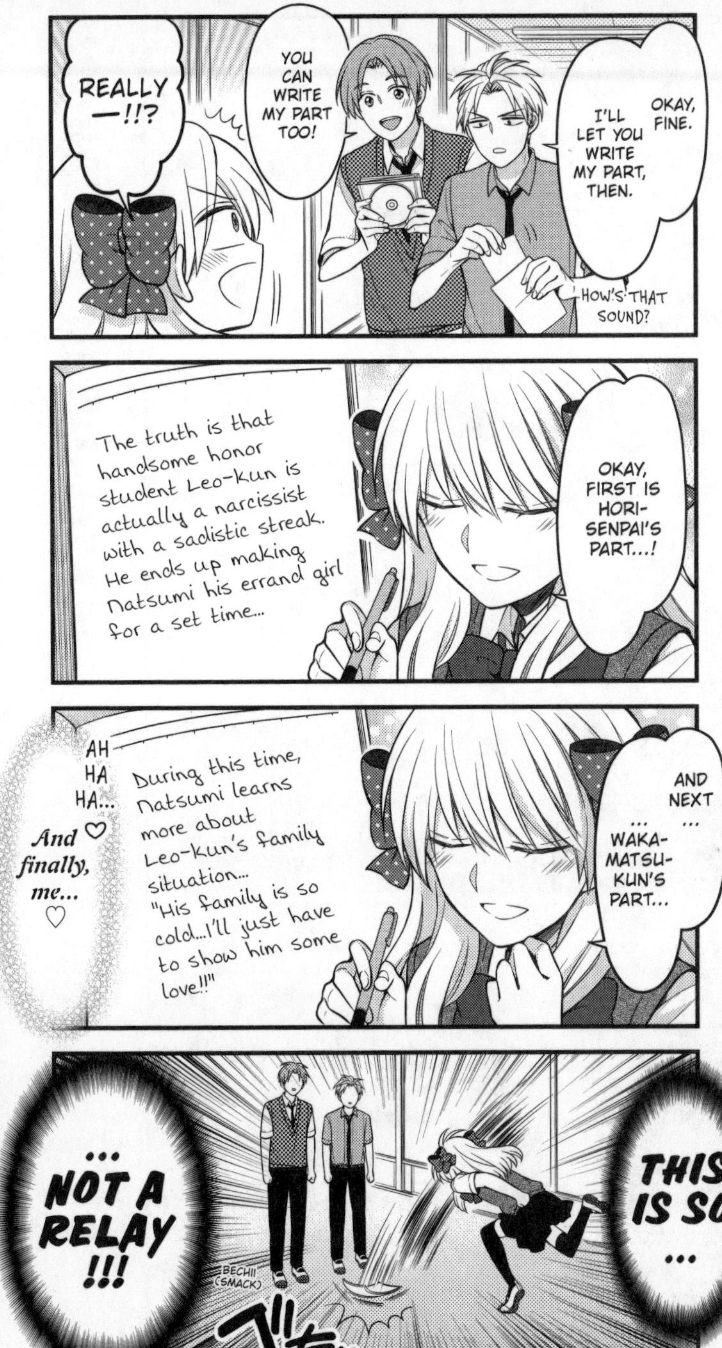
OKAY, FINE.
I'LL LET YOU WRITE MY PART, THEN.
HOW'S THAT SOUND?
YOU CAN WRITE MY PART TOO!
REALLY —!!?
OKAY, FIRST IS HORI-SENPAI'S PART...!
The truth is that handsome honor student Leo-kun is actually a narcissist with a sadistic streak. He ends up making Natsumi his errand girl for a set time...
AND NEXT... ...WAKAMATSU-KUN'S PART...
During this time, Natsumi learns more about Leo-kun's family situation... "His family is so cold...I'll just have to show him some love!!"
AH HA HA...♡
And finally, me...♡
THIS IS SO...
...NOT A RELAY!!!
BECHII (SMACK)

NO ULTERIOR MOTIVE

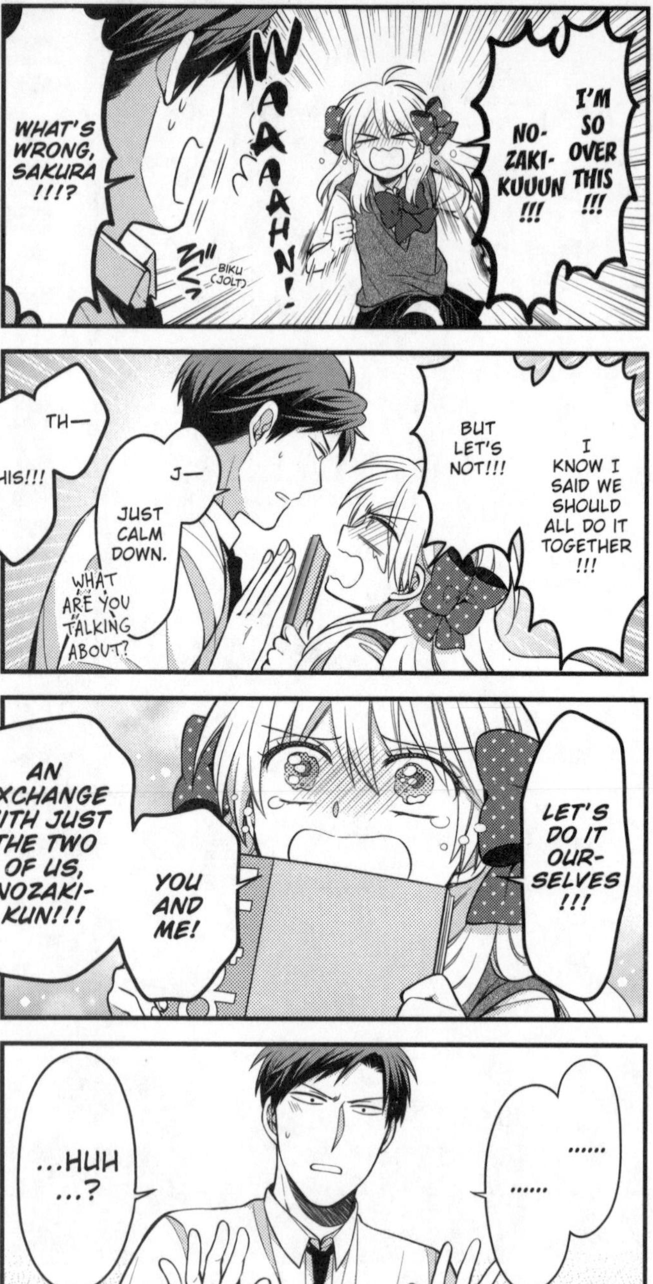
I'M SO OVER THIS!!!
NO-ZAKI-KUUUN!!!
WAAAAAAHN!
WHAT'S WRONG, SAKURA!!!?
BIKU (JOLT)
I KNOW I SAID WE SHOULD ALL DO IT TOGETHER!!!
BUT LET'S NOT!!!
J— JUST CALM DOWN.
TH— THIS!!!
WHAT ARE YOU TALKING ABOUT?
LET'S DO IT OURSELVES!!!
YOU AND ME!
AN EXCHANGE WITH JUST THE TWO OF US, NOZAKI-KUN!!!
....
...HUH ...?

YOU SURPRISE ME EVERY DAY

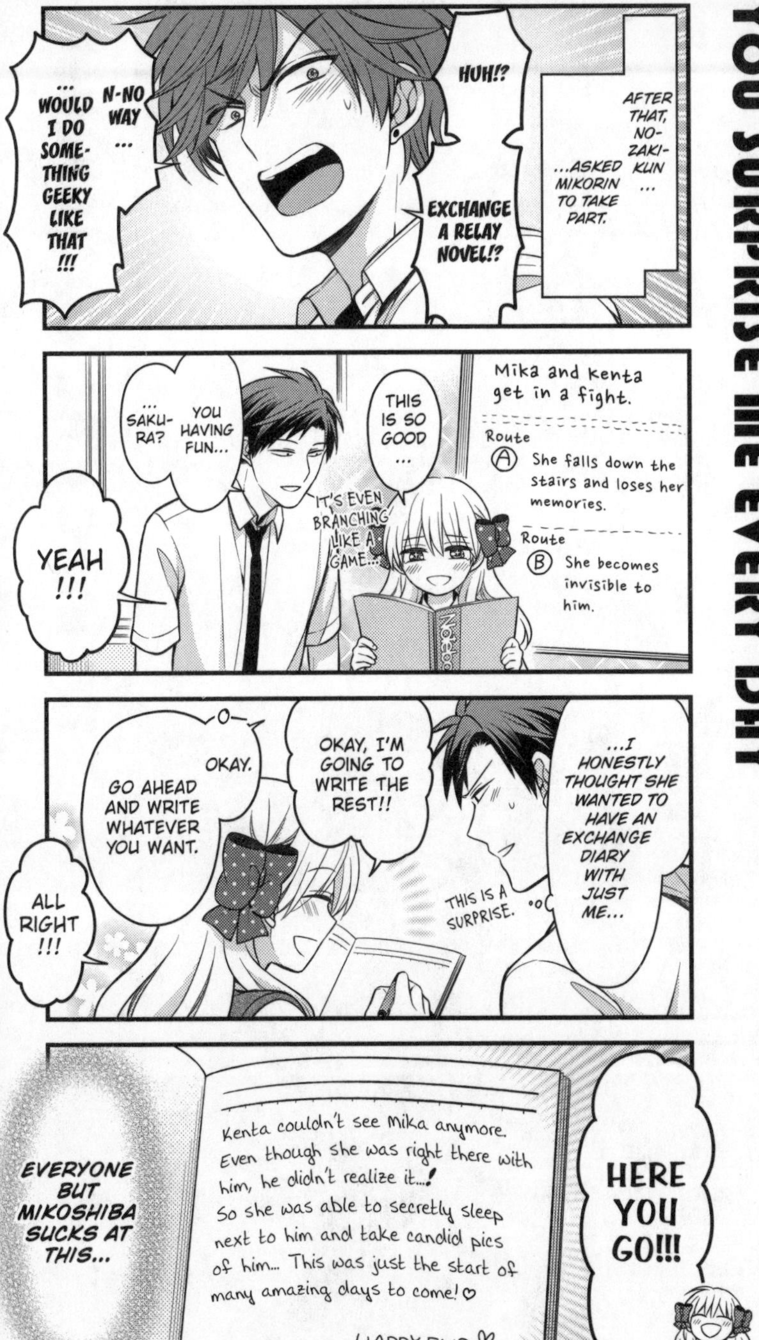

AFTER THAT, NOZAKI-KUN ...
...ASKED MIKORIN TO TAKE PART.
HUH!?
EXCHANGE A RELAY NOVEL!?
N-NO WAY ...
...WOULD I DO SOMETHING GEEKY LIKE THAT!!!
Mika and Kenta get in a fight.
Route
A She falls down the stairs and loses her memories.
Route
B She becomes invisible to him.
THIS IS SO GOOD ...
IT'S EVEN BRANCHING LIKE A GAME...
YOU HAVING FUN...
...SAKURA?
YEAH!!!
...I HONESTLY THOUGHT SHE WANTED TO HAVE AN EXCHANGE DIARY WITH JUST ME...
THIS IS A SURPRISE.
OKAY, I'M GOING TO WRITE THE REST!!
O—
OKAY.
GO AHEAD AND WRITE WHATEVER YOU WANT.
ALL RIGHT!!!
HERE YOU GO!!!
Kenta couldn't see Mika anymore. Even though she was right there with him, he didn't realize it...! So she was able to secretly sleep next to him and take candid pics of him... This was just the start of many amazing days to come! ♡
HAPPY END
EVERYONE BUT MIKOSHIBA SUCKS AT THIS...

[Extra]

LEAVE IT TO CHIYO-CHAN!

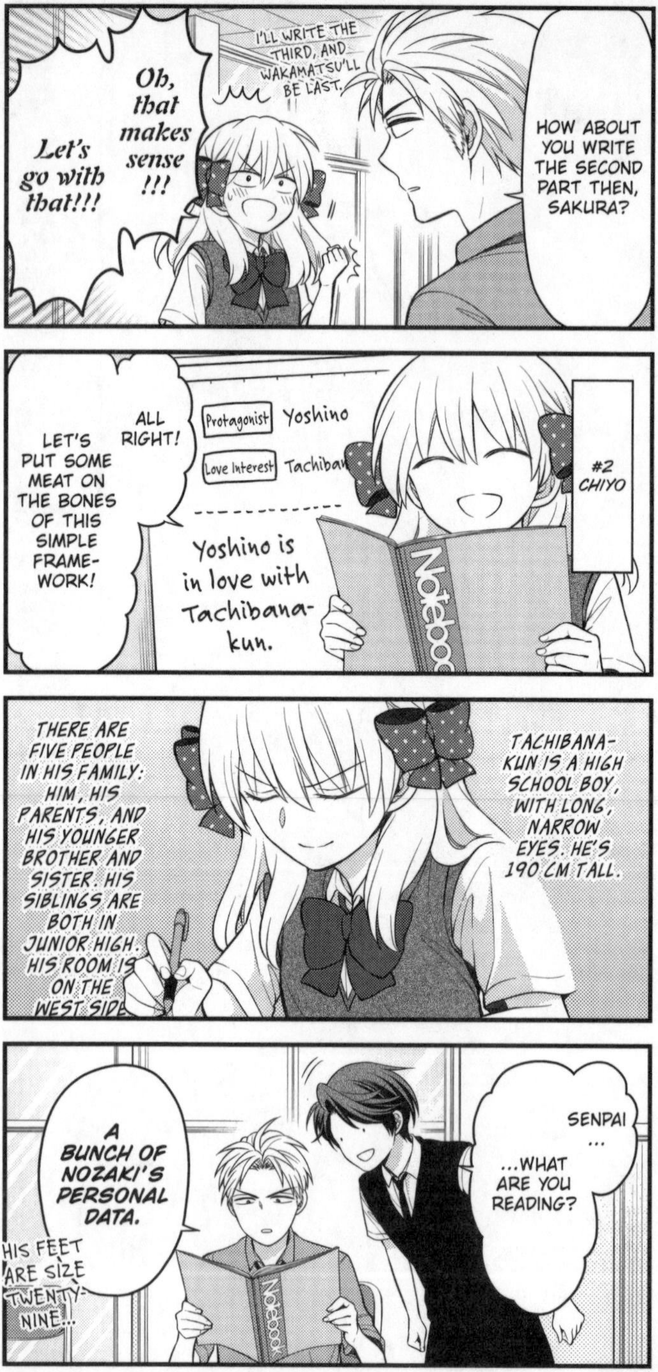

HOW ABOUT YOU WRITE THE SECOND PART THEN, SAKURA?
I'LL WRITE THE THIRD, AND WAKAMATSU'LL BE LAST.
Oh, that makes sense!!!
Let's go with that!!!
#2 CHIYO
ALL RIGHT!
LET'S PUT SOME MEAT ON THE BONES OF THIS SIMPLE FRAME-WORK!
Protagonist Yoshino
Love Interest Tachiban
Yoshino is in love with Tachibana-kun.
Notebook
TACHIBANA-KUN IS A HIGH SCHOOL BOY, WITH LONG, NARROW EYES. HE'S 190 CM TALL.
THERE ARE FIVE PEOPLE IN HIS FAMILY: HIM, HIS PARENTS, AND HIS YOUNGER BROTHER AND SISTER. HIS SIBLINGS ARE BOTH IN JUNIOR HIGH. HIS ROOM IS ON THE WEST SIDE
SENPAI ... ...WHAT ARE YOU READING?
A BUNCH OF NOZAKI'S PERSONAL DATA.
HIS FEET ARE SIZE TWENTY-NINE...
Notebook

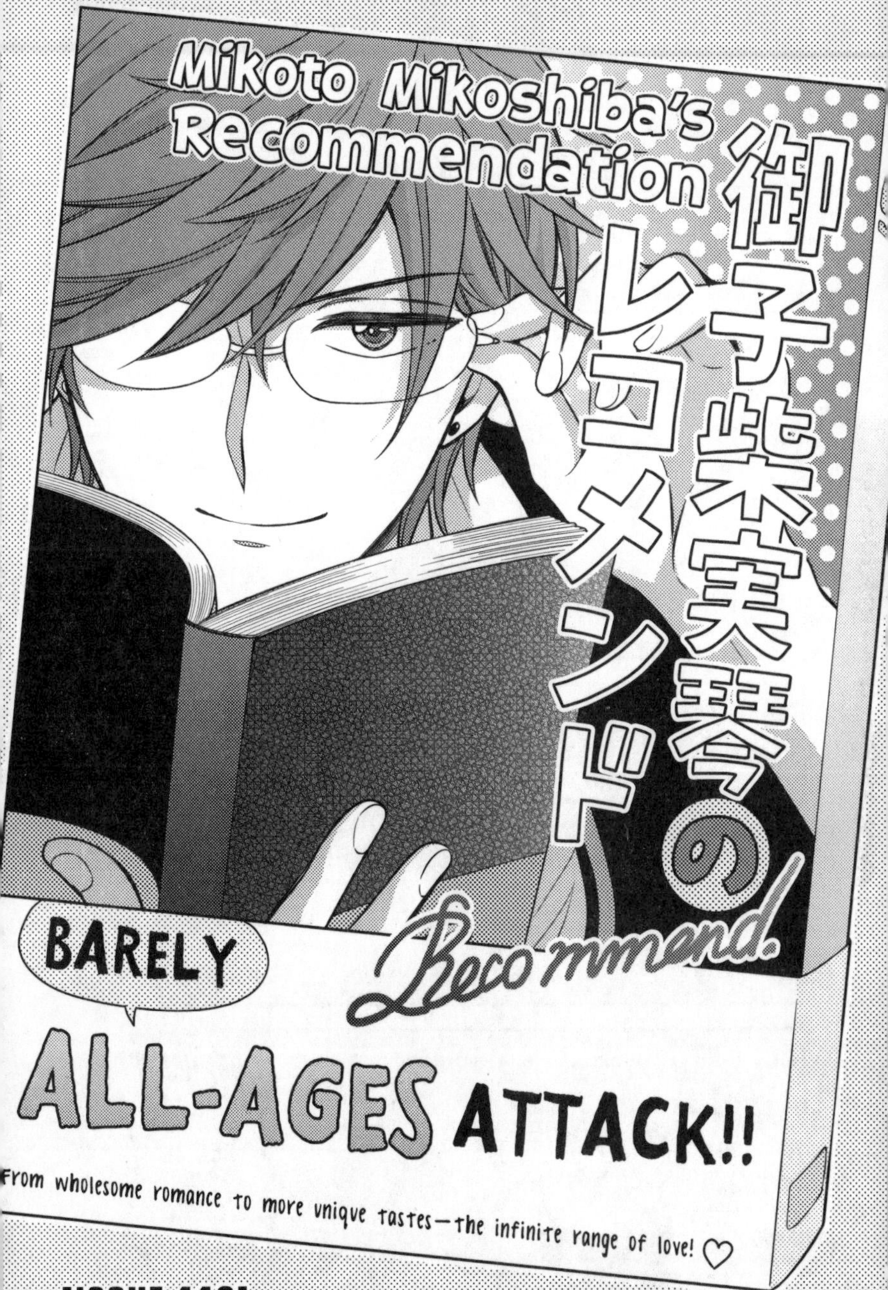
Mikoto Mikoshiba's Recommendation
御子柴実琴のレコメンド
Recommend.
BARELY
ALL-AGES ATTACK!!
From wholesome romance to more unique tastes—the infinite range of love! ♡

[ISSUE 110]

A HEART-POUNDING CONFESSION

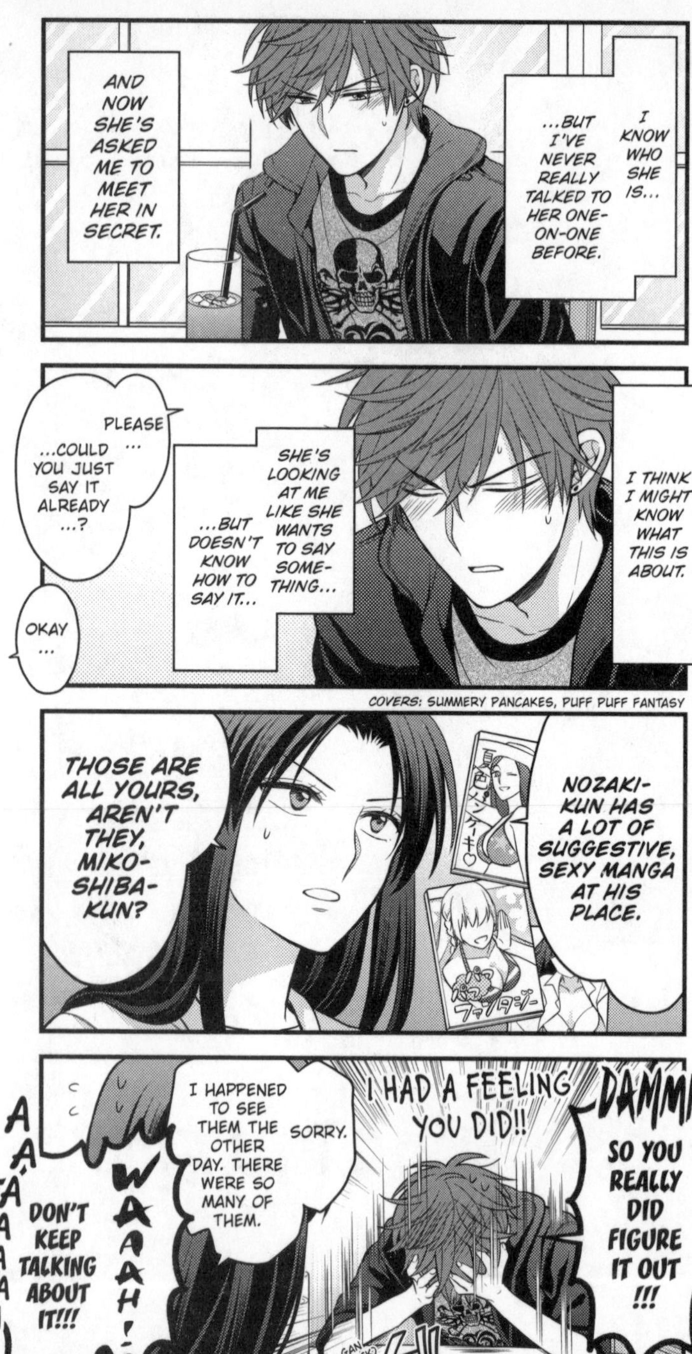
I KNOW WHO SHE IS...
...BUT I'VE NEVER REALLY TALKED TO HER ONE-ON-ONE BEFORE.
AND NOW SHE'S ASKED ME TO MEET HER IN SECRET.
I THINK I MIGHT KNOW WHAT THIS IS ABOUT.
SHE'S LOOKING AT ME LIKE SHE WANTS TO SAY SOMETHING...
...BUT DOESN'T KNOW HOW TO SAY IT...
PLEASE... ...COULD YOU JUST SAY IT ALREADY...?
OKAY...
COVERS: SUMMERY PANCAKES, PUFF PUFF FANTASY
NOZAKI-KUN HAS A LOT OF SUGGESTIVE, SEXY MANGA AT HIS PLACE.
THOSE ARE ALL YOURS, AREN'T THEY, MIKO-SHIBA-KUN?
DAMMIT!
SO YOU REALLY DID FIGURE IT OUT!!!
I HAD A FEELING YOU DID!!
SORRY.
I HAPPENED TO SEE THEM THE OTHER DAY. THERE WERE SO MANY OF THEM.
WAAAH!
DON'T KEEP TALKING ABOUT IT!!!
AAAAAAAAH!
GAN (SHOCK)

MIKOSHIBA'S EXPERT CLASSIFICATION

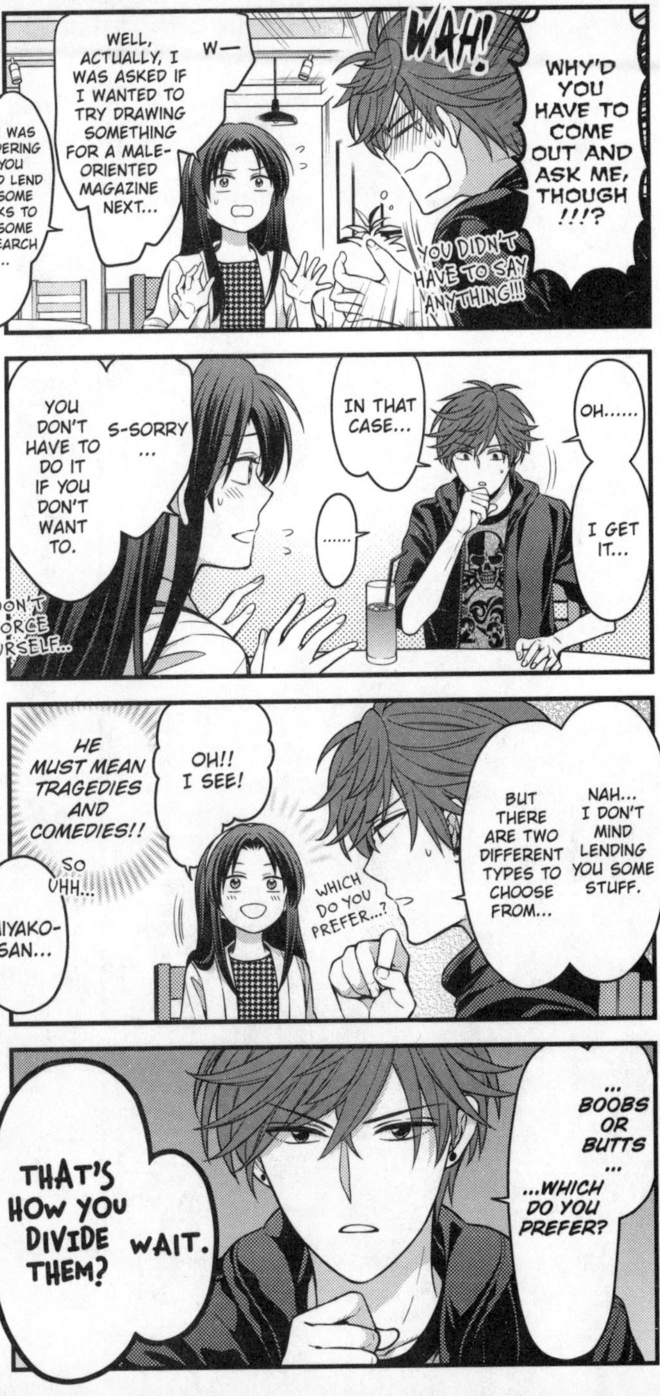
WAH!
WHY'D YOU HAVE TO COME OUT AND ASK ME, THOUGH !!!?
YOU DIDN'T HAVE TO SAY ANYTHING!!!
W—
WELL, ACTUALLY, I WAS ASKED IF I WANTED TO TRY DRAWING SOMETHING FOR A MALE-ORIENTED MAGAZINE NEXT...
SO I WAS WONDERING IF YOU COULD LEND ME SOME BOOKS TO DO SOME RESEARCH ...
OH......
I GET IT...
IN THAT CASE...
......
S-SORRY ...
YOU DON'T HAVE TO DO IT IF YOU DON'T WANT TO.
DON'T FORCE YOURSELF...
NAH... I DON'T MIND LENDING YOU SOME STUFF.
BUT THERE ARE TWO DIFFERENT TYPES TO CHOOSE FROM...
WHICH DO YOU PREFER...?
OH!! I SEE!
HE MUST MEAN TRAGEDIES AND COMEDIES!!
SO UHH...
MIYAKO-SAN...
... BOOBS OR BUTTS ...
...WHICH DO YOU PREFER?
WAIT.
THAT'S HOW YOU DIVIDE THEM?

IN A REFINED ATMOSPHERE

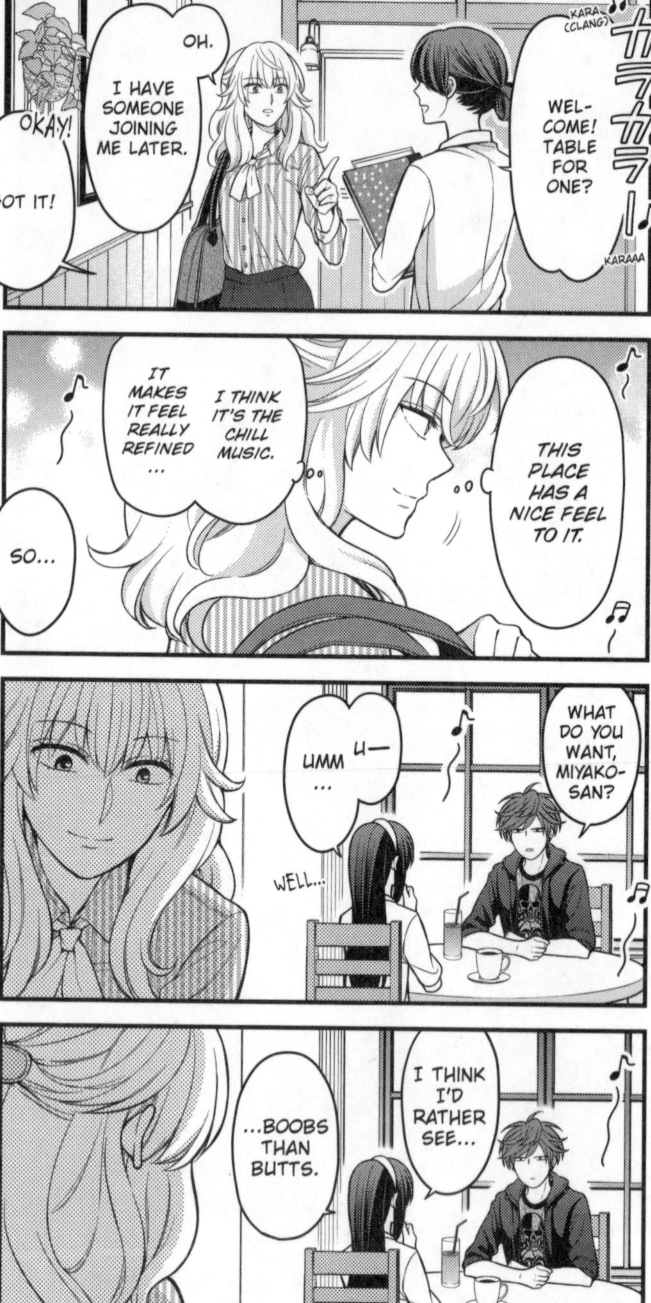
KARA (CLANG)
KARAAA
WEL-COME! TABLE FOR ONE?
OH.
I HAVE SOMEONE JOINING ME LATER.
OKAY!
GOT IT!
THIS PLACE HAS A NICE FEEL TO IT.
I THINK IT'S THE CHILL MUSIC.
IT MAKES IT FEEL REALLY REFINED...
SO...
WHAT DO YOU WANT, MIYAKO-SAN?
U— UMM...
WELL...
I THINK I'D RATHER SEE...
...BOOBS THAN BUTTS.

TALKING ABOUT PORN MANGA

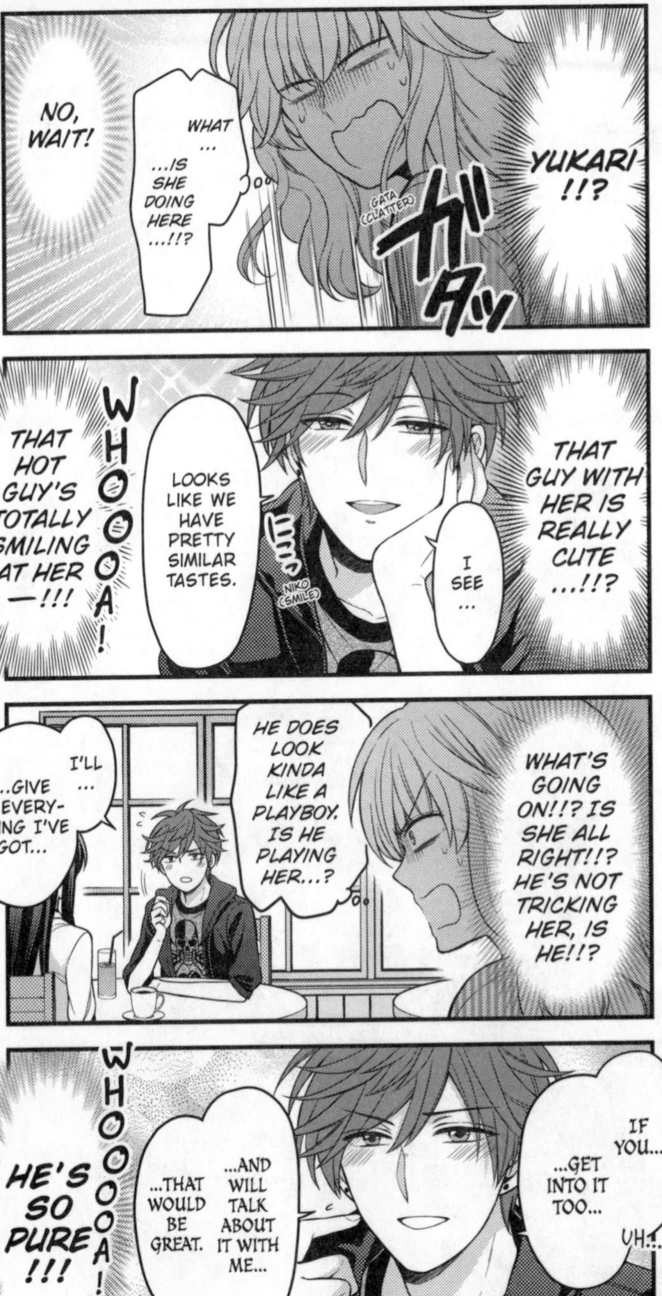
YUKARI!!?
GATA (CLATTER)
WHAT... ...IS SHE DOING HERE...!!?
NO, WAIT!
THAT GUY WITH HER IS REALLY CUTE...!!?
I SEE...
NIKO (SMILE)
LOOKS LIKE WE HAVE PRETTY SIMILAR TASTES.
WHOOOOA!
THAT HOT GUY'S TOTALLY SMILING AT HER—!!!
WHAT'S GOING ON!!? IS SHE ALL RIGHT!!? HE'S NOT TRICKING HER, IS HE!!?
HE DOES LOOK KINDA LIKE A PLAYBOY. IS HE PLAYING HER...?
I'LL... ...GIVE IT EVERYTHING I'VE GOT...
IF YOU... ...GET INTO IT TOO...
UH...
...AND WILL TALK ABOUT IT WITH ME...
...THAT WOULD BE GREAT.
WHOOOOOA!
HE'S SO PURE!!!
HEH HEH HEH.

MIYAKO-SAN'S POTENTIAL

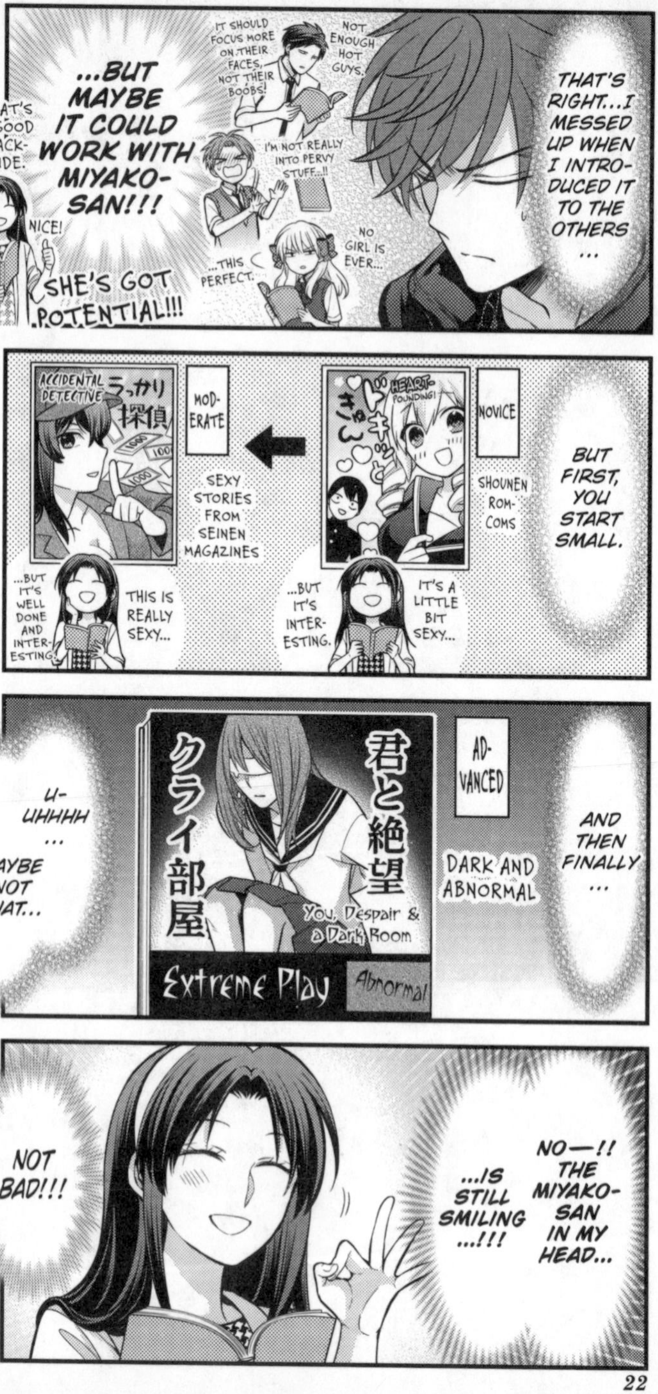
THAT'S RIGHT...I MESSED UP WHEN I INTRODUCED IT TO THE OTHERS...
NOT ENOUGH HOT GUYS.
IT SHOULD FOCUS MORE ON THEIR FACES, NOT THEIR BOOBS!
I'M NOT REALLY INTO PERVY STUFF...!!
NO GIRL IS EVER...
...THIS PERFECT.
...BUT MAYBE IT COULD WORK WITH MIYAKO-SAN!!!
THAT'S A GOOD BACKSIDE.
NICE!
SHE'S GOT POTENTIAL!!!
BUT FIRST, YOU START SMALL.
NOVICE
HEART-POUNDING!
SHOUNEN ROM-COMS
IT'S A LITTLE BIT SEXY...
...BUT IT'S INTERESTING.
MODERATE
ACCIDENTAL DETECTIVE
うっかり探偵
SEXY STORIES FROM SEINEN MAGAZINES
THIS IS REALLY SEXY...
...BUT IT'S WELL DONE AND INTERESTING
AND THEN FINALLY...
ADVANCED
DARK AND ABNORMAL
君と絶望クライ部屋
You, Despair & a Dark Room
Extreme Play
Abnormal
U-UHHHH... MAYBE NOT THAT...
NO—!! THE MIYAKO-SAN IN MY HEAD...
...IS STILL SMILING...!!!
NOT BAD!!!

A DANGEROUS PERSON

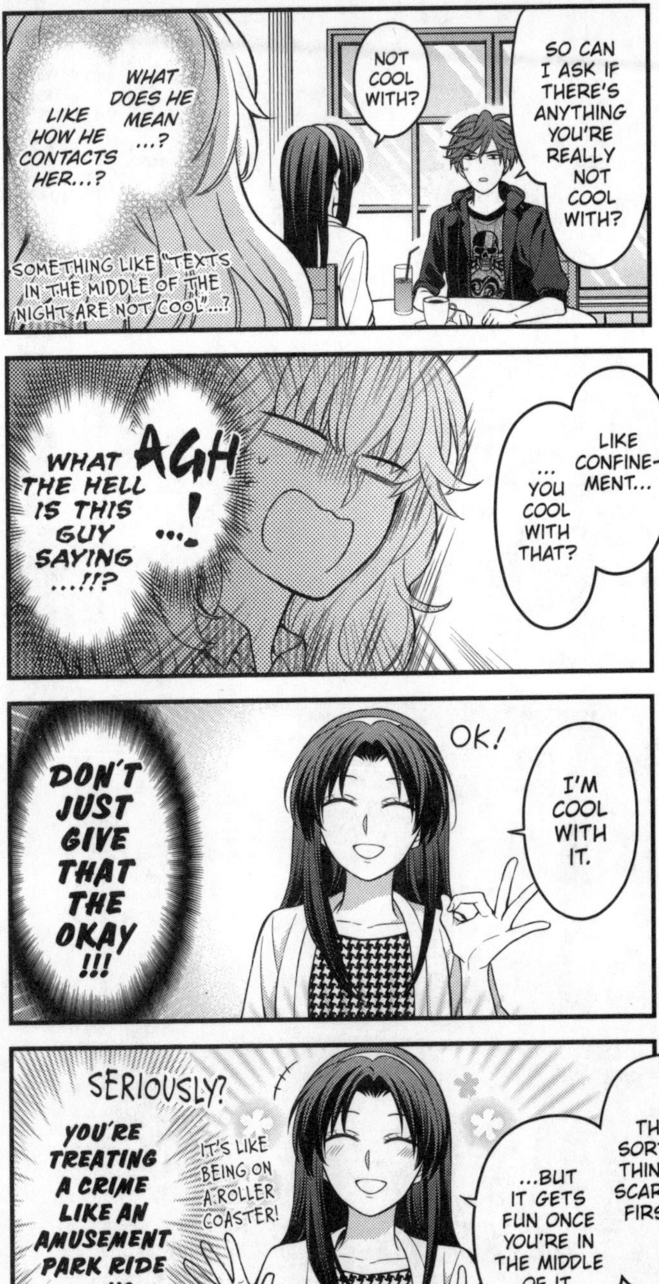
SO CAN I ASK IF THERE'S ANYTHING YOU'RE REALLY NOT COOL WITH?
NOT COOL WITH?
WHAT DOES HE MEAN ...?
LIKE HOW HE CONTACTS HER...?
SOMETHING LIKE "TEXTS IN THE MIDDLE OF THE NIGHT ARE NOT COOL"...?
LIKE CONFINEMENT...
...YOU COOL WITH THAT?
AGH...!
WHAT THE HELL IS THIS GUY SAYING...!!?
I'M COOL WITH IT.
OK!
DON'T JUST GIVE THAT THE OKAY!!!
THAT SORT OF THING IS SCARY AT FIRST...
...BUT IT GETS FUN ONCE YOU'RE IN THE MIDDLE OF IT.
IT'S LIKE BEING ON A ROLLER COASTER!
SERIOUSLY?
YOU'RE TREATING A CRIME LIKE AN AMUSEMENT PARK RIDE—!!?

A SKEWED PREFERENCE

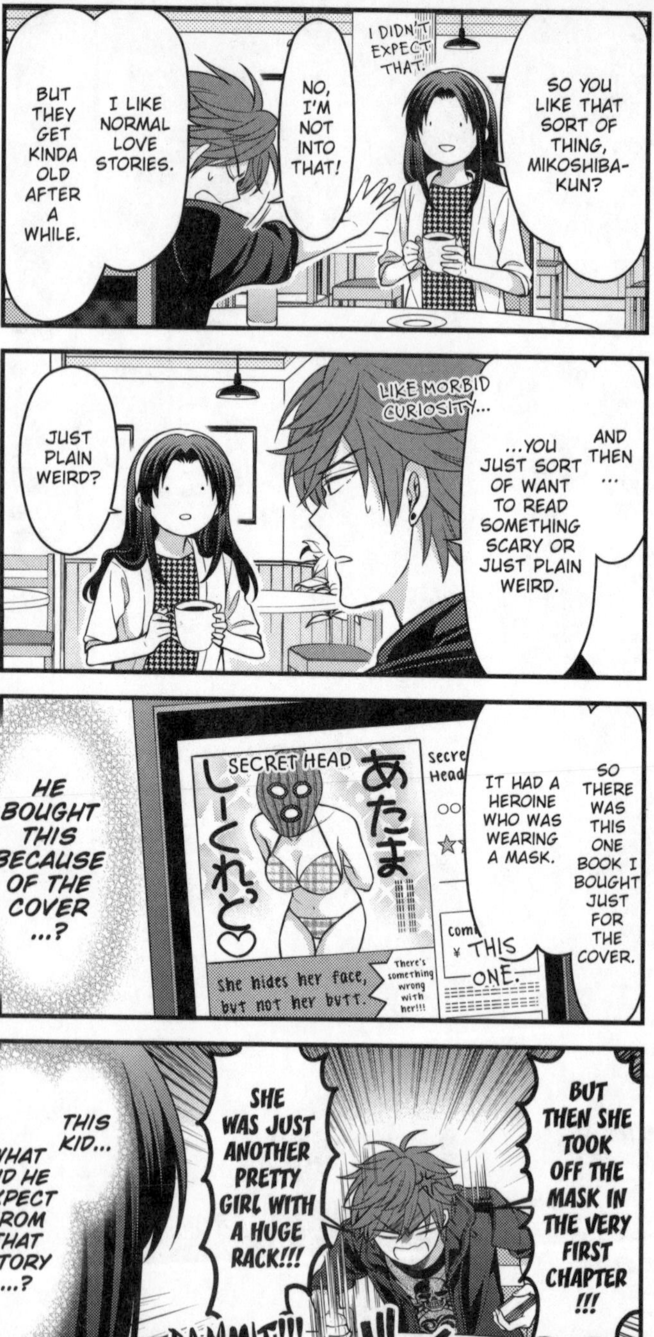
SO YOU LIKE THAT SORT OF THING, MIKOSHIBA-KUN?
I DIDN'T EXPECT THAT.
NO, I'M NOT INTO THAT!
I LIKE NORMAL LOVE STORIES.
BUT THEY GET KINDA OLD AFTER A WHILE.
AND THEN ...
...YOU JUST SORT OF WANT TO READ SOMETHING SCARY OR JUST PLAIN WEIRD.
LIKE MORBID CURIOSITY...
JUST PLAIN WEIRD?
SO THERE WAS THIS ONE BOOK I BOUGHT JUST FOR THE COVER.
IT HAD A HEROINE WHO WAS WEARING A MASK.
THIS ONE.
Secret Head
SECRET HEAD
あたま しーくれっど
There's something wrong with her!!!
She hides her face, but not her butt.
HE BOUGHT THIS BECAUSE OF THE COVER ...?
BUT THEN SHE TOOK OFF THE MASK IN THE VERY FIRST CHAPTER!!!
SHE WAS JUST ANOTHER PRETTY GIRL WITH A HUGE RACK!!!
DAMMIT!!!...
ドンッ
DON (SLAM)
THIS KID...
WHAT DID HE EXPECT FROM THAT STORY ...?

RIGHT NOW, THE GIRL I LIKE IS...

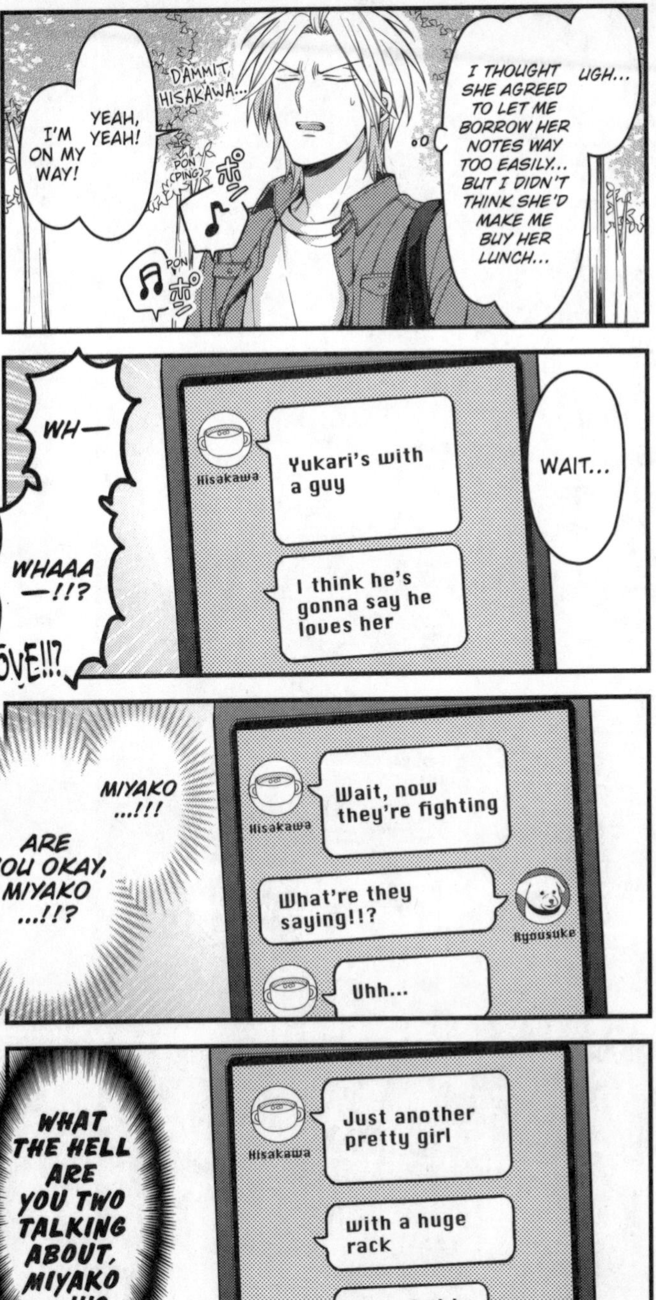
UGH...
I THOUGHT SHE AGREED TO LET ME BORROW HER NOTES WAY TOO EASILY... BUT I DIDN'T THINK SHE'D MAKE ME BUY HER LUNCH...
PON (PING)
PON
DAMMIT, HISAKAWA...
YEAH, YEAH! I'M ON MY WAY!
WAIT...
Hisakawa
Yukari's with a guy
I think he's gonna say he loves her
WH—
WHAAA—!!?
LOVE!!?
Hisakawa
Wait, now they're fighting
What're they saying!!?
Ryousuke
Uhh...
MIYAKO...!!!
ARE YOU OKAY, MIYAKO...!!?
Hisakawa
Just another pretty girl
with a huge rack
Not what he expected
WHAT THE HELL ARE YOU TWO TALKING ABOUT, MIYAKO—!!!?

THE MOOD BETWEEN THEM

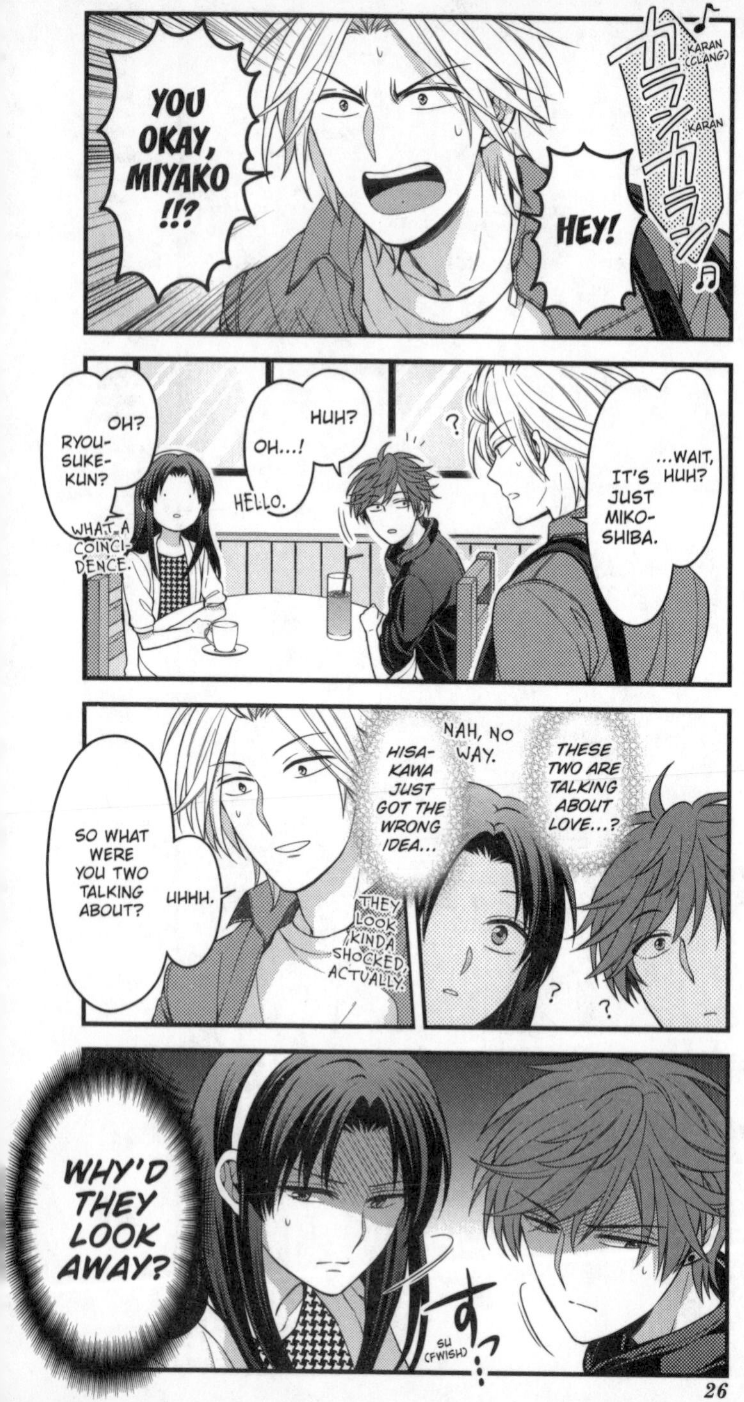
カランカラン♪
KARAN (CLANG) KARAN
HEY!
YOU OKAY, MIYAKO!!?
...WAIT, HUH? IT'S JUST MIKO-SHIBA.
?
HUH? OH...!
HELLO.
OH? RYOU-SUKE-KUN?
WHAT A COINCI-DENCE.
THESE TWO ARE TALKING ABOUT LOVE...?
NAH, NO WAY.
HISA-KAWA JUST GOT THE WRONG IDEA...
THEY LOOK KINDA SHOCKED, ACTUALLY.
UHHH.
SO WHAT WERE YOU TWO TALKING ABOUT?
すっ
SU (FWISH)
WHY'D THEY LOOK AWAY?

THE TABOO WORD: MANGA

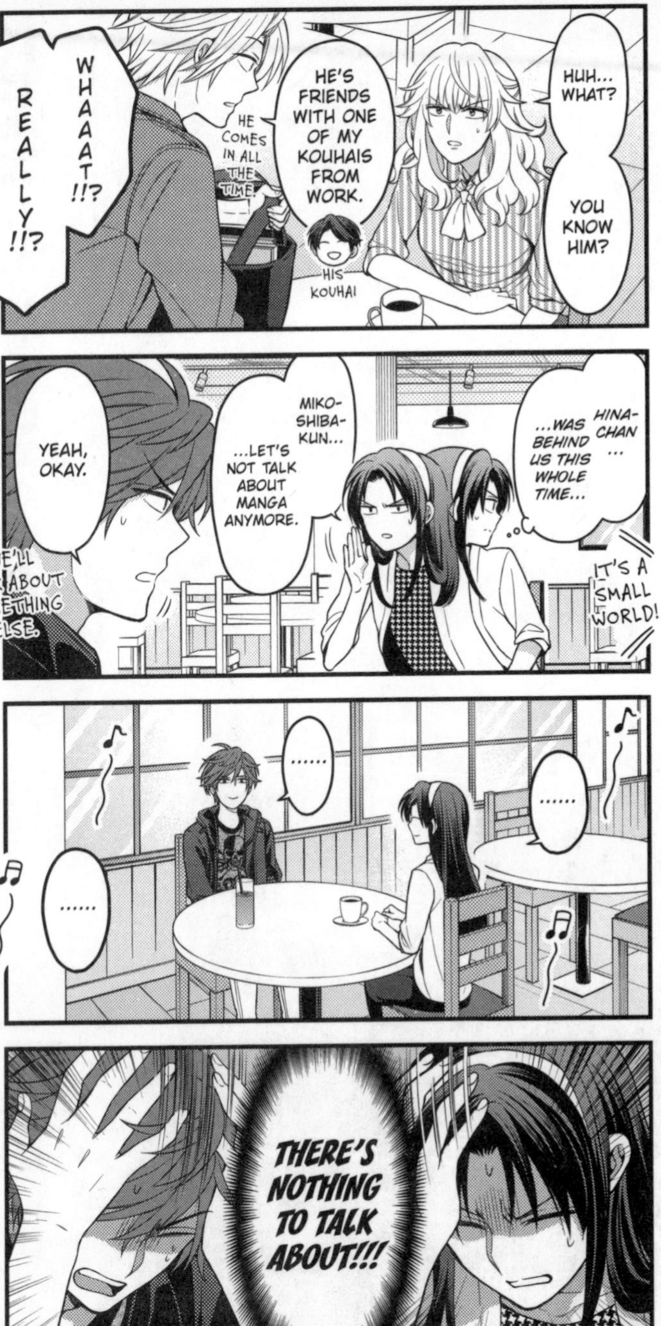
HUH... WHAT?
YOU KNOW HIM?
HE'S FRIENDS WITH ONE OF MY KOUHAIS FROM WORK.
HIS KOUHAI
HE COMES IN ALL THE TIME.
WHAAAT!!?
REALLY!!?
HINA-CHAN...
...WAS BEHIND US THIS WHOLE TIME...
IT'S A SMALL WORLD!
MIKO-SHIBA-KUN...
...LET'S NOT TALK ABOUT MANGA ANYMORE.
YEAH, OKAY.
WE'LL TALK ABOUT SOMETHING ELSE.
......
......
......
THERE'S NOTHING TO TALK ABOUT!!!

EXCESSIVE PRECAUTIONS

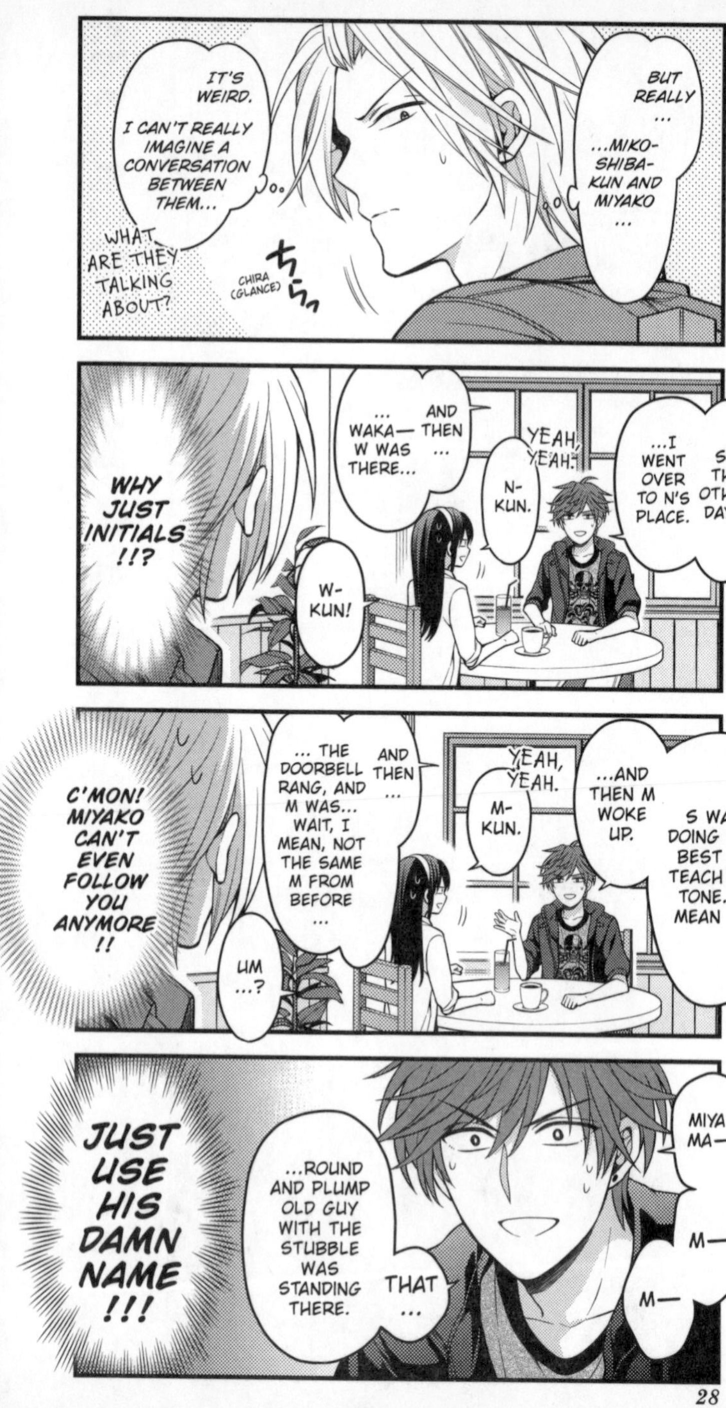
BUT REALLY ... ...MIKO-SHIBA-KUN AND MIYAKO ...
IT'S WEIRD. I CAN'T REALLY IMAGINE A CONVERSATION BETWEEN THEM...
CHIRA (GLANCE)
WHAT ARE THEY TALKING ABOUT?
SO THE OTHER DAY... ...I WENT OVER TO N'S PLACE.
YEAH, YEAH.
N-KUN.
AND THEN ...
... WAKA— W WAS THERE...
W-KUN!
WHY JUST INITIALS!!?
S WAS DOING HER BEST TO TEACH HIM TONE...I MEAN T...
...AND THEN M WOKE UP.
YEAH, YEAH.
M-KUN.
AND THEN ...
... THE DOORBELL RANG, AND M WAS... WAIT, I MEAN, NOT THE SAME M FROM BEFORE ...
UM ...?
C'MON! MIYAKO CAN'T EVEN FOLLOW YOU ANYMORE!!
MIYA-MA—
M—
M—
THAT ...
...ROUND AND PLUMP OLD GUY WITH THE STUBBLE WAS STANDING THERE.
JUST USE HIS DAMN NAME!!!

UNNECESSARY CAUTION

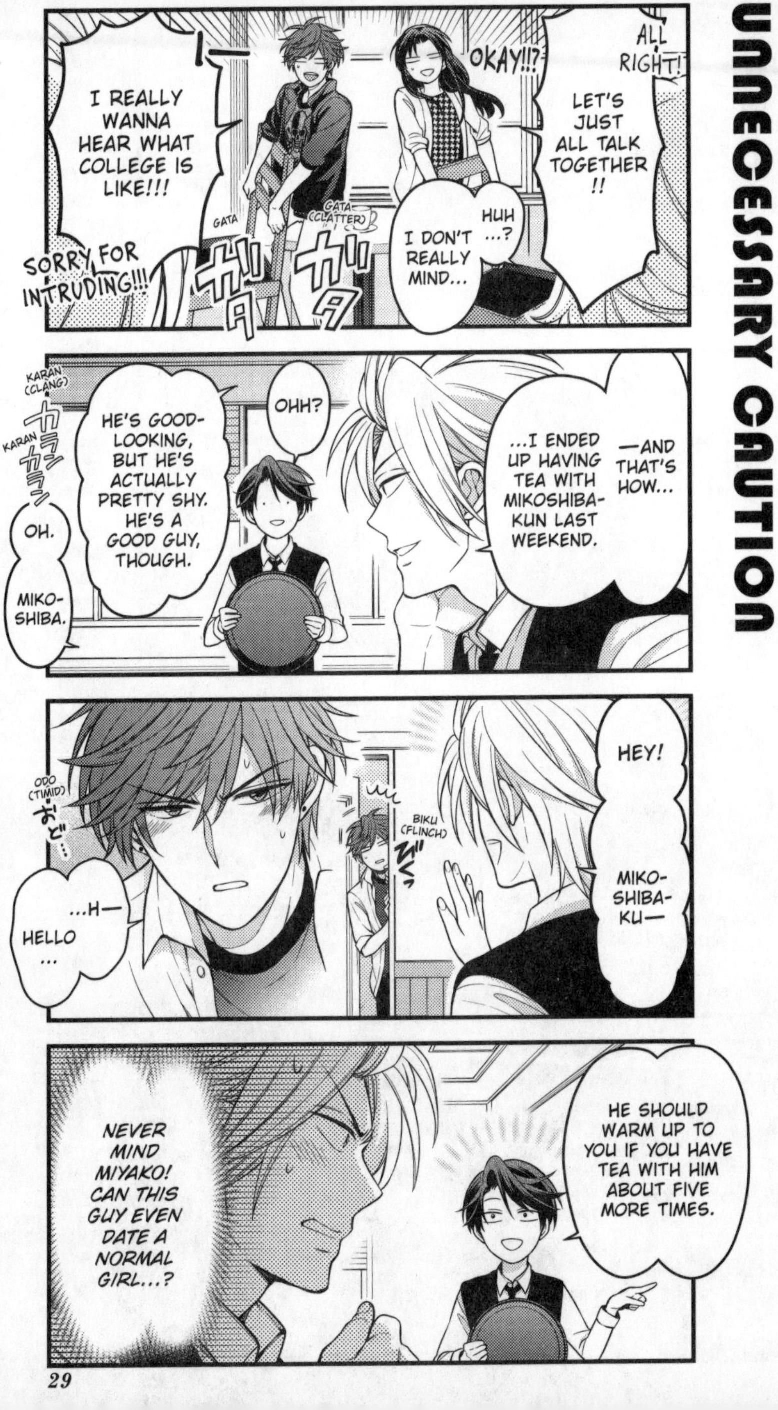

ALL RIGHT!
LET'S JUST ALL TALK TOGETHER!!
OKAY!!?
HUH ...?
I DON'T REALLY MIND...
GATA (CLATTER)
ガタ
GATA
ガタ
I REALLY WANNA HEAR WHAT COLLEGE IS LIKE!!!
SORRY FOR INTRUDING!!!
—AND THAT'S HOW...
...I ENDED UP HAVING TEA WITH MIKOSHIBA-KUN LAST WEEKEND.
OHH?
HE'S GOOD-LOOKING, BUT HE'S ACTUALLY PRETTY SHY. HE'S A GOOD GUY, THOUGH.
KARAN (CLANG)
カラン
KARAN
カラン
OH.
MIKO-SHIBA.
HEY!
MIKO-SHIBA-KU—
BIKU (FLINCH)
ビクッ
ODO (TIMID)
おど…
...H—
HELLO ...
HE SHOULD WARM UP TO YOU IF YOU HAVE TEA WITH HIM ABOUT FIVE MORE TIMES.
NEVER MIND MIYAKO! CAN THIS GUY EVEN DATE A NORMAL GIRL...?

THE RESULTS OF MIKOSHIBA'S HELP

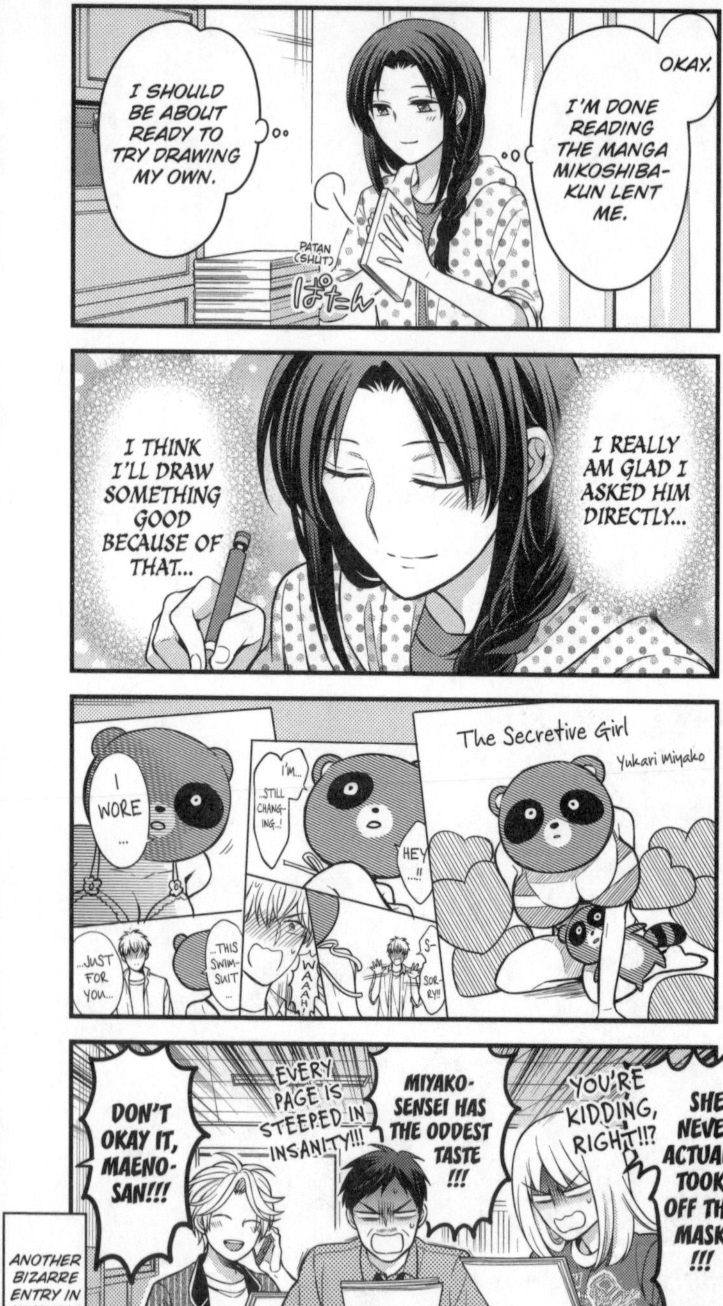
OKAY.
I'M DONE READING THE MANGA MIKOSHIBA-KUN LENT ME.
I SHOULD BE ABOUT READY TO TRY DRAWING MY OWN.
PATAN (SHUT)
ぱたん
I REALLY AM GLAD I ASKED HIM DIRECTLY...
I THINK I'LL DRAW SOMETHING GOOD BECAUSE OF THAT...
The Secretive Girl
Yukari Miyako
I'M... ...STILL CHANGING...!
HEY...!!
I WORE...
S-SORRY!!
WAAAH!
...THIS SWIMSUIT...
...JUST FOR YOU...
SHE NEVER ACTUALLY TOOK OFF THE MASK!!!
YOU'RE KIDDING, RIGHT!!?
MIYAKO-SENSEI HAS THE ODDEST TASTE!!!
EVERY PAGE IS STEEPED IN INSANITY!!!
DON'T OKAY IT, MAENO-SAN!!!
ANOTHER BIZARRE ENTRY IN MIYAKO'S PORT-FOLIO.

MONTHLY GIRLS' × NOZAKI-KUN

[Extra]

TRAITOR

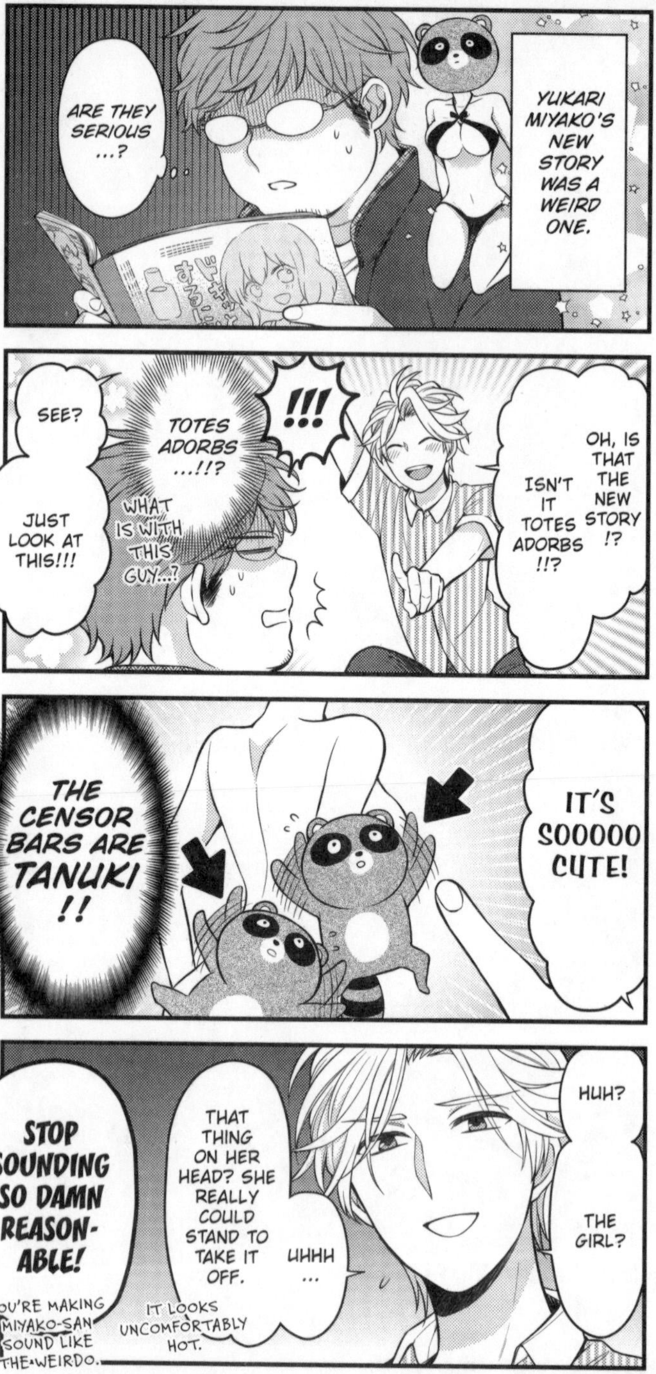
YUKARI MIYAKO'S NEW STORY WAS A WEIRD ONE.
ARE THEY SERIOUS ...?
OH, IS THAT THE NEW STORY !?
ISN'T IT TOTES ADORBS !!?
!!!
TOTES ADORBS ...!!?
WHAT IS WITH THIS GUY...?
SEE?
JUST LOOK AT THIS!!!
IT'S SOOOOO CUTE!
THE CENSOR BARS ARE TANUKI !!
HUH?
THE GIRL?
THAT THING ON HER HEAD? SHE REALLY COULD STAND TO TAKE IT OFF.
UHHH ...
IT LOOKS UNCOMFORTABLY HOT.
STOP SOUNDING SO DAMN REASON-ABLE!
YOU'RE MAKING MIYAKO-SAN SOUND LIKE THE WEIRDO.

[Extra]

THINGS THAT SET HIM ON EDGE

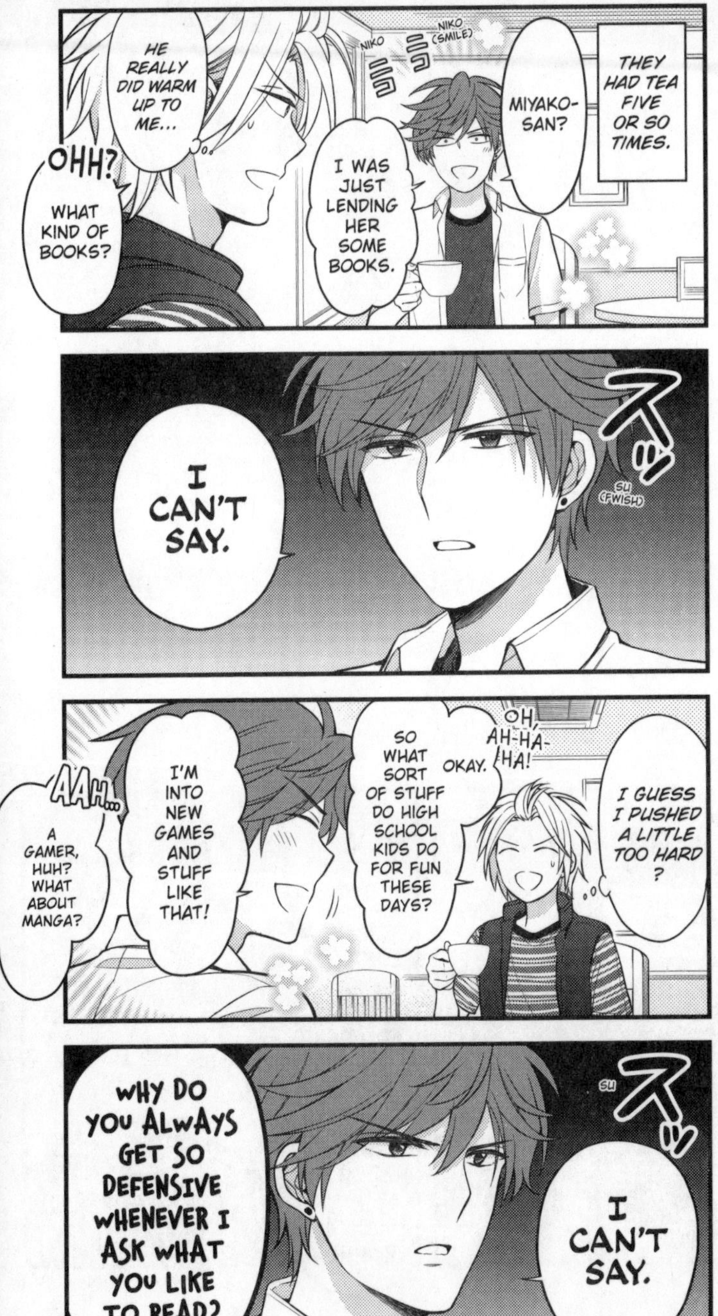
THEY HAD TEA FIVE OR SO TIMES.
MIYAKO-SAN?
NIKO NIKO (SMILE)
I WAS JUST LENDING HER SOME BOOKS.
HE REALLY DID WARM UP TO ME...
OHH? WHAT KIND OF BOOKS?
SU (FWISH)
I CAN'T SAY.
I GUESS I PUSHED A LITTLE TOO HARD?
OH, AH-HA-HA!
OKAY.
SO WHAT SORT OF STUFF DO HIGH SCHOOL KIDS DO FOR FUN THESE DAYS?
I'M INTO NEW GAMES AND STUFF LIKE THAT!
AAH... A GAMER, HUH? WHAT ABOUT MANGA?
SU
I CAN'T SAY.
WHY DO YOU ALWAYS GET SO DEFENSIVE WHENEVER I ASK WHAT YOU LIKE TO READ?

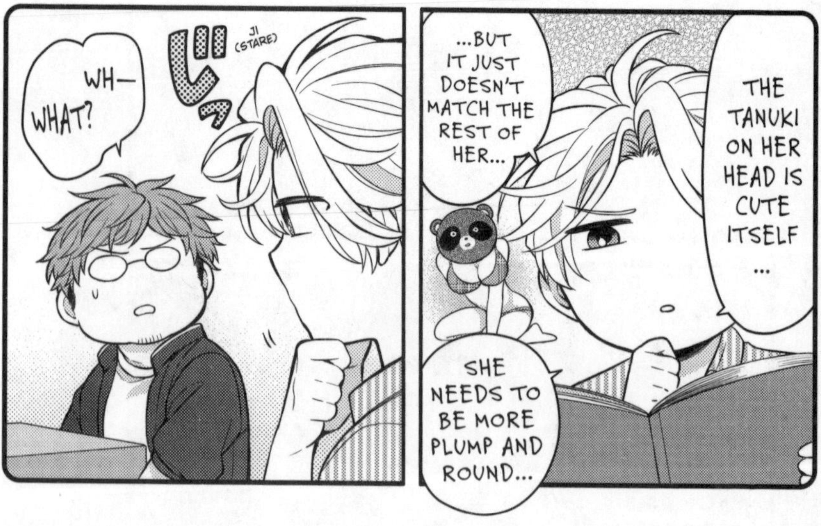
THE TANUKI ON HER HEAD IS CUTE ITSELF ...
...BUT IT JUST DOESN'T MATCH THE REST OF HER...
SHE NEEDS TO BE MORE PLUMP AND ROUND...
JI (STARE)
WH— WHAT?

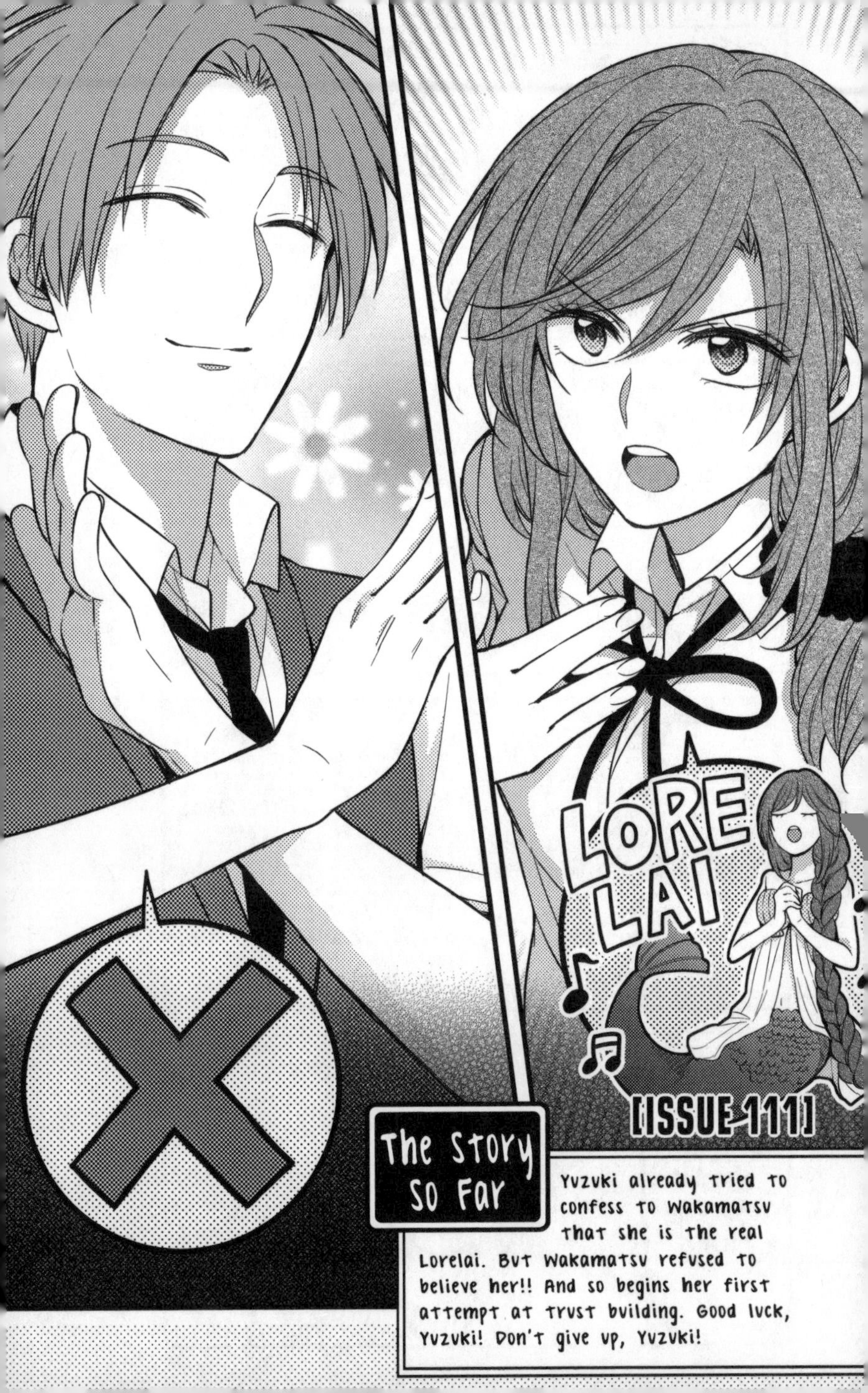
LORELAI
[ISSUE 111]
The Story So Far
Yuzuki already tried to confess to Wakamatsu that she is the real Lorelai. But Wakamatsu refused to believe her!! And so begins her first attempt at trust building. Good luck, Yuzuki! Don't give up, Yuzuki!

THE TRUTH SHE JUST REALIZED

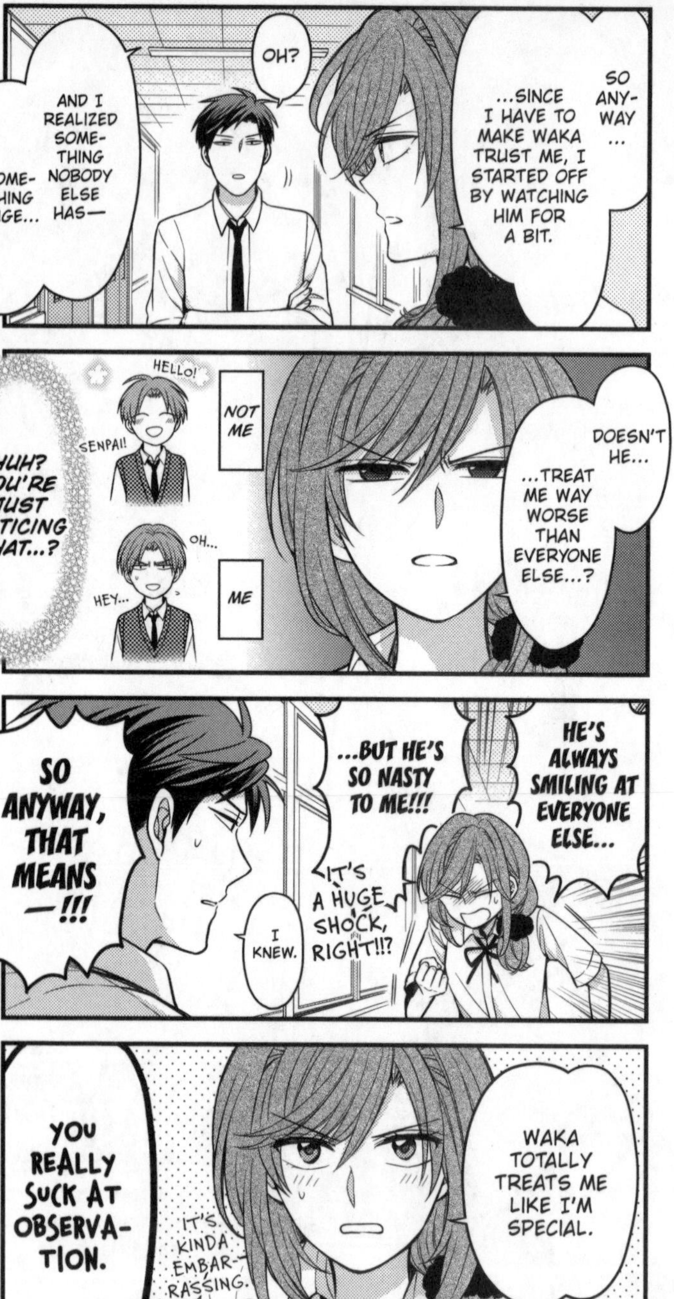
SO ANYWAY...
...SINCE I HAVE TO MAKE WAKA TRUST ME, I STARTED OFF BY WATCHING HIM FOR A BIT.
OH?
AND I REALIZED SOMETHING NOBODY ELSE HAS—
SOMETHING HUGE...
DOESN'T HE...
...TREAT ME WAY WORSE THAN EVERYONE ELSE...?
NOT ME
HELLO!
SENPAI!
ME
OH...
HEY...
HUH? YOU'RE JUST NOTICING THAT...?
HE'S ALWAYS SMILING AT EVERYONE ELSE...
...BUT HE'S SO NASTY TO ME!!!
IT'S A HUGE SHOCK, RIGHT!!?
I KNEW.
SO ANYWAY, THAT MEANS—!!!
WAKA TOTALLY TREATS ME LIKE I'M SPECIAL.
IT'S KINDA EMBARRASSING.
YOU REALLY SUCK AT OBSERVATION.

AN EMOTIONAL CONNECTION

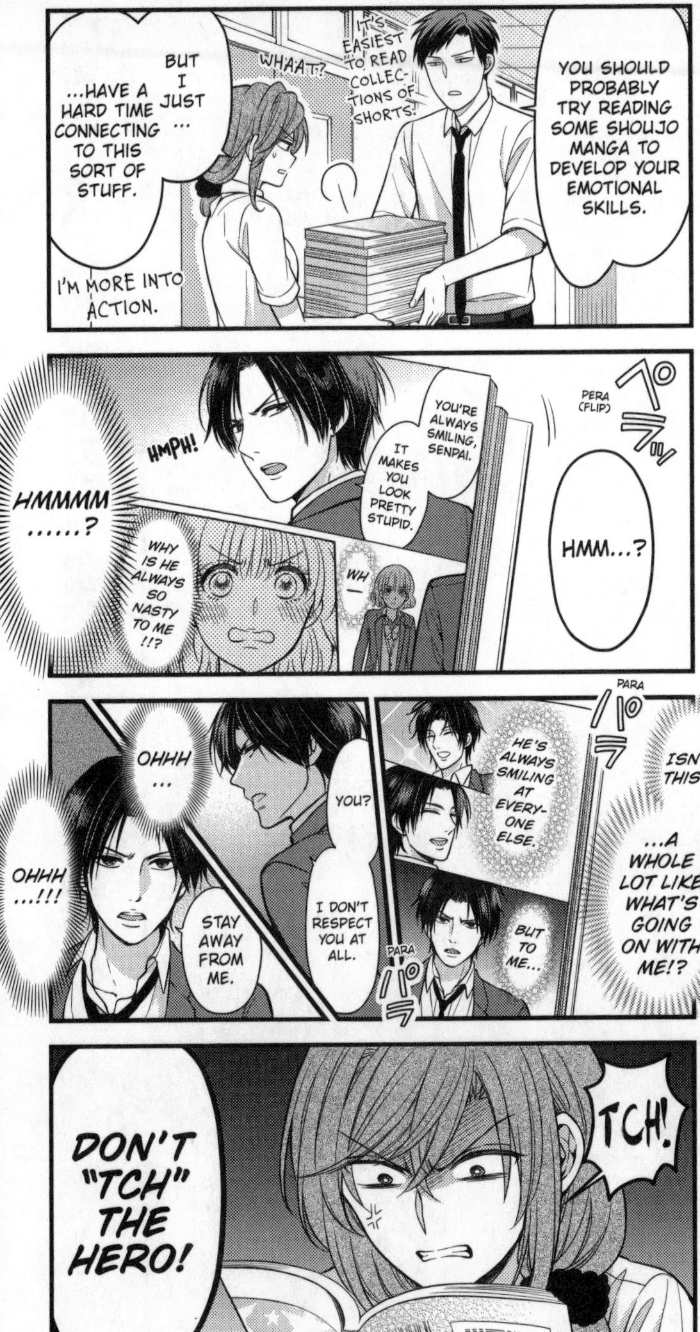
YOU SHOULD PROBABLY TRY READING SOME SHOUJO MANGA TO DEVELOP YOUR EMOTIONAL SKILLS.
IT'S EASIEST TO READ COLLECTIONS OF SHORTS!
WHAAT?
BUT I JUST ...
...HAVE A HARD TIME CONNECTING TO THIS SORT OF STUFF.
I'M MORE INTO ACTION.
PERA (FLIP)
HMM...?
YOU'RE ALWAYS SMILING, SENPAI.
IT MAKES YOU LOOK PRETTY STUPID.
HMPH!
WH—
WHY IS HE ALWAYS SO NASTY TO ME !!?
HMMMM ......?
PARA
ISN'T THIS...
...A WHOLE LOT LIKE WHAT'S GOING ON WITH ME!?
HE'S ALWAYS SMILING AT EVERY-ONE ELSE.
BUT TO ME...
PARA
YOU?
I DON'T RESPECT YOU AT ALL.
STAY AWAY FROM ME.
OHHH ...
OHHH ...!!!
TCH!
DON'T "TCH" THE HERO!

CHIYO-CHAN, PROFESSIONAL READER

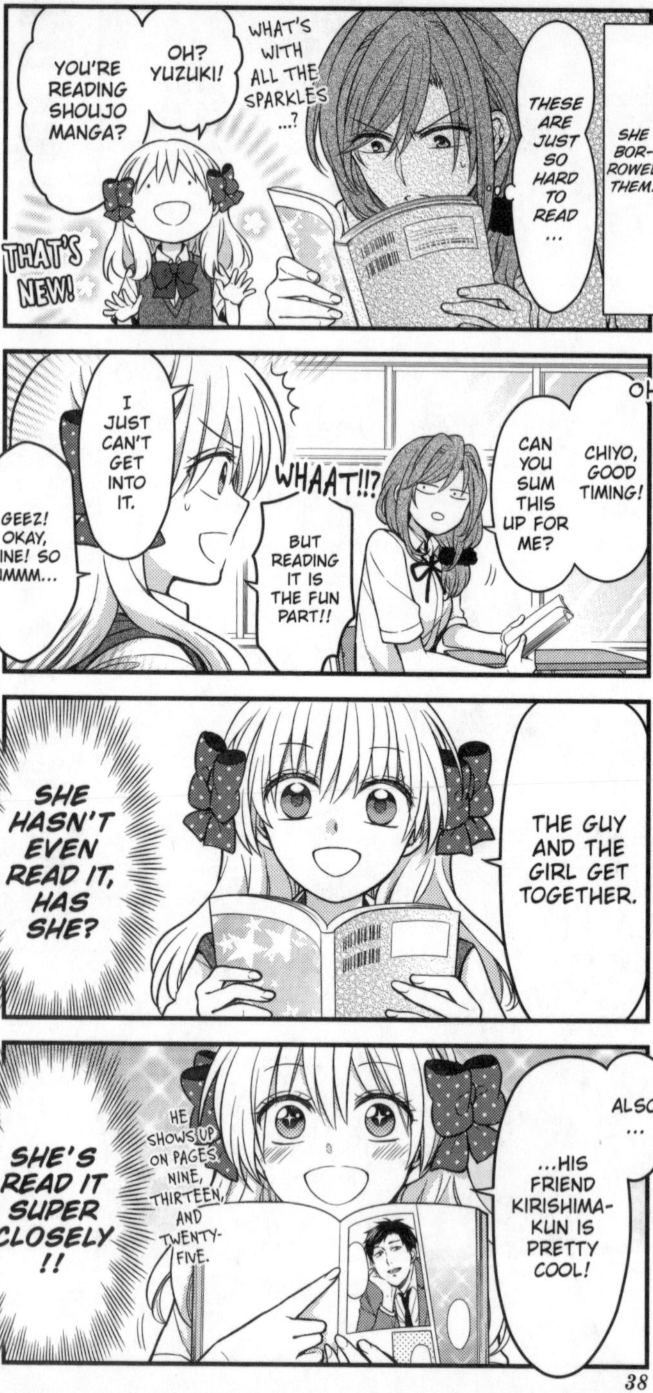
SHE BORROWED THEM.
THESE ARE JUST SO HARD TO READ…
WHAT'S WITH ALL THE SPARKLES…?
OH? YUZUKI!
YOU'RE READING SHOUJO MANGA?
THAT'S NEW!
OH.
CHIYO, GOOD TIMING!
CAN YOU SUM THIS UP FOR ME?
WHAAT!!?
BUT READING IT IS THE FUN PART!!
I JUST CAN'T GET INTO IT.
GEEZ! OKAY, FINE! SO UMMM…
THE GUY AND THE GIRL GET TOGETHER.
SHE HASN'T EVEN READ IT, HAS SHE?
ALSO…
…HIS FRIEND KIRISHIMA-KUN IS PRETTY COOL!
HE SHOWS UP ON PAGES NINE, THIRTEEN, AND TWENTY-FIVE.
SHE'S READ IT SUPER CLOSELY!!

YOU CAN'T ESCAPE

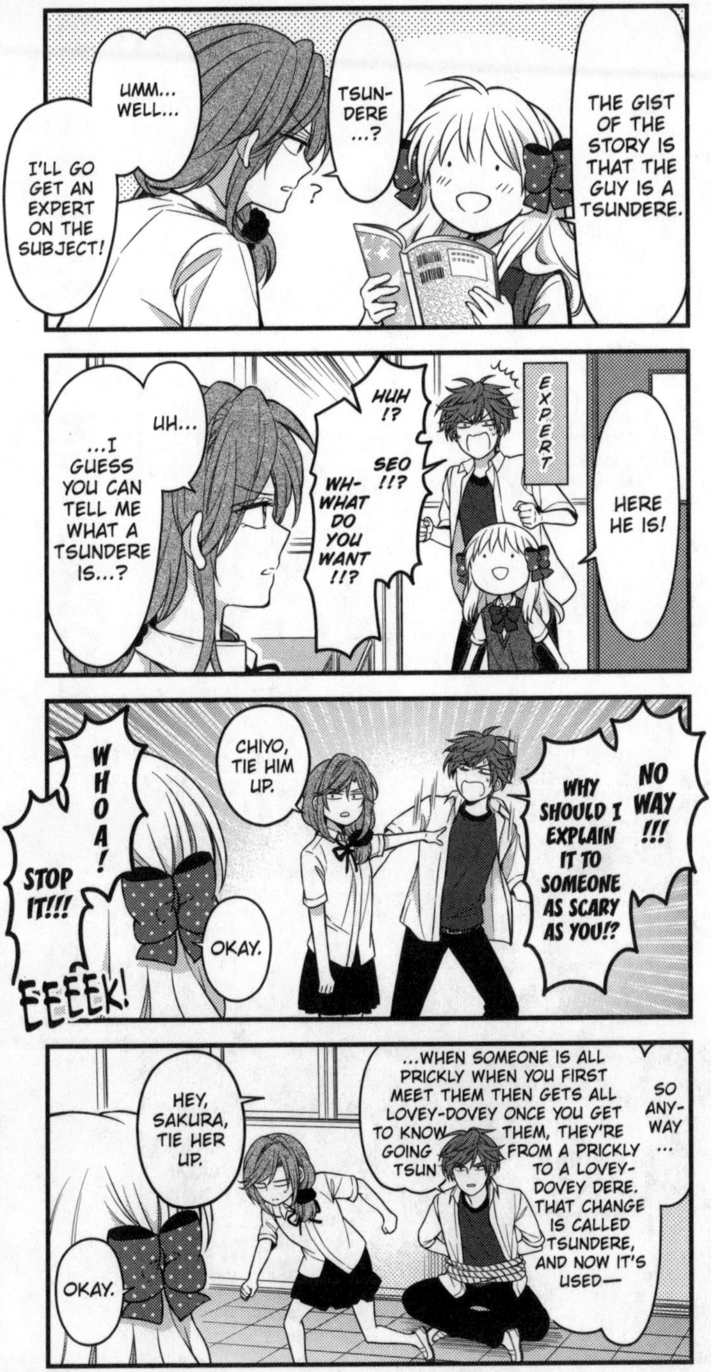
THE GIST OF THE STORY IS THAT THE GUY IS A TSUNDERE.
TSUN-DERE ...?
?
UMM... WELL...
I'LL GO GET AN EXPERT ON THE SUBJECT!
HERE HE IS!
EXPERT
HUH!?
SEO!!?
WH-WHAT DO YOU WANT!!?
UH...
...I GUESS YOU CAN TELL ME WHAT A TSUNDERE IS...?
NO WAY!!!
WHY SHOULD I EXPLAIN IT TO SOMEONE AS SCARY AS YOU!?
CHIYO, TIE HIM UP.
WHOA! STOP IT!!!
OKAY.
EEEEK!
SO ANYWAY...
...WHEN SOMEONE IS ALL PRICKLY WHEN YOU FIRST MEET THEM THEN GETS ALL LOVEY-DOVEY ONCE YOU GET TO KNOW THEM, THEY'RE GOING FROM A PRICKLY TSUN TO A LOVEY-DOVEY DERE. THAT CHANGE IS CALLED TSUNDERE, AND NOW IT'S USED—
HEY, SAKURA, TIE HER UP.
OKAY.

THE FRUITS OF HER LABOR

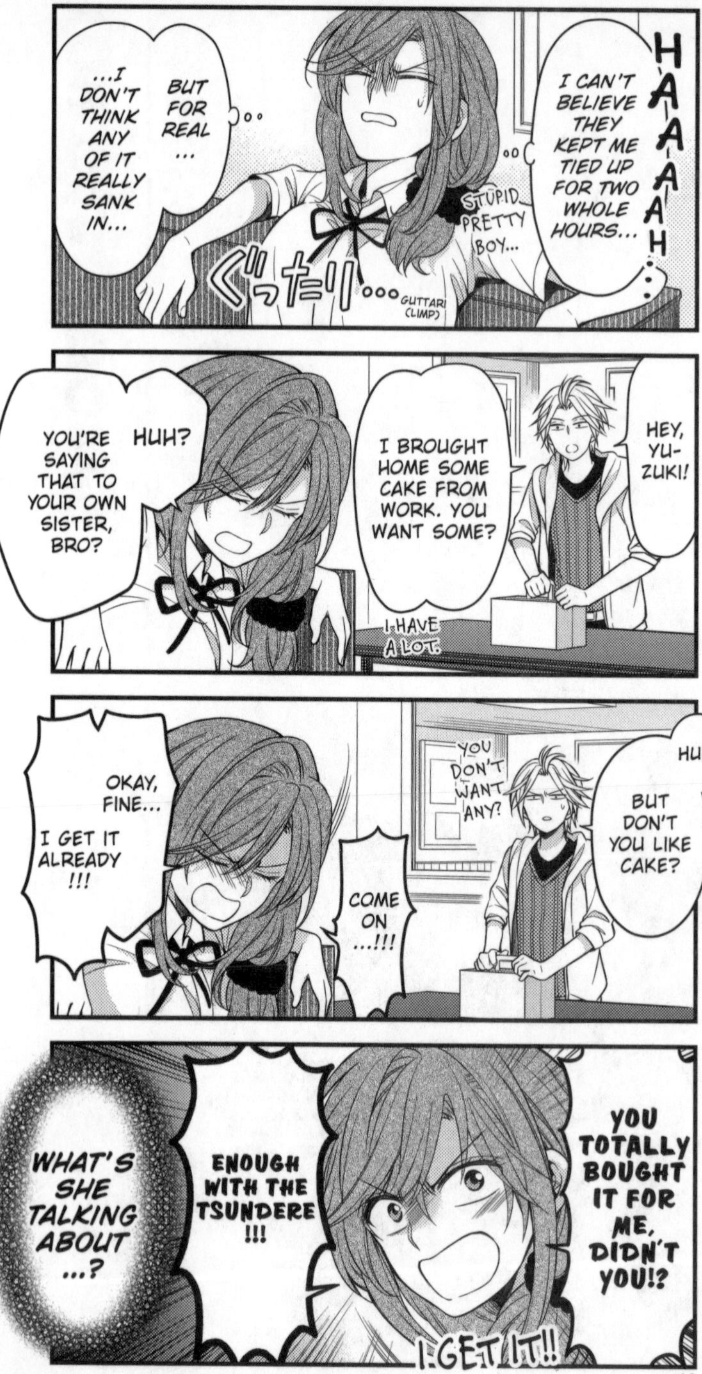
HAAAAH...
I CAN'T BELIEVE THEY KEPT ME TIED UP FOR TWO WHOLE HOURS...
STUPID PRETTY BOY...
BUT FOR REAL...
...I DON'T THINK ANY OF IT REALLY SANK IN...
ぐったり...
GUTTARI (LIMP)
HEY, YU-ZUKI!
I BROUGHT HOME SOME CAKE FROM WORK. YOU WANT SOME?
I HAVE A LOT.
HUH?
YOU'RE SAYING THAT TO YOUR OWN SISTER, BRO?
HUH?
BUT DON'T YOU LIKE CAKE?
YOU DON'T WANT ANY?
COME ON ...!!!
OKAY, FINE...
I GET IT ALREADY !!!
YOU TOTALLY BOUGHT IT FOR ME, DIDN'T YOU!?
I GET IT!!
ENOUGH WITH THE TSUNDERE !!!
WHAT'S SHE TALKING ABOUT ...?

SENPAI'S GROWTH

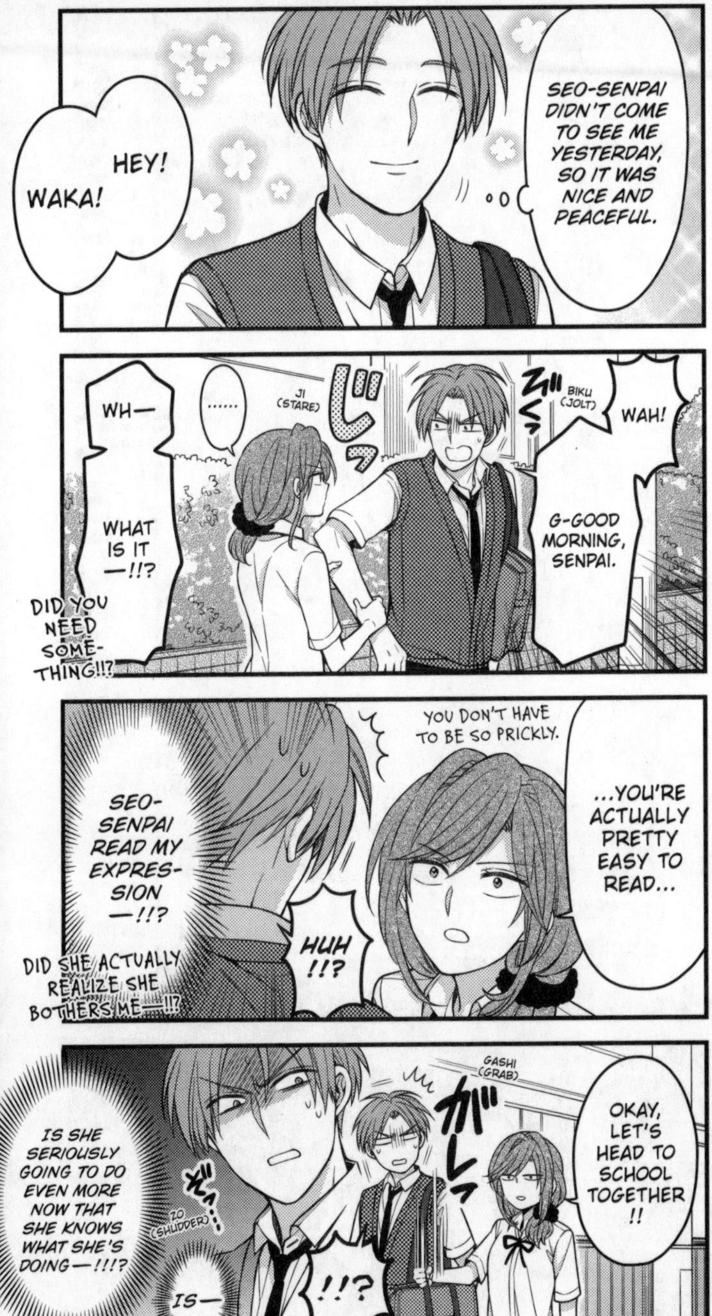
SEO-SENPAI DIDN'T COME TO SEE ME YESTERDAY, SO IT WAS NICE AND PEACEFUL.
HEY! WAKA!
WAH!
G-GOOD MORNING, SENPAI.
BIKU (JOLT)
JI (STARE)
......
WH— WHAT IS IT—!!?
DID YOU NEED SOME-THING!!?
YOU DON'T HAVE TO BE SO PRICKLY.
...YOU'RE ACTUALLY PRETTY EASY TO READ...
HUH !!?
SEO-SENPAI READ MY EXPRES-SION—!!?
DID SHE ACTUALLY REALIZE SHE BOTHERS ME—!!?
OKAY, LET'S HEAD TO SCHOOL TOGETHER!!
GASHI (GRAB)
!!?
ZO (SHUDDER)
IS—
IS SHE SERIOUSLY GOING TO DO EVEN MORE NOW THAT SHE KNOWS WHAT SHE'S DOING—!!!?

A GRAND PERFORMANCE

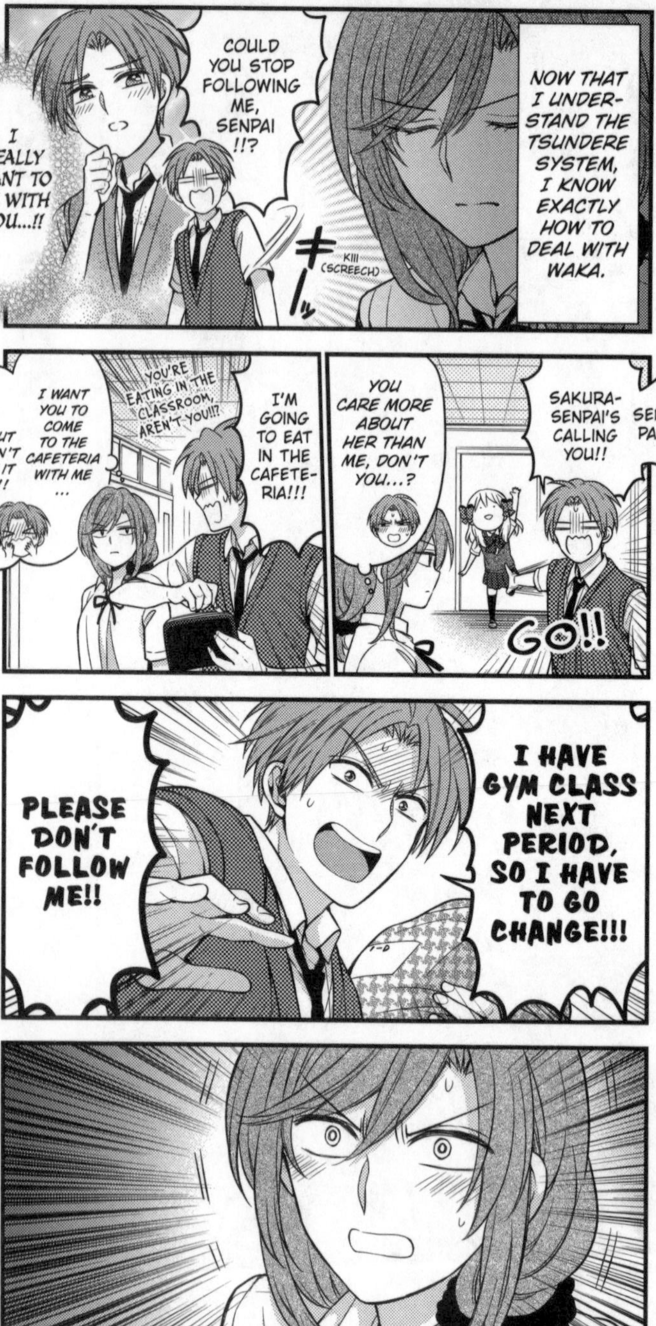
NOW THAT I UNDERSTAND THE TSUNDERE SYSTEM, I KNOW EXACTLY HOW TO DEAL WITH WAKA.
COULD YOU STOP FOLLOWING ME, SENPAI!!?
I REALLY WANT TO BE WITH YOU...!!
KIII (SCREECH)
SEN-PAI!
SAKURA-SENPAI'S CALLING YOU!!
YOU CARE MORE ABOUT HER THAN ME, DON'T YOU...?
GO!!
I'M GOING TO EAT IN THE CAFETERIA!!!
YOU'RE EATING IN THE CLASSROOM, AREN'T YOU!!?
I WANT YOU TO COME TO THE CAFETERIA WITH ME ...
...BUT I CAN'T SAY IT—!!
I HAVE GYM CLASS NEXT PERIOD, SO I HAVE TO GO CHANGE!!!
PLEASE DON'T FOLLOW ME!!

FALSE ACCUSATION

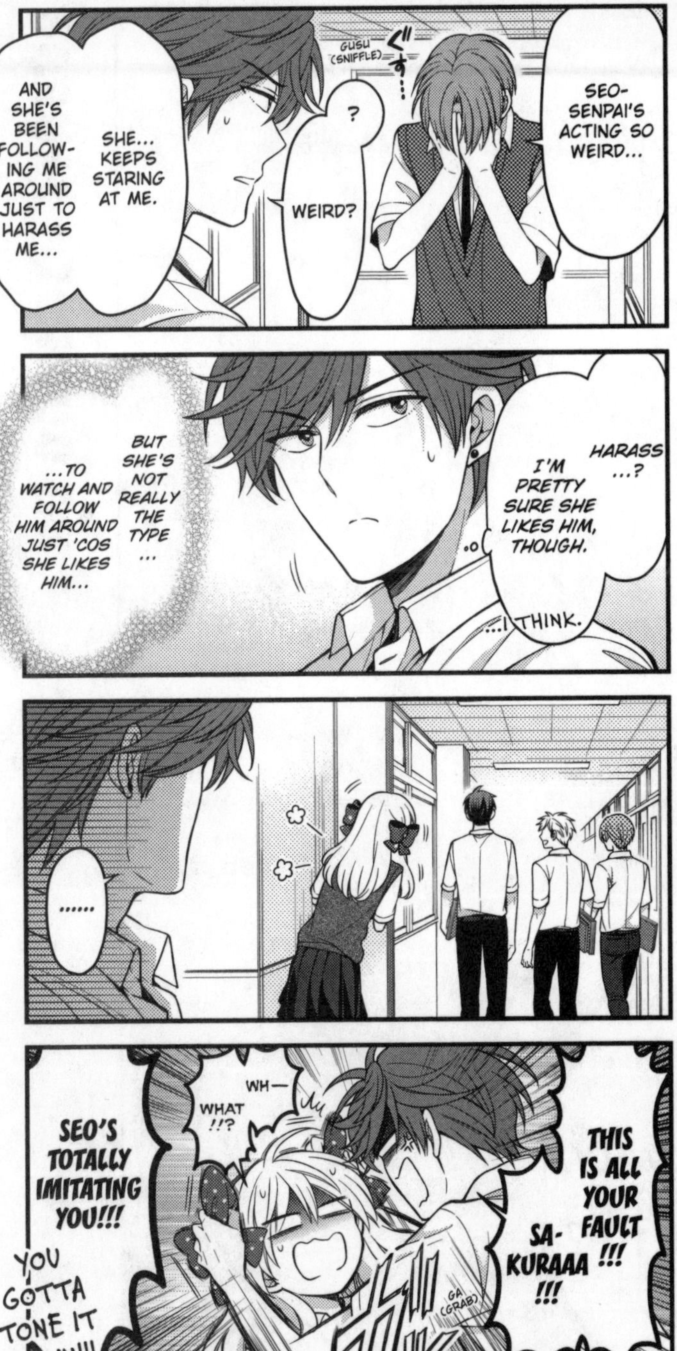
SEO-SENPAI'S ACTING SO WEIRD...
GUSU (SNIFFLE)
? WEIRD?
SHE... KEEPS STARING AT ME.
AND SHE'S BEEN FOLLOWING ME AROUND JUST TO HARASS ME...
HARASS ...?
I'M PRETTY SURE SHE LIKES HIM, THOUGH.
...I THINK.
BUT SHE'S NOT REALLY THE TYPE ...
...TO WATCH AND FOLLOW HIM AROUND JUST 'COS SHE LIKES HIM...
......
THIS IS ALL YOUR FAULT!!!
SA-KURAAA!!!
WH—
WHAT!!?
SEO'S TOTALLY IMITATING YOU!!!
YOU GOTTA TONE IT DOWN!!!
GA (GRAB)

ALWAYS LOOKING UP

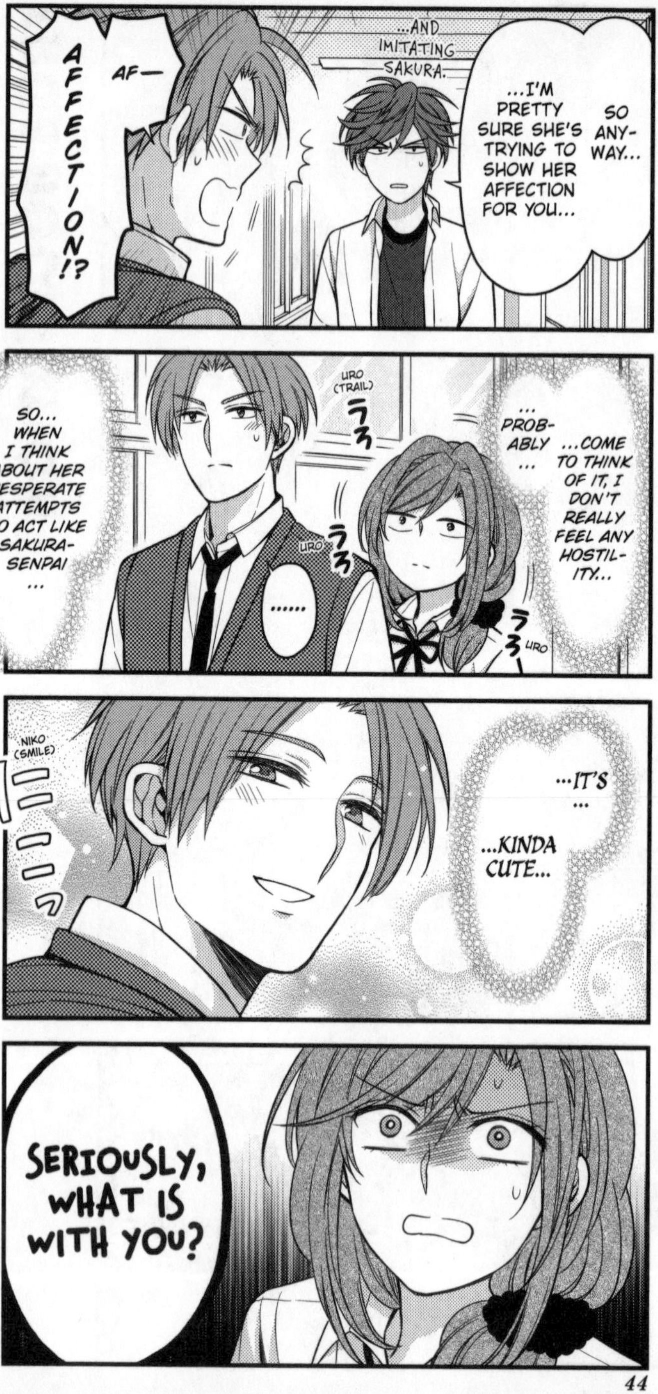
SO ANY-WAY...
...I'M PRETTY SURE SHE'S TRYING TO SHOW HER AFFECTION FOR YOU...
...AND IMITATING SAKURA.
AF—
AFFECTION!?
...COME TO THINK OF IT, I DON'T REALLY FEEL ANY HOSTIL-ITY...
...PROB-ABLY...
URO (TRAIL)
URO
URO
......
SO... WHEN I THINK ABOUT HER DESPERATE ATTEMPTS TO ACT LIKE SAKURA-SENPAI...
...IT'S... ...KINDA CUTE...
NIKO (SMILE)
SERIOUSLY, WHAT IS WITH YOU?

THE EVENTUAL CONCLUSION ①

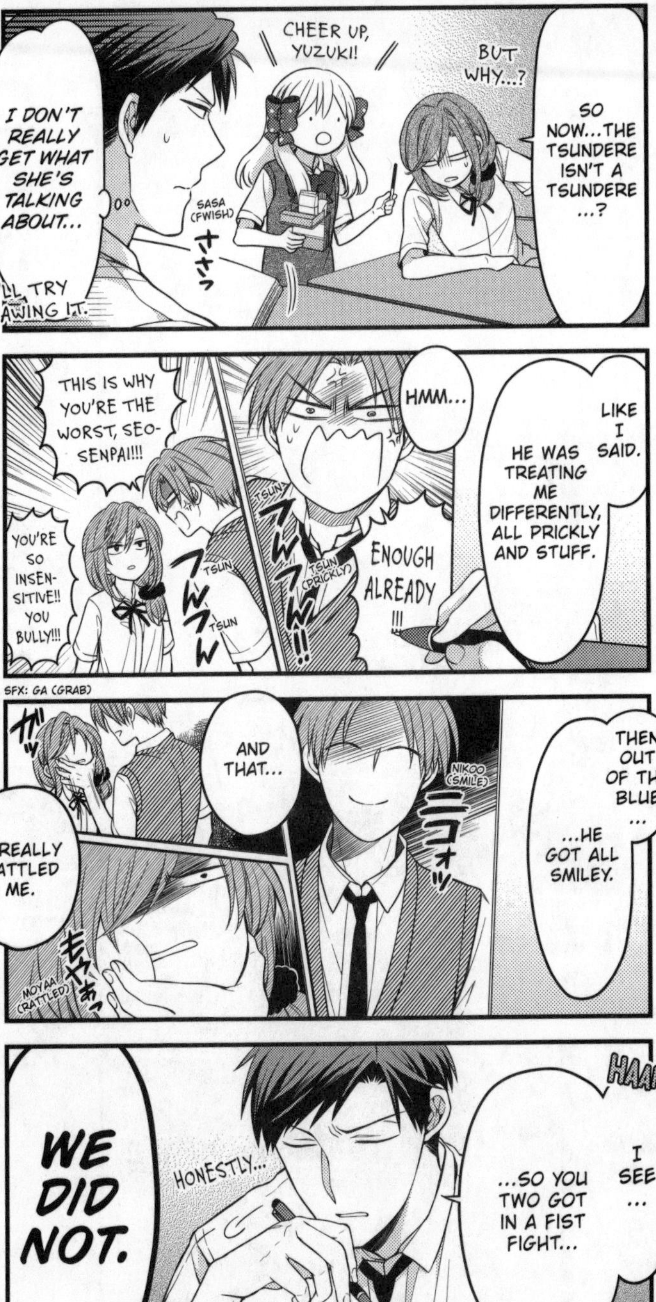

SO NOW...THE TSUNDERE ISN'T A TSUNDERE...?
BUT WHY...?
CHEER UP, YUZUKI!
SASA (FWISH)
I DON'T REALLY GET WHAT SHE'S TALKING ABOUT...
I'LL TRY DRAWING IT.
LIKE I SAID.
HE WAS TREATING ME DIFFERENTLY, ALL PRICKLY AND STUFF.
HMM...
ENOUGH ALREADY!!!
TSUN (PRICKLY)
TSUN
TSUN
TSUN
THIS IS WHY YOU'RE THE WORST, SEO-SENPAI!!!
YOU'RE SO INSENSITIVE!! YOU BULLY!!!
SFX: GA (GRAB)
THEN OUT OF THE BLUE...
...HE GOT ALL SMILEY.
NIKOO (SMILE)
AND THAT...
...REALLY RATTLED ME.
MOYAA (RATTLED)
HAAH...
I SEE...
...SO YOU TWO GOT IN A FIST FIGHT...
HONESTLY...
WE DID NOT.

THE EVENTUAL CONCLUSION ②

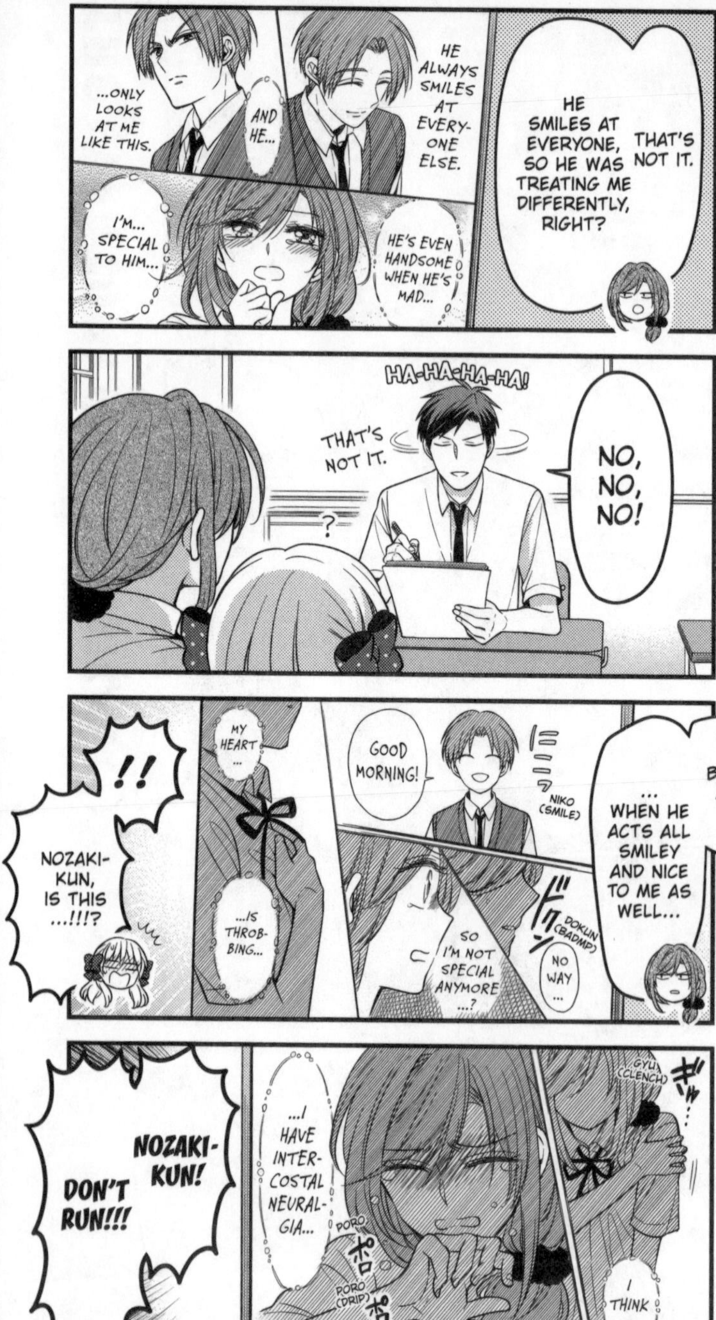
THAT'S NOT IT.
HE SMILES AT EVERYONE, SO HE WAS TREATING ME DIFFERENTLY, RIGHT?
HE ALWAYS SMILES AT EVERY-ONE ELSE.
AND HE...
...ONLY LOOKS AT ME LIKE THIS.
HE'S EVEN HANDSOME WHEN HE'S MAD...
I'M... SPECIAL TO HIM...
HA-HA-HA-HA!
NO, NO, NO!
THAT'S NOT IT.
?
BUT ...
... WHEN HE ACTS ALL SMILEY AND NICE TO ME AS WELL...
GOOD MORNING!
NIKO (SMILE)
DOKUN (BADMP)
NO WAY ...
SO I'M NOT SPECIAL ANYMORE ...?
MY HEART ...
...IS THROB-BING...
!!
NOZAKI-KUN, IS THIS ...!!!?
GYU (CLENCH)
I THINK ...
...I HAVE INTER-COSTAL NEURAL-GIA...
PORO
PORO (DRIP)
NOZAKI-KUN!
DON'T RUN!!!

TSUNDERE SUSPICIONS

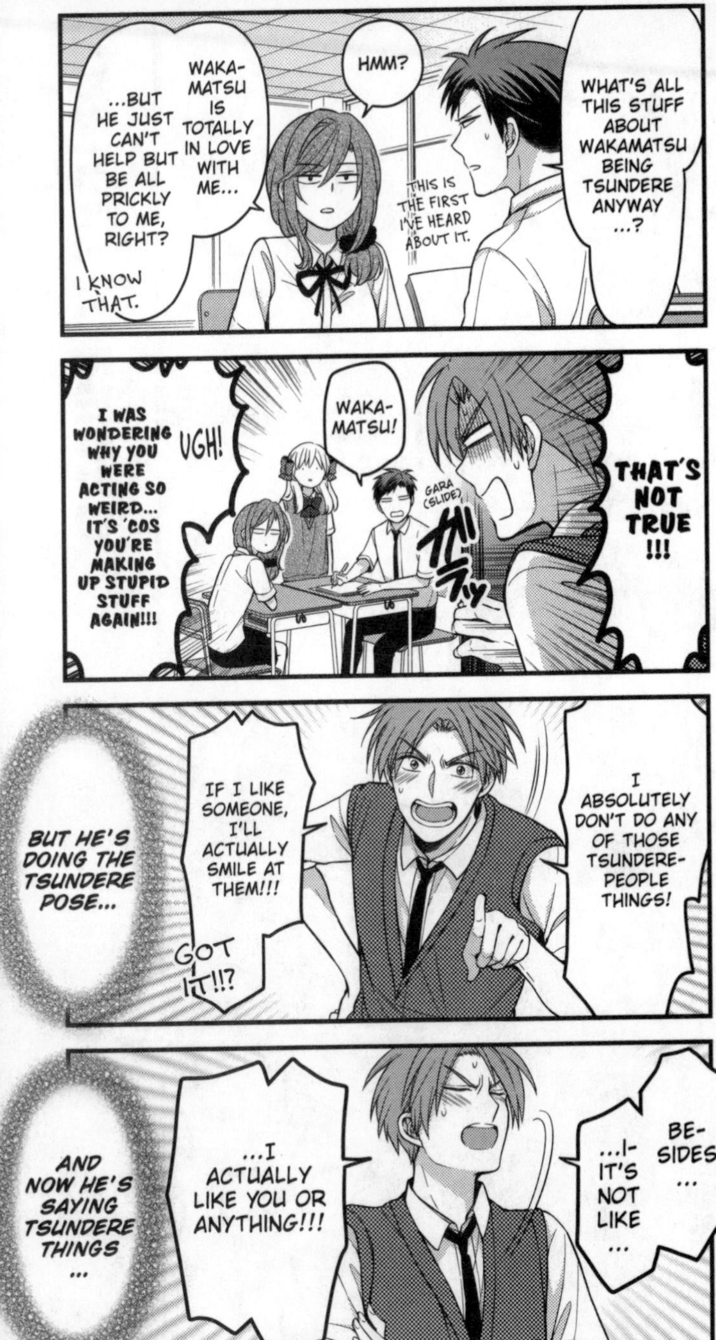
WHAT'S ALL THIS STUFF ABOUT WAKAMATSU BEING TSUNDERE ANYWAY ...?
THIS IS THE FIRST I'VE HEARD ABOUT IT.
HMM?
WAKAMATSU IS TOTALLY IN LOVE WITH ME...
...BUT HE JUST CAN'T HELP BUT BE ALL PRICKLY TO ME, RIGHT?
I KNOW THAT.
THAT'S NOT TRUE!!!
GARA (SLIDE)
WAKAMATSU!
UGH!
I WAS WONDERING WHY YOU WERE ACTING SO WEIRD... IT'S 'COS YOU'RE MAKING UP STUPID STUFF AGAIN!!!
I ABSOLUTELY DON'T DO ANY OF THOSE TSUNDERE-PEOPLE THINGS!
IF I LIKE SOMEONE, I'LL ACTUALLY SMILE AT THEM!!!
GOT IT!!?
BUT HE'S DOING THE TSUNDERE POSE...
BE-SIDES ...
...I-IT'S NOT LIKE ...
...I ACTUALLY LIKE YOU OR ANYTHING!!!
AND NOW HE'S SAYING TSUNDERE THINGS ...

STRAIGHTFORWARD

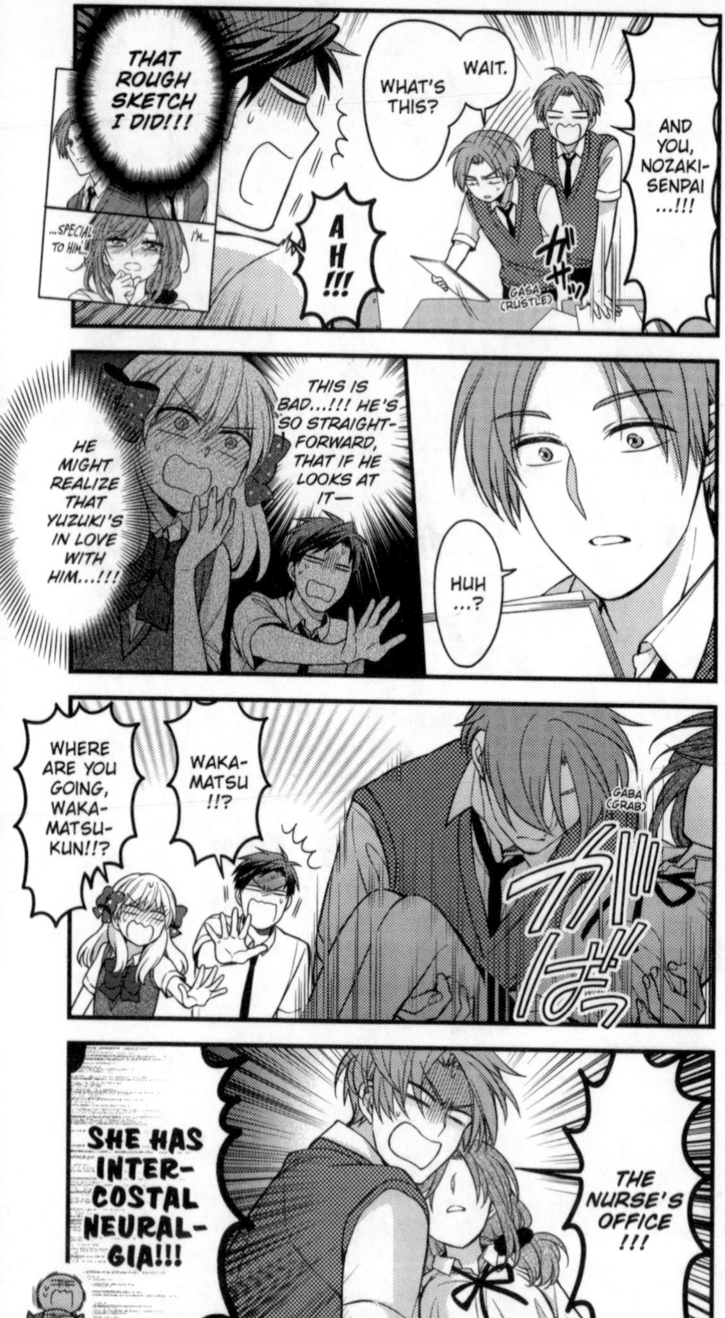

AND YOU, NOZAKI-SENPAI...!!!
GASA (RUSTLE)
WAIT. WHAT'S THIS?
AH!!!
I'M...
...SPECIAL TO HIM...
THAT ROUGH SKETCH I DID!!!
HUH...?
THIS IS BAD...!!! HE'S SO STRAIGHT-FORWARD, THAT IF HE LOOKS AT IT—
HE MIGHT REALIZE THAT YUZUKI'S IN LOVE WITH HIM...!!!
GABA (GRAB)
WAKAMATSU!!?
WHERE ARE YOU GOING, WAKAMATSU-KUN!!?
THE NURSE'S OFFICE!!!
SHE HAS INTER-COSTAL NEURAL-GIA!!!

HER ETERNAL MISSION

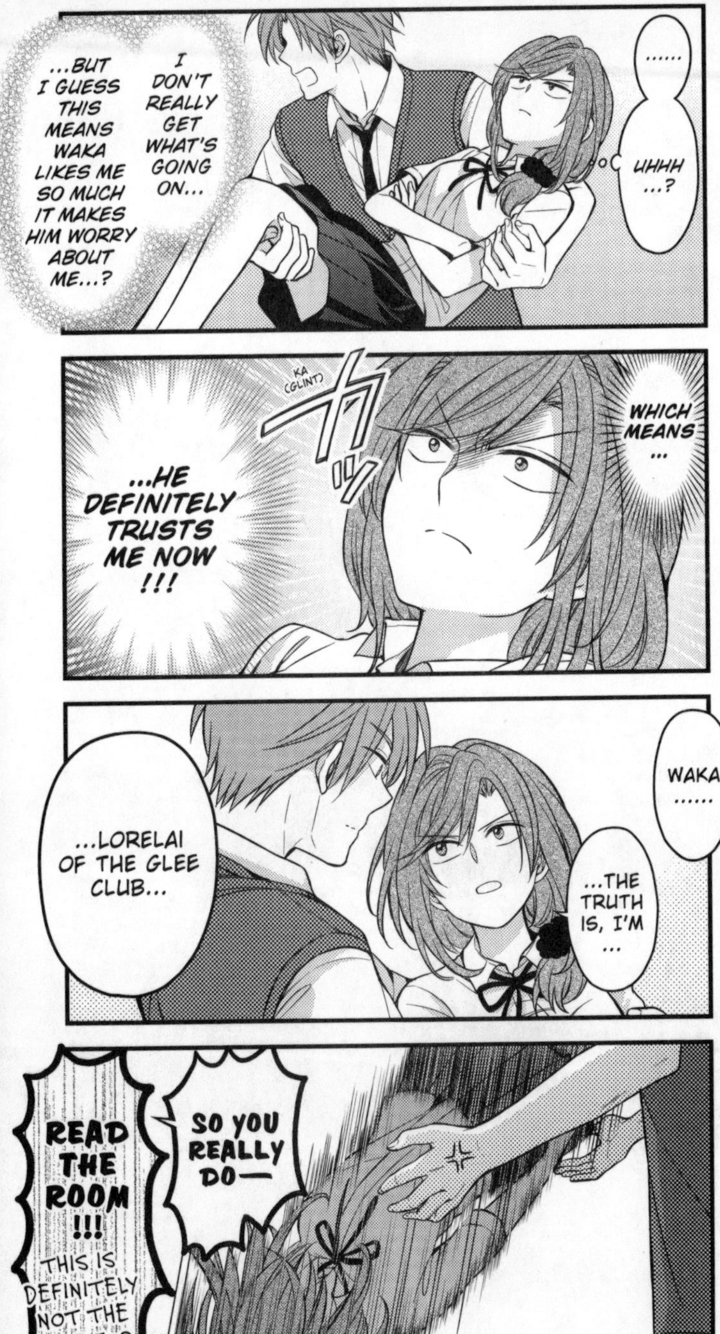

......
UHHH ...?
I DON'T REALLY GET WHAT'S GOING ON...
...BUT I GUESS THIS MEANS WAKA LIKES ME SO MUCH IT MAKES HIM WORRY ABOUT ME...?
WHICH MEANS ...
KA (GLINT)
...HE DEFINITELY TRUSTS ME NOW !!!
WAKA ......
...THE TRUTH IS, I'M ...
...LORELAI OF THE GLEE CLUB...
SO YOU REALLY DO—
READ THE ROOM !!!
THIS IS DEFINITELY NOT THE TIME FOR THAT!!!

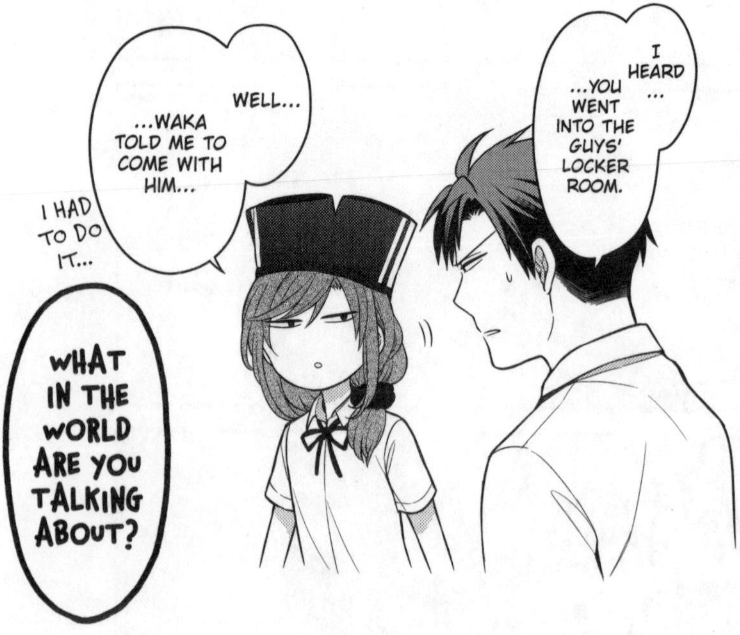
I HEARD... ...YOU WENT INTO THE GUYS' LOCKER ROOM.
WELL... ...WAKA TOLD ME TO COME WITH HIM...
I HAD TO DO IT...
WHAT IN THE WORLD ARE YOU TALKING ABOUT?

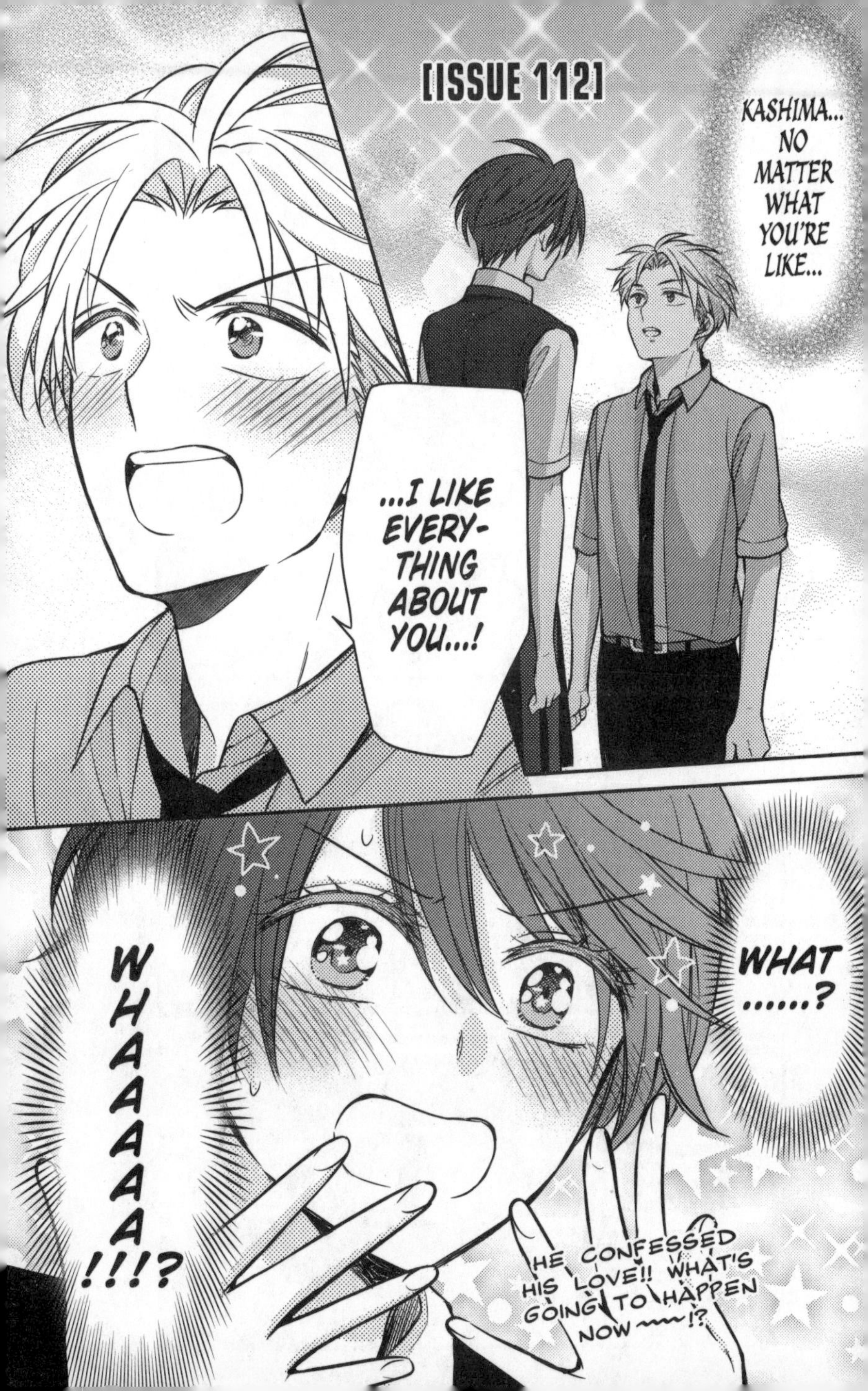
[ISSUE 112]
KASHIMA... NO MATTER WHAT YOU'RE LIKE...
...I LIKE EVERY-THING ABOUT YOU...!
WHAT ......?
WHAAAAAAA!!!?
HE CONFESSED HIS LOVE!! WHAT'S GOING TO HAPPEN NOW~~!?

RIGHT NOW, SHE'S...

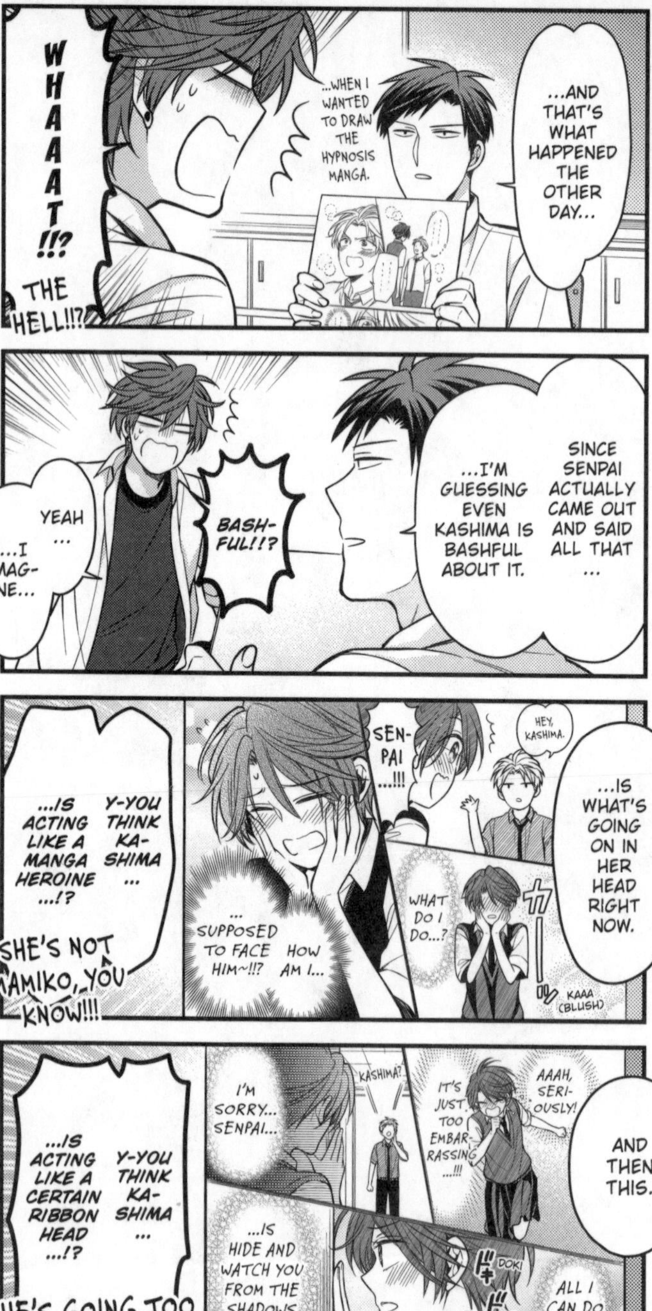

...AND THAT'S WHAT HAPPENED THE OTHER DAY...
...WHEN I WANTED TO DRAW THE HYPNOSIS MANGA.
WHAAAAT!!?
THE HELL!!?
SINCE SENPAI ACTUALLY CAME OUT AND SAID ALL THAT...
...I'M GUESSING EVEN KASHIMA IS BASHFUL ABOUT IT.
BASH-FUL!!?
YEAH... ...I IMAGINE...
...THIS... ...IS WHAT'S GOING ON IN HER HEAD RIGHT NOW.
HEY, KASHIMA.
SEN-PAI...!!!
KAAA (BLUSH)
WHAT DO I DO...?
HOW AM I... ...SUPPOSED TO FACE HIM~!!?
Y-YOU THINK KA-SHIMA... ...IS ACTING LIKE A MANGA HEROINE...!?
SHE'S NOT MAMIKO, YOU KNOW!!!
AND THEN THIS.
AAAH, SERI-OUSLY!
IT'S JUST TOO EMBAR-RASSING...!!!
KASHIMA?
I'M SORRY... SENPAI...
ALL I CAN DO NOW...
...IS HIDE AND WATCH YOU FROM THE SHADOWS...
DOKI
DOKI (BADMP)
Y-YOU THINK KA-SHIMA... ...IS ACTING LIKE A CERTAIN RIBBON HEAD...!?
SHE'S GOING TOO FAR, YOU KNOW!!!

THE CHANGE IN HIS BEST FRIEND

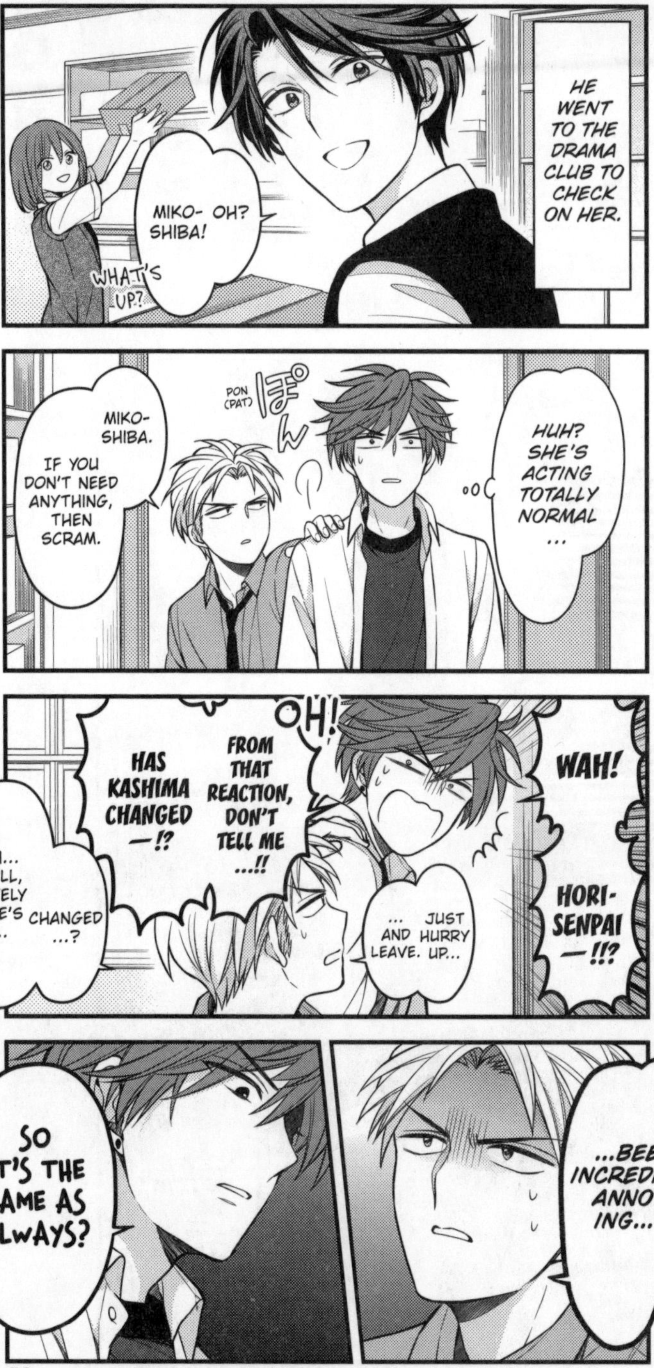
HE WENT TO THE DRAMA CLUB TO CHECK ON HER.
OH?
MIKO-SHIBA!
WHAT'S UP?
HUH? SHE'S ACTING TOTALLY NORMAL ...
PON (PAT)
ぽん
MIKO-SHIBA.
IF YOU DON'T NEED ANYTHING, THEN SCRAM.
WAH!
HORI-SENPAI—!!?
OH!
FROM THAT REACTION, DON'T TELL ME ...!!
HAS KASHIMA CHANGED—!?
JUST HURRY UP... ... AND LEAVE.
OH... WELL, LATELY SHE'S ...
CHANGED ...?
...BEEN INCREDIBLY ANNOY-ING...
SO IT'S THE SAME AS ALWAYS?

SO MEAN

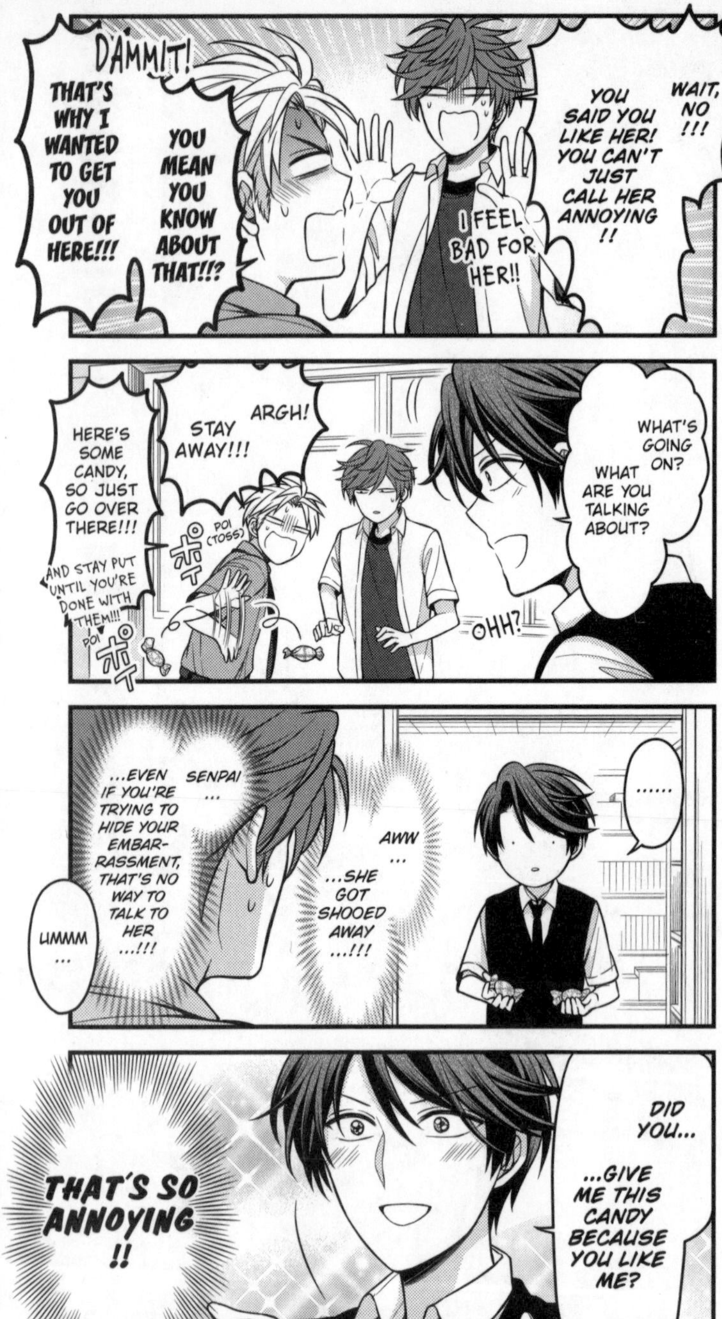

WAIT, NO !!!
YOU SAID YOU LIKE HER! YOU CAN'T JUST CALL HER ANNOYING !!
I FEEL BAD FOR HER!!
YOU MEAN YOU KNOW ABOUT THAT!!?
D'AMMIT!
THAT'S WHY I WANTED TO GET YOU OUT OF HERE!!!
WHAT'S GOING ON?
WHAT ARE YOU TALKING ABOUT?
OHH?
ARGH!
STAY AWAY!!!
HERE'S SOME CANDY, SO JUST GO OVER THERE!!!
ポイ
POI (TOSS)
AND STAY PUT UNTIL YOU'RE DONE WITH THEM!!!
ポイ
POI
......
AWW ...
...SHE GOT SHOOED AWAY ...!!!
SENPAI ...
...EVEN IF YOU'RE TRYING TO HIDE YOUR EMBARRASSMENT, THAT'S NO WAY TO TALK TO HER ...!!!
UMMM ...
DID YOU...
...GIVE ME THIS CANDY BECAUSE YOU LIKE ME?
THAT'S SO ANNOYING !!

BECAUSE HE LIKES HER?

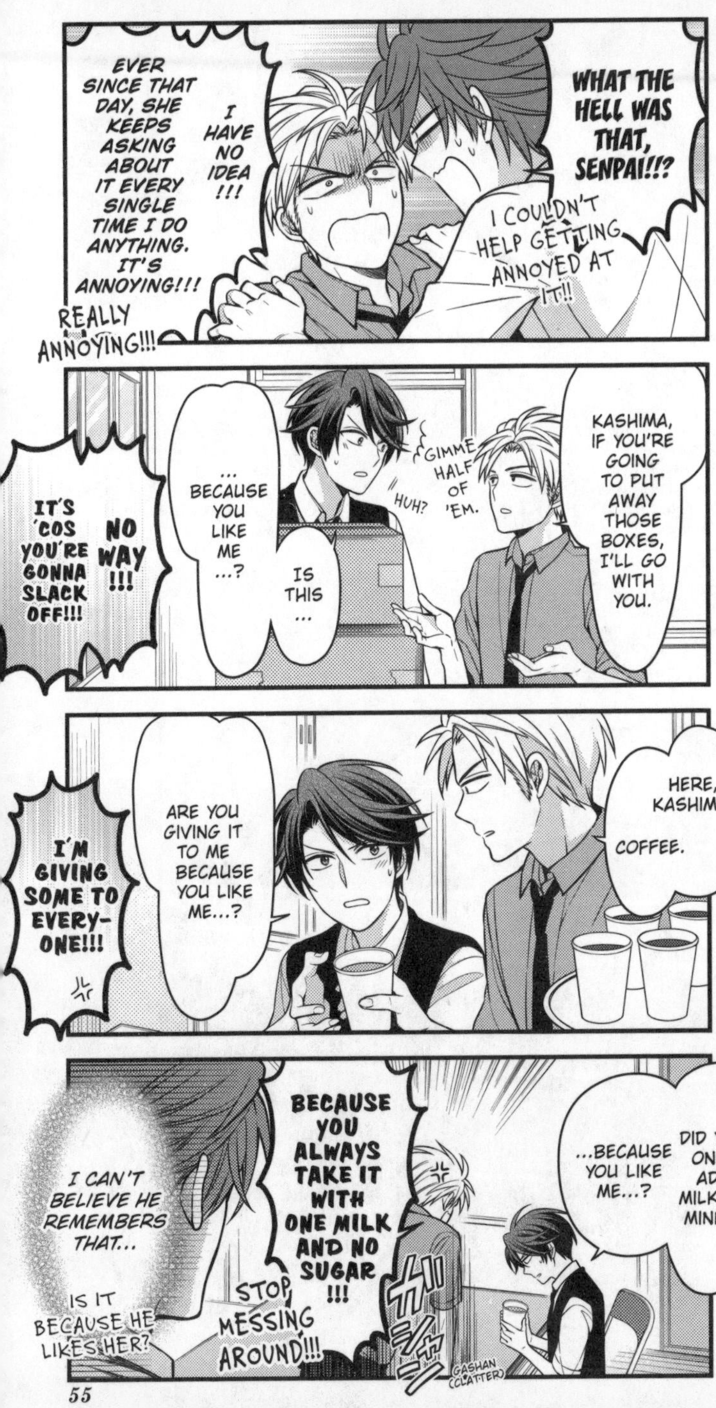

WHAT THE HELL WAS THAT, SENPAI!!?
I COULDN'T HELP GETTING ANNOYED AT IT!!
I HAVE NO IDEA!!!
EVER SINCE THAT DAY, SHE KEEPS ASKING ABOUT IT EVERY SINGLE TIME I DO ANYTHING. IT'S ANNOYING!!!
REALLY ANNOYING!!!
KASHIMA, IF YOU'RE GOING TO PUT AWAY THOSE BOXES, I'LL GO WITH YOU.
GIMME HALF OF 'EM.
HUH?
IS THIS ...
... BECAUSE YOU LIKE ME ...?
NO WAY!!!
IT'S 'COS YOU'RE GONNA SLACK OFF!!!
HERE, KASHIMA.
COFFEE.
ARE YOU GIVING IT TO ME BECAUSE YOU LIKE ME...?
I'M GIVING SOME TO EVERYONE!!!
DID YOU ONLY ADD MILK TO MINE...
...BECAUSE YOU LIKE ME...?
BECAUSE YOU ALWAYS TAKE IT WITH ONE MILK AND NO SUGAR!!!
GASHAN (CLATTER)
STOP MESSING AROUND!!!
I CAN'T BELIEVE HE REMEMBERS THAT...
IS IT BECAUSE HE LIKES HER?

AN EMBARRASSING MOOD

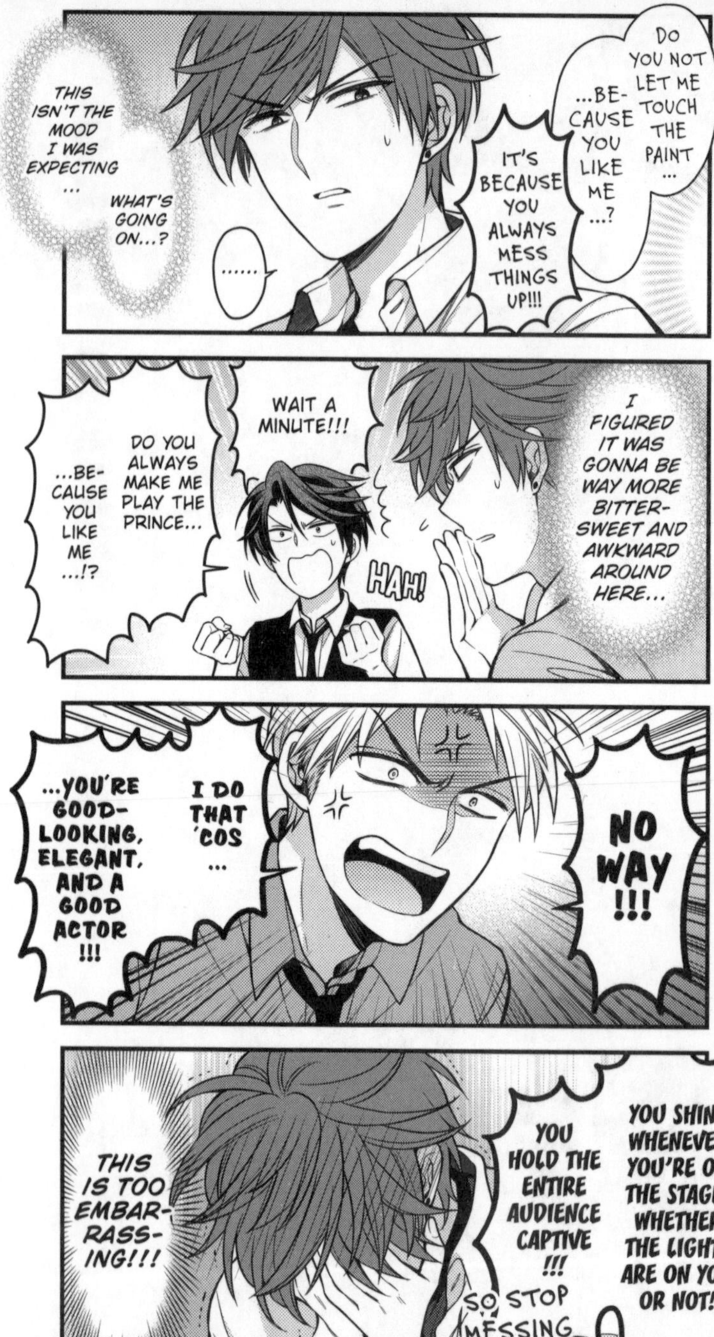

DO YOU NOT LET ME TOUCH THE PAINT...
...BE-CAUSE YOU LIKE ME ...?
IT'S BECAUSE YOU ALWAYS MESS THINGS UP!!!
......
THIS ISN'T THE MOOD I WAS EXPECTING...
WHAT'S GOING ON...?
I FIGURED IT WAS GONNA BE WAY MORE BITTER-SWEET AND AWKWARD AROUND HERE...
WAIT A MINUTE!!!
HAH!
DO YOU ALWAYS MAKE ME PLAY THE PRINCE...
...BE-CAUSE YOU LIKE ME ...!?
NO WAY !!!
I DO THAT 'COS ...
...YOU'RE GOOD-LOOKING, ELEGANT, AND A GOOD ACTOR !!!
YOU SHINE WHENEVER YOU'RE ON THE STAGE, WHETHER THE LIGHTS ARE ON YOU OR NOT!
YOU HOLD THE ENTIRE AUDIENCE CAPTIVE !!!
SO STOP MESSING AROUND!!
THIS IS TOO EMBAR-RASS-ING!!!

HOW TO SOOTHE HER WORRIES

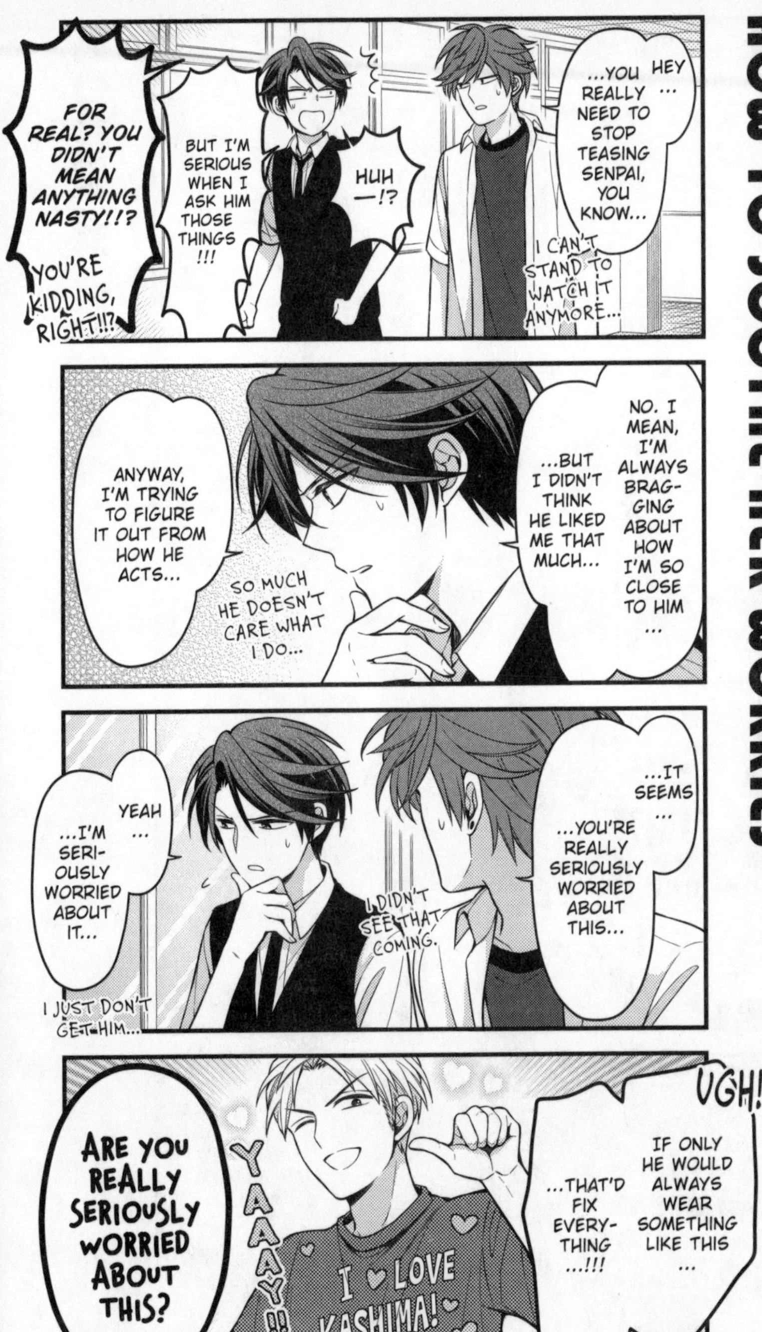
HEY ... ...YOU REALLY NEED TO STOP TEASING SENPAI, YOU KNOW...
I CAN'T STAND TO WATCH IT ANYMORE...
HUH—!?
BUT I'M SERIOUS WHEN I ASK HIM THOSE THINGS!!!
FOR REAL? YOU DIDN'T MEAN ANYTHING NASTY!!?
YOU'RE KIDDING, RIGHT!!?
NO. I MEAN, I'M ALWAYS BRAG-GING ABOUT HOW I'M SO CLOSE TO HIM ...
...BUT I DIDN'T THINK HE LIKED ME THAT MUCH...
SO MUCH HE DOESN'T CARE WHAT I DO...
ANYWAY, I'M TRYING TO FIGURE IT OUT FROM HOW HE ACTS...
...IT SEEMS ... ...YOU'RE REALLY SERIOUSLY WORRIED ABOUT THIS...
I DIDN'T SEE THAT COMING.
YEAH ... ...I'M SERI-OUSLY WORRIED ABOUT IT...
I JUST DON'T GET HIM...
UGH!
IF ONLY HE WOULD ALWAYS WEAR SOMETHING LIKE THIS ... ...THAT'D FIX EVERY-THING ...!!!
YAAAAY!!
I LOVE KASHIMA!
ARE YOU REALLY SERIOUSLY WORRIED ABOUT THIS?

WORSENING LOVE

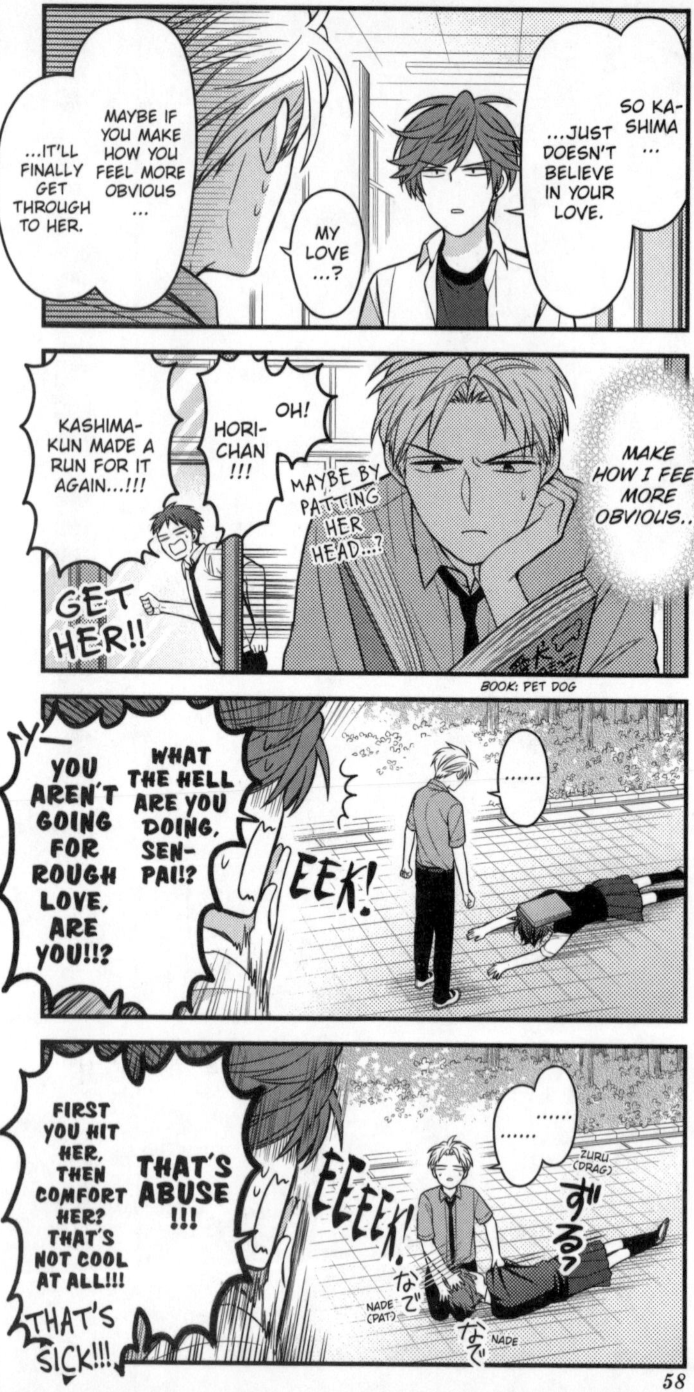
SO KA-SHIMA ...
...JUST DOESN'T BELIEVE IN YOUR LOVE.
MY LOVE ...?
MAYBE IF YOU MAKE HOW YOU FEEL MORE OBVIOUS ...
...IT'LL FINALLY GET THROUGH TO HER.
MAKE HOW I FEEL MORE OBVIOUS...
MAYBE BY PATTING HER HEAD...?
OH! HORI-CHAN !!!
KASHIMA-KUN MADE A RUN FOR IT AGAIN...!!!
GET HER!!
BOOK: PET DOG
......
EEK!
WHAT THE HELL ARE YOU DOING, SEN-PAI!?
Y— YOU AREN'T GOING FOR ROUGH LOVE, ARE YOU!!?
....
ZURU (DRAG)
ずるっ
EEEEK!
なで
NADE (PAT)
なで
NADE
THAT'S ABUSE !!!
FIRST YOU HIT HER, THEN COMFORT HER? THAT'S NOT COOL AT ALL!!!
THAT'S SICK!!!

WHAT IS WITH YOU TWO?

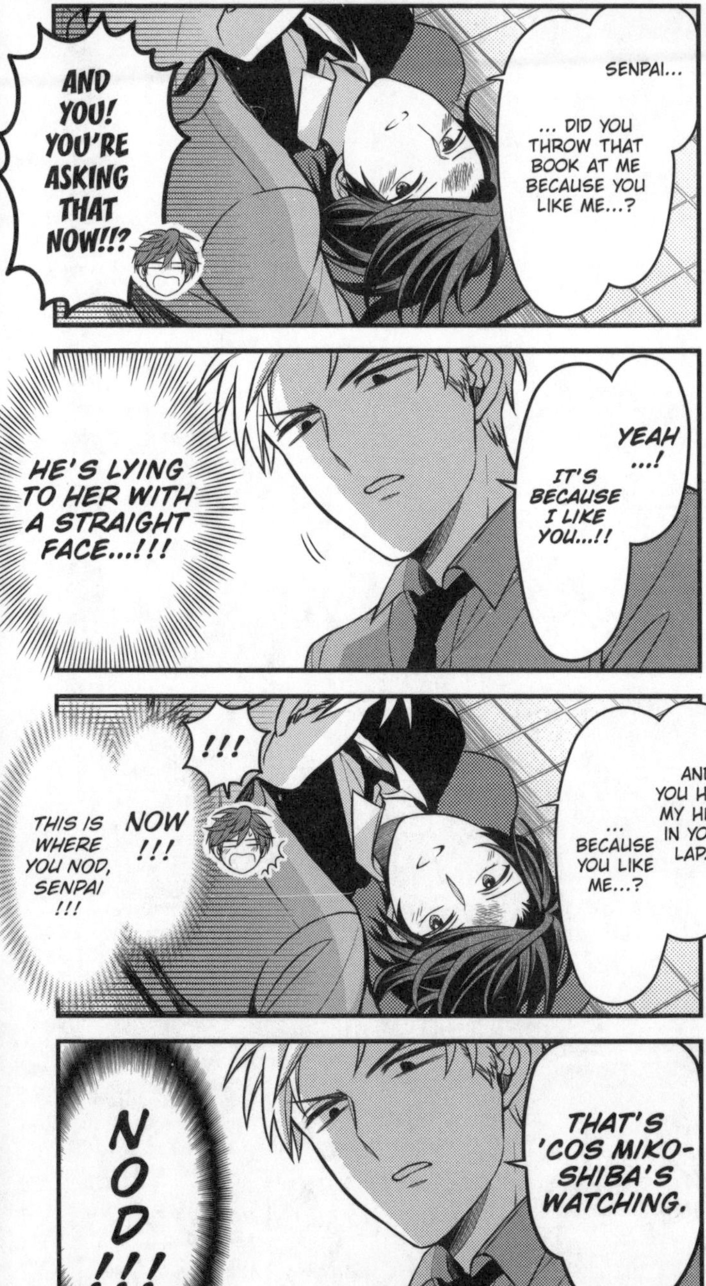
SENPAI...
... DID YOU THROW THAT BOOK AT ME BECAUSE YOU LIKE ME...?
AND YOU! YOU'RE ASKING THAT NOW!!?
YEAH ...!
IT'S BECAUSE I LIKE YOU...!!
HE'S LYING TO HER WITH A STRAIGHT FACE...!!!
AND YOU HAVE MY HEAD IN YOUR LAP...
... BECAUSE YOU LIKE ME...?
!!!
NOW !!!
THIS IS WHERE YOU NOD, SENPAI !!!
THAT'S 'COS MIKO-SHIBA'S WATCHING.
NOD !!!

ADVANCED DEVELOPMENTS

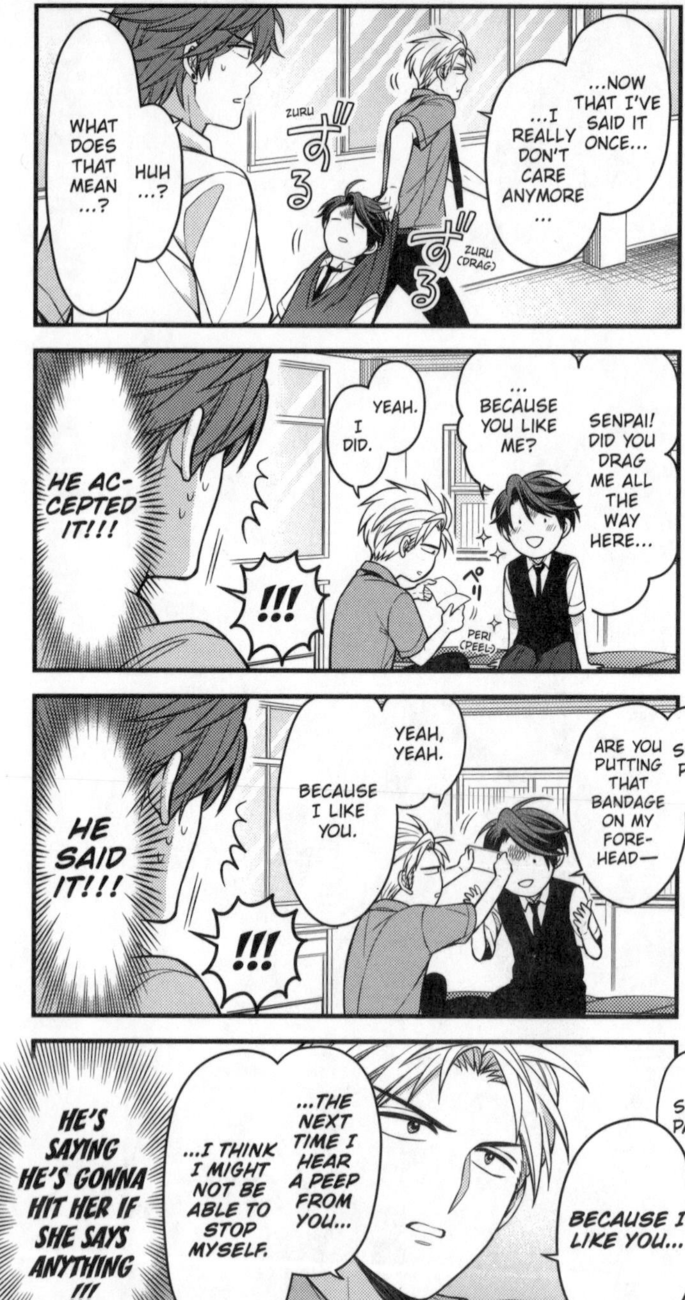
...NOW THAT I'VE SAID IT ONCE...
...I REALLY DON'T CARE ANYMORE...
ZURU
ずる
ずる
ZURU (DRAG)
HUH...?
WHAT DOES THAT MEAN...?
SENPAI! DID YOU DRAG ME ALL THE WAY HERE...
...BECAUSE YOU LIKE ME?
YEAH. I DID.
ペリ
PERI (PEEL-)
!!!
HE ACCEPTED IT!!!
SENPAI!
ARE YOU PUTTING THAT BANDAGE ON MY FOREHEAD—
YEAH, YEAH.
BECAUSE I LIKE YOU.
!!!
HE SAID IT!!!
SENPA—
BECAUSE I LIKE YOU...
...THE NEXT TIME I HEAR A PEEP FROM YOU...
...I THINK I MIGHT NOT BE ABLE TO STOP MYSELF.
HE'S SAYING HE'S GONNA HIT HER IF SHE SAYS ANYTHING!!!

A SHOCKING STATEMENT

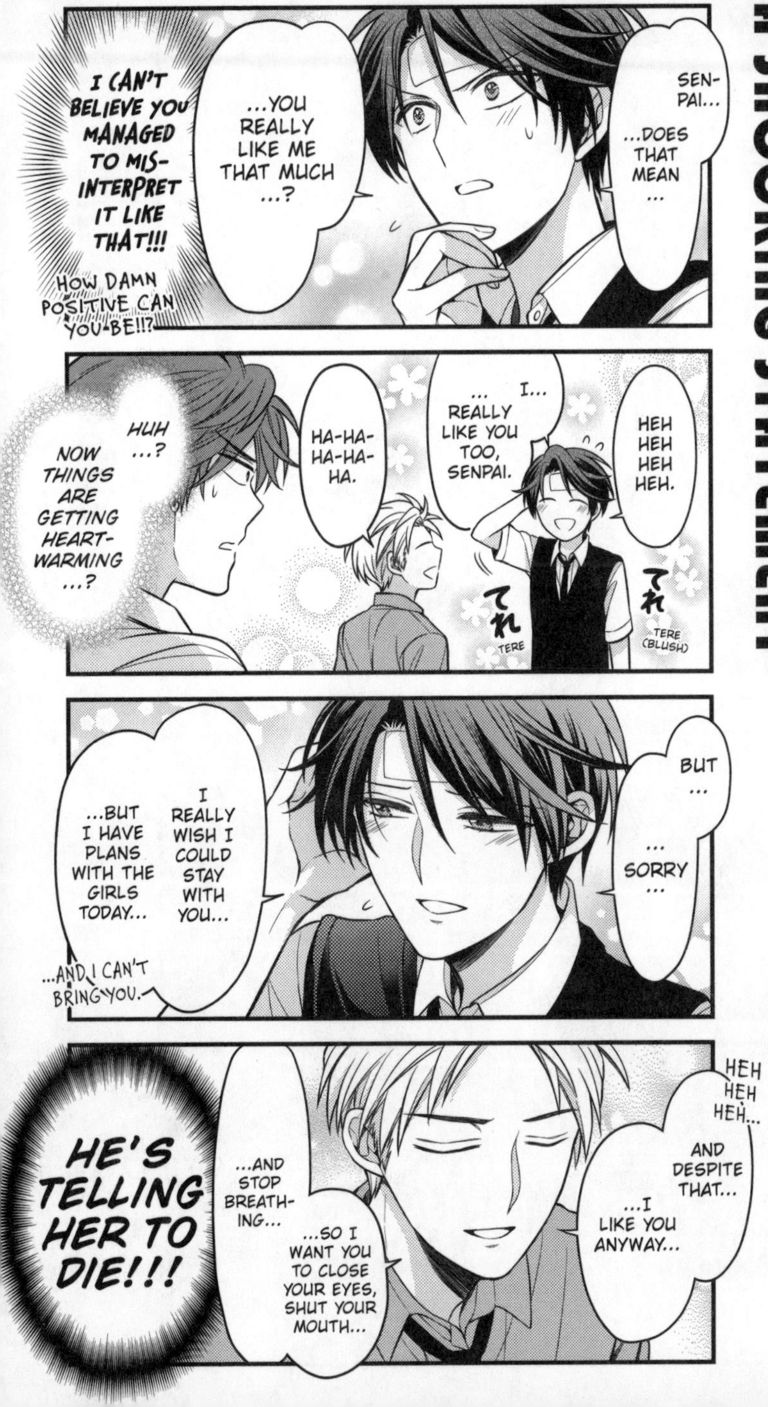
SEN-PAI... ...DOES THAT MEAN ...
...YOU REALLY LIKE ME THAT MUCH ...?
I CAN'T BELIEVE YOU MANAGED TO MIS-INTERPRET IT LIKE THAT!!!
HOW DAMN POSITIVE CAN YOU BE!!?
HEH HEH HEH HEH.
てれ
TERE (BLUSH)
I... ...REALLY LIKE YOU TOO, SENPAI.
てれ
TERE
HA-HA-HA-HA-HA.
HUH ...?
NOW THINGS ARE GETTING HEART-WARMING ...?
BUT ... ...SORRY ...
I REALLY WISH I COULD STAY WITH YOU...
...BUT I HAVE PLANS WITH THE GIRLS TODAY...
...AND I CAN'T BRING YOU.
HEH HEH HEH...
AND DESPITE THAT... ...I LIKE YOU ANYWAY...
...SO I WANT YOU TO CLOSE YOUR EYES, SHUT YOUR MOUTH...
...AND STOP BREATHING...
HE'S TELLING HER TO DIE!!!

A DIFFERENT GENRE

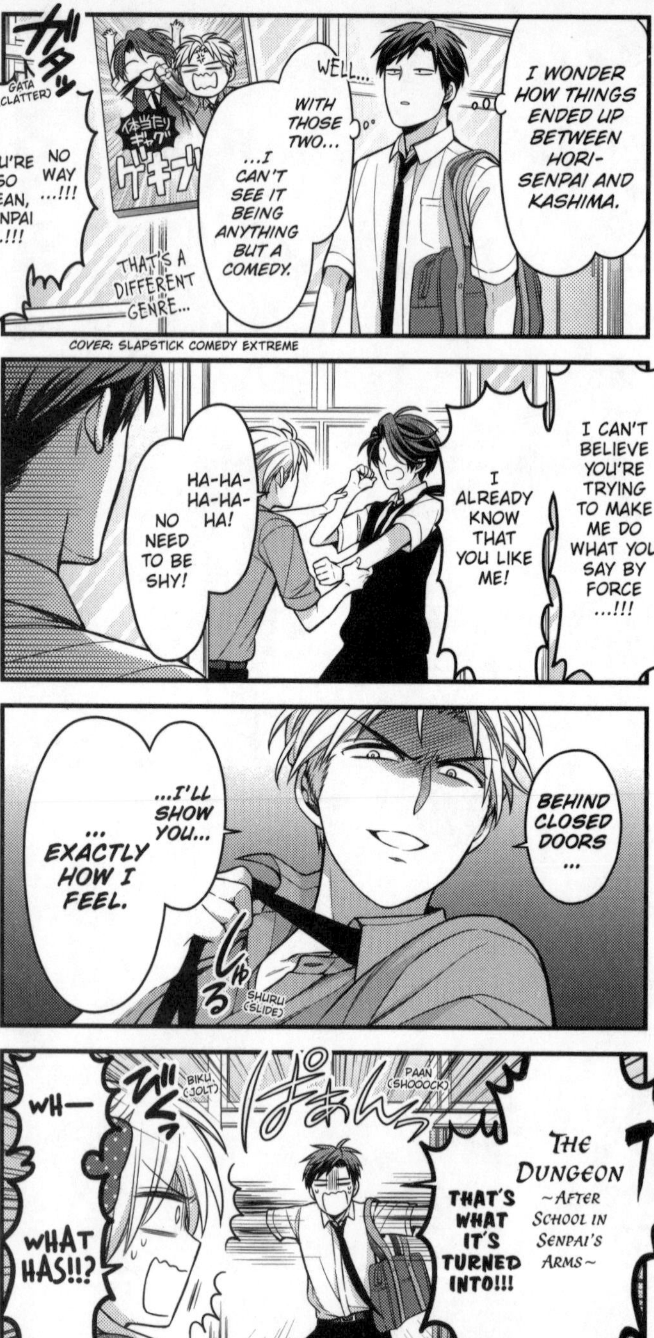
I WONDER HOW THINGS ENDED UP BETWEEN HORI-SENPAI AND KASHIMA.
WELL...
WITH THOSE TWO...
...I CAN'T SEE IT BEING ANYTHING BUT A COMEDY.
体当たりギャグ
THAT'S A DIFFERENT GENRE...
NO WAY...!!!
YOU'RE SO MEAN, SENPAI...!!!
ガタッ
GATA (CLATTER)
COVER: SLAPSTICK COMEDY EXTREME
I CAN'T BELIEVE YOU'RE TRYING TO MAKE ME DO WHAT YOU SAY BY FORCE...!!!
I ALREADY KNOW THAT YOU LIKE ME!
HA-HA-HA-HA-HA!
NO NEED TO BE SHY!
BEHIND CLOSED DOORS...
...I'LL SHOW YOU...
...EXACTLY HOW I FEEL.
しゅる
SHURU (SLIDE)
TH—
THE DUNGEON ~AFTER SCHOOL IN SENPAI'S ARMS~
THAT'S WHAT IT'S TURNED INTO!!!
ぱあんっ
PAAN (SHOOOCK)
びくっ
BIKU (JOLT)
WH—
WHAT HAS!!?

I CAN TELL

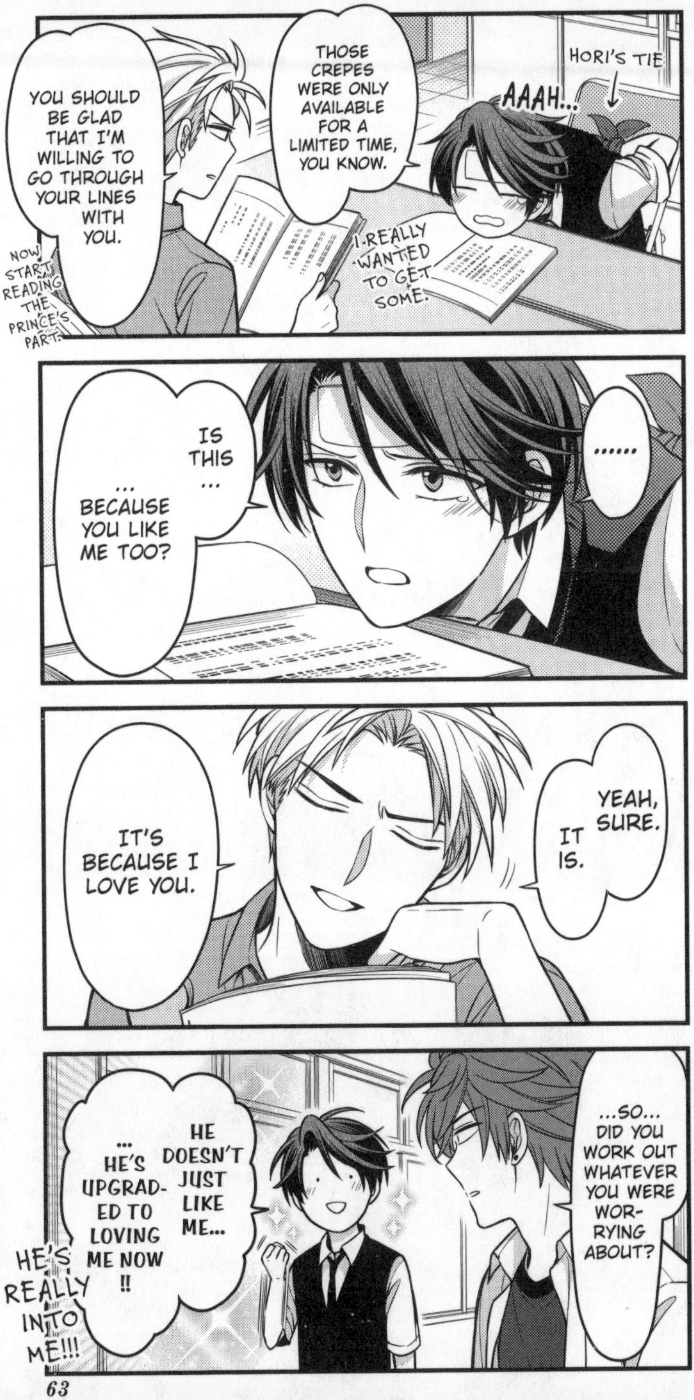

HORI'S TIE
AAAH!...
I REALLY WANTED TO GET SOME.
THOSE CREPES WERE ONLY AVAILABLE FOR A LIMITED TIME, YOU KNOW.
YOU SHOULD BE GLAD THAT I'M WILLING TO GO THROUGH YOUR LINES WITH YOU.
NOW START READING THE PRINCE'S PART.
......
IS THIS ... ... BECAUSE YOU LIKE ME TOO?
YEAH, SURE. IT IS.
IT'S BECAUSE I LOVE YOU.
...SO... DID YOU WORK OUT WHATEVER YOU WERE WOR-RYING ABOUT?
HE DOESN'T JUST LIKE ME... ... HE'S UPGRAD-ED TO LOVING ME NOW !!
HE'S REALLY INTO ME!!!

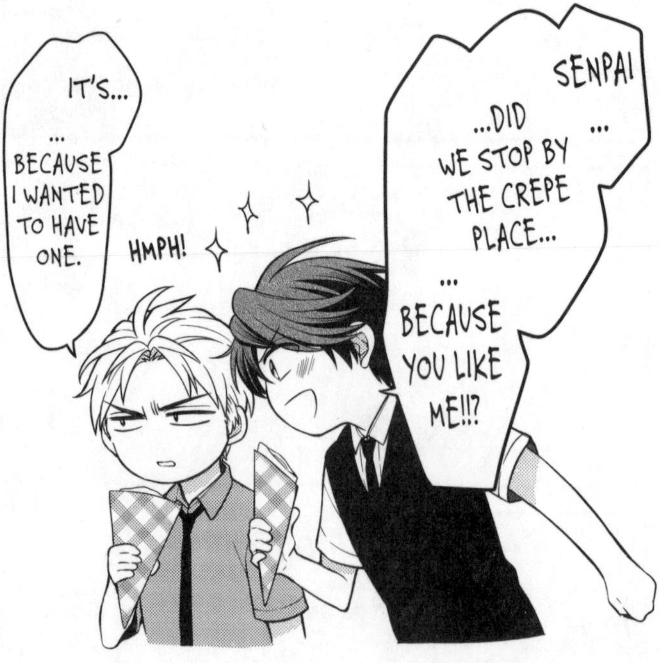
SENPAI ... ...DID WE STOP BY THE CREPE PLACE... ...BECAUSE YOU LIKE ME!!?
IT'S... ...BECAUSE I WANTED TO HAVE ONE.
HMPH!

[Extra]

KASHIMA'S LOVE

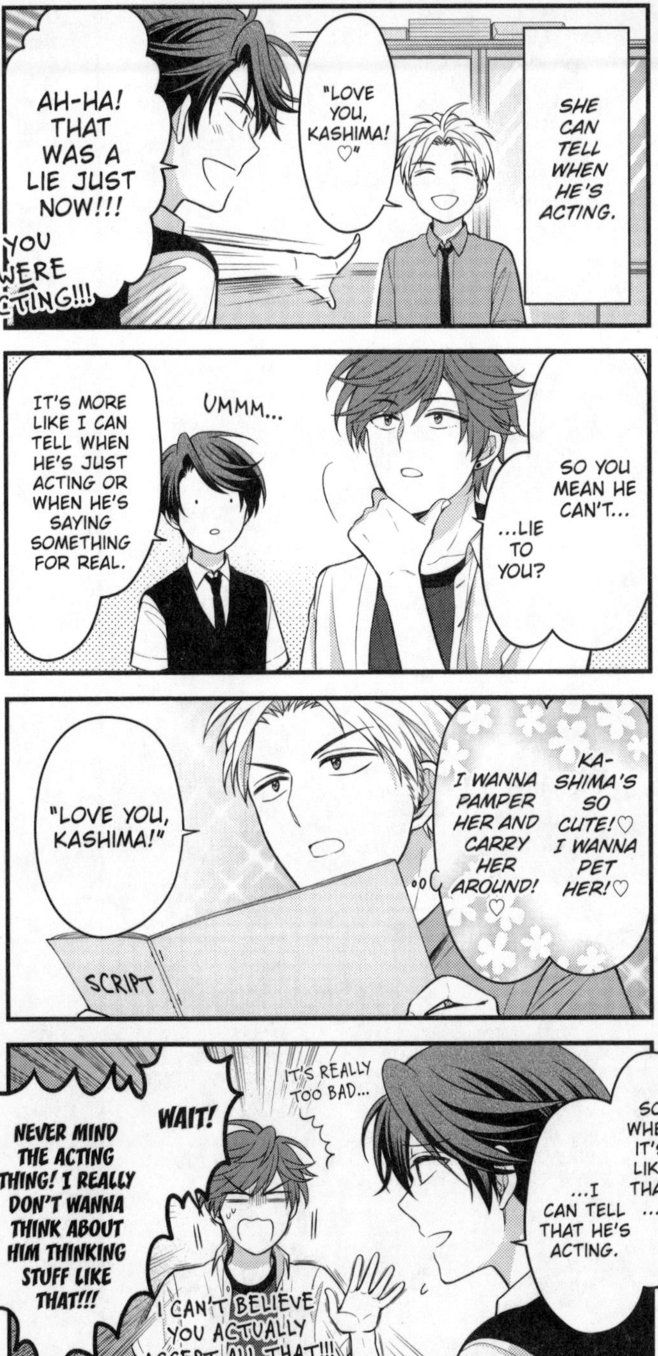
SHE CAN TELL WHEN HE'S ACTING.
"LOVE YOU, KASHIMA! ♡"
AH-HA! THAT WAS A LIE JUST NOW!!!
YOU WERE ACTING!!!
SO YOU MEAN HE CAN'T... ...LIE TO YOU?
UMMM...
IT'S MORE LIKE I CAN TELL WHEN HE'S JUST ACTING OR WHEN HE'S SAYING SOMETHING FOR REAL.
KA-SHIMA'S SO CUTE!♡ I WANNA PET HER!♡
I WANNA PAMPER HER AND CARRY HER AROUND! ♡
"LOVE YOU, KASHIMA!"
SCRIPT
SO WHEN IT'S LIKE THAT ... ...I CAN TELL THAT HE'S ACTING.
IT'S REALLY TOO BAD...
WAIT!
NEVER MIND THE ACTING THING! I REALLY DON'T WANNA THINK ABOUT HIM THINKING STUFF LIKE THAT!!!
I CAN'T BELIEVE YOU ACTUALLY ACCEPT ALL THAT!!!

[Extra]

I CAN TELL

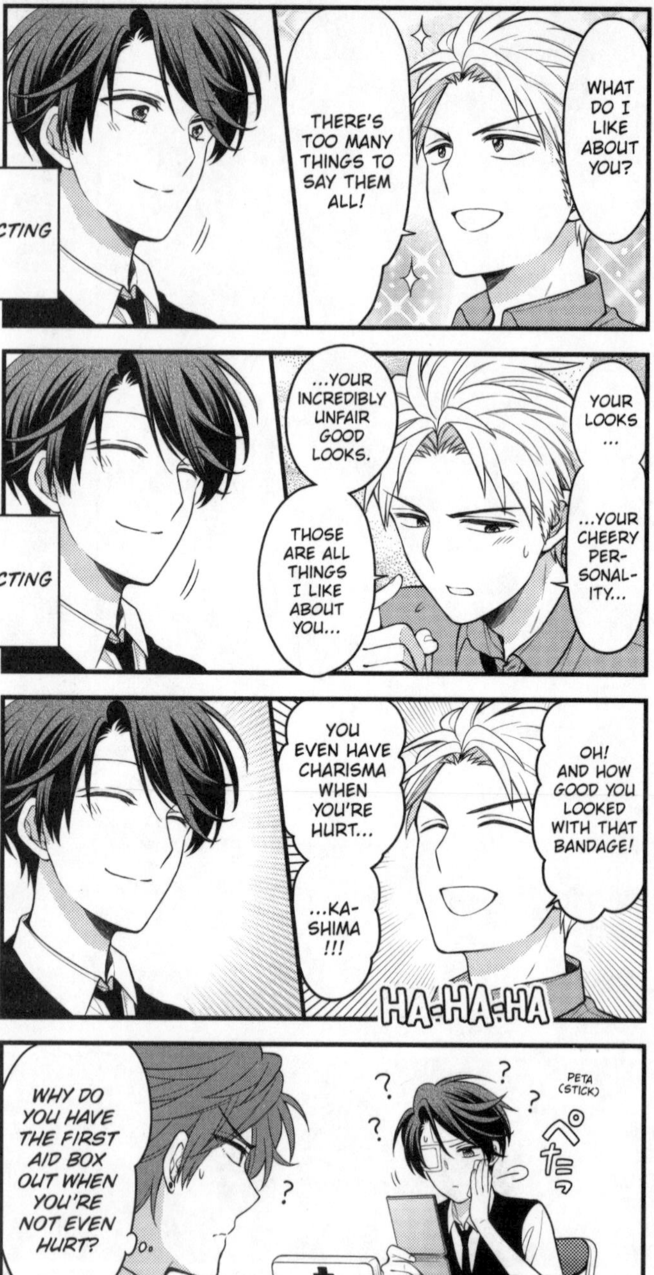

WHAT DO I LIKE ABOUT YOU?
THERE'S TOO MANY THINGS TO SAY THEM ALL!
ACTING
YOUR LOOKS...
...YOUR CHEERY PERSONALITY...
...YOUR INCREDIBLY UNFAIR GOOD LOOKS.
THOSE ARE ALL THINGS I LIKE ABOUT YOU...
ACTING
OH! AND HOW GOOD YOU LOOKED WITH THAT BANDAGE!
YOU EVEN HAVE CHARISMA WHEN YOU'RE HURT...
...KASHIMA!!!
HA-HA-HA
PETA (STICK)
ペタッ
WHY DO YOU HAVE THE FIRST AID BOX OUT WHEN YOU'RE NOT EVEN HURT?

KINDRED SOULS?

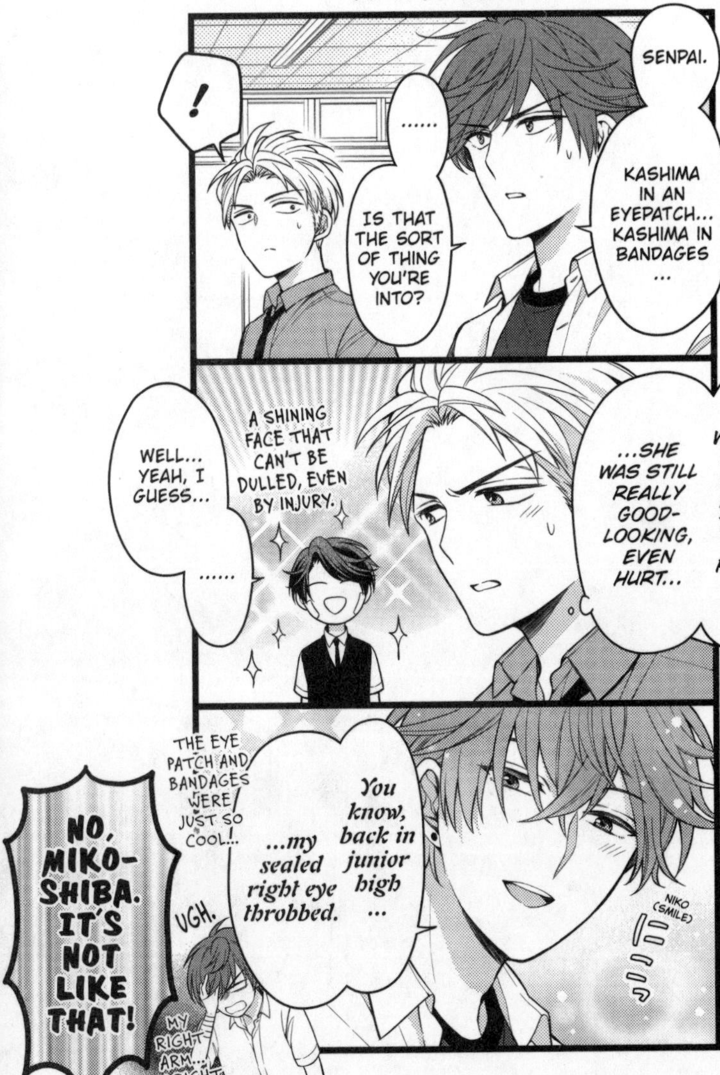
SENPAI.
KASHIMA IN AN EYEPATCH... KASHIMA IN BANDAGES ...
......
IS THAT THE SORT OF THING YOU'RE INTO?
!
WHEN SHE WAS LIKE THAT BEFORE ...
...SHE WAS STILL REALLY GOOD-LOOKING, EVEN HURT...
A SHINING FACE THAT CAN'T BE DULLED, EVEN BY INJURY.
WELL... YEAH, I GUESS...
......
NIKO (SMILE)
You know, back in junior high ...
...my sealed right eye throbbed.
THE EYE PATCH AND BANDAGES WERE JUST SO COOL...!
UGH.
MY RIGHT ARM... MY RIGHT EYE...
NO, MIKO-SHIBA. IT'S NOT LIKE THAT!

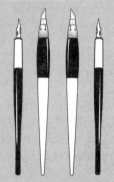

MONTHLY GIRLS' ✕ NOZAKI-KUN

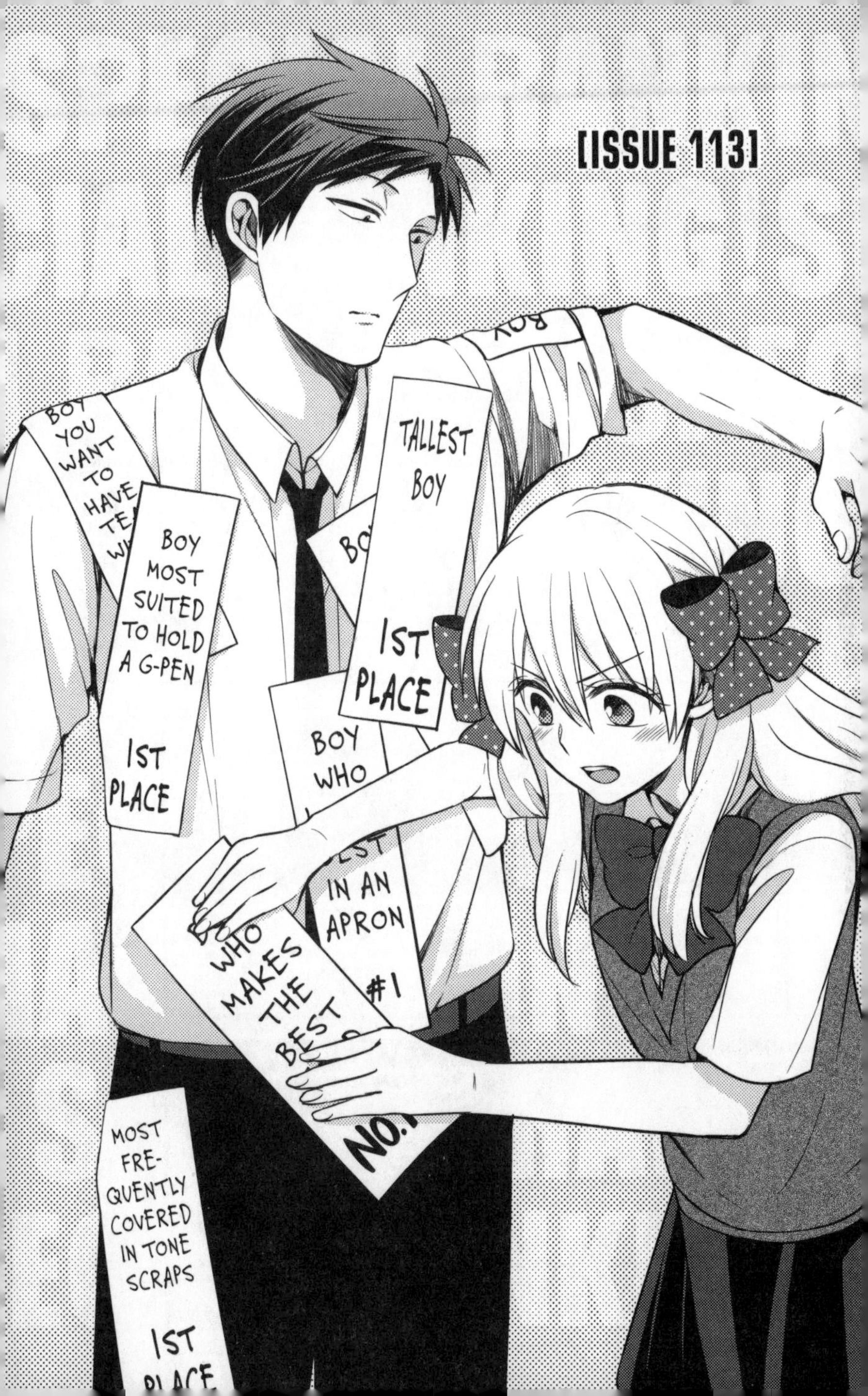
[ISSUE 113]
BOY
TALLEST BOY 1ST PLACE
BOY YOU WANT TO HAVE
BOY MOST SUITED TO HOLD A G-PEN 1ST PLACE
BOY WHO
IN AN APRON #1
WHO MAKES THE BEST
MOST FRE-QUENTLY COVERED IN TONE SCRAPS 1ST PLACE

LET'S HAVE A POPULARITY CONTEST♡

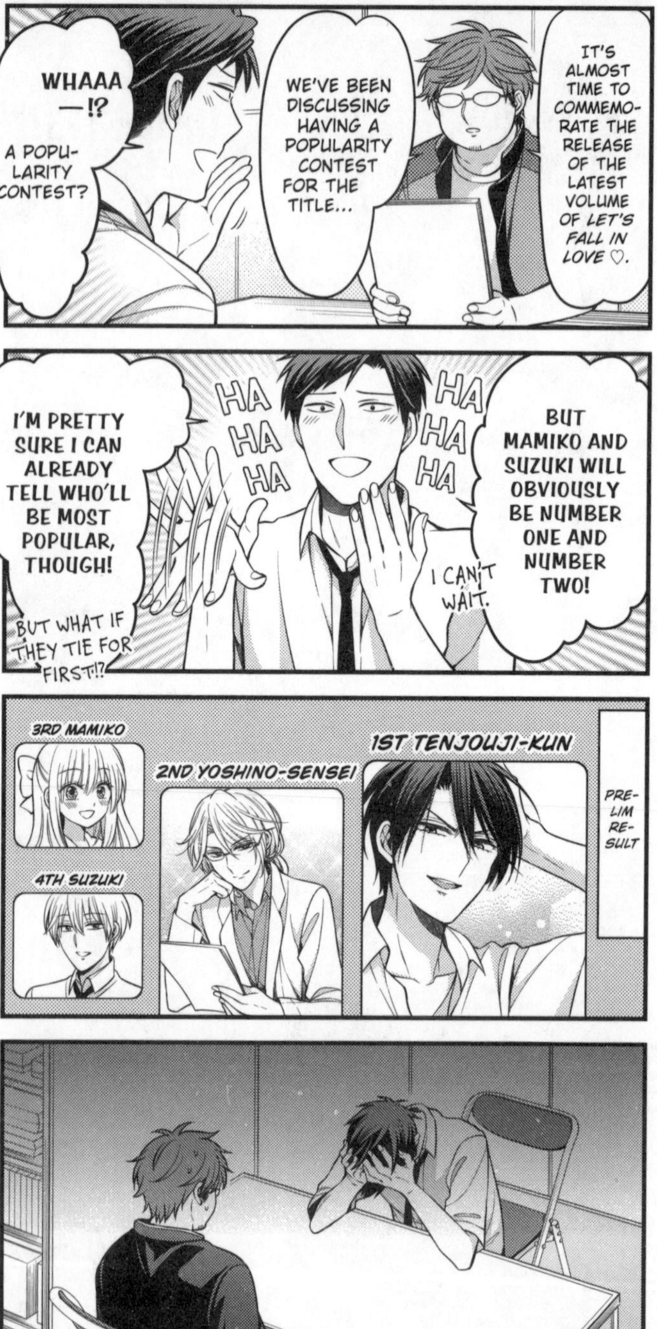

IT'S ALMOST TIME TO COMMEMORATE THE RELEASE OF THE LATEST VOLUME OF *LET'S FALL IN LOVE* ♡.
WE'VE BEEN DISCUSSING HAVING A POPULARITY CONTEST FOR THE TITLE...
WHAAA—!?
A POPULARITY CONTEST?
BUT MAMIKO AND SUZUKI WILL OBVIOUSLY BE NUMBER ONE AND NUMBER TWO!
HA HA HA
I CAN'T WAIT.
HA HA HA
I'M PRETTY SURE I CAN ALREADY TELL WHO'LL BE MOST POPULAR, THOUGH!
BUT WHAT IF THEY TIE FOR FIRST!?
PRELIM RESULT
1ST TENJOUJI-KUN
2ND YOSHINO-SENSEI
3RD MAMIKO
4TH SUZUKI

THE CREATOR'S POINT OF VIEW

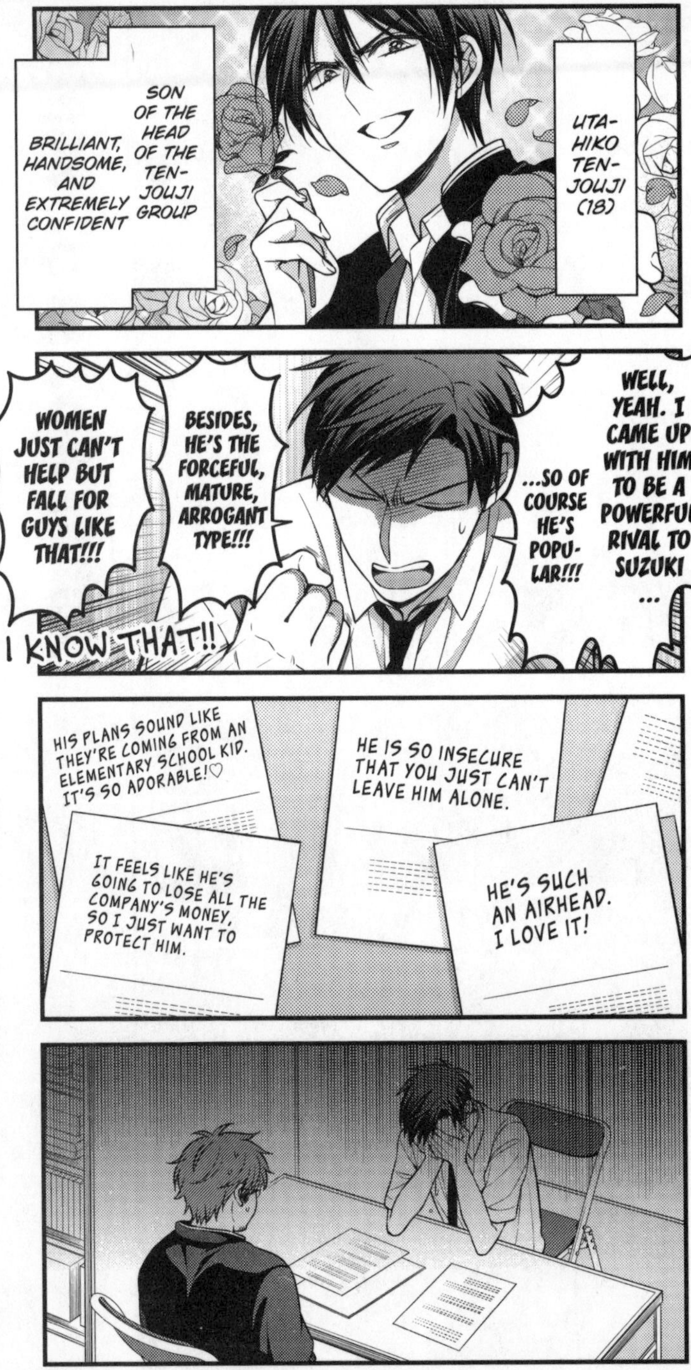
UTA-HIKO TEN-JOUJI (18)
SON OF THE HEAD OF THE TEN-JOUJI GROUP
BRILLIANT, HANDSOME, AND EXTREMELY CONFIDENT
WELL, YEAH. I CAME UP WITH HIM TO BE A POWERFUL RIVAL TO SUZUKI ...
...SO OF COURSE HE'S POPU-LAR!!!
BESIDES, HE'S THE FORCEFUL, MATURE, ARROGANT TYPE!!!
WOMEN JUST CAN'T HELP BUT FALL FOR GUYS LIKE THAT!!!
I KNOW THAT!!
HE IS SO INSECURE THAT YOU JUST CAN'T LEAVE HIM ALONE.
HIS PLANS SOUND LIKE THEY'RE COMING FROM AN ELEMENTARY SCHOOL KID. IT'S SO ADORABLE!♡
HE'S SUCH AN AIRHEAD. I LOVE IT!
IT FEELS LIKE HE'S GOING TO LOSE ALL THE COMPANY'S MONEY, SO I JUST WANT TO PROTECT HIM.

A PURE VOTE FOR SUZUKI

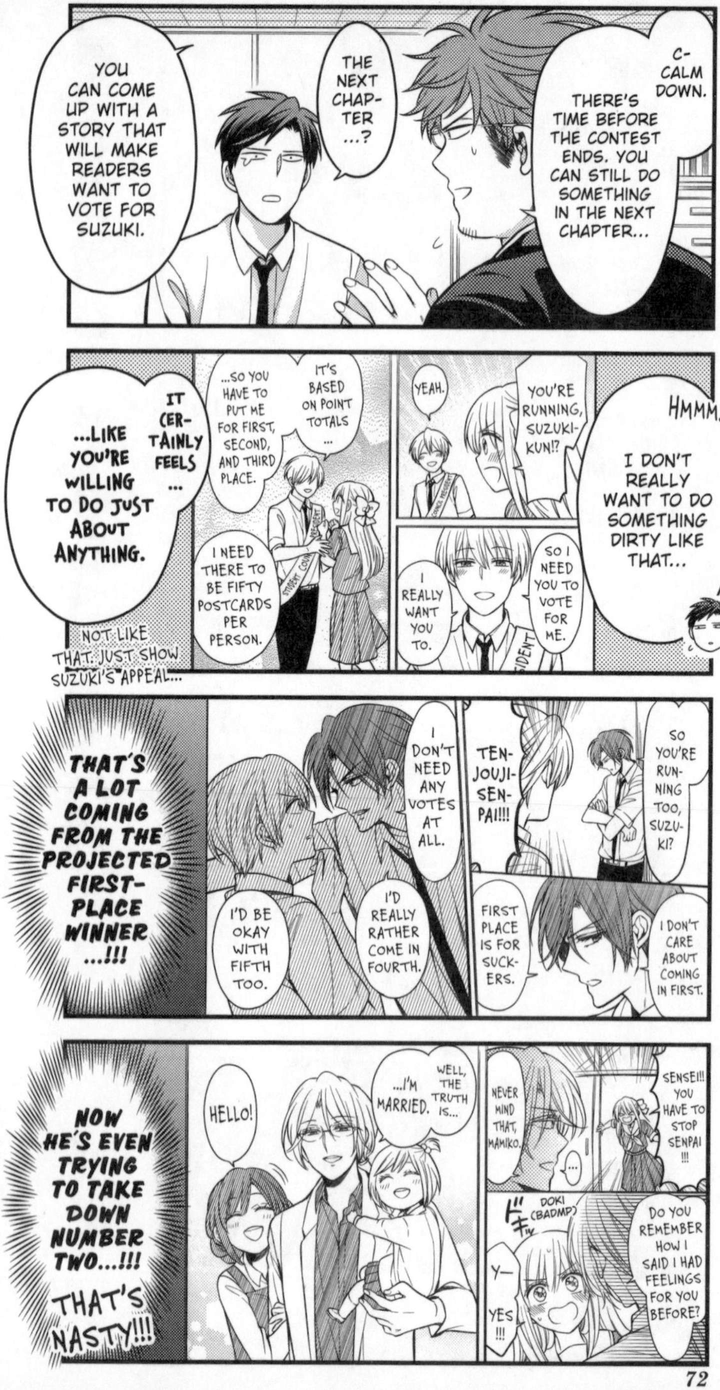
C-CALM DOWN.
THERE'S TIME BEFORE THE CONTEST ENDS. YOU CAN STILL DO SOMETHING IN THE NEXT CHAPTER...
THE NEXT CHAPTER...?
YOU CAN COME UP WITH A STORY THAT WILL MAKE READERS WANT TO VOTE FOR SUZUKI.
HMMM...
I DON'T REALLY WANT TO DO SOMETHING DIRTY LIKE THAT...
YOU'RE RUNNING, SUZUKI-KUN!?
YEAH.
SO I NEED YOU TO VOTE FOR ME.
I REALLY WANT YOU TO.
IT'S BASED ON POINT TOTALS...
...SO YOU HAVE TO PUT ME FOR FIRST, SECOND, AND THIRD PLACE.
I NEED THERE TO BE FIFTY POSTCARDS PER PERSON.
IT CERTAINLY FEELS...
...LIKE YOU'RE WILLING TO DO JUST ABOUT ANYTHING.
NOT LIKE THAT. JUST SHOW SUZUKI'S APPEAL...
SO YOU'RE RUNNING TOO, SUZUKI?
TENJOUJI-SENPAI!!!
I DON'T CARE ABOUT COMING IN FIRST.
FIRST PLACE IS FOR SUCKERS.
I DON'T NEED ANY VOTES AT ALL.
I'D REALLY RATHER COME IN FOURTH.
I'D BE OKAY WITH FIFTH TOO.
THAT'S A LOT COMING FROM THE PROJECTED FIRST-PLACE WINNER...!!!
SENSEI!!! YOU HAVE TO STOP SENPAI!!!
NEVER MIND THAT, MAMIKO.
...
DO YOU REMEMBER HOW I SAID I HAD FEELINGS FOR YOU BEFORE?
ドキ
DOKI (BADMP)
Y— YES!!!
WELL, THE TRUTH IS...
...I'M MARRIED.
HELLO!
NOW HE'S EVEN TRYING TO TAKE DOWN NUMBER TWO...!!!
THAT'S NASTY!!!

YOU'RE ALL SO MEAN

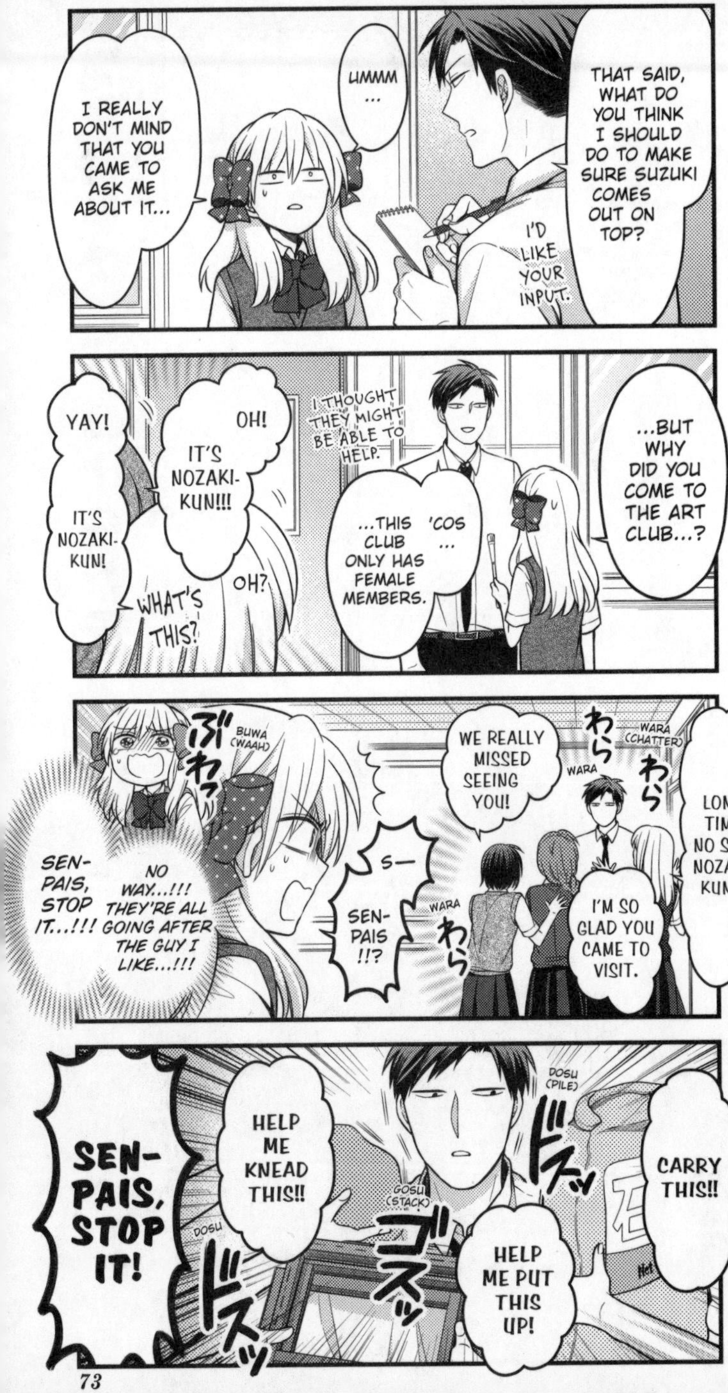

THAT SAID, WHAT DO YOU THINK I SHOULD DO TO MAKE SURE SUZUKI COMES OUT ON TOP?
I'D LIKE YOUR INPUT.
UMMM ...
I REALLY DON'T MIND THAT YOU CAME TO ASK ME ABOUT IT...
...BUT WHY DID YOU COME TO THE ART CLUB...?
'COS ...
I THOUGHT THEY MIGHT BE ABLE TO HELP.
...THIS CLUB ONLY HAS FEMALE MEMBERS.
OH!
IT'S NOZAKI-KUN!!!
OH?
WHAT'S THIS?
YAY!
IT'S NOZAKI-KUN!
わら WARA (CHATTER)
LONG TIME NO SEE, NOZAKI-KUN!!!
わら WARA
WE REALLY MISSED SEEING YOU!
I'M SO GLAD YOU CAME TO VISIT.
わら WARA
S—
SEN-PAIS !!?
ぶわっ BUWA (WAAH)
NO WAY...!!! THEY'RE ALL GOING AFTER THE GUY I LIKE...!!!
SEN-PAIS, STOP IT...!!!
CARRY THIS!!
ドスッ DOSU (PILE)
HELP ME PUT THIS UP!
ゴスッ GOSU (STACK)
HELP ME KNEAD THIS!!
ドスッ DOSU
SEN-PAIS, STOP IT!

GIVE ME YOUR OPINIONS

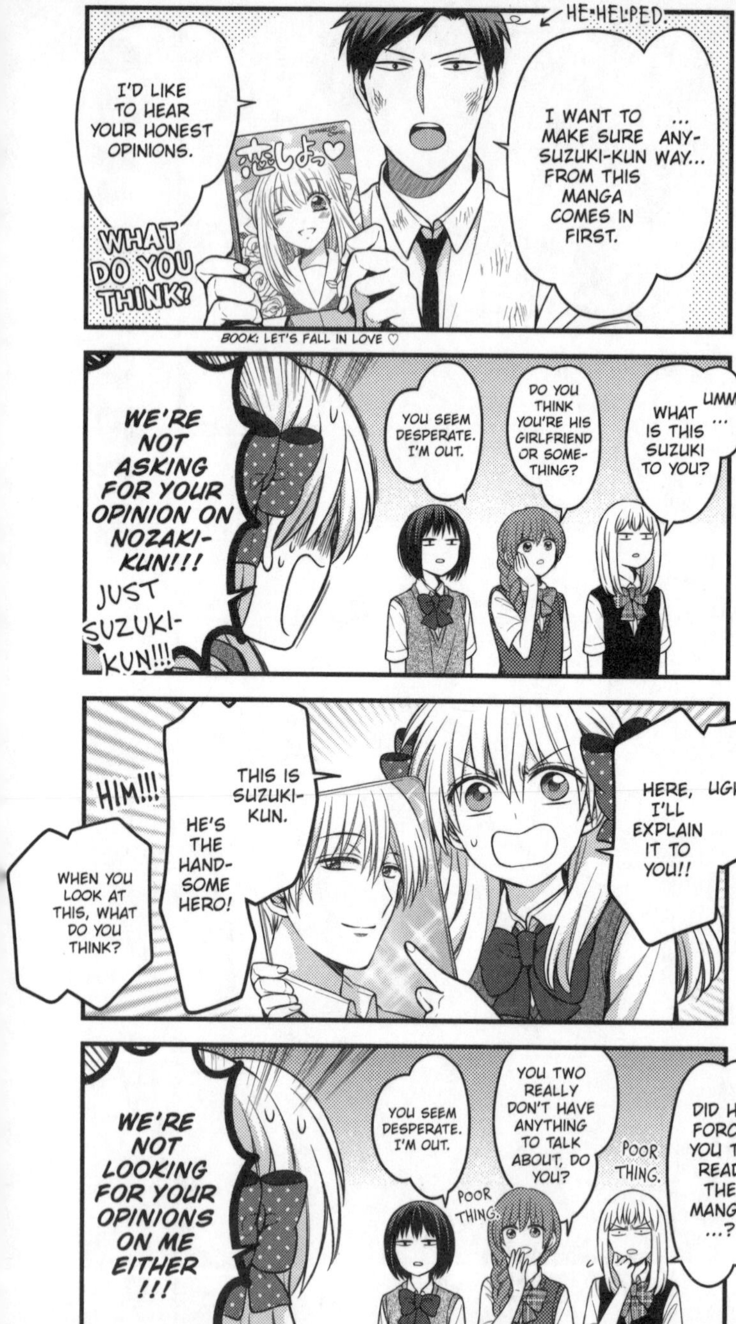
HE-HELPED.
... ANY-WAY...
I WANT TO MAKE SURE SUZUKI-KUN FROM THIS MANGA COMES IN FIRST.
I'D LIKE TO HEAR YOUR HONEST OPINIONS.
WHAT DO YOU THINK?
UMM...
WHAT IS THIS SUZUKI TO YOU?
DO YOU THINK YOU'RE HIS GIRLFRIEND OR SOME-THING?
YOU SEEM DESPERATE. I'M OUT.
WE'RE NOT ASKING FOR YOUR OPINION ON NOZAKI-KUN!!!
JUST SUZUKI-KUN!!!
UGH!
HERE, I'LL EXPLAIN IT TO YOU!!
THIS IS SUZUKI-KUN.
HE'S THE HAND-SOME HERO!
HIM!!!
WHEN YOU LOOK AT THIS, WHAT DO YOU THINK?
DID HE FORCE YOU TO READ THE MANGA ...?
POOR THING.
YOU TWO REALLY DON'T HAVE ANYTHING TO TALK ABOUT, DO YOU?
POOR THING.
YOU SEEM DESPERATE. I'M OUT.
WE'RE NOT LOOKING FOR YOUR OPINIONS ON ME EITHER !!!

BOOK: LET'S FALL IN LOVE ♡

BECAUSE IT'S THE ART CLUB

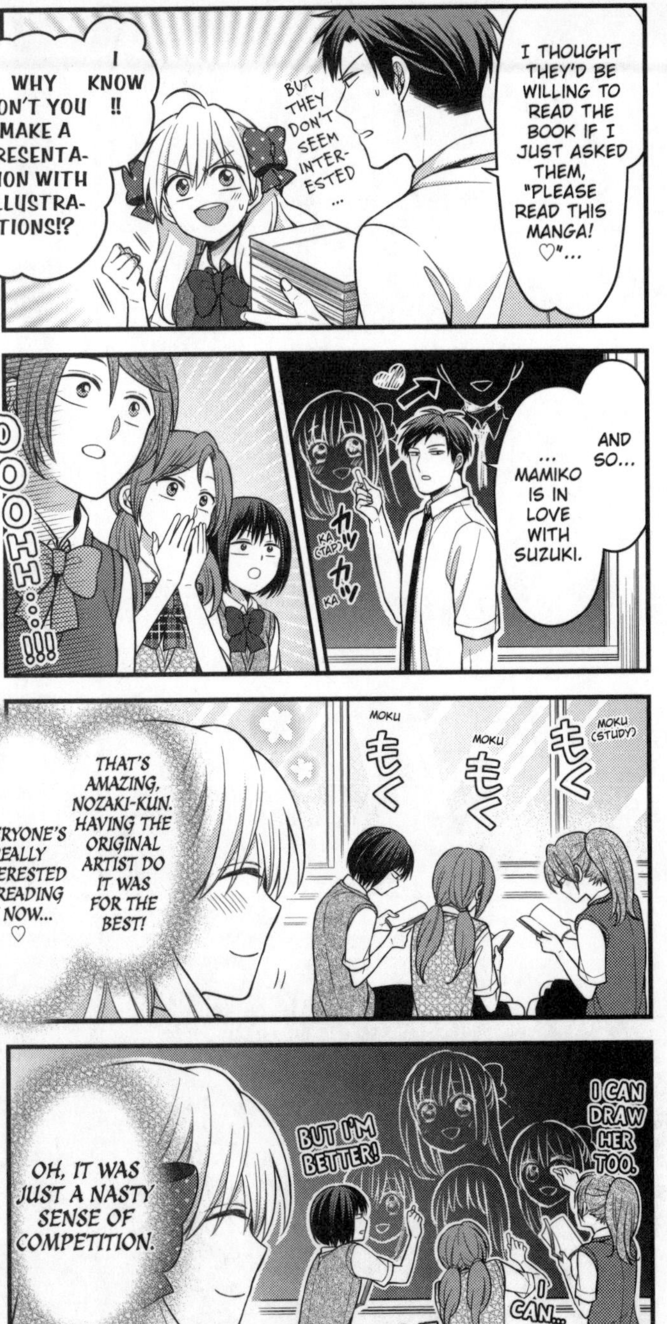
I THOUGHT THEY'D BE WILLING TO READ THE BOOK IF I JUST ASKED THEM, "PLEASE READ THIS MANGA! ♡"...
BUT THEY DON'T SEEM INTERESTED...
I KNOW!!
WHY DON'T YOU MAKE A PRESENTATION WITH ILLUSTRATIONS!?
AND SO...
...MAMIKO IS IN LOVE WITH SUZUKI.
KA (TAP) カッ
カッ KA
OOOHH...!!!
MOKU (STUDY) もく
MOKU もく
MOKU もく
THAT'S AMAZING, NOZAKI-KUN. HAVING THE ORIGINAL ARTIST DO IT WAS FOR THE BEST!
EVERYONE'S REALLY INTERESTED IN READING IT NOW... ♡
I CAN DRAW HER TOO.
BUT I'M BETTER!
I CAN...
...DO IT TOO!
OH, IT WAS JUST A NASTY SENSE OF COMPETITION.

THE BEST FROM MY MANGA

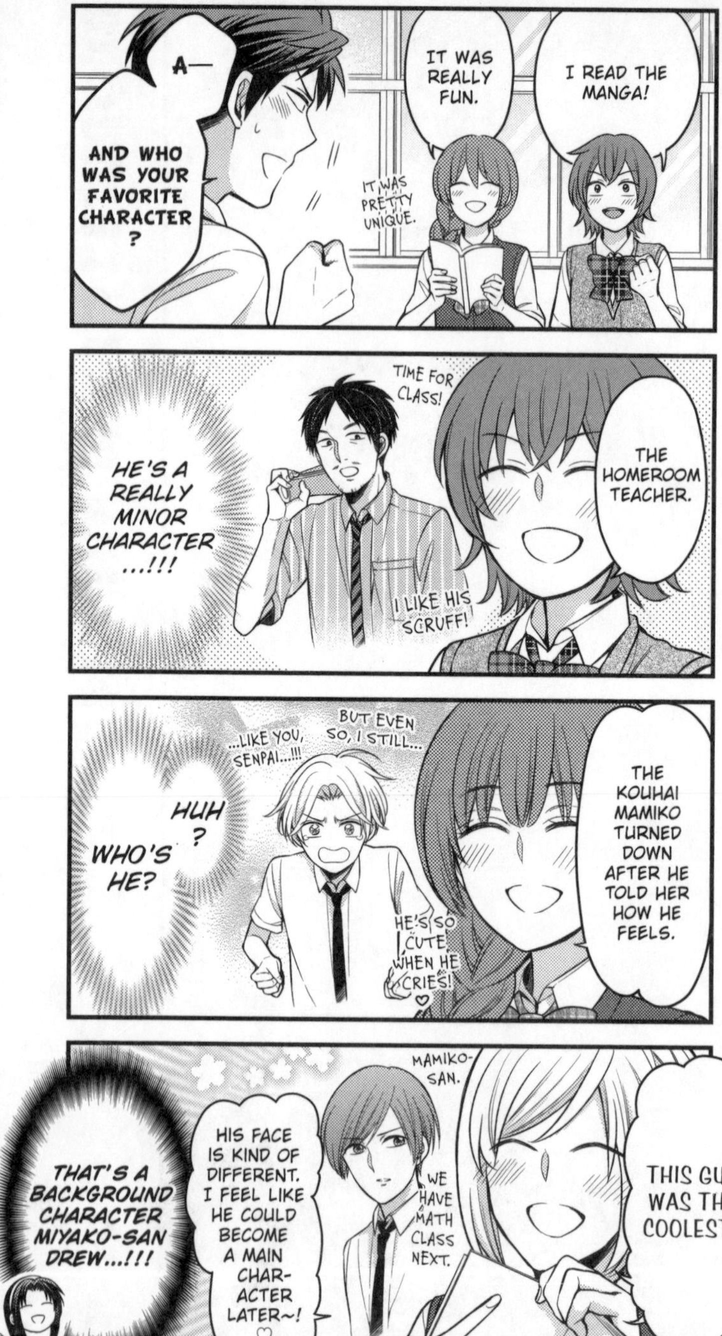

I READ THE MANGA!
IT WAS REALLY FUN.
IT WAS PRETTY UNIQUE.
A—
AND WHO WAS YOUR FAVORITE CHARACTER?
THE HOMEROOM TEACHER.
TIME FOR CLASS!
I LIKE HIS SCRUFF!
HE'S A REALLY MINOR CHARACTER ...!!!
THE KOUHAI MAMIKO TURNED DOWN AFTER HE TOLD HER HOW HE FEELS.
BUT EVEN SO, I STILL...
...LIKE YOU, SENPAI...!!!
HE'S SO CUTE WHEN HE CRIES! ♡
HUH?
WHO'S HE?
THIS GUY WAS THE COOLEST!!
MAMIKO-SAN.
WE HAVE MATH CLASS NEXT.
HIS FACE IS KIND OF DIFFERENT. I FEEL LIKE HE COULD BECOME A MAIN CHAR-ACTER LATER~! ♡
THAT'S A BACKGROUND CHARACTER MIYAKO-SAN DREW...!!!
HELPING OUT

THAT'S NOT FUNNY

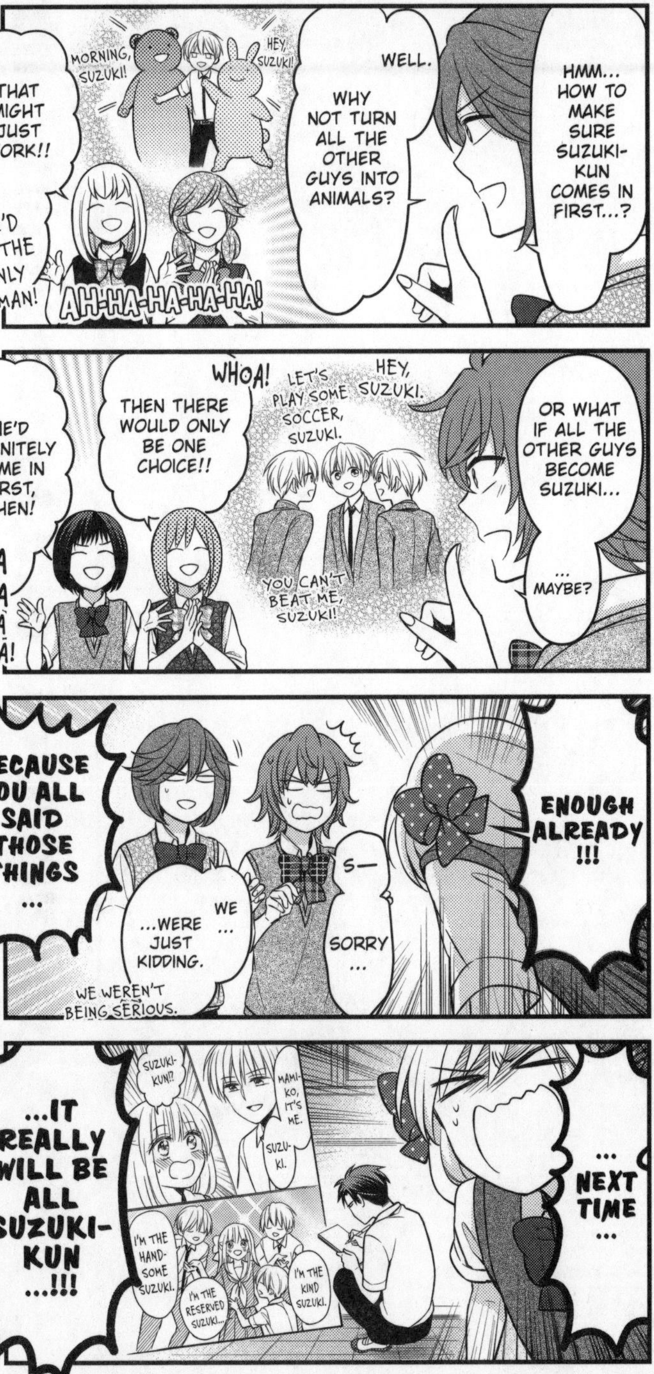
HMM... HOW TO MAKE SURE SUZUKI-KUN COMES IN FIRST...?
WELL.
WHY NOT TURN ALL THE OTHER GUYS INTO ANIMALS?
HEY, SUZUKI!
MORNING, SUZUKI!
THAT MIGHT JUST WORK!!
HE'D BE THE ONLY HUMAN!
AH-HA-HA-HA-HA!
OR WHAT IF ALL THE OTHER GUYS BECOME SUZUKI...
...MAYBE?
HEY, SUZUKI.
LET'S PLAY SOME SOCCER, SUZUKI.
WHOA!
YOU CAN'T BEAT ME, SUZUKI!
THEN THERE WOULD ONLY BE ONE CHOICE!!
HE'D DEFINITELY COME IN FIRST, THEN!
HA HA HA HA!
ENOUGH ALREADY!!!
S— SORRY...
WE... ...WERE JUST KIDDING.
WE WEREN'T BEING SERIOUS.
BECAUSE YOU ALL SAID THOSE THINGS...
...NEXT TIME...
MAMIKO, IT'S ME. SUZUKI.
SUZUKI-KUN!?
I'M THE KIND SUZUKI.
I'M THE RESERVED SUZUKI...
I'M THE HANDSOME SUZUKI.
...IT REALLY WILL BE ALL SUZUKI-KUN...!!!

GUERRILLA TROOPS AND COMMANDOS

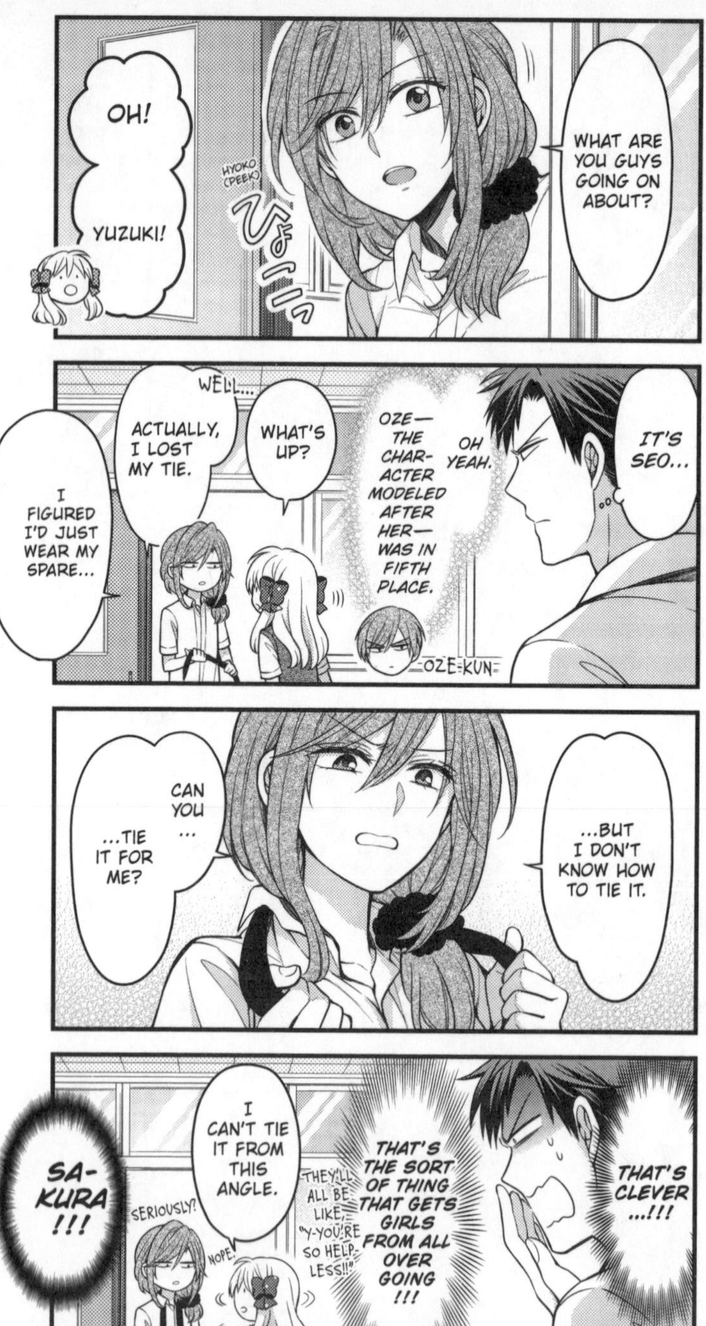
WHAT ARE YOU GUYS GOING ON ABOUT?
HYOKO (PEEK)
ひょこっ
OH! YUZUKI!
IT'S SEO...
OH YEAH.
OZE—THE CHARACTER MODELED AFTER HER—WAS IN FIFTH PLACE.
WHAT'S UP?
WELL...
ACTUALLY, I LOST MY TIE.
I FIGURED I'D JUST WEAR MY SPARE...
OZE-KUN
...BUT I DON'T KNOW HOW TO TIE IT.
CAN YOU ...
...TIE IT FOR ME?
THAT'S CLEVER...!!!
THAT'S THE SORT OF THING THAT GETS GIRLS FROM ALL OVER GOING!!!
THEY'LL ALL BE LIKE, "Y-YOU'RE SO HELPLESS!!"
I CAN'T TIE IT FROM THIS ANGLE.
NOPE.
SERIOUSLY?
SA-KURA!!!

SEO-SAN'S ADVICE

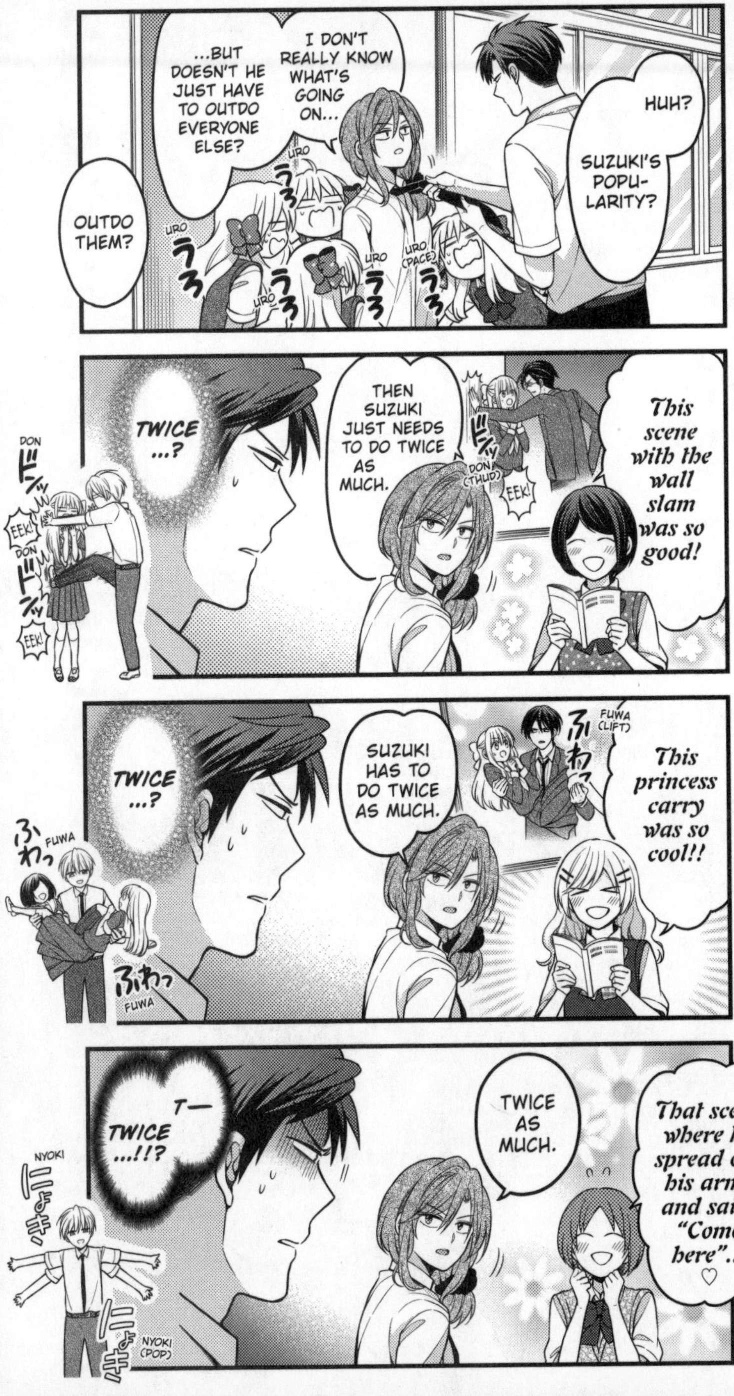
HUH?
SUZUKI'S POPULARITY?
I DON'T REALLY KNOW WHAT'S GOING ON...
...BUT DOESN'T HE JUST HAVE TO OUTDO EVERYONE ELSE?
URO (PACE)
URO
URO
URO
URO
OUTDO THEM?
This scene with the wall slam was so good!
DON (THUD)
EEK!
THEN SUZUKI JUST NEEDS TO DO TWICE AS MUCH.
TWICE ...?
DON
EEK!
DON
EEK!
This princess carry was so cool!!
FUWA (LIFT)
SUZUKI HAS TO DO TWICE AS MUCH.
TWICE ...?
FUWA
FUWA
That scene where he spread out his arms and said, "Come here"... ♡
TWICE AS MUCH.
T— TWICE ...!!?
NYOKI
NYOKI (POP)

AT THE EDGE OF HIS VISION

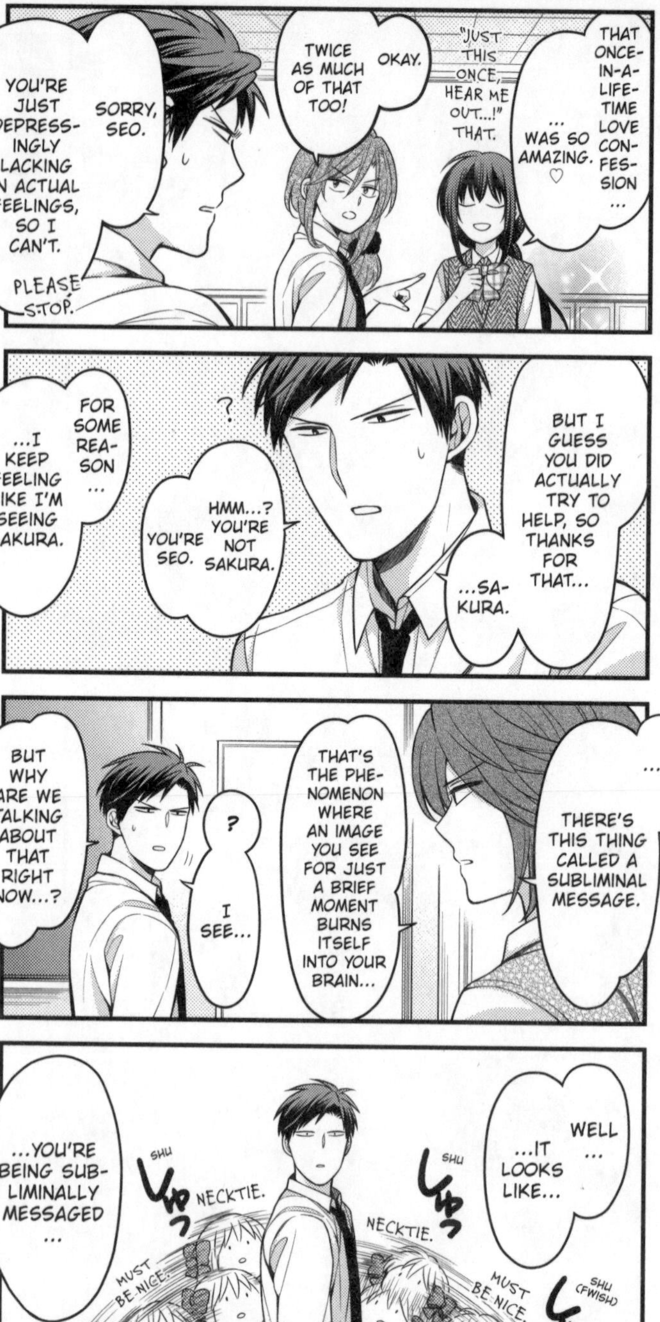
THAT ONCE-IN-A-LIFETIME LOVE CONFESSION...
...WAS SO AMAZING. ♡
"JUST THIS ONCE, HEAR ME OUT...!" THAT.
OKAY.
TWICE AS MUCH OF THAT TOO!
SORRY, SEO.
YOU'RE JUST DEPRESSINGLY LACKING IN ACTUAL FEELINGS, SO I CAN'T.
PLEASE STOP.
BUT I GUESS YOU DID ACTUALLY TRY TO HELP, SO THANKS FOR THAT...
...SAKURA.
HMM...? YOU'RE NOT SAKURA.
YOU'RE SEO.
?
FOR SOME REASON...
...I KEEP FEELING LIKE I'M SEEING SAKURA.
......
THERE'S THIS THING CALLED A SUBLIMINAL MESSAGE.
THAT'S THE PHENOMENON WHERE AN IMAGE YOU SEE FOR JUST A BRIEF MOMENT BURNS ITSELF INTO YOUR BRAIN...
?
I SEE...
BUT WHY ARE WE TALKING ABOUT THAT RIGHT NOW...?
WELL...
...IT LOOKS LIKE...
SHU (FWISH)
MUST BE NICE.
SHU
NECKTIE.
NECKTIE.
SHU
MUST BE NICE.
SHU
...YOU'RE BEING SUBLIMINALLY MESSAGED...

SUBLIMINAL MESSAGING

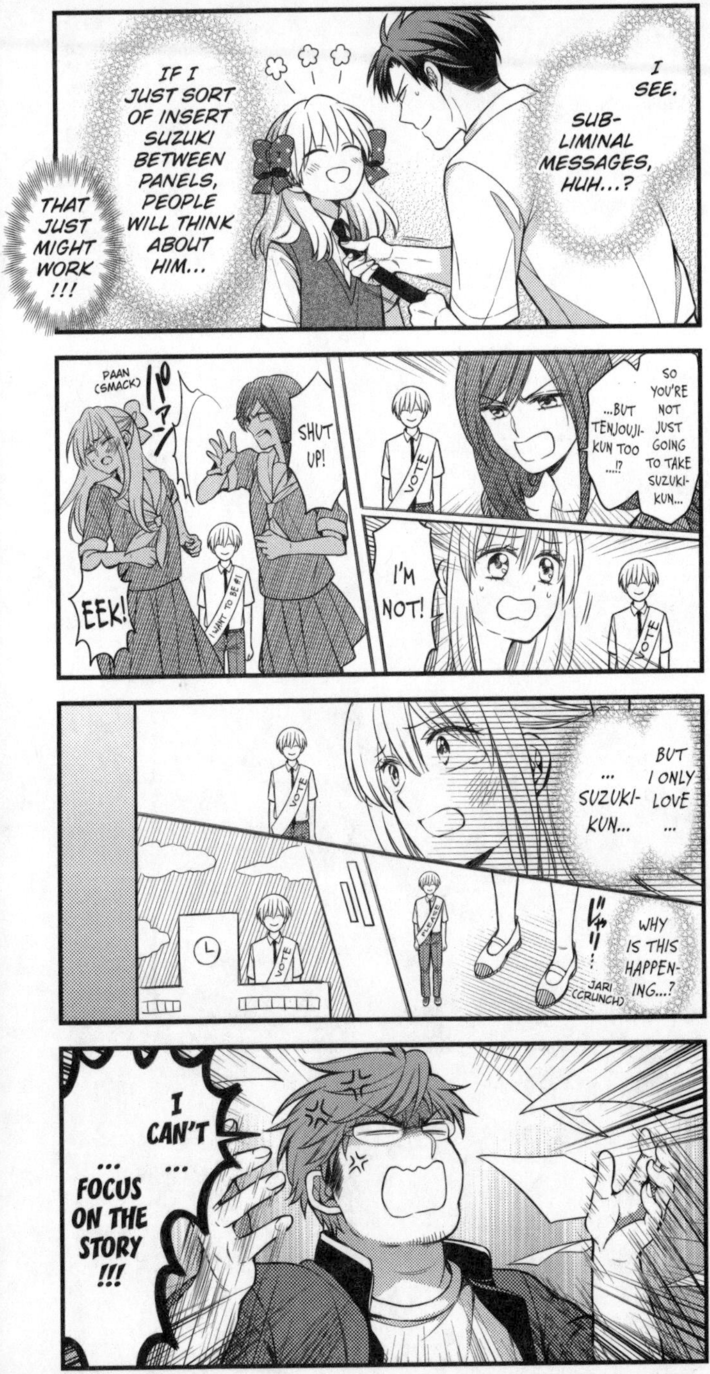
I SEE.
SUB-LIMINAL MESSAGES, HUH...?
IF I JUST SORT OF INSERT SUZUKI BETWEEN PANELS, PEOPLE WILL THINK ABOUT HIM...
THAT JUST MIGHT WORK!!!
SO YOU'RE NOT JUST GOING TO TAKE SUZUKI-KUN...
...BUT TENJOUJI-KUN TOO ...!?
VOTE
I'M NOT!
VOTE
SHUT UP!
PAAN (SMACK)
I WANT TO BE #1
EEK!
BUT I ONLY LOVE ...
... SUZUKI-KUN...
VOTE
WHY IS THIS HAPPEN-ING...?
JARI (CRUNCH)
PLEASE
VOTE
I CAN'T ...
... FOCUS ON THE STORY!!!

THE REAL #1

THE RESULTS OF THE POPULARITY CONTEST

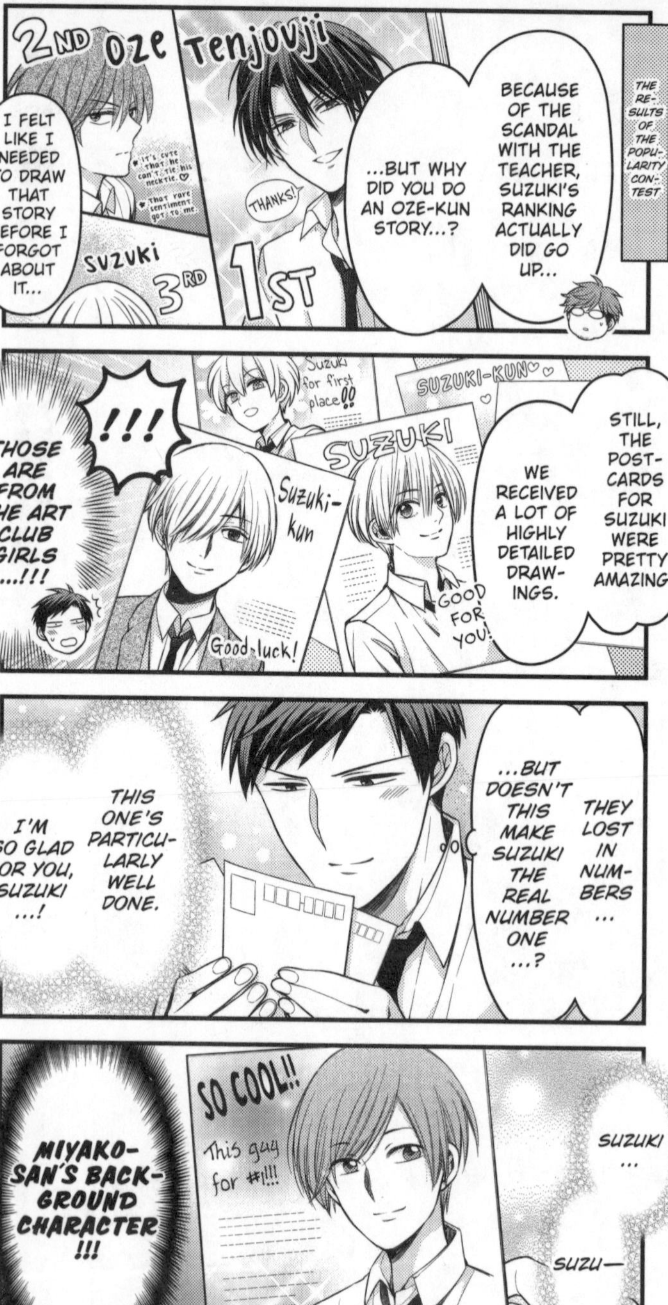

BECAUSE OF THE SCANDAL WITH THE TEACHER, SUZUKI'S RANKING ACTUALLY DID GO UP...
...BUT WHY DID YOU DO AN OZE-KUN STORY...?
Tenjouji
1ST
THANKS!
2ND Oze
It's cute that he can't tie his necktie.
That rare sentiment got to me.
SUZUKI 3RD
I FELT LIKE I NEEDED TO DRAW THAT STORY BEFORE I FORGOT ABOUT IT...
STILL, THE POSTCARDS FOR SUZUKI WERE PRETTY AMAZING.
WE RECEIVED A LOT OF HIGHLY DETAILED DRAWINGS.
SUZUKI-KUN
Suzuki for first place!!
SUZUKI
GOOD FOR YOU!
Suzuki-kun
Good luck!
!!!
THOSE ARE FROM THE ART CLUB GIRLS...!!!
THEY LOST IN NUMBERS...
...BUT DOESN'T THIS MAKE SUZUKI THE REAL NUMBER ONE...?
THIS ONE'S PARTICULARLY WELL DONE.
I'M SO GLAD FOR YOU, SUZUKI...!
SUZUKI...
SUZU—
SO COOL!!
This guy for #1!!!
MIYAKO-SAN'S BACKGROUND CHARACTER!!!

MONTHLY GIRLS' ✕ NOZAKI-KUN

[Extra]

JUST RUN WITH IT!

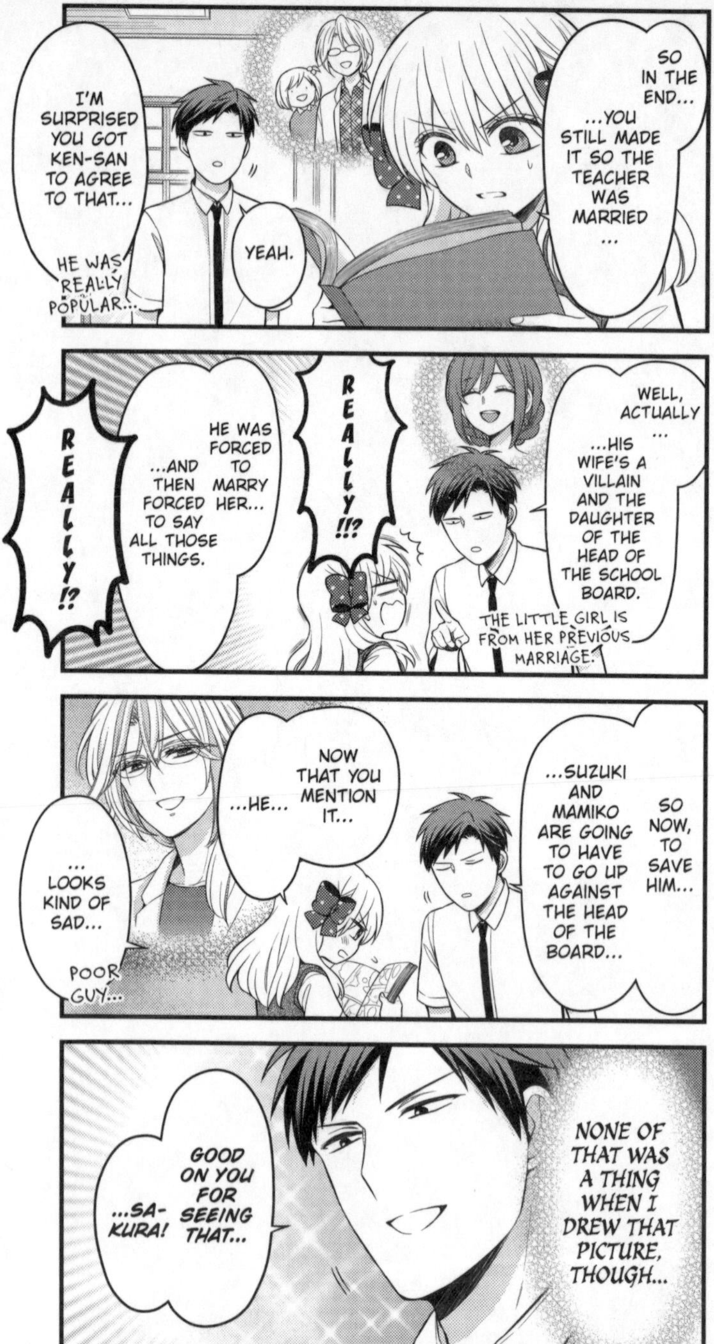
SO IN THE END... ...YOU STILL MADE IT SO THE TEACHER WAS MARRIED ...
YEAH.
I'M SURPRISED YOU GOT KEN-SAN TO AGREE TO THAT...
HE WAS REALLY POPULAR...
WELL, ACTUALLY ... ...HIS WIFE'S A VILLAIN AND THE DAUGHTER OF THE HEAD OF THE SCHOOL BOARD.
THE LITTLE GIRL IS FROM HER PREVIOUS MARRIAGE.
REALLY!!?
HE WAS FORCED TO MARRY HER... ...AND THEN FORCED TO SAY ALL THOSE THINGS.
REALLY!?
SO NOW, TO SAVE HIM... ...SUZUKI AND MAMIKO ARE GOING TO HAVE TO GO UP AGAINST THE HEAD OF THE BOARD...
NOW THAT YOU MENTION IT... ...HE...
...LOOKS KIND OF SAD...
POOR GUY...
NONE OF THAT WAS A THING WHEN I DREW THAT PICTURE, THOUGH...
GOOD ON YOU FOR SEEING THAT... ...SA-KURA!

[Extra]

GO FOR IT, TENJOUJI-KUN!!

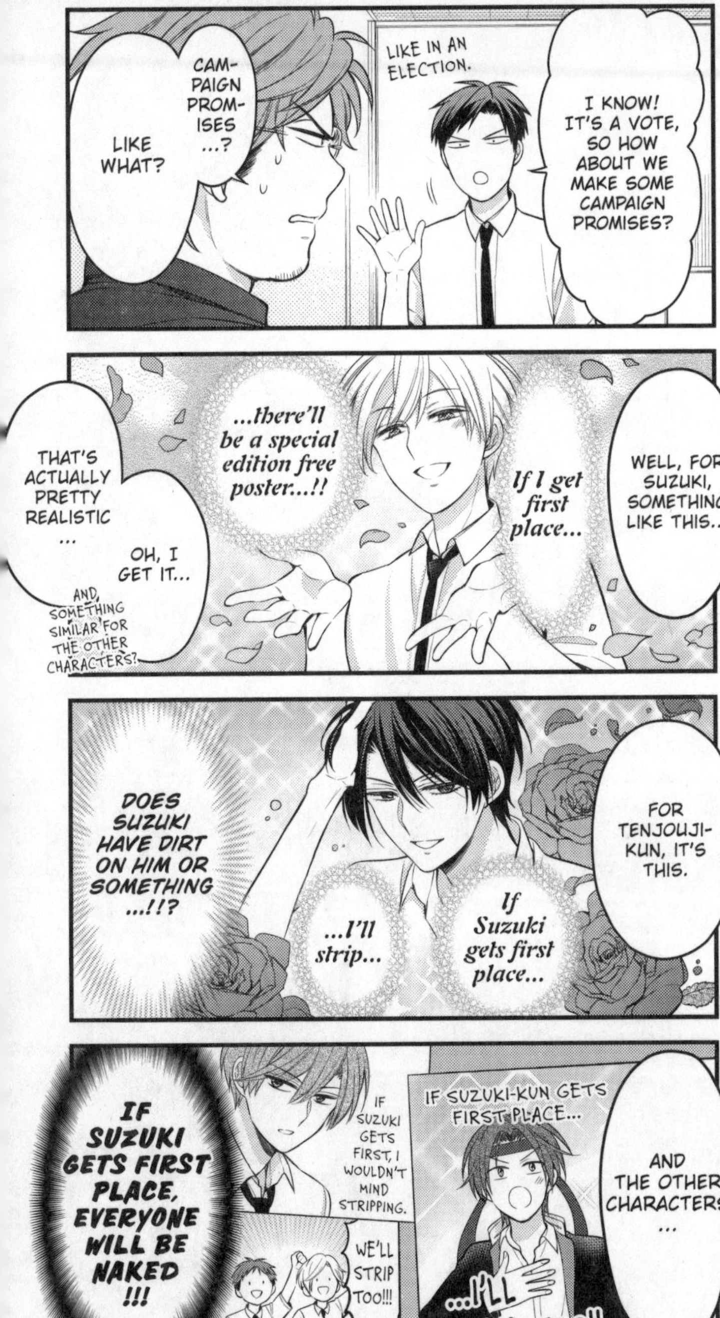
I KNOW! IT'S A VOTE, SO HOW ABOUT WE MAKE SOME CAMPAIGN PROMISES?
LIKE IN AN ELECTION.
CAM-PAIGN PROM-ISES ...?
LIKE WHAT?
WELL, FOR SUZUKI, SOMETHING LIKE THIS...
If I get first place...
...there'll be a special edition free poster...!!
THAT'S ACTUALLY PRETTY REALISTIC ...
OH, I GET IT...
AND, SOMETHING SIMILAR FOR THE OTHER CHARACTERS?
FOR TENJOUJI-KUN, IT'S THIS.
If Suzuki gets first place...
...I'll strip...
DOES SUZUKI HAVE DIRT ON HIM OR SOMETHING ...!!?
AND THE OTHER CHARACTERS ...
IF SUZUKI-KUN GETS FIRST PLACE...
...I'LL STRIP TOO!!
IF SUZUKI GETS FIRST, I WOULDN'T MIND STRIPPING.
WE'LL STRIP TOO!!!
IF SUZUKI GETS FIRST PLACE, EVERYONE WILL BE NAKED !!!

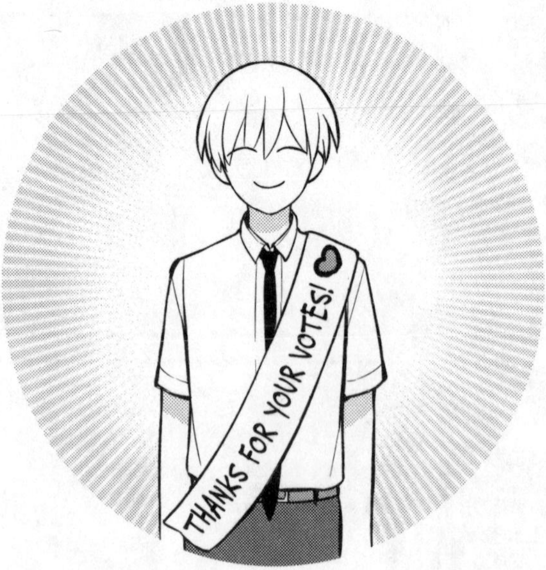
THANKS FOR YOUR VOTES!

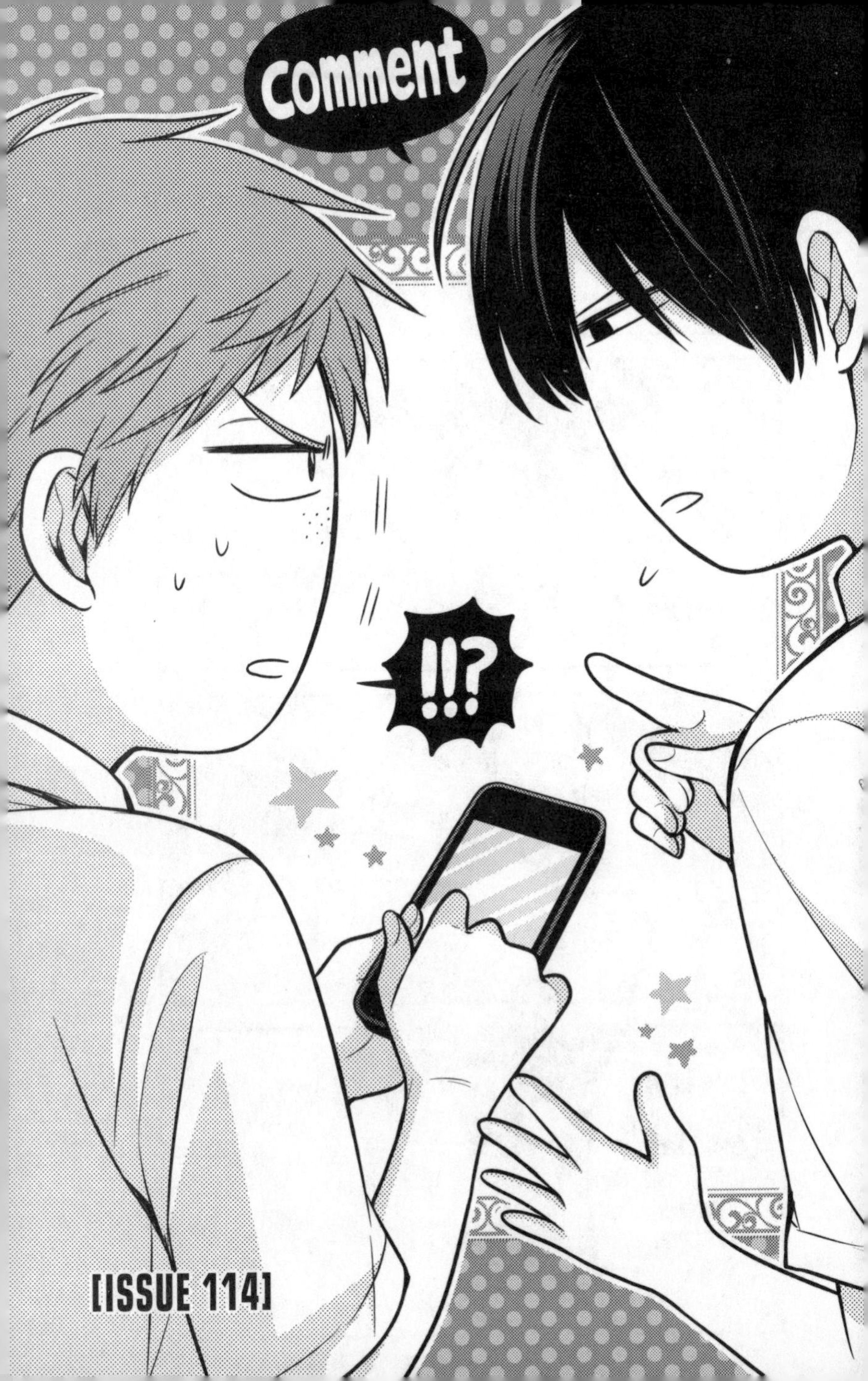
Comment
!!?
[ISSUE 114]

MAYU'S A BAD KID

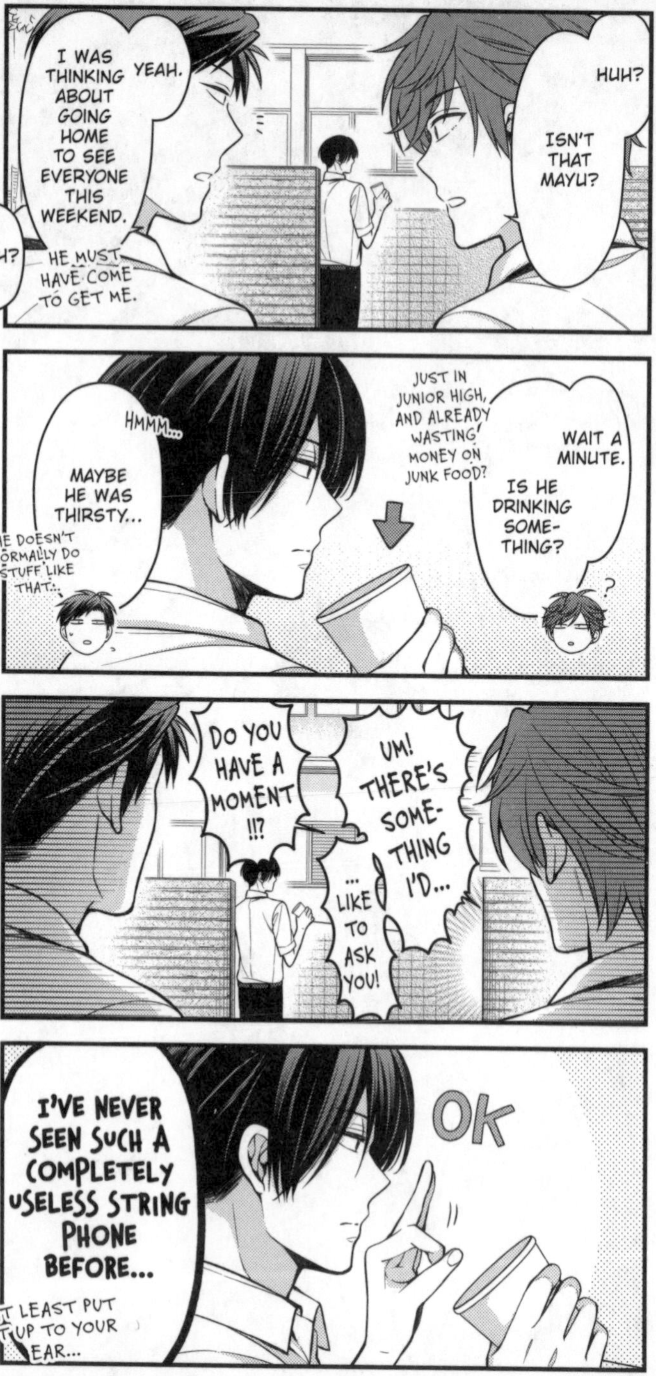
HUH?
ISN'T THAT MAYU?
YEAH.
I WAS THINKING ABOUT GOING HOME TO SEE EVERYONE THIS WEEKEND.
OH?
HE MUST HAVE COME TO GET ME.
WAIT A MINUTE.
IS HE DRINKING SOME-THING?
JUST IN JUNIOR HIGH, AND ALREADY WASTING MONEY ON JUNK FOOD?
HMMM...
MAYBE HE WAS THIRSTY...
HE DOESN'T NORMALLY DO STUFF LIKE THAT...
UM! THERE'S SOME-THING I'D...
...LIKE TO ASK YOU!
DO YOU HAVE A MOMENT!!?
OK
I'VE NEVER SEEN SUCH A COMPLETELY USELESS STRING PHONE BEFORE...
AT LEAST PUT IT UP TO YOUR EAR...

SHE WAS RAISED RIGHT. SUPPOSEDLY

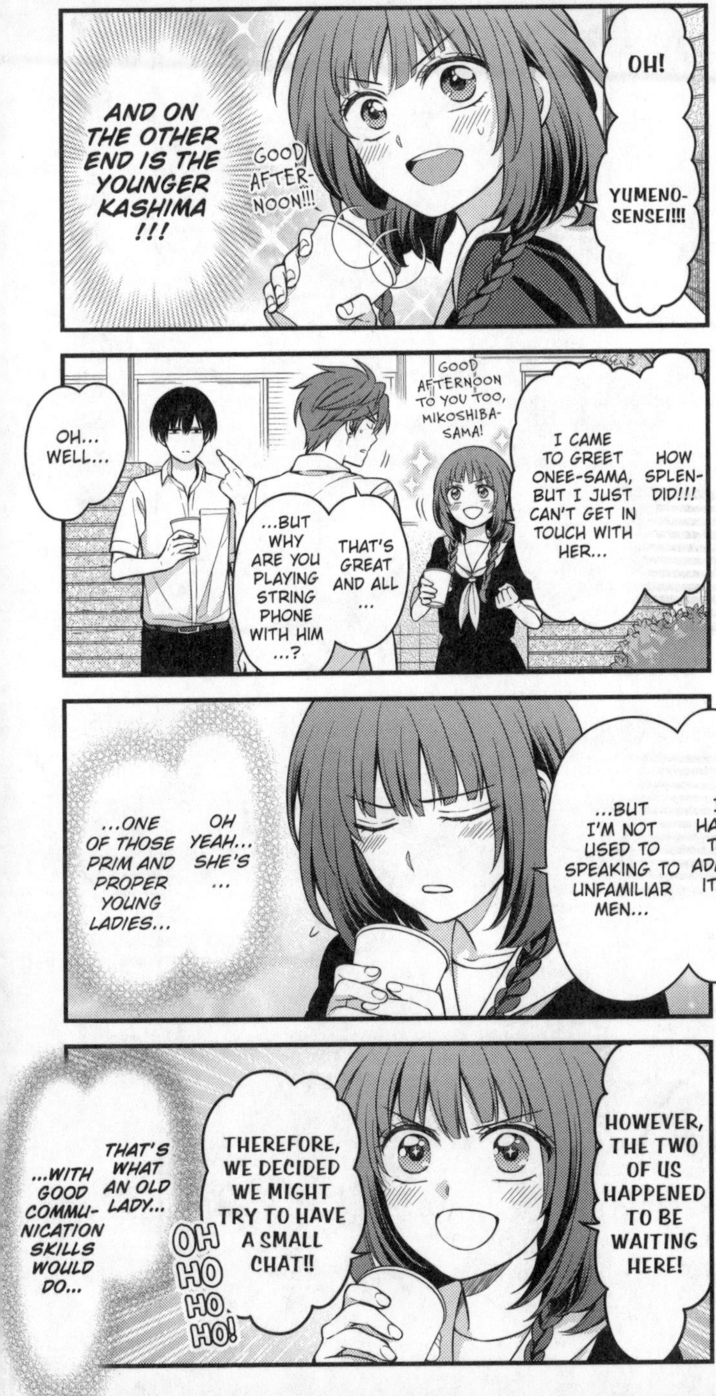
OH! YUMENO-SENSEI!!!
GOOD AFTER-NOON!!!
AND ON THE OTHER END IS THE YOUNGER KASHIMA !!!
HOW SPLEN-DID!!!
I CAME TO GREET ONEE-SAMA, BUT I JUST CAN'T GET IN TOUCH WITH HER...
GOOD AFTERNOON TO YOU TOO, MIKOSHIBA-SAMA!
THAT'S GREAT AND ALL ...
...BUT WHY ARE YOU PLAYING STRING PHONE WITH HIM ...?
OH... WELL...
I HATE TO ADMIT IT...
...BUT I'M NOT USED TO SPEAKING TO UNFAMILIAR MEN...
OH YEAH... SHE'S ...
...ONE OF THOSE PRIM AND PROPER YOUNG LADIES...
HOWEVER, THE TWO OF US HAPPENED TO BE WAITING HERE!
THEREFORE, WE DECIDED WE MIGHT TRY TO HAVE A SMALL CHAT!!
OH HO HO HO HO!
THAT'S WHAT AN OLD LADY...
...WITH GOOD COMMUNICATION SKILLS WOULD DO...

A JUNIOR HIGH GIRL

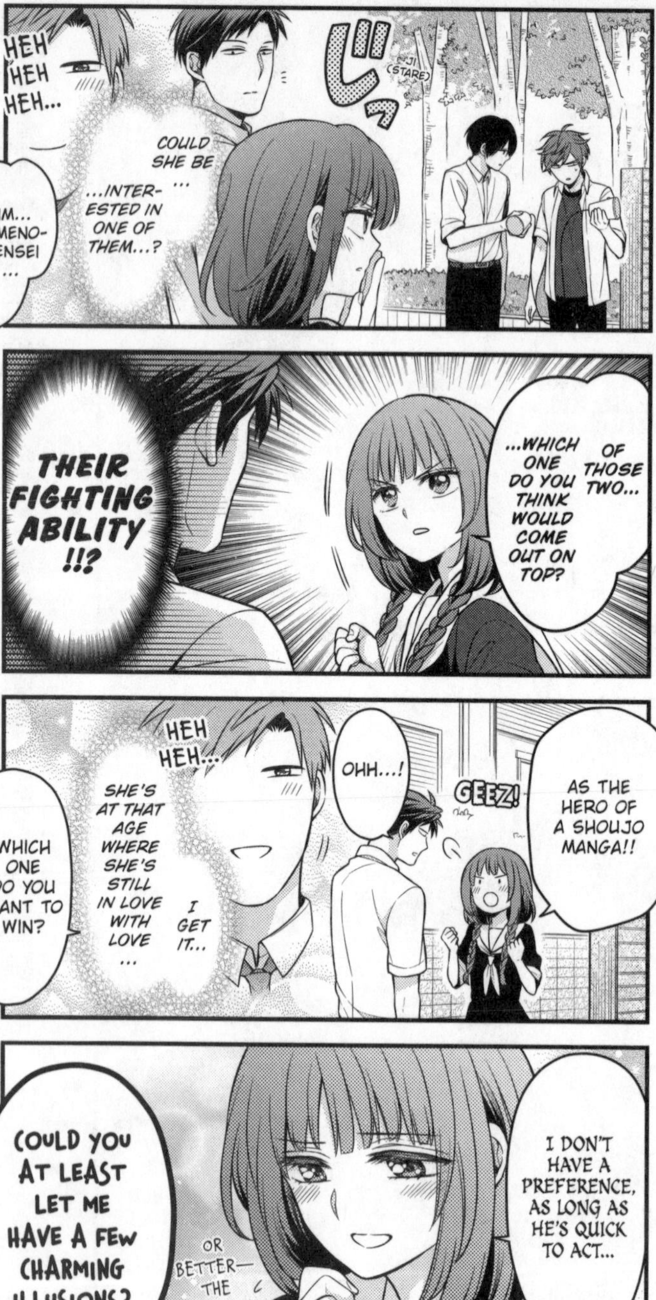
JI (STARE)
じっ
COULD SHE BE ...
...INTER-ESTED IN ONE OF THEM...?
HEH HEH HEH...
UM... YUMENO-SENSEI ...
OF THOSE TWO...
...WHICH ONE DO YOU THINK WOULD COME OUT ON TOP?
THEIR FIGHTING ABILITY !!?
NO!!
AS THE HERO OF A SHOUJO MANGA!!
GEEZ!
OHH...!
HEH HEH...
I GET IT...
SHE'S AT THAT AGE WHERE SHE'S STILL IN LOVE WITH LOVE ...
WHICH ONE DO YOU WANT TO WIN?
I DON'T HAVE A PREFERENCE, AS LONG AS HE'S QUICK TO ACT...
OR BETTER—THE ACCIDENTAL PERVERT...
COULD YOU AT LEAST LET ME HAVE A FEW CHARMING ILLUSIONS?

SPEAKING FROM EXPERIENCE

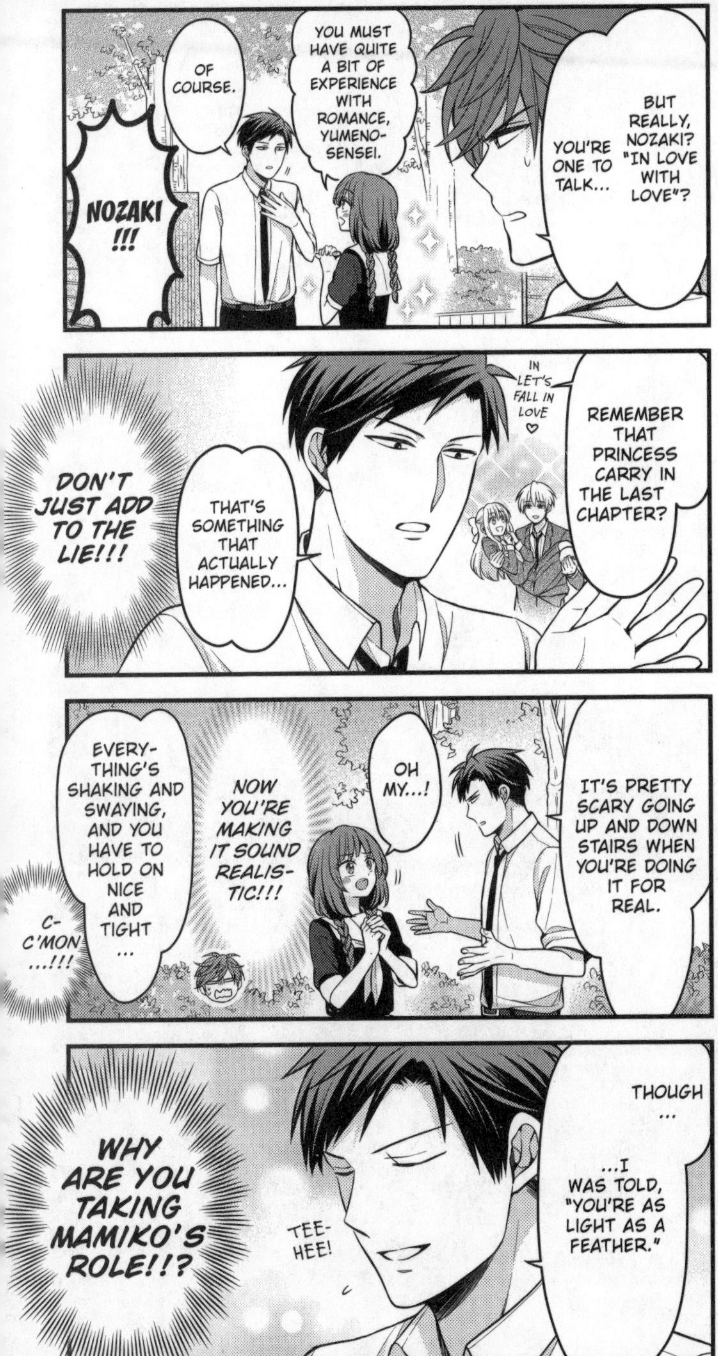
BUT REALLY, NOZAKI? "IN LOVE WITH LOVE"?
YOU'RE ONE TO TALK...
YOU MUST HAVE QUITE A BIT OF EXPERIENCE WITH ROMANCE, YUMENO-SENSEI.
OF COURSE.
NOZAKI!!!
REMEMBER THAT PRINCESS CARRY IN THE LAST CHAPTER?
IN LET'S FALL IN LOVE
THAT'S SOMETHING THAT ACTUALLY HAPPENED...
DON'T JUST ADD TO THE LIE!!!
IT'S PRETTY SCARY GOING UP AND DOWN STAIRS WHEN YOU'RE DOING IT FOR REAL.
OH MY...!
NOW YOU'RE MAKING IT SOUND REALIS-TIC!!!
EVERY-THING'S SHAKING AND SWAYING, AND YOU HAVE TO HOLD ON NICE AND TIGHT...
C-C'MON...!!!
THOUGH...
...I WAS TOLD, "YOU'RE AS LIGHT AS A FEATHER."
TEE-HEE!
WHY ARE YOU TAKING MAMIKO'S ROLE!!?

OVER AND OVER AGAIN IN THREE YEARS OF LOVE

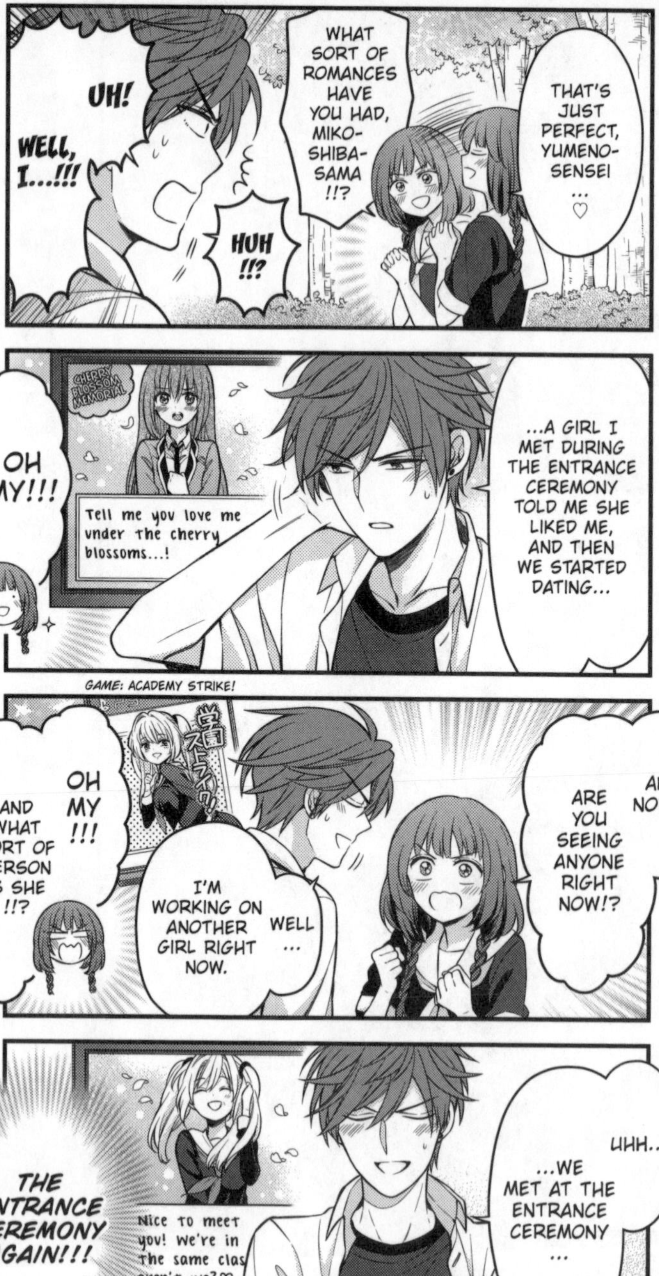
THAT'S JUST PERFECT, YUMENO-SENSEI ...♡
WHAT SORT OF ROMANCES HAVE YOU HAD, MIKO-SHIBA-SAMA !!?
HUH !!?
UH!
WELL, I...!!!
...A GIRL I MET DURING THE ENTRANCE CEREMONY TOLD ME SHE LIKED ME, AND THEN WE STARTED DATING...
CHERRY BLOSSOM MEMORIAL
Tell me you love me under the cherry blossoms...!
OH MY!!!
GAME: ACADEMY STRIKE!
AND NOW!?
ARE YOU SEEING ANYONE RIGHT NOW!?
WELL ...
I'M WORKING ON ANOTHER GIRL RIGHT NOW.
学園ストライク!
OH MY !!!
AND WHAT SORT OF PERSON IS SHE !!?
UHH...
...WE MET AT THE ENTRANCE CEREMONY ...
Nice to meet you! We're in the same clas aren't we?♡
THE ENTRANCE CEREMONY AGAIN!!!

MAYU DOESN'T LIE

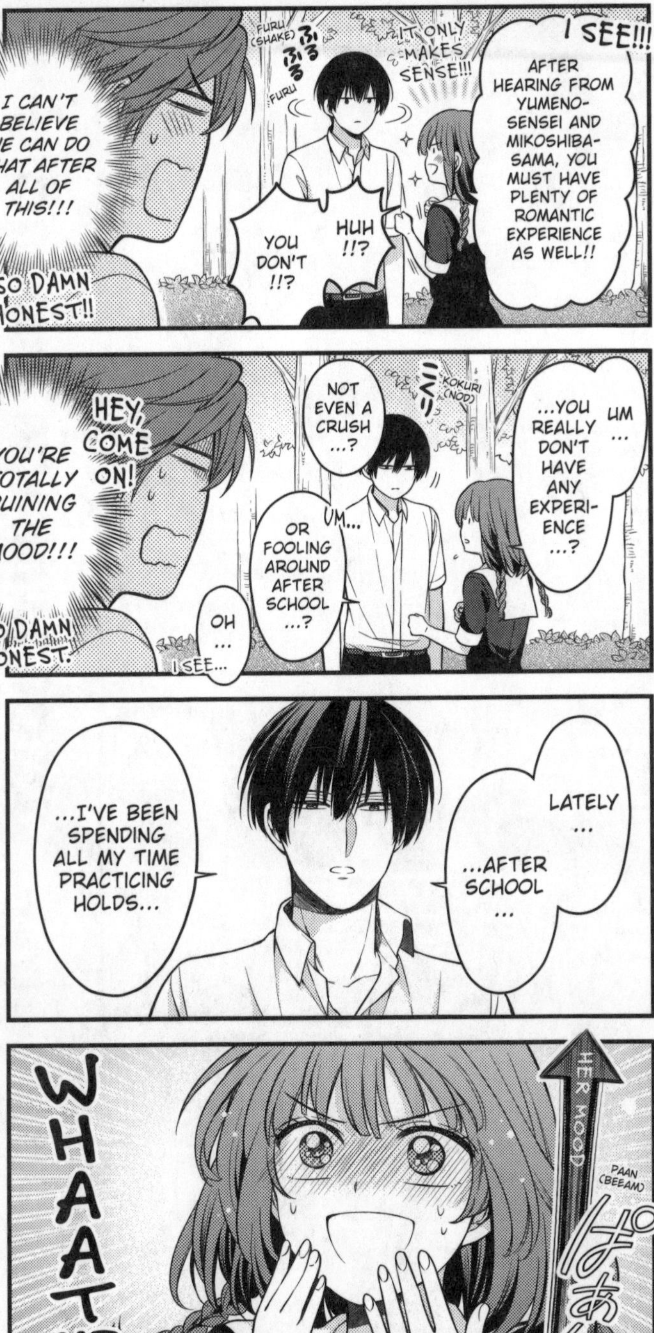
I SEE!!!
AFTER HEARING FROM YUMENO-SENSEI AND MIKOSHIBA-SAMA, YOU MUST HAVE PLENTY OF ROMANTIC EXPERIENCE AS WELL!!
IT ONLY MAKES SENSE!!!
FURU (SHAKE) ふるふる FURU
HUH !!?
YOU DON'T !!?
I CAN'T BELIEVE HE CAN DO THAT AFTER ALL OF THIS!!!
SO DAMN HONEST!!
UM ...
...YOU REALLY DON'T HAVE ANY EXPERIENCE ...?
KOKURI (NOD)
NOT EVEN A CRUSH ...?
UM...
OR FOOLING AROUND AFTER SCHOOL ...?
OH ... I SEE...
HEY, COME ON!
YOU'RE TOTALLY RUINING THE MOOD!!!
SO DAMN HONEST.
LATELY ... ...AFTER SCHOOL ...
...I'VE BEEN SPENDING ALL MY TIME PRACTICING HOLDS...
HER MOOD
PAAN (BEEAM)
ぱあん
WHAAT!!?

I'LL SHOW YOU WITH MY BODY

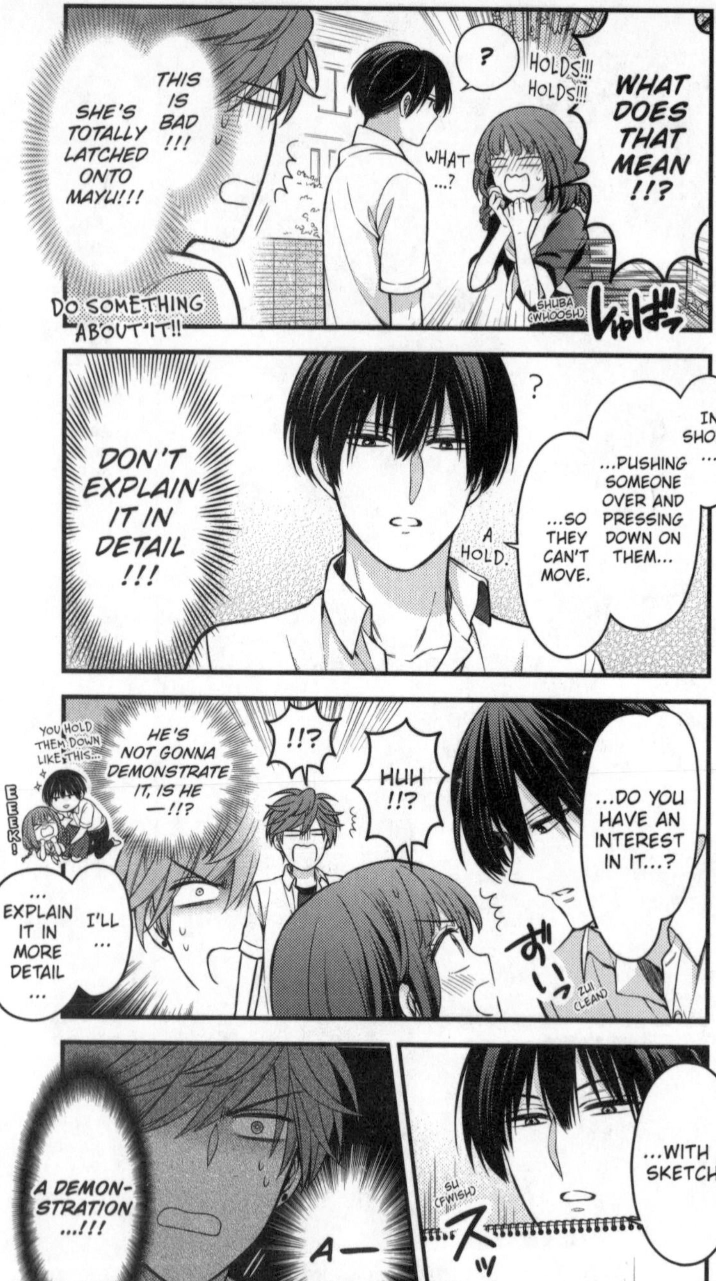
WHAT DOES THAT MEAN!!?
HOLDS!!! HOLDS!!!
?
WHAT...?
SHUBA (WHOOSH)
THIS IS BAD!!!
SHE'S TOTALLY LATCHED ONTO MAYU!!!
DO SOMETHING ABOUT IT!!
IN SHORT...
...PUSHING SOMEONE OVER AND PRESSING DOWN ON THEM...
...SO THEY CAN'T MOVE.
A HOLD.
?
DON'T EXPLAIN IT IN DETAIL!!!
...DO YOU HAVE AN INTEREST IN IT...?
ZUI (LEAN)
HUH!!?
!!?
HE'S NOT GONNA DEMONSTRATE IT, IS HE—!!?
YOU HOLD THEM DOWN LIKE THIS...
EEEK!
I'LL...
...EXPLAIN IT IN MORE DETAIL...
...WITH A SKETCH.
SU (FWISH)
A DEMON-STRATION...!!!
A—

PRO TECHNIQUES

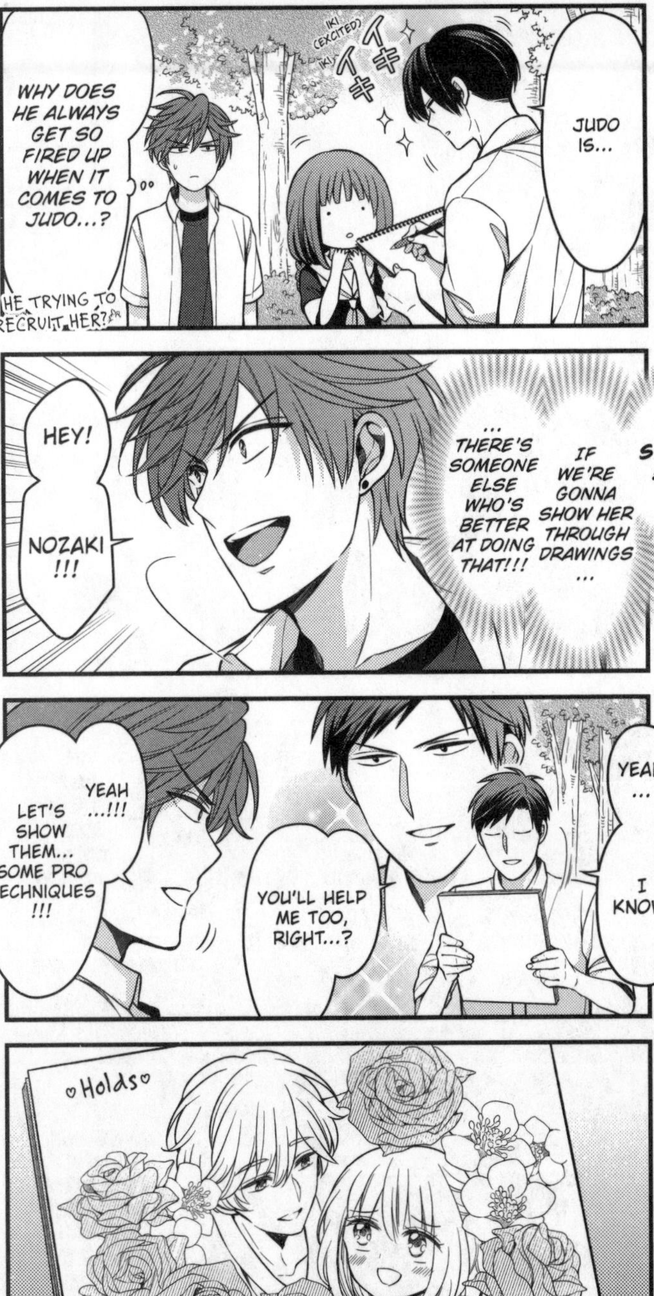
JUDO IS...
IKI (EXCITED)
IKI
WHY DOES HE ALWAYS GET SO FIRED UP WHEN IT COMES TO JUDO...?
IS HE TRYING TO RECRUIT HER?
STILL!!!
IF WE'RE GONNA SHOW HER THROUGH DRAWINGS...
...THERE'S SOMEONE ELSE WHO'S BETTER AT DOING THAT!!!
HEY!
NOZAKI!!!
YEAH...
I KNOW.
YOU'LL HELP ME TOO, RIGHT...?
YEAH...!!!
LET'S SHOW THEM... SOME PRO TECHNIQUES!!!
♡Holds♡

INCRIMINATING TESTIMONY

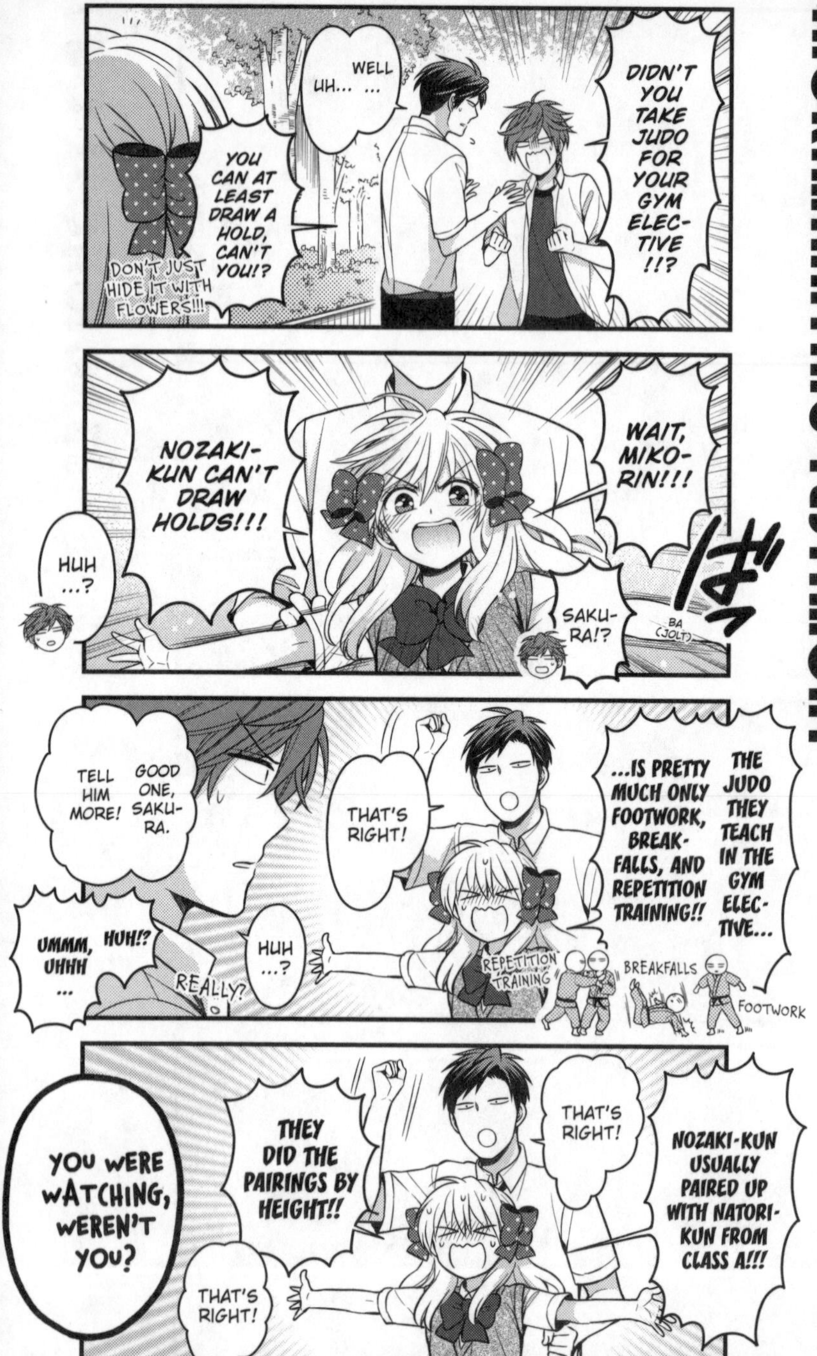
DIDN'T YOU TAKE JUDO FOR YOUR GYM ELECTIVE!!?
WELL UH... ...
YOU CAN AT LEAST DRAW A HOLD, CAN'T YOU!?
DON'T JUST HIDE IT WITH FLOWERS!!!
ぱっ
BA (JOLT)
WAIT, MIKO-RIN!!!
SAKU-RA!?
NOZAKI-KUN CAN'T DRAW HOLDS!!!
HUH ...?
THE JUDO THEY TEACH IN THE GYM ELECTIVE...
...IS PRETTY MUCH ONLY FOOTWORK, BREAK-FALLS, AND REPETITION TRAINING!!
FOOTWORK
BREAKFALLS
REPETITION TRAINING
THAT'S RIGHT!
HUH ...?
GOOD ONE, SAKU-RA.
TELL HIM MORE!
REALLY?
HUH!?
UMMM, UHHH ...
NOZAKI-KUN USUALLY PAIRED UP WITH NATORI-KUN FROM CLASS A!!!
THAT'S RIGHT!
THEY DID THE PAIRINGS BY HEIGHT!!
THAT'S RIGHT!
YOU WERE WATCHING, WEREN'T YOU?

WHAT HE WANTS TO GET ACROSS

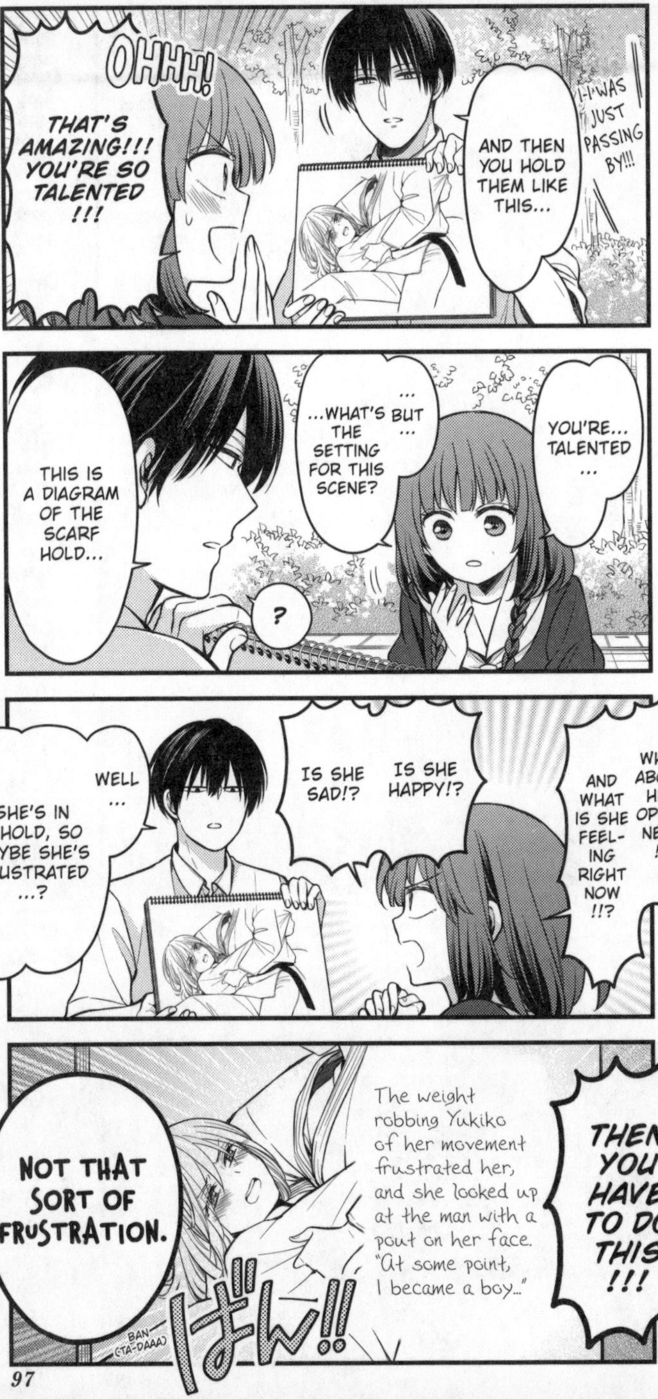
I-I WAS JUST PASSING BY!!!
AND THEN YOU HOLD THEM LIKE THIS...
OHHH!
THAT'S AMAZING!!! YOU'RE SO TALENTED !!!
YOU'RE... TALENTED ...
... BUT ...
...WHAT'S THE SETTING FOR THIS SCENE?
?
THIS IS A DIAGRAM OF THE SCARF HOLD...
WHAT ABOUT HER OPPONENT !?
AND WHAT IS SHE FEELING RIGHT NOW !!?
IS SHE HAPPY!?
IS SHE SAD!?
WELL ...
SHE'S IN A HOLD, SO MAYBE SHE'S FRUSTRATED ...?
THEN YOU HAVE TO DO THIS !!!
The weight robbing Yukiko of her movement frustrated her, and she looked up at the man with a pout on her face. "At some point, I became a boy..."
NOT THAT SORT OF FRUSTRATION.
ばん!!
BAN (TA-DAAA)

CASUALLY ADDING A STORY

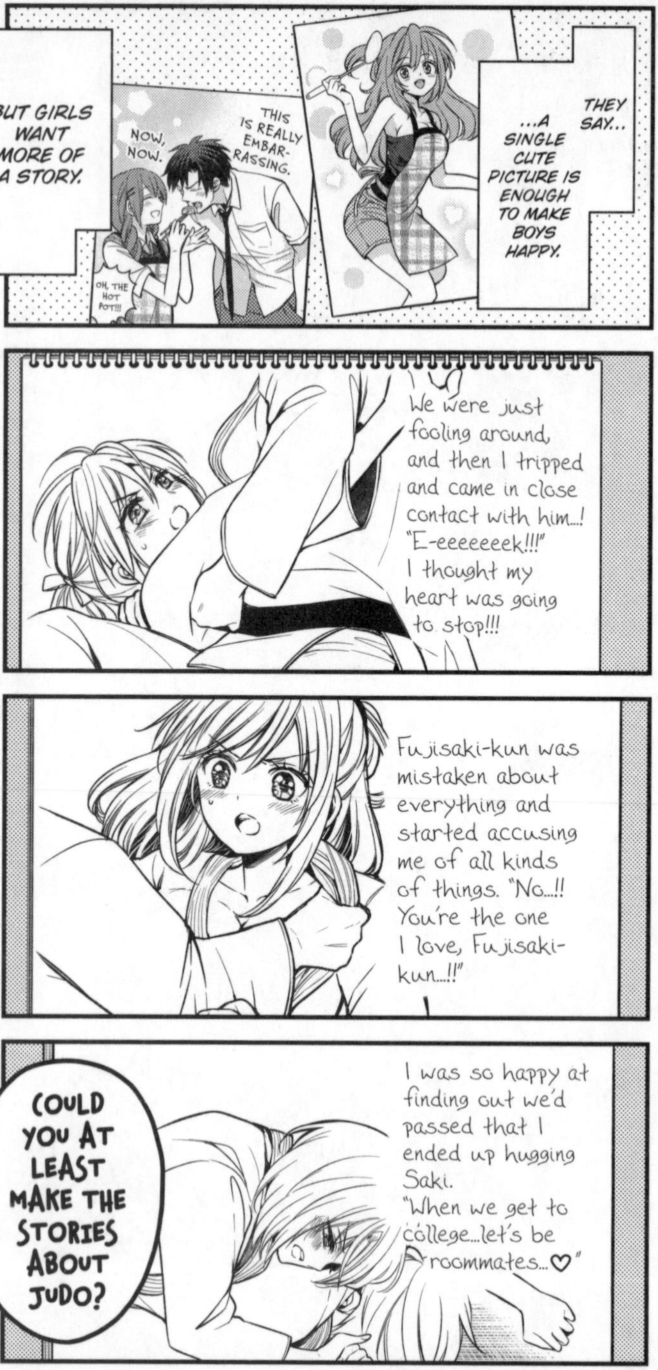
THEY SAY...
...A SINGLE CUTE PICTURE IS ENOUGH TO MAKE BOYS HAPPY.
THIS IS REALLY EMBAR-RASSING.
NOW, NOW.
OH, THE HOT POT!!!
BUT GIRLS WANT MORE OF A STORY.
We were just fooling around, and then I tripped and came in close contact with him...! "E-eeeeeeek!!!" I thought my heart was going to stop!!!
Fujisaki-kun was mistaken about everything and started accusing me of all kinds of things. "No...!! You're the one I love, Fujisaki-kun...!!"
I was so happy at finding out we'd passed that I ended up hugging Saki. "When we get to college...let's be roommates...♡"
COULD YOU AT LEAST MAKE THE STORIES ABOUT JUDO?

SHE LIKES TROUBLESOME COUPLES

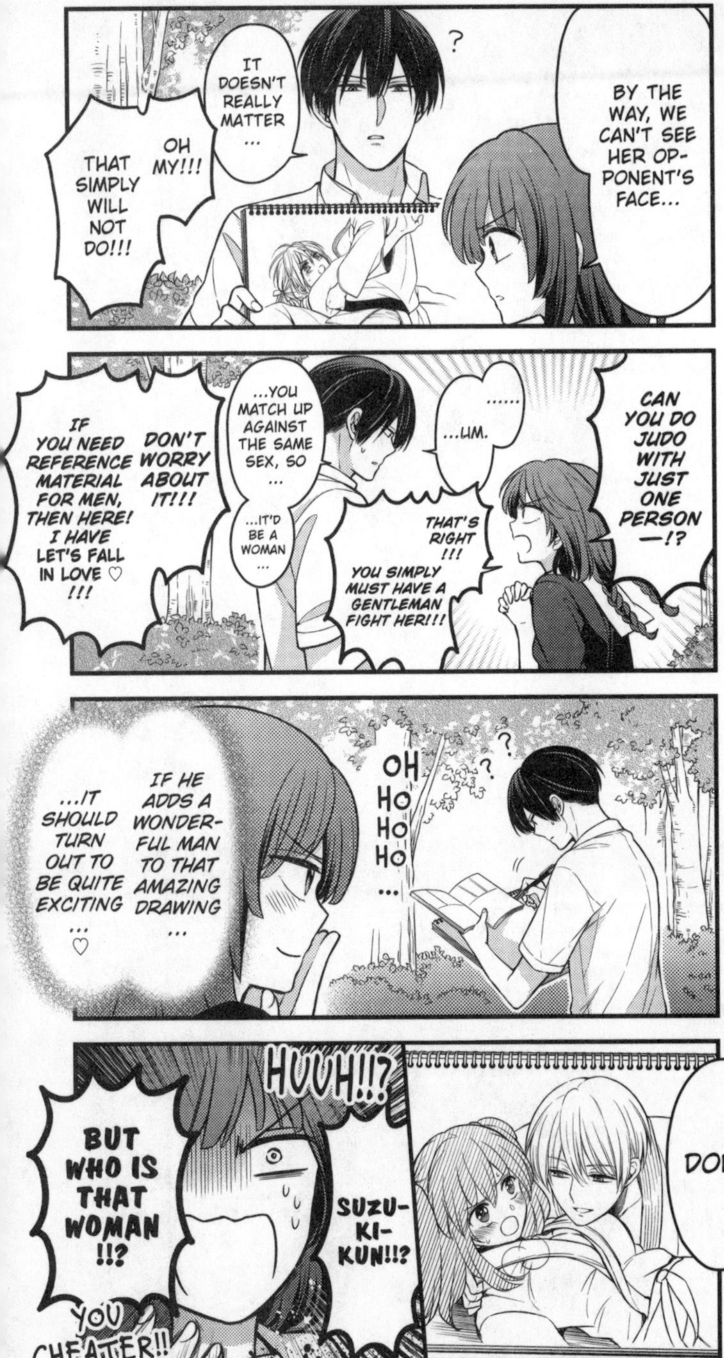
BY THE WAY, WE CAN'T SEE HER OP-PONENT'S FACE...
?
IT DOESN'T REALLY MATTER ...
OH MY!!!
THAT SIMPLY WILL NOT DO!!!
CAN YOU DO JUDO WITH JUST ONE PERSON—!?
....UM.
...YOU MATCH UP AGAINST THE SAME SEX, SO ...
...IT'D BE A WOMAN ...
THAT'S RIGHT !!!
YOU SIMPLY MUST HAVE A GENTLEMAN FIGHT HER!!!
DON'T WORRY ABOUT IT!!!
IF YOU NEED REFERENCE MATERIAL FOR MEN, THEN HERE! I HAVE LET'S FALL IN LOVE ♡ !!!
? ?
OH HO HO HO ...
IF HE ADDS A WONDERFUL MAN TO THAT AMAZING DRAWING ...
...IT SHOULD TURN OUT TO BE QUITE EXCITING ... ♡
DONE.
SUZUKI-KUN!!?
HUUH!!?
BUT WHO IS THAT WOMAN !!?
YOU CHEATER!!

A FAN'S GAZE

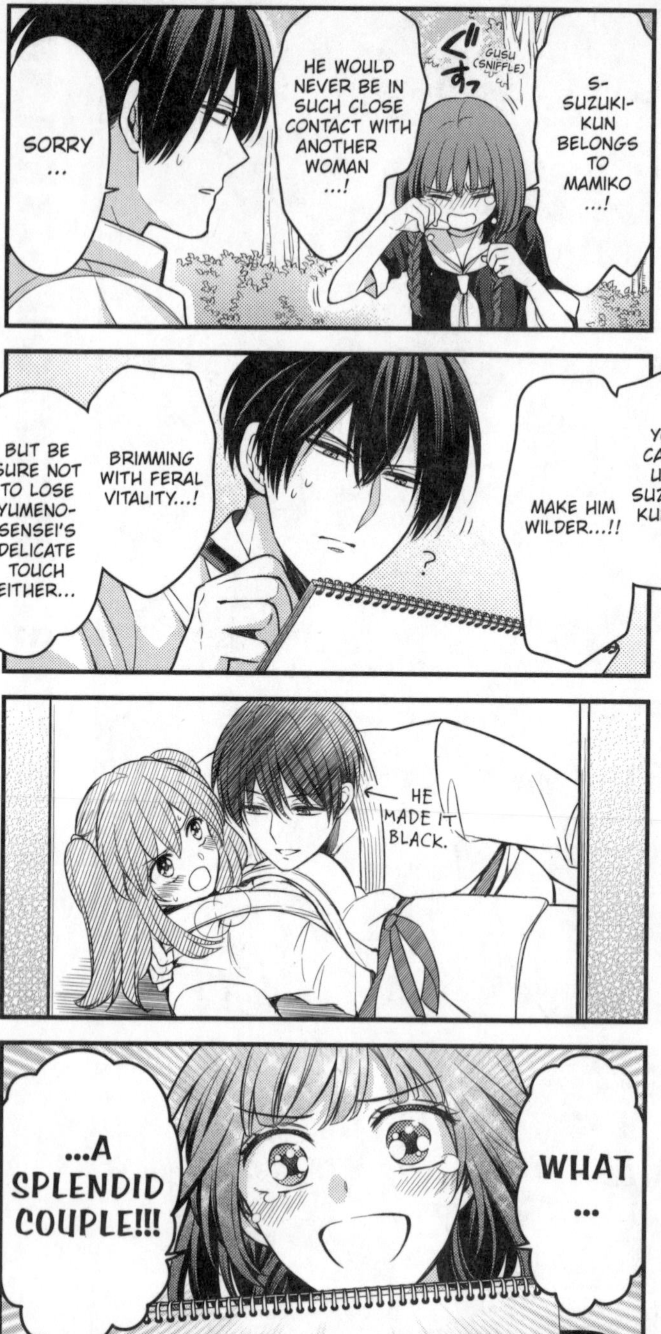
ぐすっ
GUSU (SNIFFLE)
S-SUZUKI-KUN BELONGS TO MAMIKO ...!
HE WOULD NEVER BE IN SUCH CLOSE CONTACT WITH ANOTHER WOMAN ...!
SORRY ...
GUSU ぐすっ
YOU CAN'T USE SUZUKI-KUN...!
MAKE HIM WILDER...!!
?
BRIMMING WITH FERAL VITALITY...!
BUT BE SURE NOT TO LOSE YUMENO-SENSEI'S DELICATE TOUCH EITHER...
HE MADE IT BLACK.
WHAT ...
...A SPLENDID COUPLE!!!

THE PROPER LADY AND THE KID BROTHER

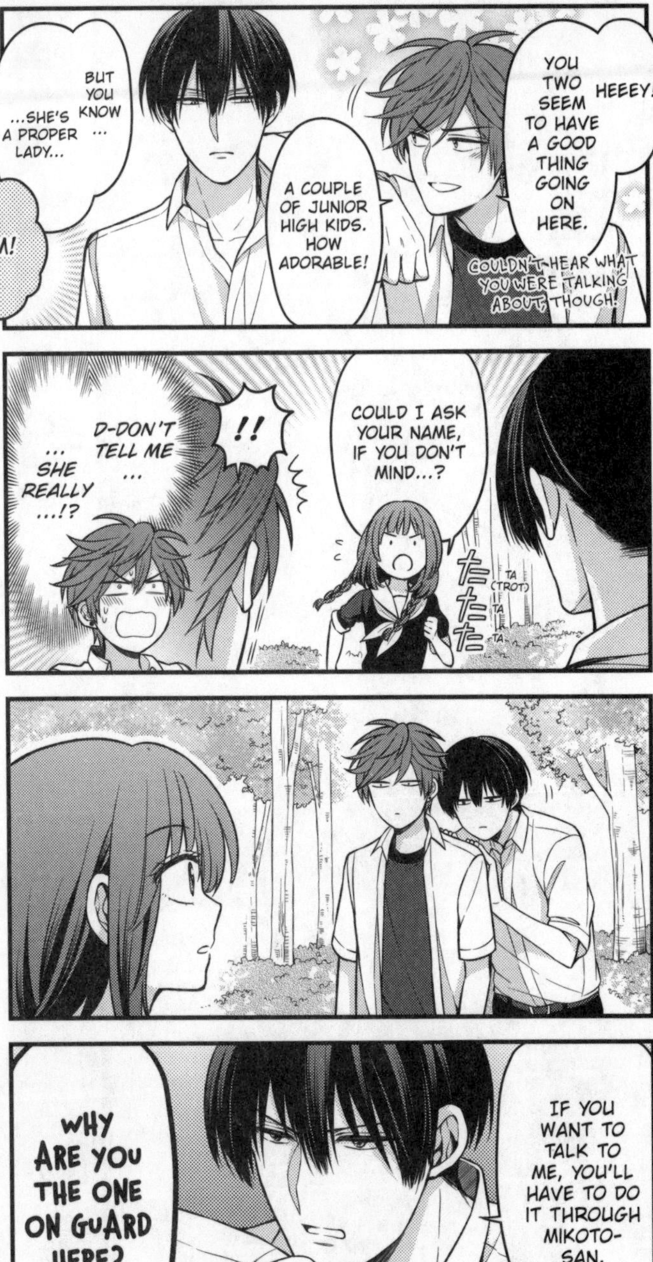
HEEEY!
YOU TWO SEEM TO HAVE A GOOD THING GOING ON HERE.
COULDN'T HEAR WHAT YOU WERE TALKING ABOUT, THOUGH!
A COUPLE OF JUNIOR HIGH KIDS. HOW ADORABLE!
BUT YOU KNOW ...
...SHE'S A PROPER LADY...
UM!
COULD I ASK YOUR NAME, IF YOU DON'T MIND...?
たたた
TA (TROT) TA TA
!!
D-DON'T TELL ME ...
... SHE REALLY ...!?
IF YOU WANT TO TALK TO ME, YOU'LL HAVE TO DO IT THROUGH MIKOTO-SAN.
WHY ARE YOU THE ONE ON GUARD HERE?

THE AFTEREFFECTS

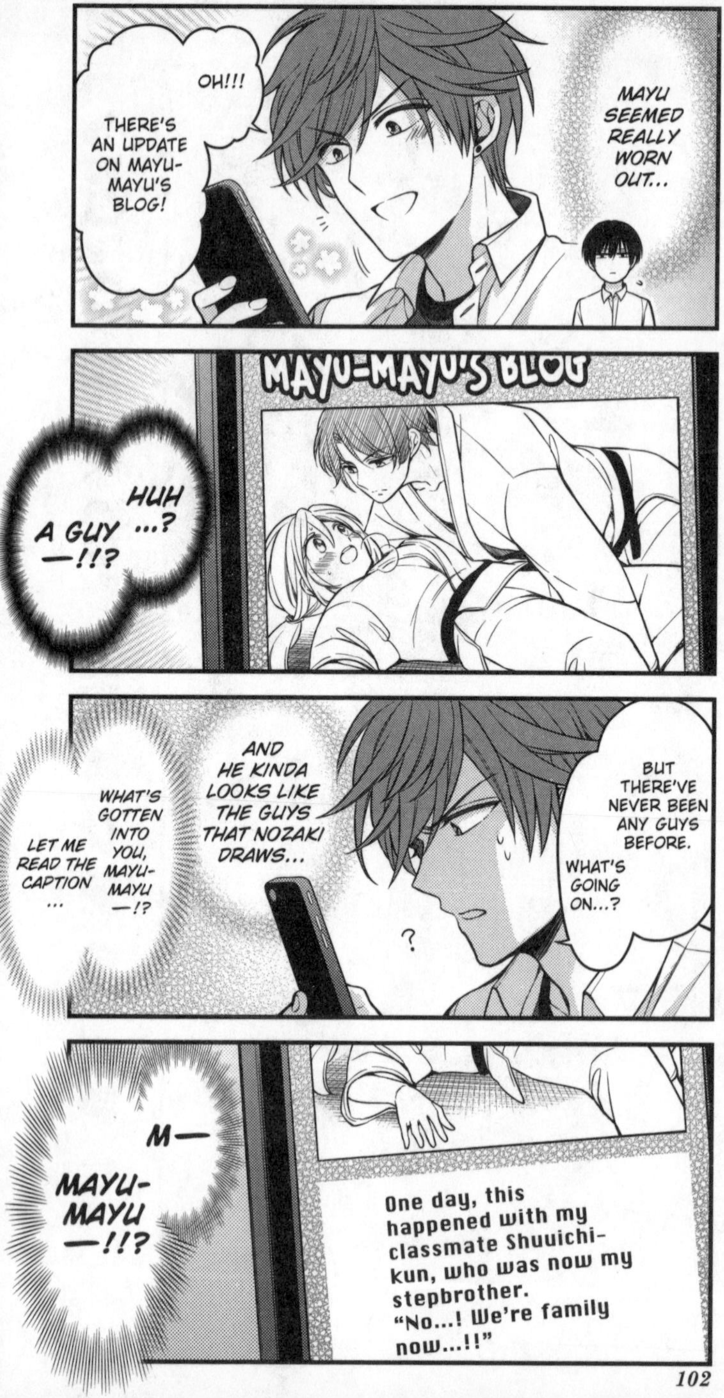
MAYU SEEMED REALLY WORN OUT...
OH!!! THERE'S AN UPDATE ON MAYU-MAYU'S BLOG!
MAYU-MAYU'S BLOG
HUH...? A GUY—!!?
BUT THERE'VE NEVER BEEN ANY GUYS BEFORE. WHAT'S GOING ON...?
?
AND HE KINDA LOOKS LIKE THE GUYS THAT NOZAKI DRAWS...
WHAT'S GOTTEN INTO YOU, MAYU-MAYU—!?
LET ME READ THE CAPTION...
One day, this happened with my classmate Shuuichi-kun, who was now my stepbrother. "No...! We're family now...!!"
M— MAYU-MAYU—!!?

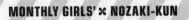

MONTHLY GIRLS' ✂ NOZAKI-KUN

[Extra]

A GAME OF TELEPHONE

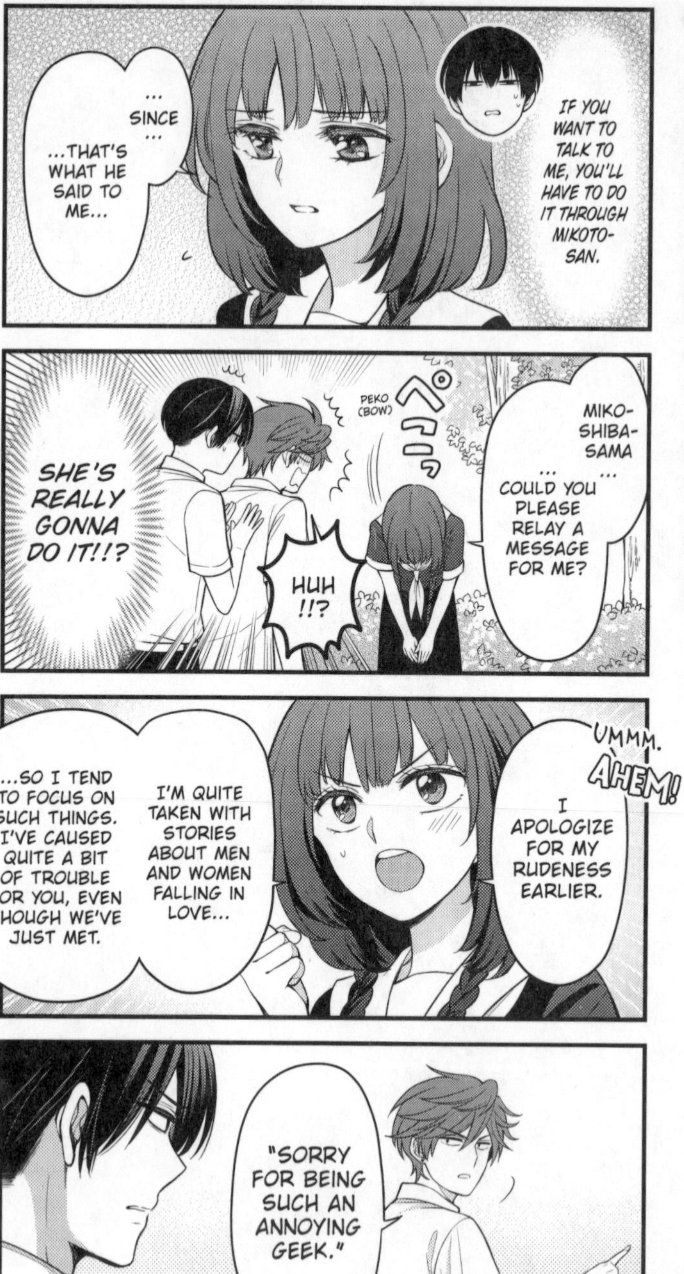
IF YOU WANT TO TALK TO ME, YOU'LL HAVE TO DO IT THROUGH MIKOTO-SAN.
... SINCE ...
...THAT'S WHAT HE SAID TO ME...
MIKO-SHIBA-SAMA ... ... COULD YOU PLEASE RELAY A MESSAGE FOR ME?
PEKO (BOW)
HUH !!?
SHE'S REALLY GONNA DO IT!!?
UMMM. AHEM!
I APOLOGIZE FOR MY RUDENESS EARLIER.
I'M QUITE TAKEN WITH STORIES ABOUT MEN AND WOMEN FALLING IN LOVE...
...SO I TEND TO FOCUS ON SUCH THINGS. I'VE CAUSED QUITE A BIT OF TROUBLE FOR YOU, EVEN THOUGH WE'VE JUST MET.
"SORRY FOR BEING SUCH AN ANNOYING GEEK."
THAT'S WHAT SHE SAID.

[Extra]

A GAME OF TELEPHONE X 2

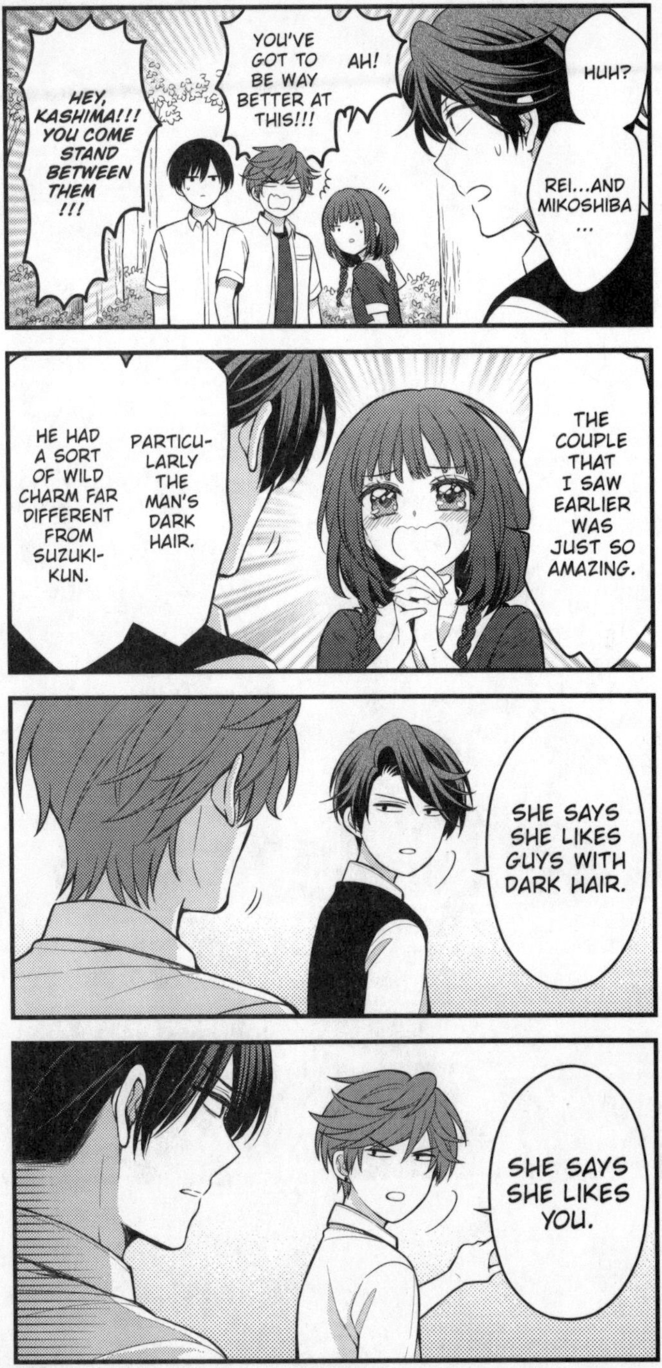
HUH?
REI...AND MIKOSHIBA...
AH!
YOU'VE GOT TO BE WAY BETTER AT THIS!!!
HEY, KASHIMA!!! YOU COME STAND BETWEEN THEM!!!
THE COUPLE THAT I SAW EARLIER WAS JUST SO AMAZING.
PARTICU-LARLY THE MAN'S DARK HAIR.
HE HAD A SORT OF WILD CHARM FAR DIFFERENT FROM SUZUKI-KUN.
SHE SAYS SHE LIKES GUYS WITH DARK HAIR.
SHE SAYS SHE LIKES YOU.

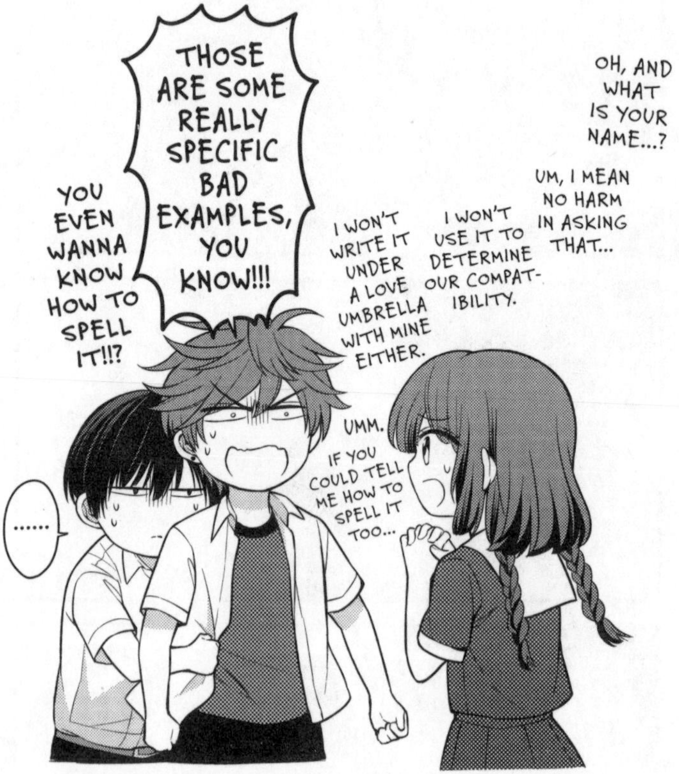
OH, AND WHAT IS YOUR NAME...?
UM, I MEAN NO HARM IN ASKING THAT...
I WON'T USE IT TO DETERMINE OUR COMPAT-IBILITY.
I WON'T WRITE IT UNDER A LOVE UMBRELLA WITH MINE EITHER.
UMM. IF YOU COULD TELL ME HOW TO SPELL IT TOO...
THOSE ARE SOME REALLY SPECIFIC BAD EXAMPLES, YOU KNOW!!!
YOU EVEN WANNA KNOW HOW TO SPELL IT!!?
......

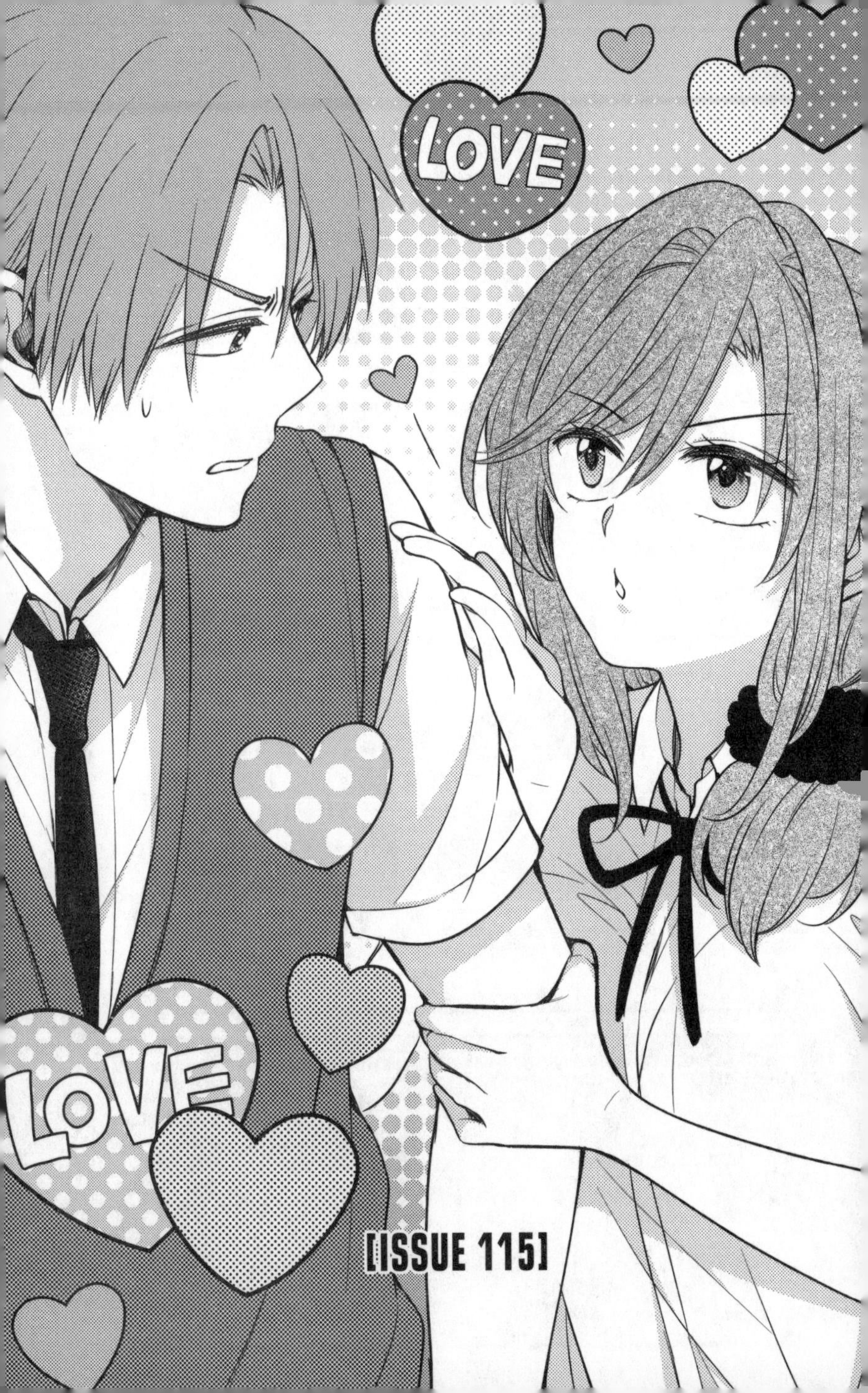
LOVE
LOVE
[ISSUE 115]

THAT WILL PUT HIM EVEN MORE ON GUARD

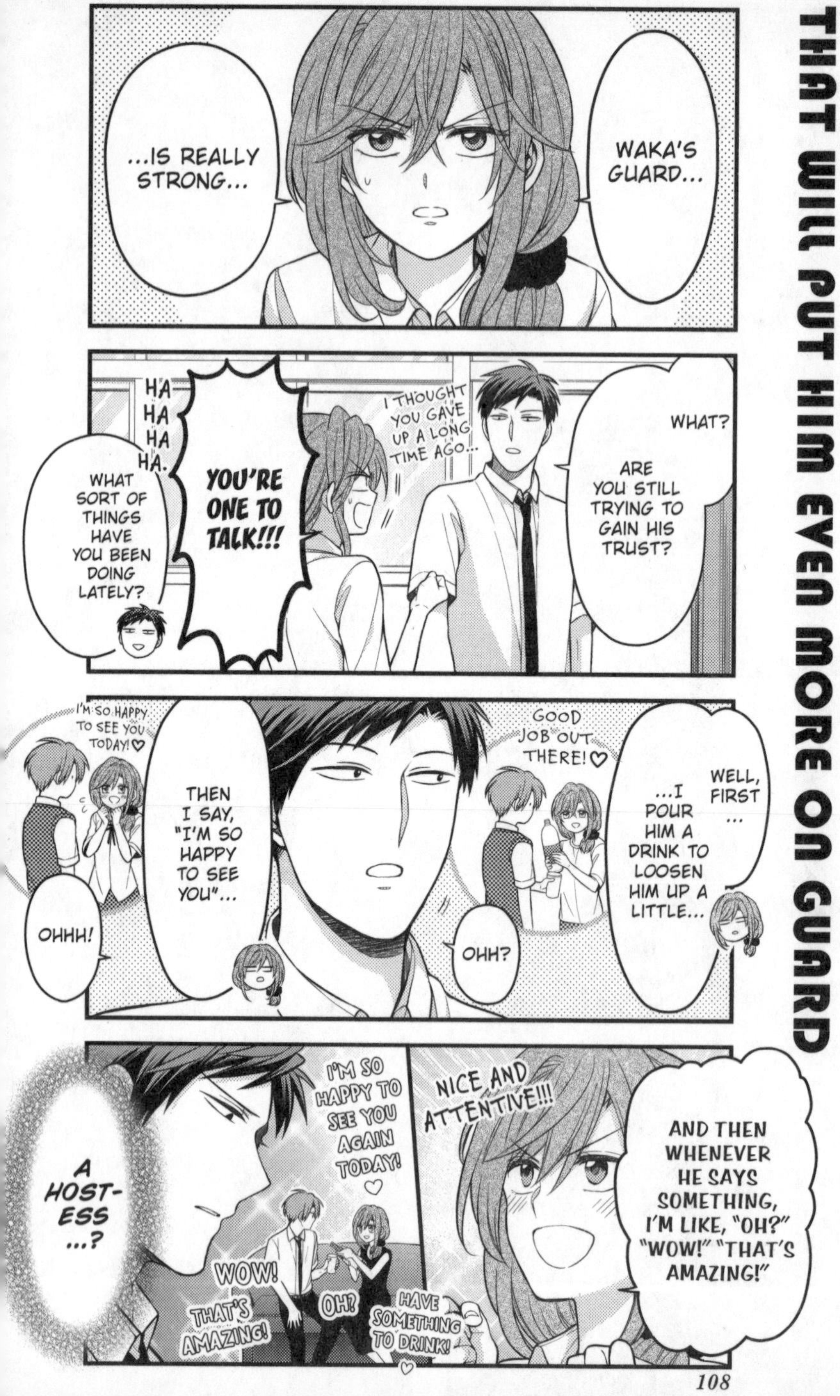
WAKA'S GUARD...
...IS REALLY STRONG...
WHAT?
ARE YOU STILL TRYING TO GAIN HIS TRUST?
I THOUGHT YOU GAVE UP A LONG TIME AGO...
YOU'RE ONE TO TALK!!!
HA HA HA HA.
WHAT SORT OF THINGS HAVE YOU BEEN DOING LATELY?
WELL, FIRST...
...I POUR HIM A DRINK TO LOOSEN HIM UP A LITTLE...
GOOD JOB OUT THERE! ♡
OHH?
THEN I SAY, "I'M SO HAPPY TO SEE YOU"...
I'M SO HAPPY TO SEE YOU TODAY! ♡
OHHH!
AND THEN WHENEVER HE SAYS SOMETHING, I'M LIKE, "OH?" "WOW!" "THAT'S AMAZING!"
NICE AND ATTENTIVE!!!
I'M SO HAPPY TO SEE YOU AGAIN TODAY! ♡
HAVE SOMETHING TO DRINK! ♡
OH?
WOW!
THAT'S AMAZING!
A HOST-ESS...?

THINK OF IT AS HIM

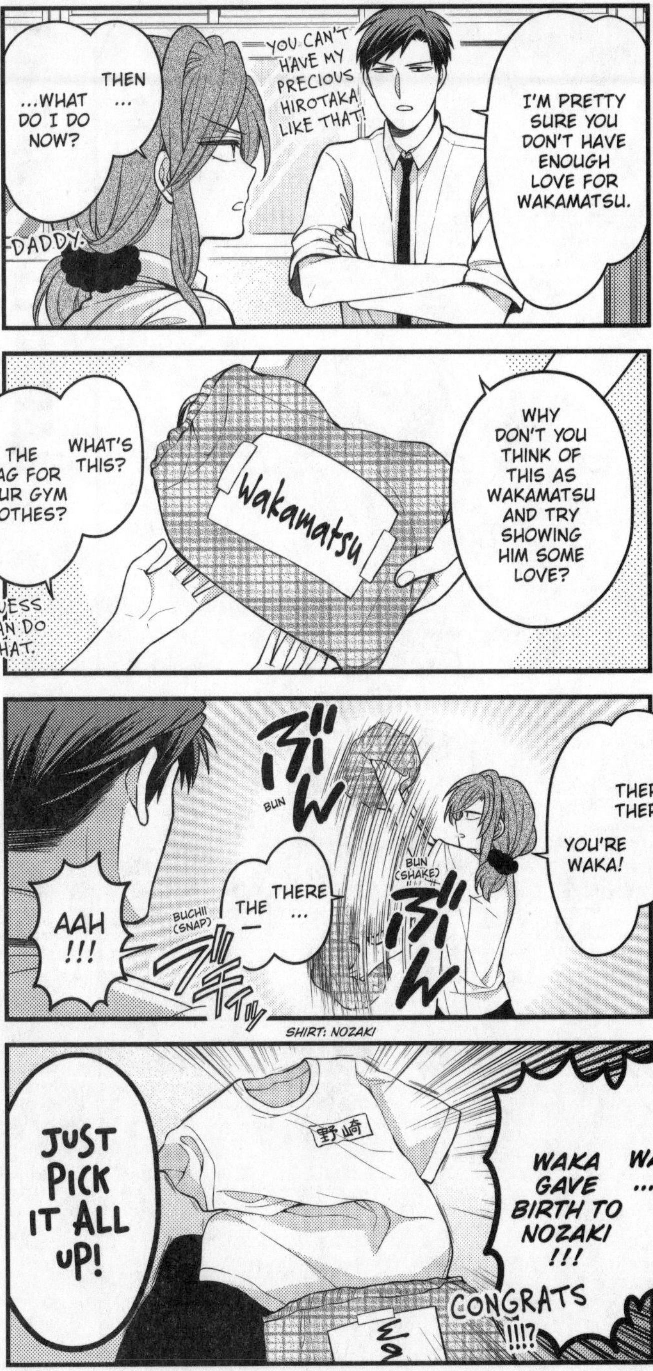
I'M PRETTY SURE YOU DON'T HAVE ENOUGH LOVE FOR WAKAMATSU.
YOU CAN'T HAVE MY PRECIOUS HIROTAKA LIKE THAT!
THEN ...
...WHAT DO I DO NOW?
DADDY.
WHY DON'T YOU THINK OF THIS AS WAKAMATSU AND TRY SHOWING HIM SOME LOVE?
Wakamatsu
WHAT'S THIS?
THE BAG FOR YOUR GYM CLOTHES?
I GUESS I CAN DO THAT.
THERE, THERE!
YOU'RE WAKA!
BUN (SHAKE)
BUN
THERE ...
THE—
BUCHII (SNAP)
AAH !!!
SHIRT: NOZAKI
WAKA ...!!!
WAKA GAVE BIRTH TO NOZAKI !!!
CONGRATS !!!?
野崎
JUST PICK IT ALL UP!

A PERFECTIONIST

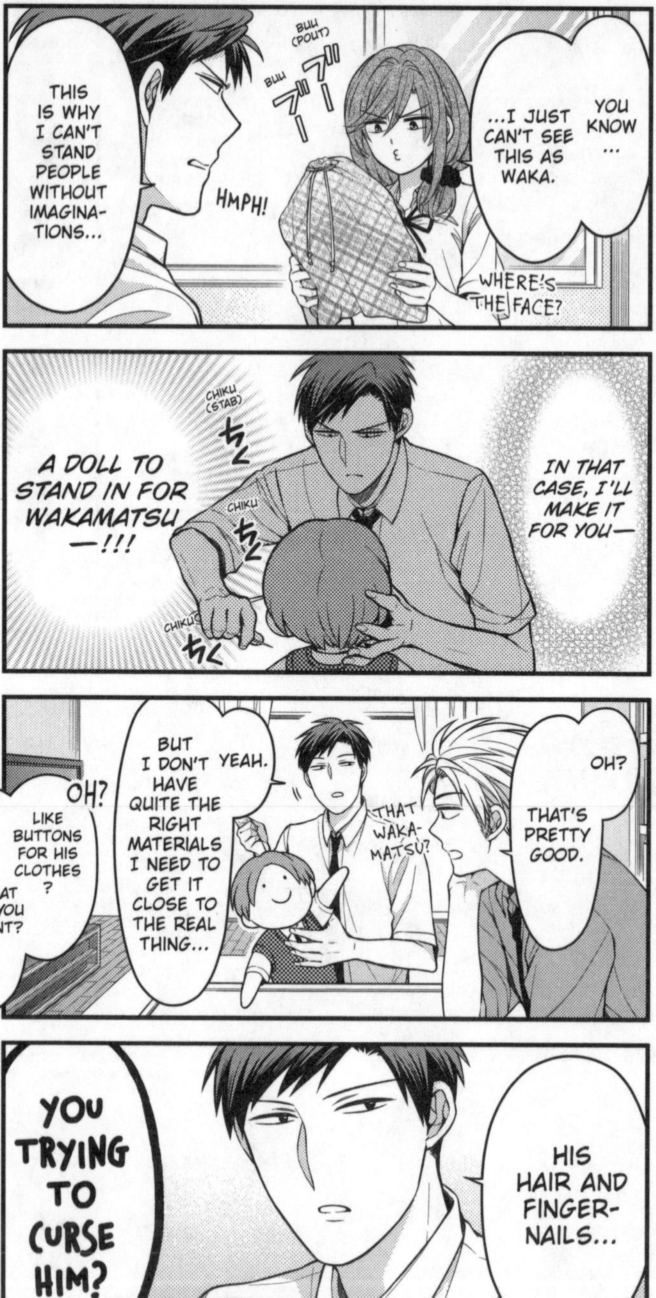

YOU KNOW...
...I JUST CAN'T SEE THIS AS WAKA.
WHERE'S THE FACE?
BUU (POUT)
BUU
HMPH!
THIS IS WHY I CAN'T STAND PEOPLE WITHOUT IMAGINA-TIONS...
IN THAT CASE, I'LL MAKE IT FOR YOU—
CHIKU (STAB)
CHIKU
CHIKU
A DOLL TO STAND IN FOR WAKAMATSU—!!!
OH? THAT'S PRETTY GOOD.
THAT WAKA-MATSU?
YEAH.
BUT I DON'T HAVE QUITE THE RIGHT MATERIALS I NEED TO GET IT CLOSE TO THE REAL THING...
OH? LIKE BUTTONS FOR HIS CLOTHES? WHAT DO YOU WANT?
HIS HAIR AND FINGER-NAILS...
YOU TRYING TO CURSE HIM?

IT'S VERY WELL MADE

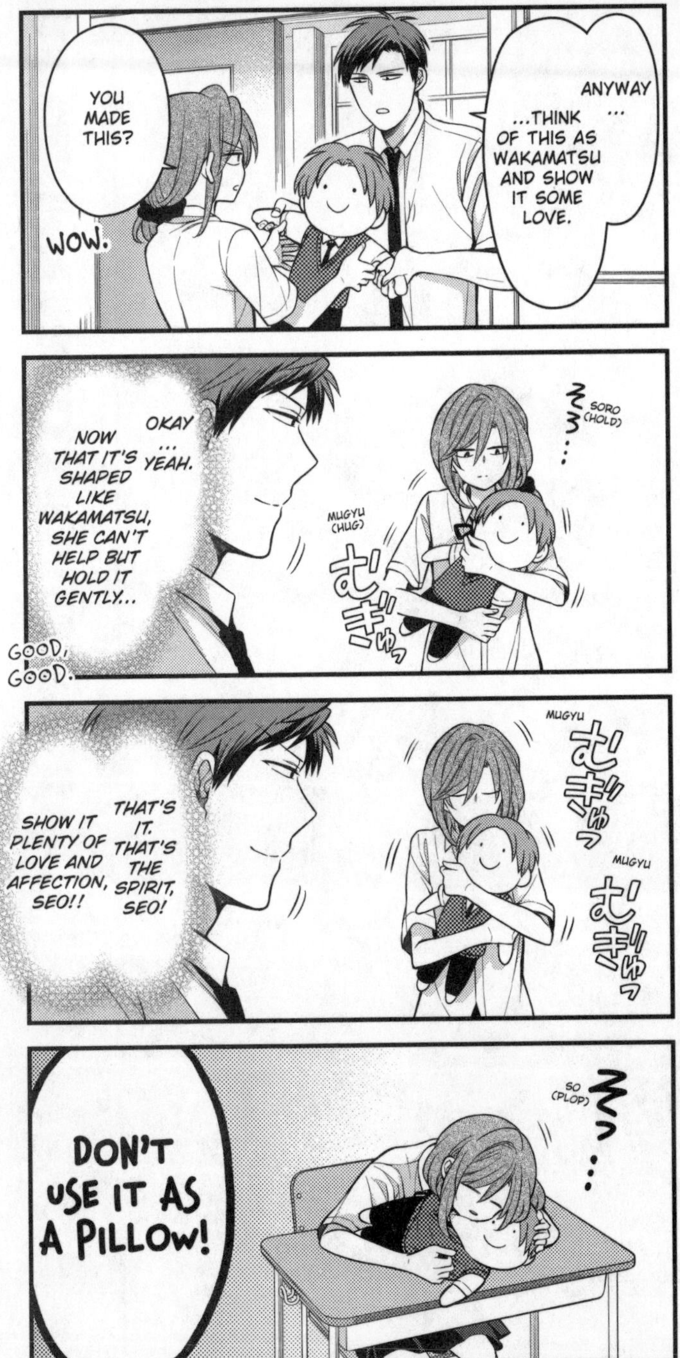
ANYWAY ... ...THINK OF THIS AS WAKAMATSU AND SHOW IT SOME LOVE.
YOU MADE THIS?
WOW.
そろ…
SORO (HOLD)
むぎゅっ
MUGYU (HUG)
OKAY ... YEAH.
NOW THAT IT'S SHAPED LIKE WAKAMATSU, SHE CAN'T HELP BUT HOLD IT GENTLY...
GOOD, GOOD.
むぎゅっ
MUGYU
むぎゅっ
MUGYU
THAT'S IT. THAT'S THE SPIRIT, SEO!
SHOW IT PLENTY OF LOVE AND AFFECTION, SEO!!
そっ…
SO (PLOP)
DON'T USE IT AS A PILLOW!

AN UNINTENDED CONFESSION

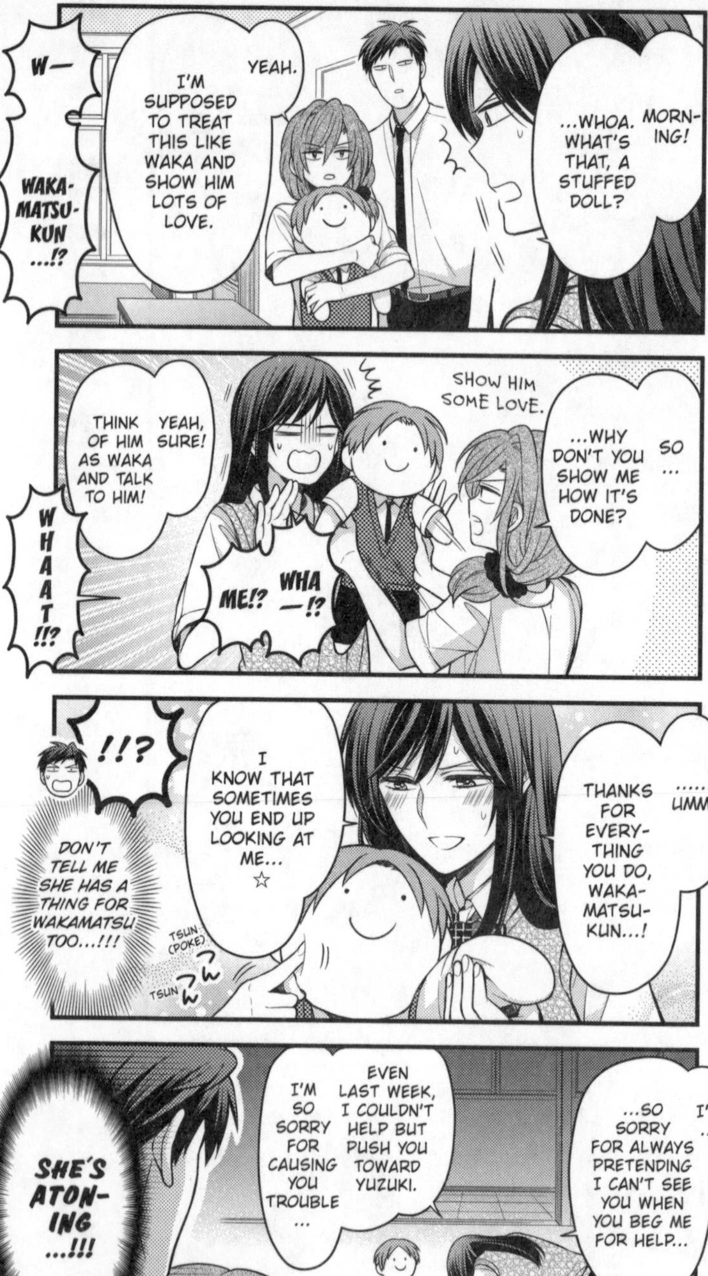
MORNING!
...WHOA. WHAT'S THAT, A STUFFED DOLL?
YEAH.
I'M SUPPOSED TO TREAT THIS LIKE WAKA AND SHOW HIM LOTS OF LOVE.
W— WAKAMATSU-KUN...!?
SO...
...WHY DON'T YOU SHOW ME HOW IT'S DONE?
SHOW HIM SOME LOVE.
YEAH, SURE!
THINK OF HIM AS WAKA AND TALK TO HIM!
WHA—!?
ME!?
WHAAAT!!?
......UMM.
THANKS FOR EVERYTHING YOU DO, WAKAMATSU-KUN...!
I KNOW THAT SOMETIMES YOU END UP LOOKING AT ME...☆
!!?
DON'T TELL ME SHE HAS A THING FOR WAKAMATSU TOO...!!!
TSUN (POKE)
TSUN
I'M...
...SO SORRY FOR ALWAYS PRETENDING I CAN'T SEE YOU WHEN YOU BEG ME FOR HELP...
EVEN LAST WEEK, I COULDN'T HELP BUT PUSH YOU TOWARD YUZUKI.
I'M SO SORRY FOR CAUSING YOU TROUBLE...
SHE'S ATONING...!!!

THE THING SHE RAISED HER HAND TO SAY

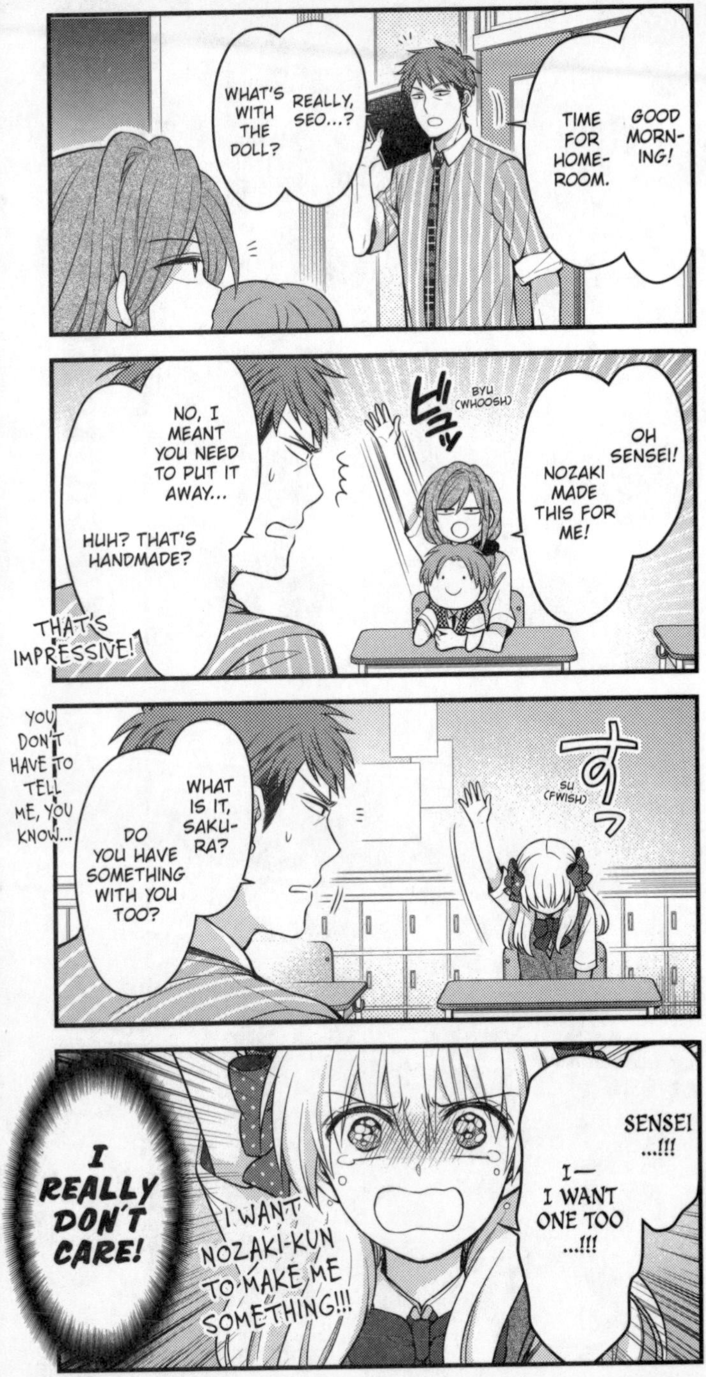

GOOD MORNING! TIME FOR HOMEROOM.
REALLY, SEO...? WHAT'S WITH THE DOLL?
BYU (WHOOSH)
OH SENSEI! NOZAKI MADE THIS FOR ME!
NO, I MEANT YOU NEED TO PUT IT AWAY...
HUH? THAT'S HANDMADE?
THAT'S IMPRESSIVE!
SU (FWISH)
WHAT IS IT, SAKURA?
DO YOU HAVE SOMETHING WITH YOU TOO?
YOU DON'T HAVE TO TELL ME, YOU KNOW...
SENSEI ...!!!
I— I WANT ONE TOO ...!!!
I WANT NOZAKI-KUN TO MAKE ME SOMETHING!!!
I REALLY DON'T CARE!

LINGERING SUSPICIONS

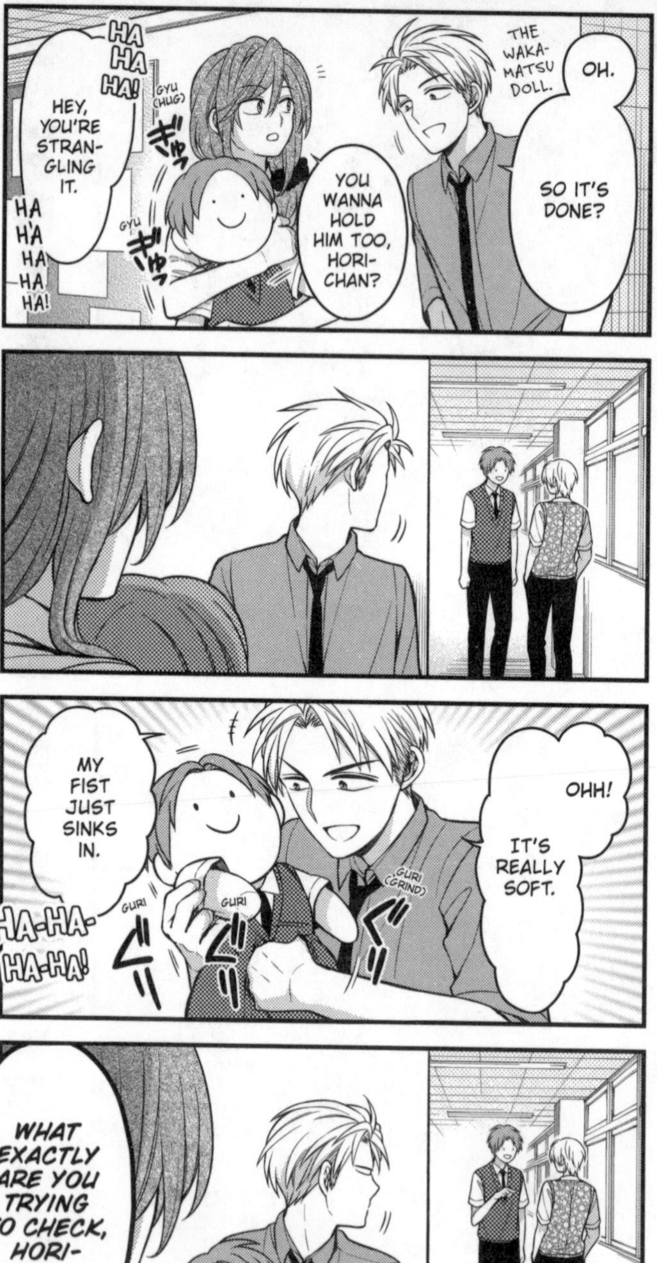
THE WAKAMATSU DOLL.
OH.
SO IT'S DONE?
YOU WANNA HOLD HIM TOO, HORI-CHAN?
GYU (HUG)
GYU
HA HA HA!
HEY, YOU'RE STRANGLING IT.
HA HA HA HA HA!
OHH!
IT'S REALLY SOFT.
GURI (GRIND)
GURI
GURI
MY FIST JUST SINKS IN.
HA-HA-HA-HA!
WHAT EXACTLY ARE YOU TRYING TO CHECK, HORI-CHAN?

HUMILIATION PLAY

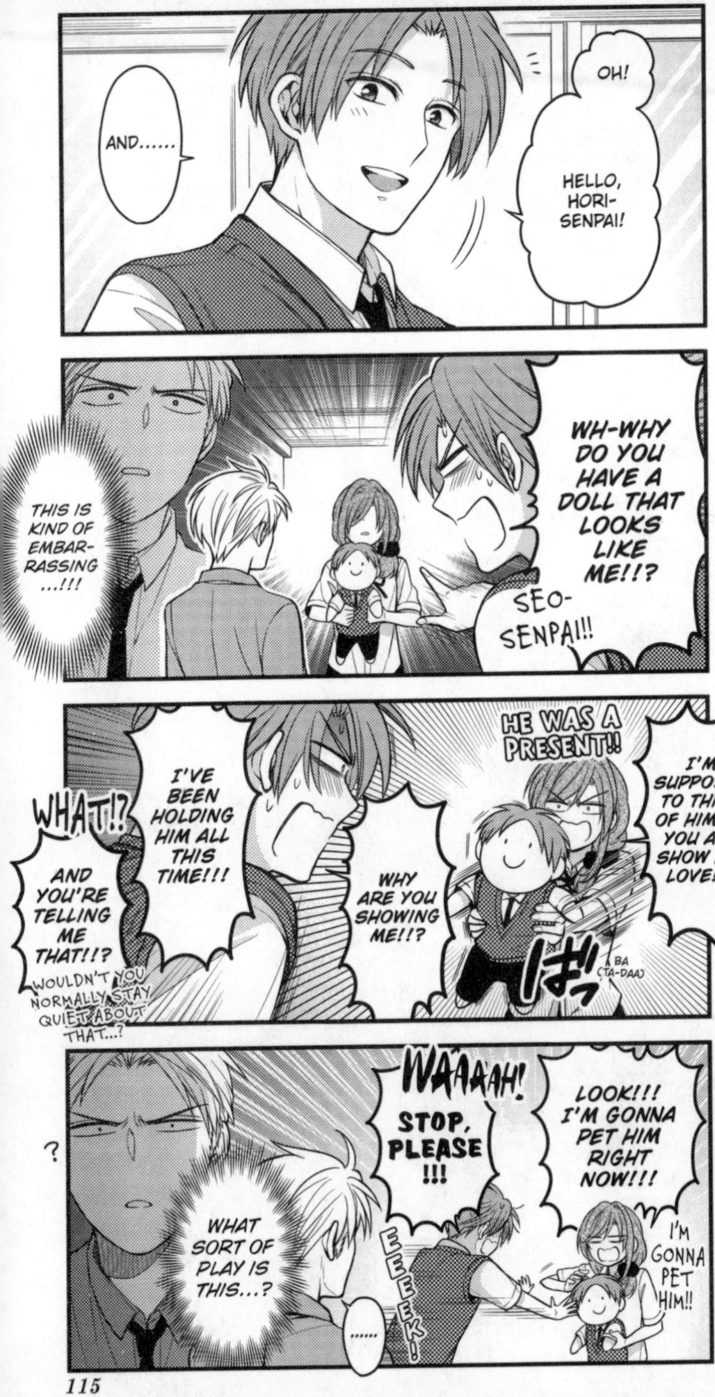
OH!
HELLO, HORI-SENPAI!
AND......
WH-WHY DO YOU HAVE A DOLL THAT LOOKS LIKE ME!!?
SEO-SENPAI!!!
THIS IS KIND OF EMBARRASSING...!!!
HE WAS A PRESENT!!
I'M SUPPOSED TO THINK OF HIM AS YOU AND SHOW HIM LOVE!!!
WHY ARE YOU SHOWING ME!!?
ばっ
BA (TA-DAA)
I'VE BEEN HOLDING HIM ALL THIS TIME!!!
WHAT!?
AND YOU'RE TELLING ME THAT!!?
WOULDN'T YOU NORMALLY STAY QUIET ABOUT THAT...?
LOOK!!! I'M GONNA PET HIM RIGHT NOW!!!
WAAAAH!
STOP, PLEASE!!!
I'M GONNA PET HIM!!
EEEEK!
WHAT SORT OF PLAY IS THIS...?
?
......

READ THE ROOM

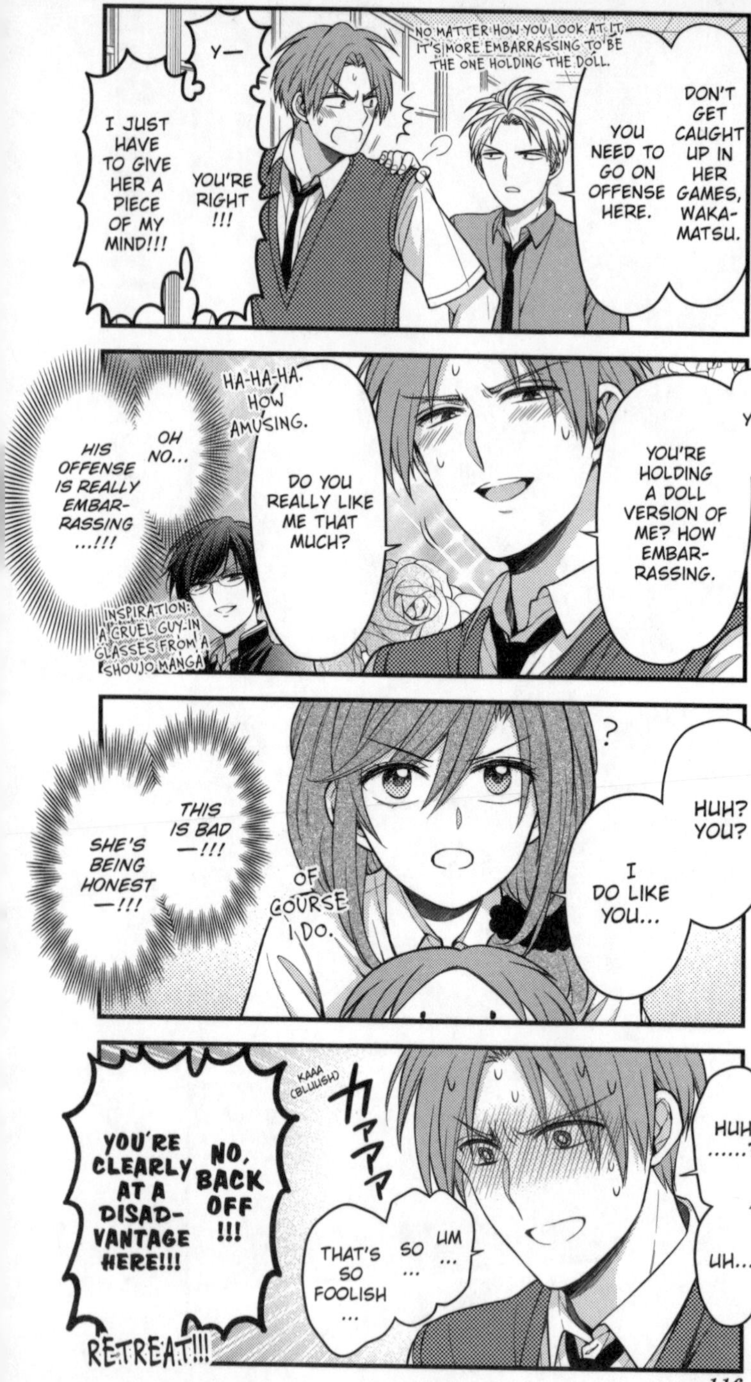
NO MATTER HOW YOU LOOK AT IT, IT'S MORE EMBARRASSING TO BE THE ONE HOLDING THE DOLL.
DON'T GET CAUGHT UP IN HER GAMES, WAKAMATSU.
YOU NEED TO GO ON OFFENSE HERE.
Y—
YOU'RE RIGHT!!!
I JUST HAVE TO GIVE HER A PIECE OF MY MIND!!!
Y—
YOU'RE HOLDING A DOLL VERSION OF ME? HOW EMBARRASSING.
HA-HA-HA. HOW AMUSING.
DO YOU REALLY LIKE ME THAT MUCH?
OH NO...
HIS OFFENSE IS REALLY EMBARRASSING...!!!
INSPIRATION: A CRUEL GUY IN GLASSES FROM A SHOUJO MANGA
?
HUH? YOU?
I DO LIKE YOU...
OF COURSE I DO.
THIS IS BAD—!!!
SHE'S BEING HONEST—!!!
HUH ......?
UH...
KAAA (BLUUSH)
UM ...
SO ...
THAT'S SO FOOLISH ...
NO, BACK OFF!!!
YOU'RE CLEARLY AT A DISADVANTAGE HERE!!!
RETREAT!!!

POOR THING

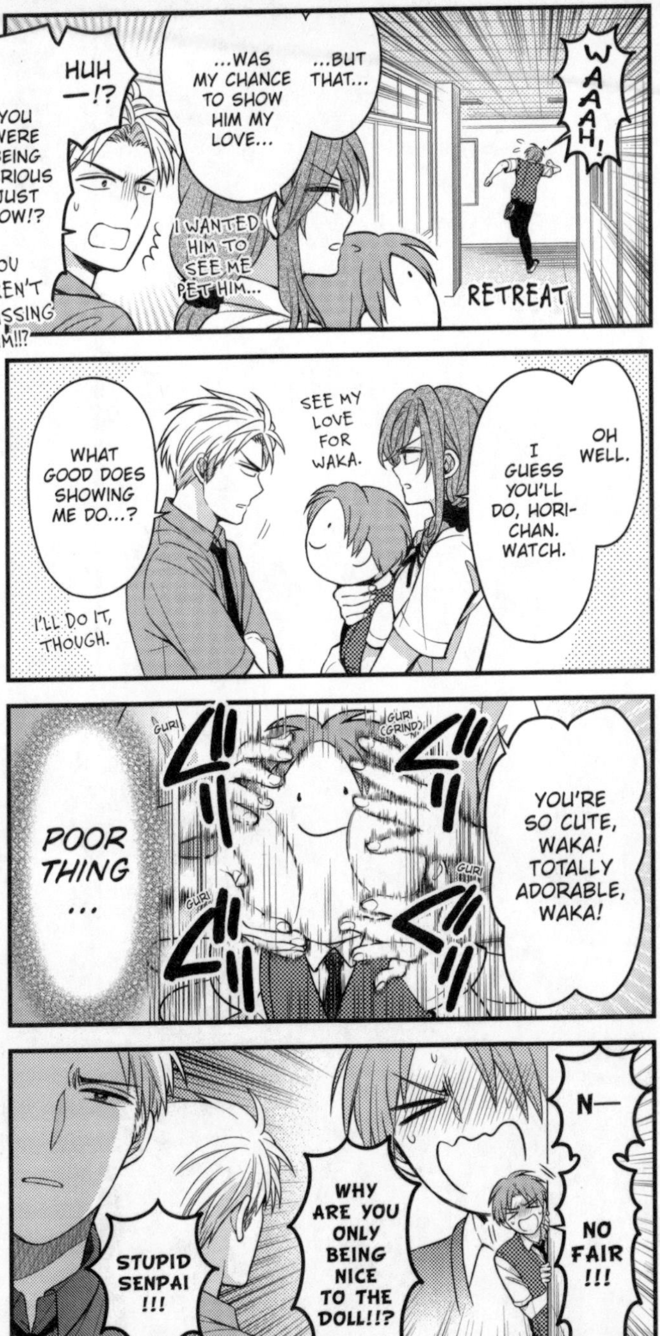
WAAAH!
RETREAT
...BUT THAT...
...WAS MY CHANCE TO SHOW HIM MY LOVE...
I WANTED HIM TO SEE ME PET HIM...
HUH—!?
YOU WERE BEING SERIOUS JUST NOW!?
YOU WEREN'T HARASSING HIM!!?
OH WELL.
I GUESS YOU'LL DO, HORI-CHAN. WATCH.
SEE MY LOVE FOR WAKA.
WHAT GOOD DOES SHOWING ME DO...?
I'LL DO IT, THOUGH.
YOU'RE SO CUTE, WAKA! TOTALLY ADORABLE, WAKA!
GURI (GRIND)
GURI
GURI
GURI
POOR THING...
N—
NO FAIR!!!
WHY ARE YOU ONLY BEING NICE TO THE DOLL!!?
STUPID SENPAI!!!

PRAISE DUTY

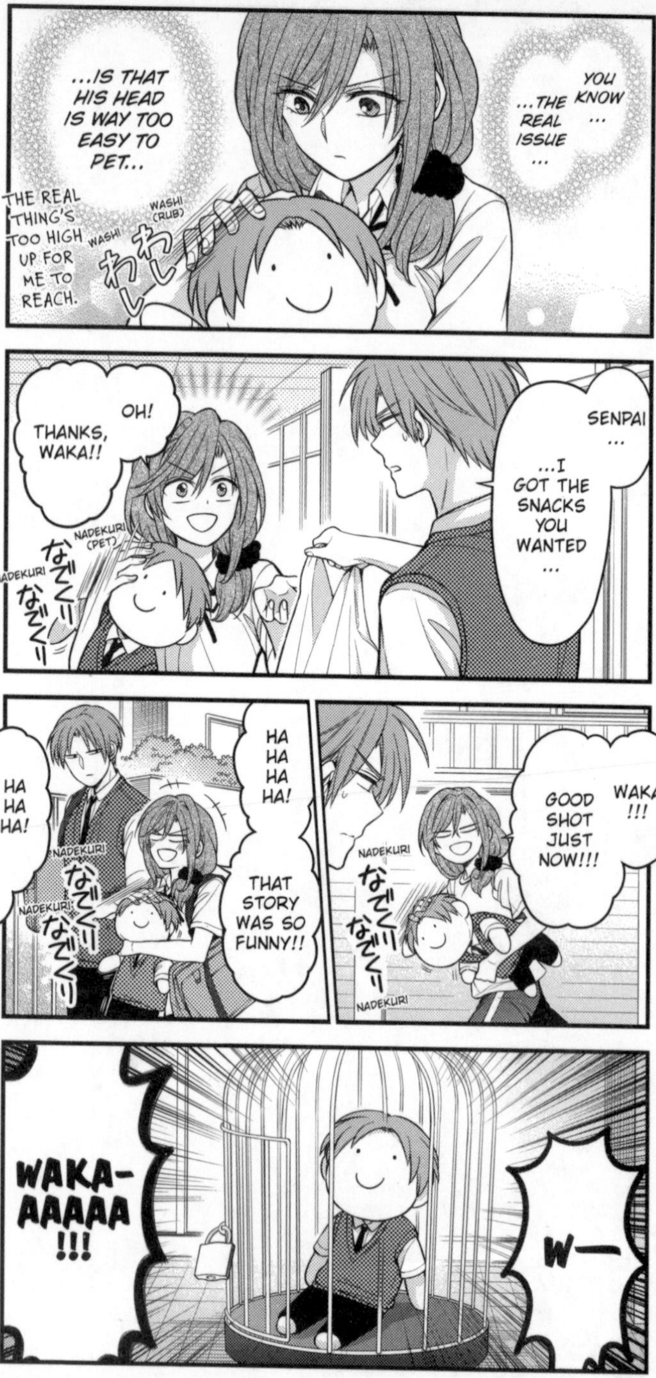
YOU KNOW ...
...THE REAL ISSUE ...
...IS THAT HIS HEAD IS WAY TOO EASY TO PET...
WASHI (RUB)
WASHI
わしわし
THE REAL THING'S TOO HIGH UP FOR ME TO REACH.
SENPAI ...
...I GOT THE SNACKS YOU WANTED ...
OH!
THANKS, WAKA!!
NADEKURI (PET)
NADEKURI
なでくり なでくり
WAKA !!!
GOOD SHOT JUST NOW!!!
NADEKURI
なでくり なでくり
NADEKURI
HA HA HA HA!
THAT STORY WAS SO FUNNY!!
HA HA HA! HA HA HA!
NADEKURI
NADEKURI
なでくり なでくり
W—
WAKA-AAAAAA!!!

PROGRESS

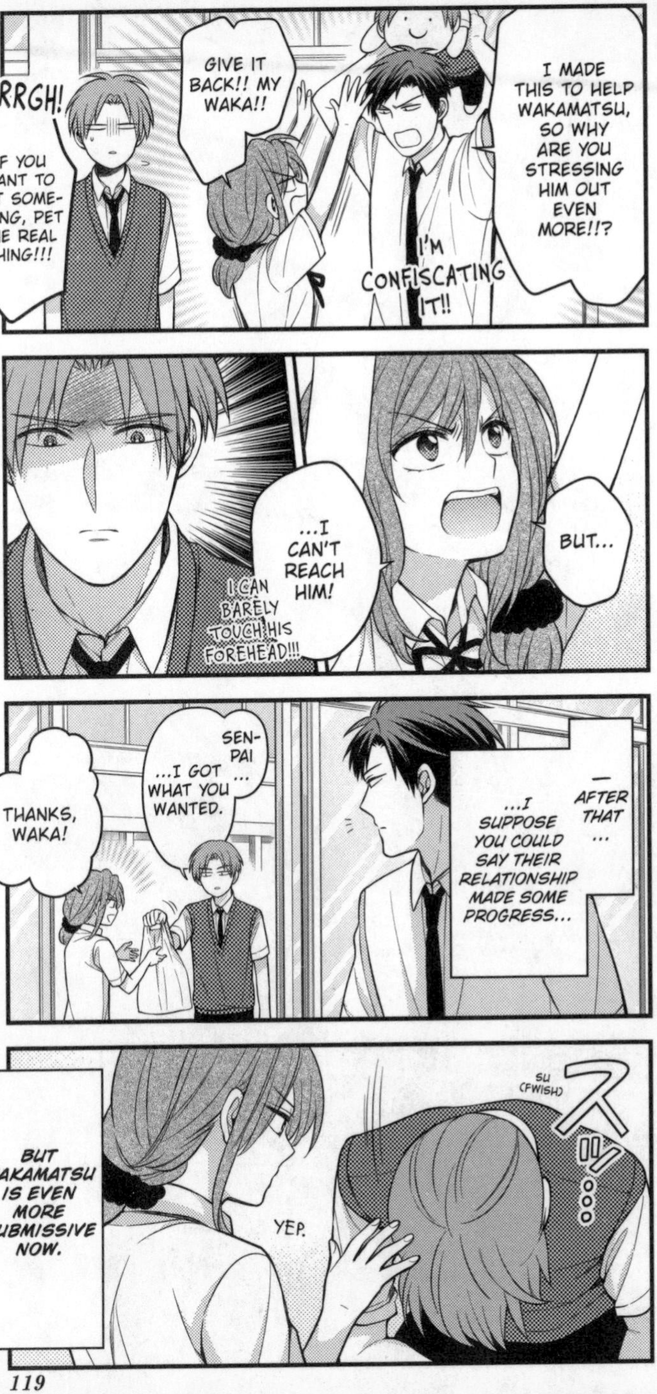

I MADE THIS TO HELP WAKAMATSU, SO WHY ARE YOU STRESSING HIM OUT EVEN MORE!!?
I'M CONFISCATING IT!!
GIVE IT BACK!! MY WAKA!!
ARRGH!
IF YOU WANT TO PET SOME-THING, PET THE REAL THING!!!
BUT...
...I CAN'T REACH HIM!
I CAN BARELY TOUCH HIS FOREHEAD!!!
—AFTER THAT...
...I SUPPOSE YOU COULD SAY THEIR RELATIONSHIP MADE SOME PROGRESS...
SEN-PAI... ...I GOT WHAT YOU WANTED.
THANKS, WAKA!
SU (FWISH)
スッ…
YEP.
BUT WAKAMATSU IS EVEN MORE SUBMISSIVE NOW.

[Extra]

SHE REALLY WANTED IT

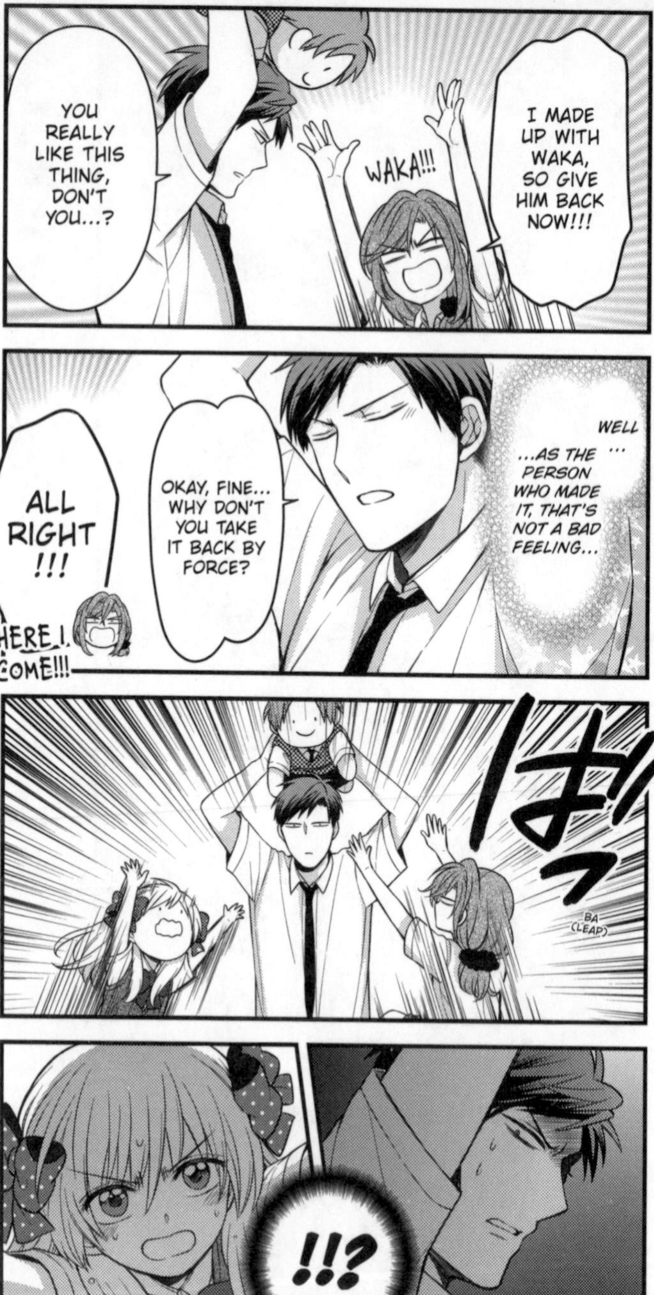

I MADE UP WITH WAKA, SO GIVE HIM BACK NOW!!!
WAKA!!!
YOU REALLY LIKE THIS THING, DON'T YOU...?
WELL ...
...AS THE PERSON WHO MADE IT, THAT'S NOT A BAD FEELING...
OKAY, FINE... WHY DON'T YOU TAKE IT BACK BY FORCE?
ALL RIGHT!!!
HERE I COME!!!
BA (LEAP)
!!?

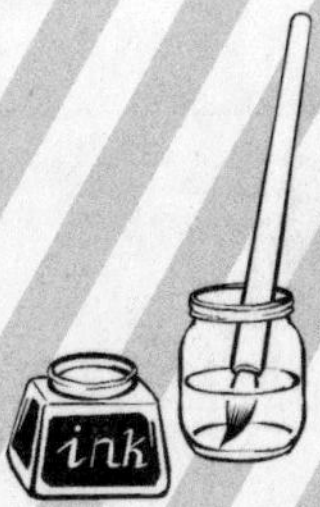
ink

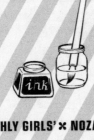

MONTHLY GIRLS' × NOZAKI-KUN

[Extra]

SEO-SAN AND THE DOLL ①

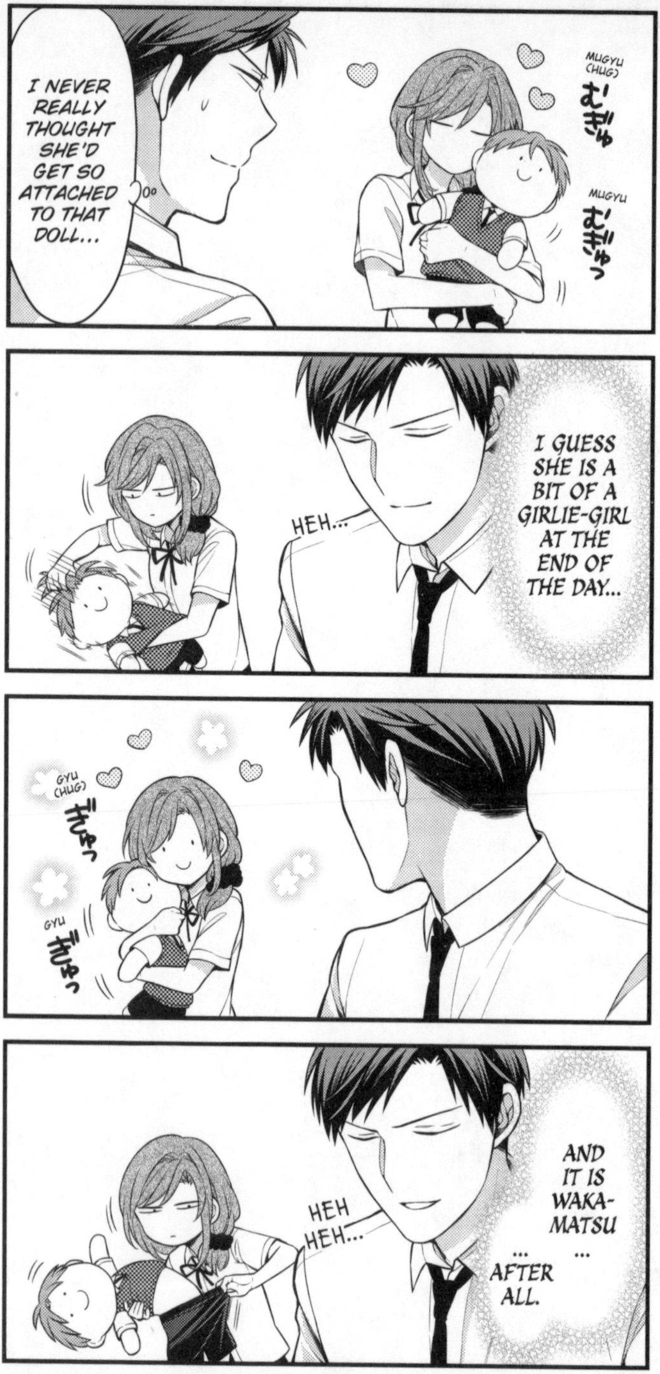
MUGYU (HUG)
むぎゅ
MUGYU
むぎゅっ
I NEVER REALLY THOUGHT SHE'D GET SO ATTACHED TO THAT DOLL...
I GUESS SHE IS A BIT OF A GIRLIE-GIRL AT THE END OF THE DAY...
HEH...
GYU (HUG)
ぎゅっ
GYU
ぎゅっ
AND IT IS WAKA-MATSU ...
... AFTER ALL.
HEH HEH...

[Extra]

SEO-SAN AND THE DOLL ②

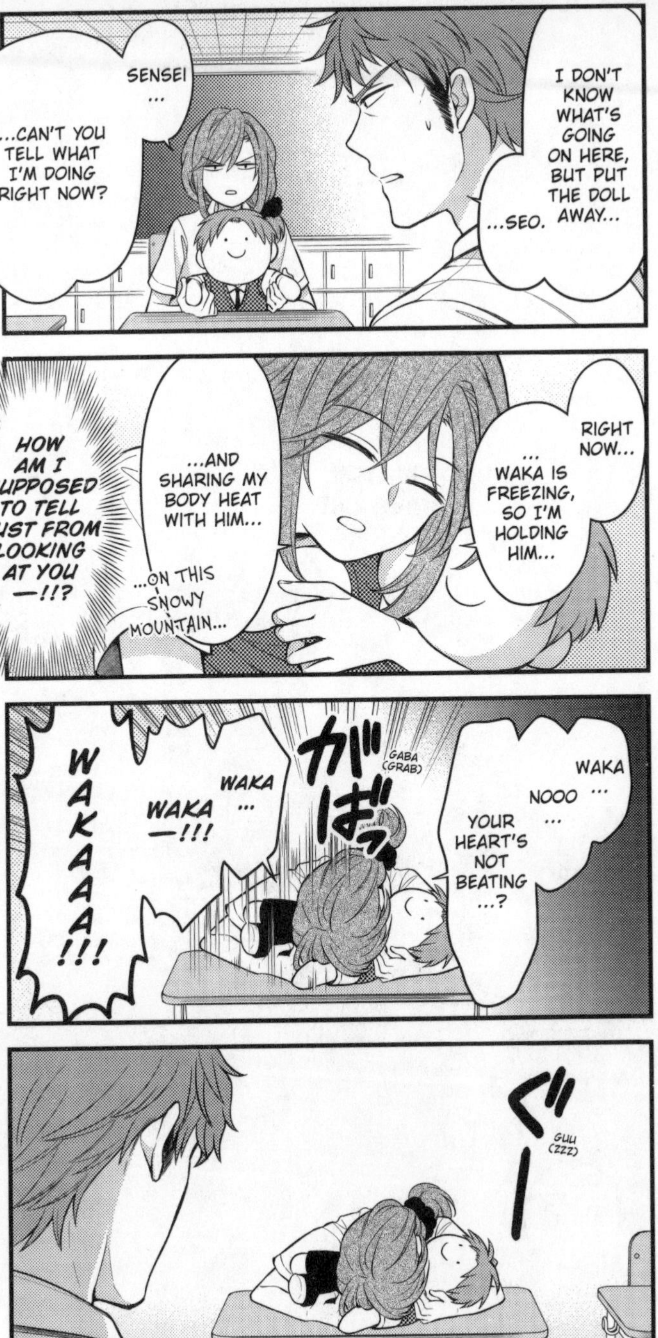
I DON'T KNOW WHAT'S GOING ON HERE, BUT PUT THE DOLL AWAY...
...SEO.
SENSEI ...
...CAN'T YOU TELL WHAT I'M DOING RIGHT NOW?
RIGHT NOW... ... WAKA IS FREEZING, SO I'M HOLDING HIM...
...AND SHARING MY BODY HEAT WITH HIM...
...ON THIS SNOWY MOUNTAIN...
HOW AM I SUPPOSED TO TELL JUST FROM LOOKING AT YOU—!!?
WAKA ...
NOOO ...
YOUR HEART'S NOT BEATING ...?
がばっ
GABA (GRAB)
WAKA ...
WAKA—!!!
WAKAAAA!!!
ぐー
GUU (ZZZ)

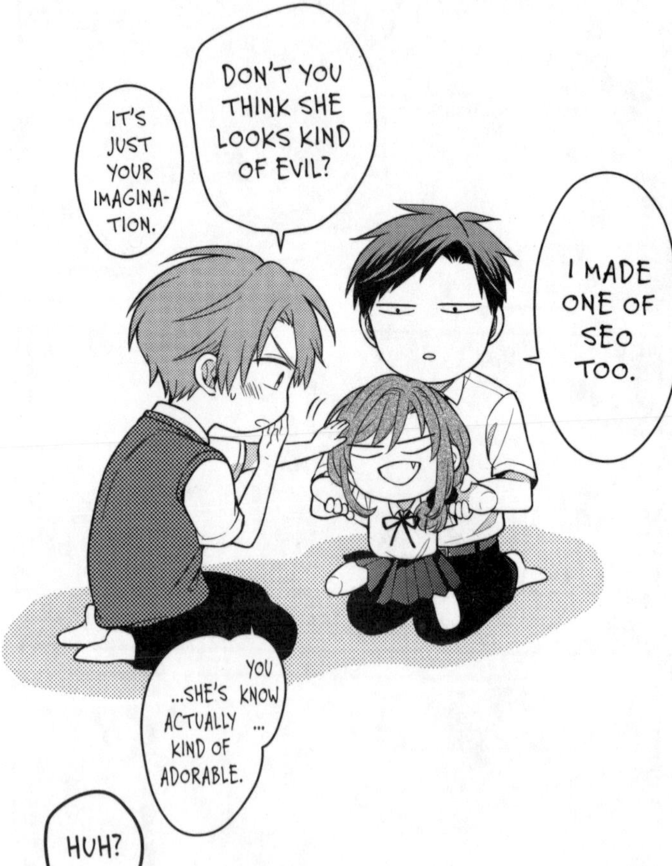
I MADE ONE OF SEO TOO.
DON'T YOU THINK SHE LOOKS KIND OF EVIL?
IT'S JUST YOUR IMAGINATION.
YOU KNOW... ...SHE'S ACTUALLY KIND OF ADORABLE.
HUH?

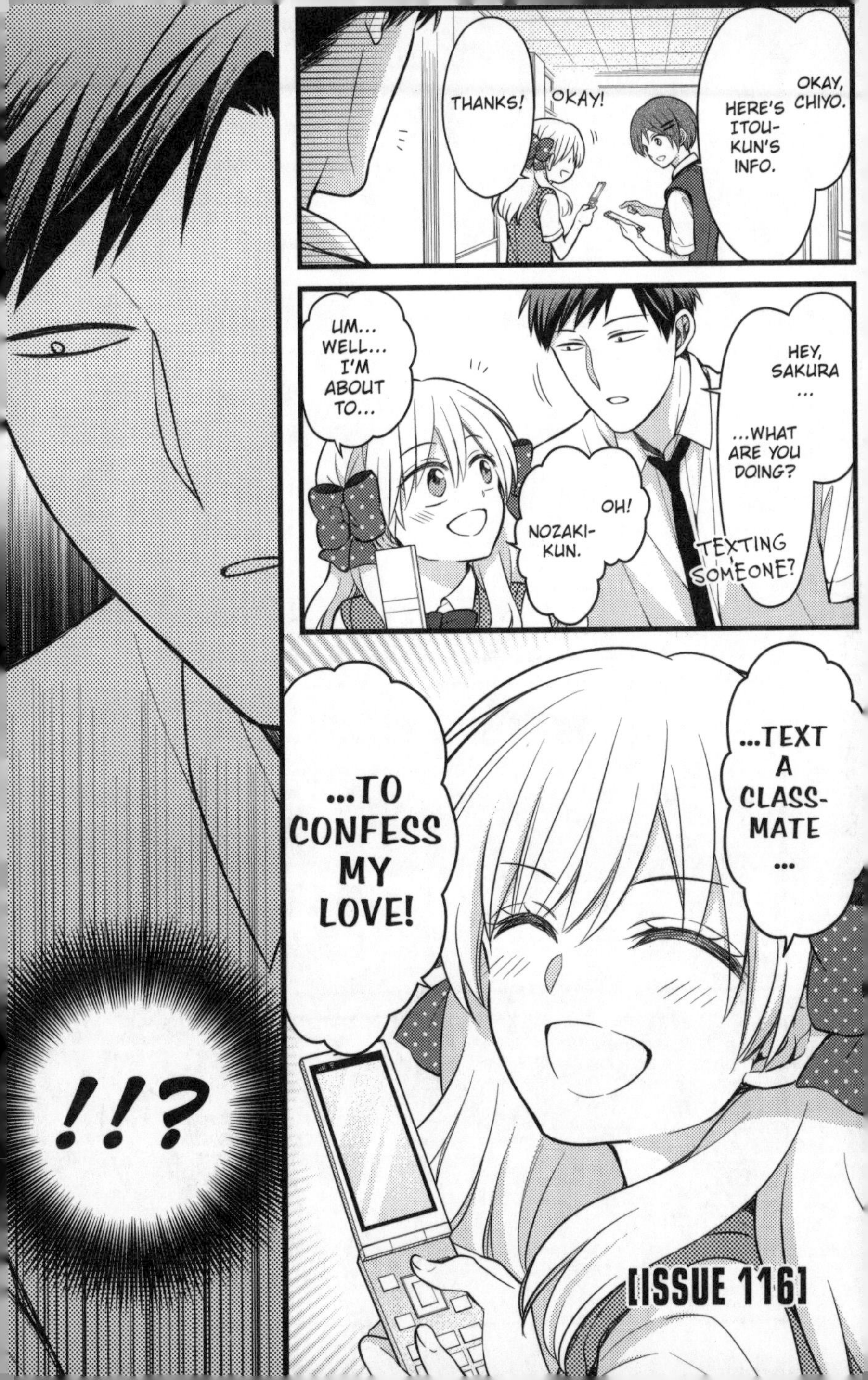
OKAY, CHIYO. HERE'S ITOU-KUN'S INFO.
OKAY!
THANKS!
HEY, SAKURA ... ...WHAT ARE YOU DOING? TEXTING SOMEONE?
OH! NOZAKI-KUN.
UM... WELL... I'M ABOUT TO...
...TEXT A CLASSMATE ...
...TO CONFESS MY LOVE!
[ISSUE 116]
!!?

CLASS A IS SUPER CLOSE

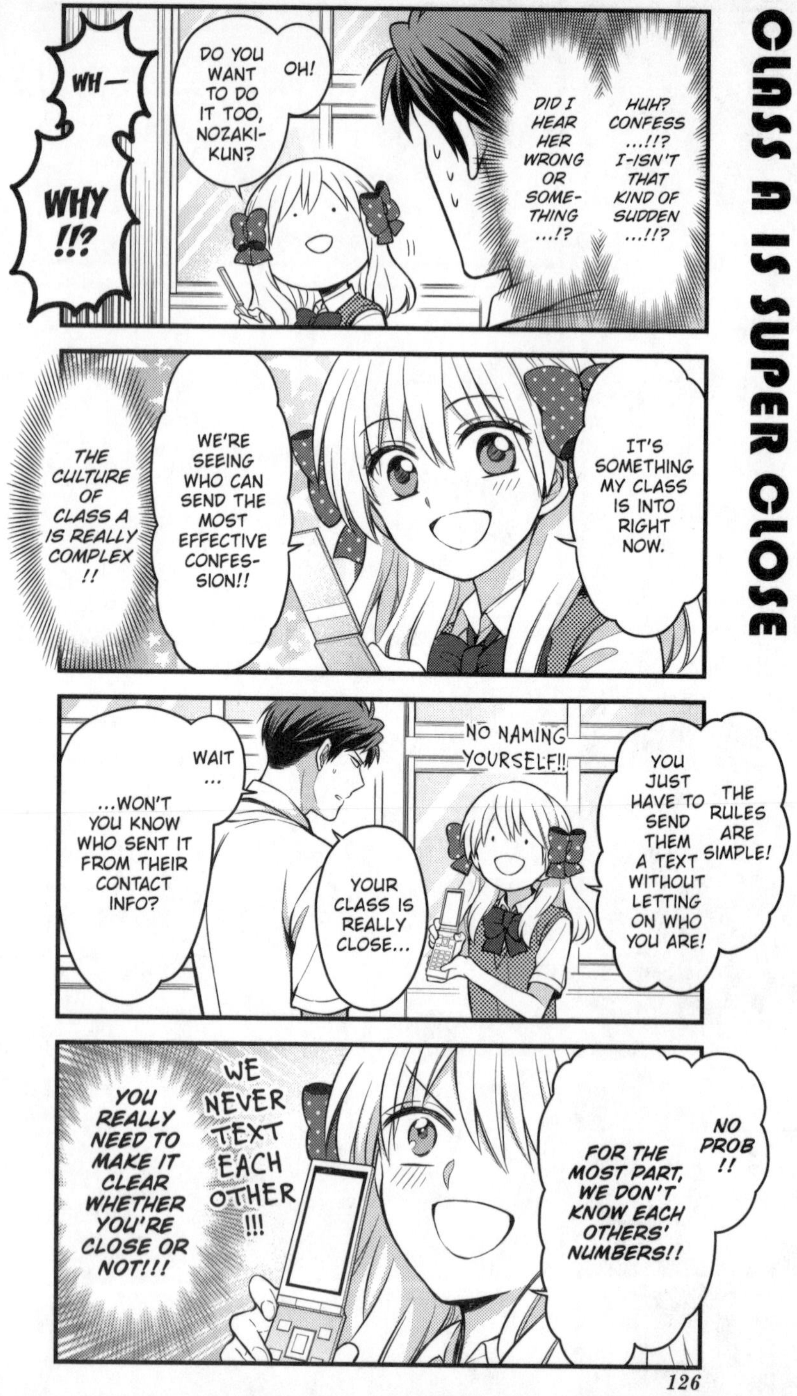
HUH? CONFESS ...!!? I-ISN'T THAT KIND OF SUDDEN ...!!?
DID I HEAR HER WRONG OR SOME-THING ...!?
OH!
DO YOU WANT TO DO IT TOO, NOZAKI-KUN?
WH— WHY!!?
IT'S SOMETHING MY CLASS IS INTO RIGHT NOW.
WE'RE SEEING WHO CAN SEND THE MOST EFFECTIVE CONFES-SION!!
THE CULTURE OF CLASS A IS REALLY COMPLEX!!
THE RULES ARE SIMPLE!
YOU JUST HAVE TO SEND THEM A TEXT WITHOUT LETTING ON WHO YOU ARE!
NO NAMING YOURSELF!!
YOUR CLASS IS REALLY CLOSE...
WAIT ...
...WON'T YOU KNOW WHO SENT IT FROM THEIR CONTACT INFO?
NO PROB!!
FOR THE MOST PART, WE DON'T KNOW EACH OTHERS' NUMBERS!!
WE NEVER TEXT EACH OTHER!!!
YOU REALLY NEED TO MAKE IT CLEAR WHETHER YOU'RE CLOSE OR NOT!!!

JUST SOME CASUAL PARTICIPATION!

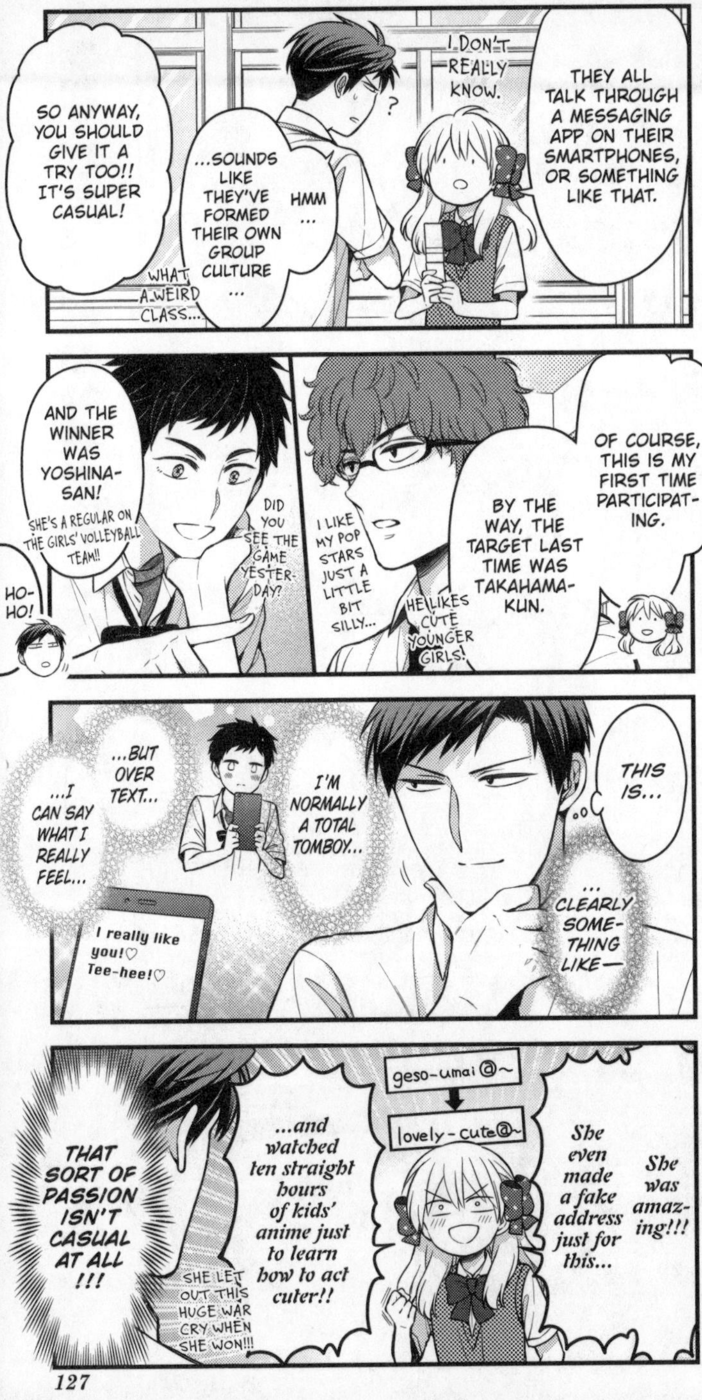
THEY ALL TALK THROUGH A MESSAGING APP ON THEIR SMARTPHONES, OR SOMETHING LIKE THAT.
I DON'T REALLY KNOW.
?
HMM ...
...SOUNDS LIKE THEY'VE FORMED THEIR OWN GROUP CULTURE ...
WHAT A WEIRD CLASS...
SO ANYWAY, YOU SHOULD GIVE IT A TRY TOO!! IT'S SUPER CASUAL!
OF COURSE, THIS IS MY FIRST TIME PARTICIPAT-ING.
BY THE WAY, THE TARGET LAST TIME WAS TAKAHAMA-KUN.
HE LIKES CUTE YOUNGER GIRLS!
I LIKE MY POP STARS JUST A LITTLE BIT SILLY...
DID YOU SEE THE GAME YESTER-DAY?
AND THE WINNER WAS YOSHINA-SAN!
SHE'S A REGULAR ON THE GIRLS' VOLLEYBALL TEAM!!
HO-HO!
THIS IS...
...CLEARLY SOME-THING LIKE—
I'M NORMALLY A TOTAL TOMBOY...
...BUT OVER TEXT...
...I CAN SAY WHAT I REALLY FEEL...
I really like you!♡ Tee-hee!♡
She was amaz-ing!!!
She even made a fake address just for this...
geso-umai@~
lovely-cute@~
...and watched ten straight hours of kids' anime just to learn how to act cuter!!
SHE LET OUT THIS HUGE WAR CRY WHEN SHE WON!!!
THAT SORT OF PASSION ISN'T CASUAL AT ALL !!!

THIS ISN'T WHAT I HEARD

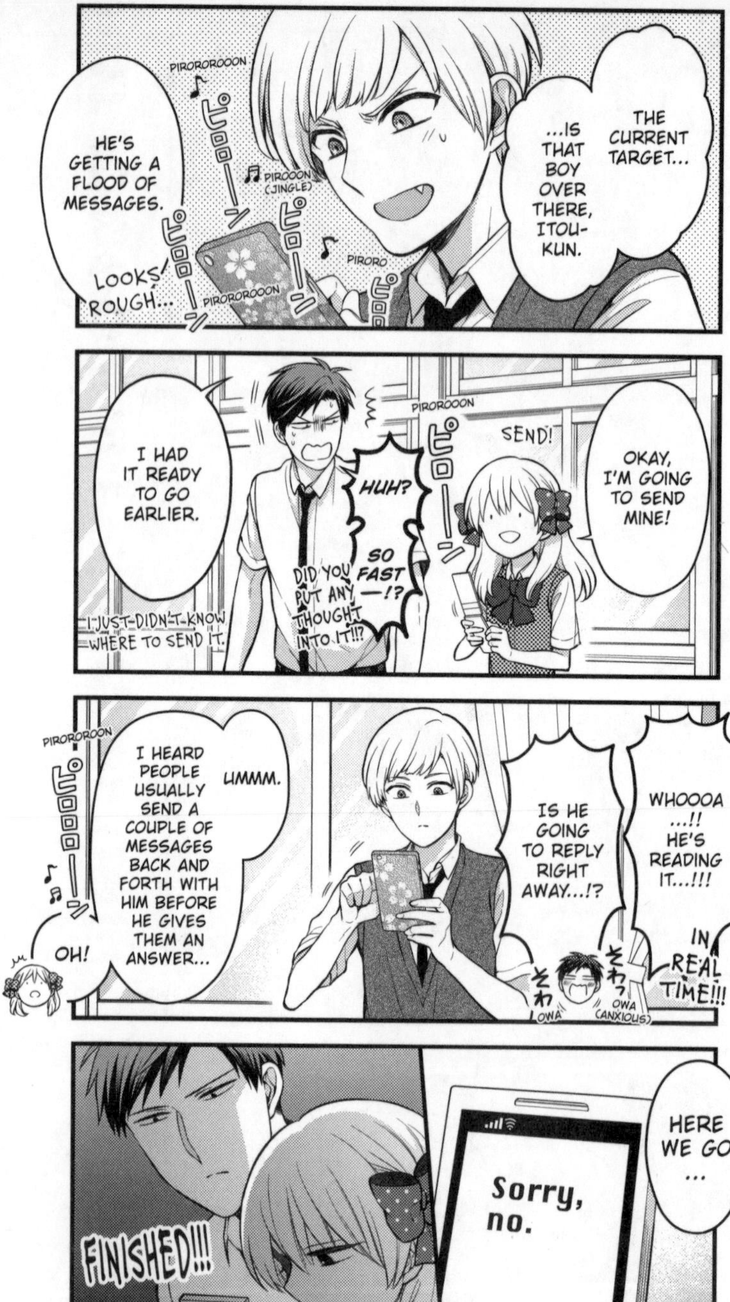

THE CURRENT TARGET...
...IS THAT BOY OVER THERE, ITOU-KUN.
PIROROROOON
PIROOON (JINGLE)
PIRORO
PIROROROOON
HE'S GETTING A FLOOD OF MESSAGES.
LOOKS ROUGH...
OKAY, I'M GOING TO SEND MINE!
SEND!
PIROROOON
HUH?
SO FAST—!?
DID YOU PUT ANY THOUGHT INTO IT!!?
I HAD IT READY TO GO EARLIER.
I JUST DIDN'T KNOW WHERE TO SEND IT.
OH, I SEE ...
WHOOOA ...!! HE'S READING IT...!!!
IN REAL TIME!!!
OWA (ANXIOUS)
OWA
IS HE GOING TO REPLY RIGHT AWAY...!?
UMMM.
I HEARD PEOPLE USUALLY SEND A COUPLE OF MESSAGES BACK AND FORTH WITH HIM BEFORE HE GIVES THEM AN ANSWER...
PIROROROON
OH!
HERE WE GO ...
Sorry, no.
FINISHED!!!

RIGHT TO HER FACE

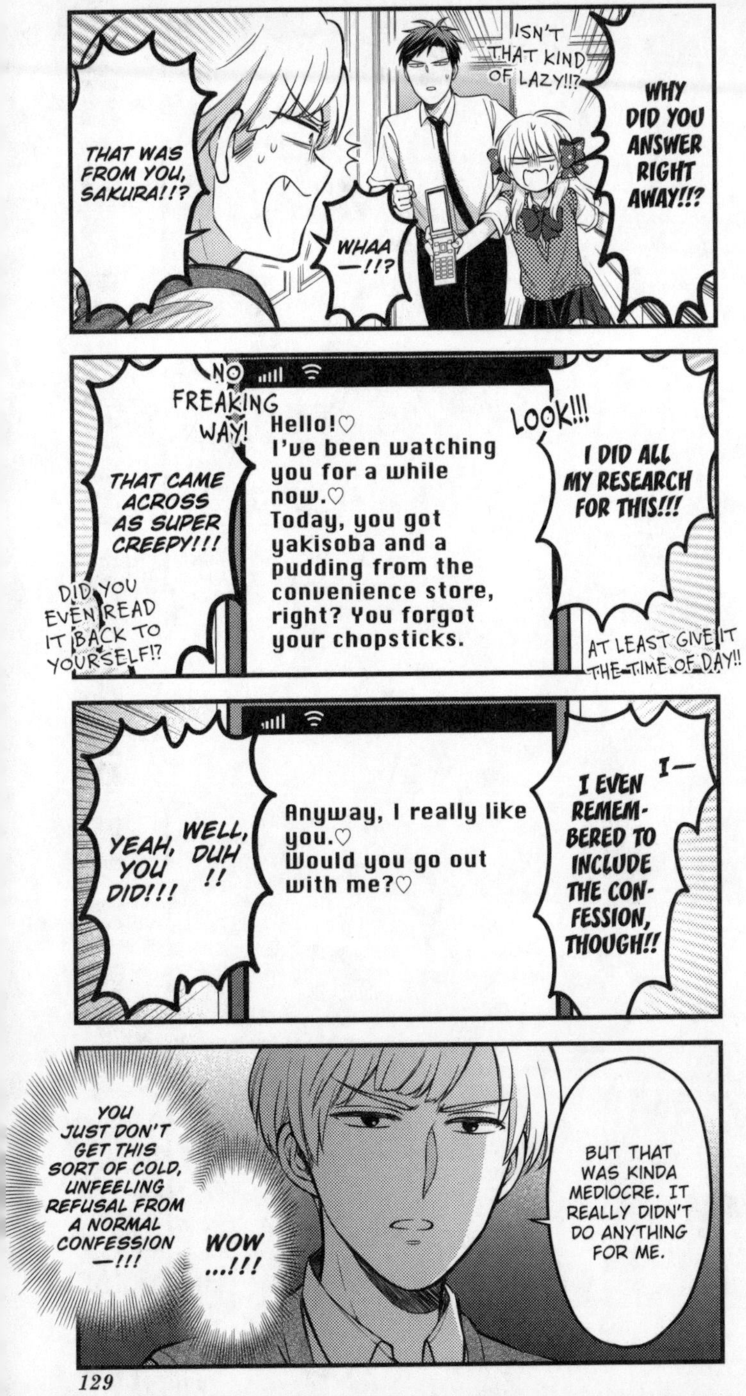
WHY DID YOU ANSWER RIGHT AWAY!!?
ISN'T THAT KIND OF LAZY!!?
WHAA—!!?
THAT WAS FROM YOU, SAKURA!!?
LOOK!!!
I DID ALL MY RESEARCH FOR THIS!!!
AT LEAST GIVE IT THE TIME OF DAY!!
Hello!♡ I've been watching you for a while now.♡ Today, you got yakisoba and a pudding from the convenience store, right? You forgot your chopsticks.
NO FREAKING WAY!
THAT CAME ACROSS AS SUPER CREEPY!!!
DID YOU EVEN READ IT BACK TO YOURSELF!?
I—
I EVEN REMEMBERED TO INCLUDE THE CONFESSION, THOUGH!!
Anyway, I really like you.♡ Would you go out with me?♡
WELL, DUH!!
YEAH, YOU DID!!!
BUT THAT WAS KINDA MEDIOCRE. IT REALLY DIDN'T DO ANYTHING FOR ME.
WOW...!!!
YOU JUST DON'T GET THIS SORT OF COLD, UNFEELING REFUSAL FROM A NORMAL CONFESSION—!!!

WHAT I CAN TELL BY LOOKING AT HIM

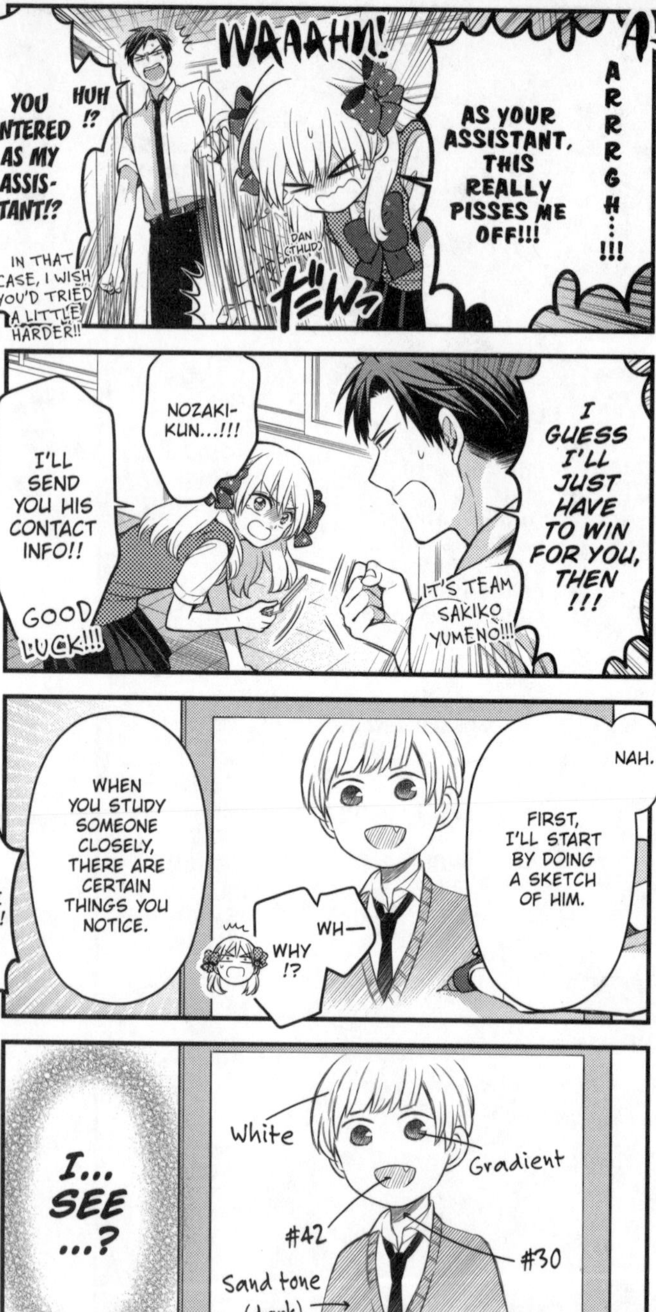

A- ARRRGH...!!!
WAAAHN!
AS YOUR ASSISTANT, THIS REALLY PISSES ME OFF!!!
DAN (THUD)
HUH!?
YOU ENTERED AS MY ASSISTANT!?
IN THAT CASE, I WISH YOU'D TRIED A LITTLE HARDER!!
I GUESS I'LL JUST HAVE TO WIN FOR YOU, THEN!!!
IT'S TEAM SAKIKO YUMENO!!!
NOZAKI-KUN...!!!
I'LL SEND YOU HIS CONTACT INFO!!
GOOD LUCK!!!
NAH.
FIRST, I'LL START BY DOING A SKETCH OF HIM.
WH—
WHY!?
WHEN YOU STUDY SOMEONE CLOSELY, THERE ARE CERTAIN THINGS YOU NOTICE.
OH, I SEE!!!
White
Gradient
#42
#30
Sand tone (dark)
I... SEE...?

CIRCUMSTANCES WE CAN'T MATCH

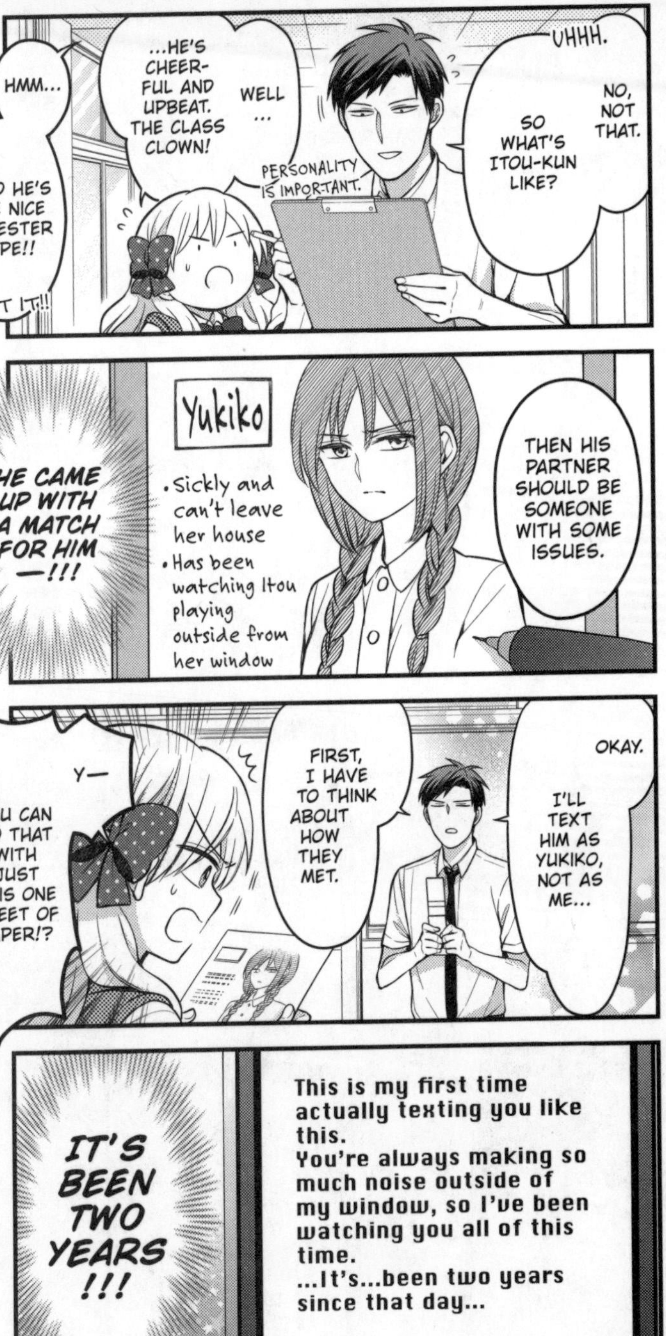
UHHH.
NO, NOT THAT.
SO WHAT'S ITOU-KUN LIKE?
PERSONALITY IS IMPORTANT.
WELL ...
...HE'S CHEERFUL AND UPBEAT. THE CLASS CLOWN!
HMM...
...SO HE'S THE NICE JOKESTER TYPE!!
GOT IT!!!
THEN HIS PARTNER SHOULD BE SOMEONE WITH SOME ISSUES.
Yukiko
•Sickly and can't leave her house
•Has been watching Itou playing outside from her window
HE CAME UP WITH A MATCH FOR HIM—!!!
OKAY.
I'LL TEXT HIM AS YUKIKO, NOT AS ME...
FIRST, I HAVE TO THINK ABOUT HOW THEY MET.
Y—
YOU CAN DO THAT WITH JUST THIS ONE SHEET OF PAPER!?
This is my first time actually texting you like this.
You're always making so much noise outside of my window, so I've been watching you all of this time.
...It's...been two years since that day...
IT'S BEEN TWO YEARS!!!

THE STORY CONNECTING US

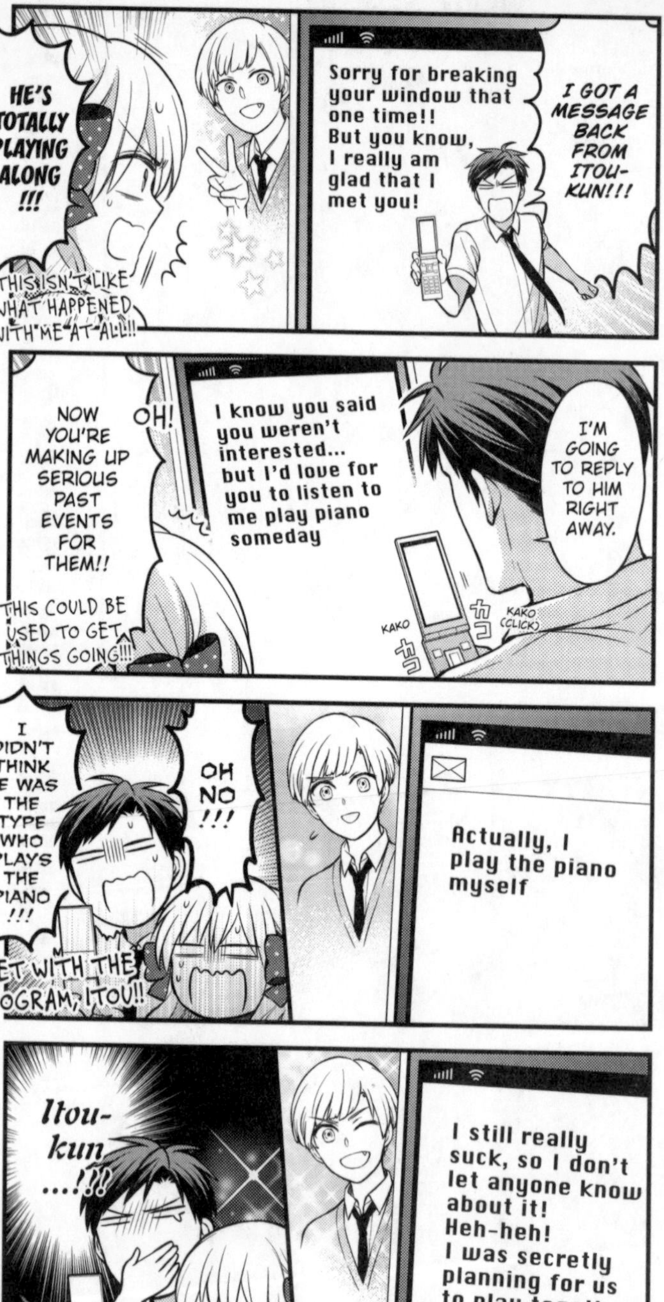
I GOT A MESSAGE BACK FROM ITOU-KUN!!!
Sorry for breaking your window that one time!! But you know, I really am glad that I met you!
HE'S TOTALLY PLAYING ALONG!!!
THIS ISN'T LIKE WHAT HAPPENED WITH ME AT ALL!!
I'M GOING TO REPLY TO HIM RIGHT AWAY.
KAKO (CLICK)
KAKO
I know you said you weren't interested... but I'd love for you to listen to me play piano someday
OH!
NOW YOU'RE MAKING UP SERIOUS PAST EVENTS FOR THEM!!
THIS COULD BE USED TO GET THINGS GOING!!!
Actually, I play the piano myself
OH NO!!!
I DIDN'T THINK HE WAS THE TYPE WHO PLAYS THE PIANO!!!
GET WITH THE PROGRAM, ITOU!!
I still really suck, so I don't let anyone know about it! Heh-heh! I was secretly planning for us to play together someday!
Itou-kun...!?!?

THEY WENT TO THE SAME JUNIOR HIGH

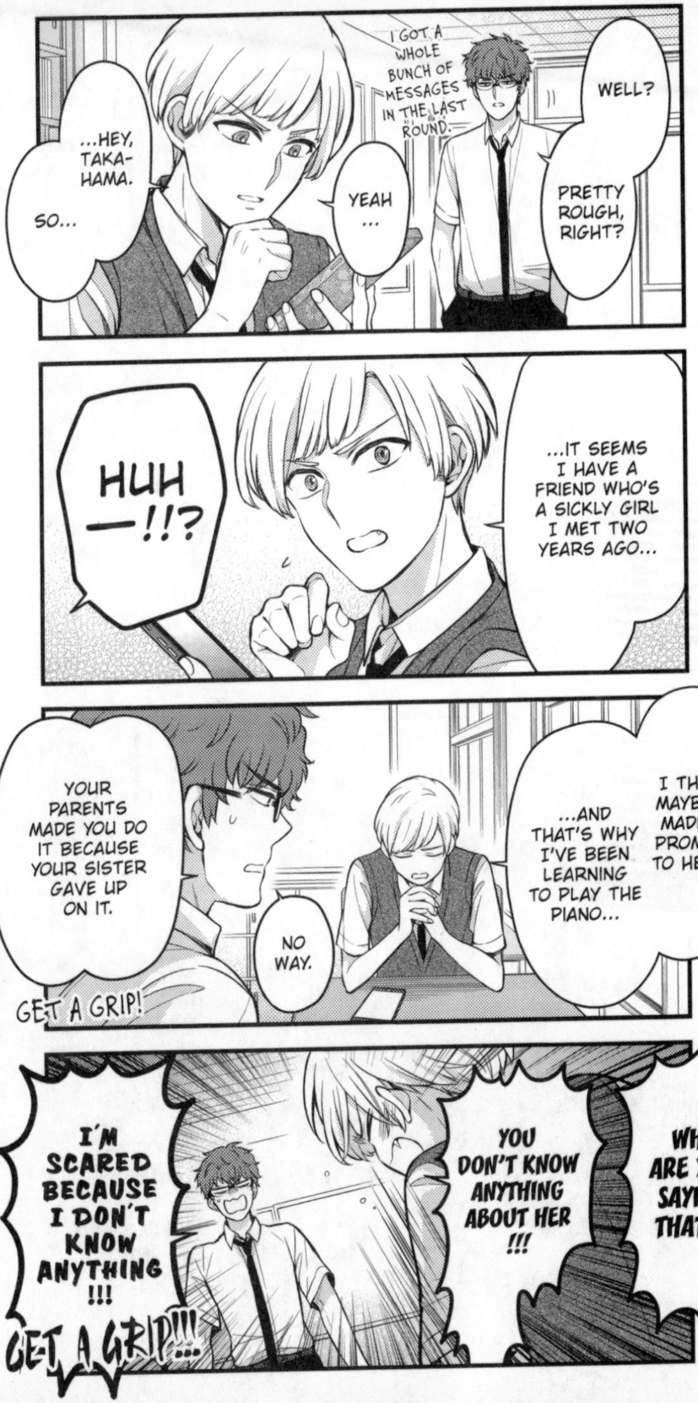
WELL?
PRETTY ROUGH, RIGHT?
I GOT A WHOLE BUNCH OF MESSAGES IN THE LAST ROUND.
YEAH ...
...HEY, TAKAHAMA.
SO...
...IT SEEMS I HAVE A FRIEND WHO'S A SICKLY GIRL I MET TWO YEARS AGO...
HUH—!!?
I THINK MAYBE I MADE A PROMISE TO HER...
...AND THAT'S WHY I'VE BEEN LEARNING TO PLAY THE PIANO...
NO WAY.
YOUR PARENTS MADE YOU DO IT BECAUSE YOUR SISTER GAVE UP ON IT.
GET A GRIP!
WHY ARE YOU SAYING THAT!!?
YOU DON'T KNOW ANYTHING ABOUT HER !!!
I'M SCARED BECAUSE I DON'T KNOW ANYTHING !!!
GET A GRIP!!!...

THE TEXT LOVE CONFESSION CHAMPION

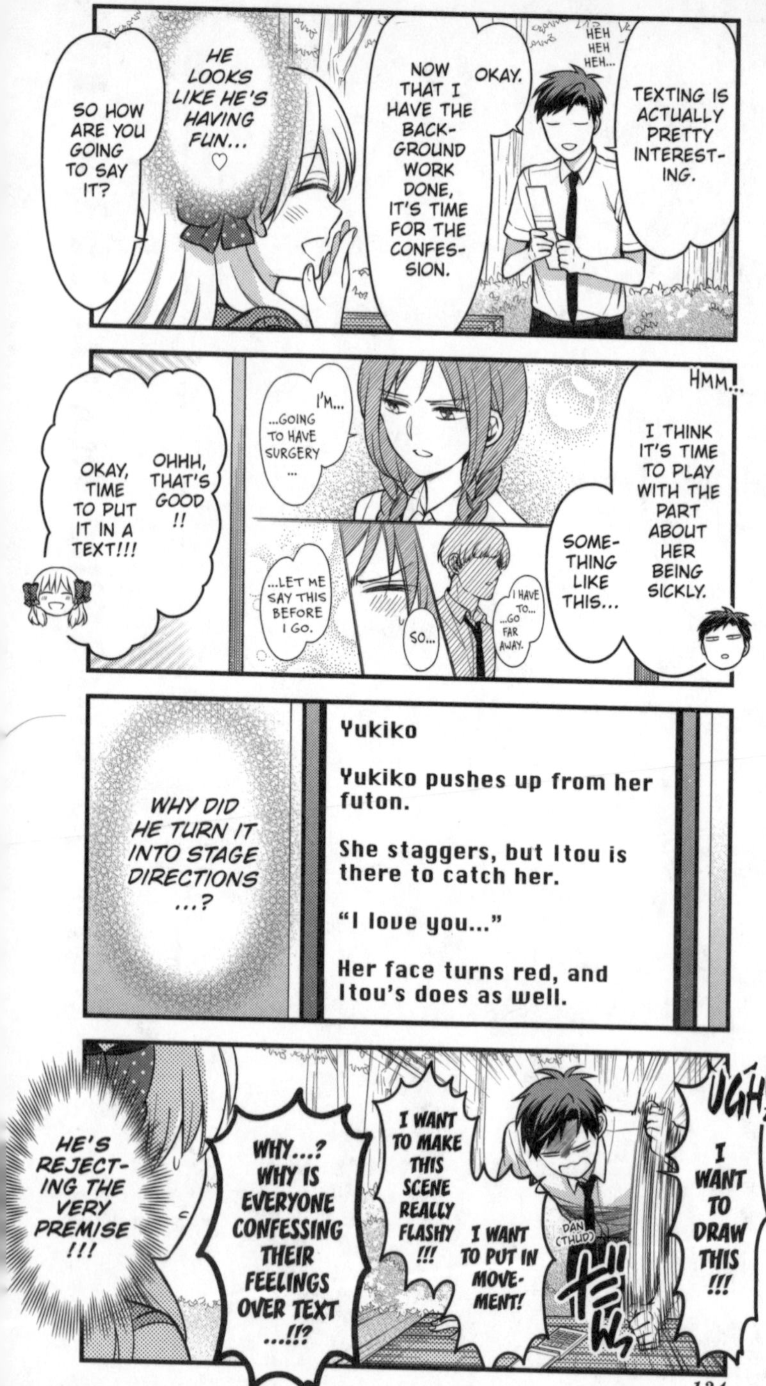
HEH HEH HEH...
TEXTING IS ACTUALLY PRETTY INTERESTING.
OKAY.
NOW THAT I HAVE THE BACKGROUND WORK DONE, IT'S TIME FOR THE CONFESSION.
HE LOOKS LIKE HE'S HAVING FUN... ♡
SO HOW ARE YOU GOING TO SAY IT?
HMM...
I THINK IT'S TIME TO PLAY WITH THE PART ABOUT HER BEING SICKLY.
SOMETHING LIKE THIS...
I'M...
...GOING TO HAVE SURGERY ...
I HAVE TO... ...GO FAR AWAY.
SO...
...LET ME SAY THIS BEFORE I GO.
OHHH, THAT'S GOOD!!
OKAY, TIME TO PUT IT IN A TEXT!!!
Yukiko
Yukiko pushes up from her futon.
She staggers, but Itou is there to catch her.
"I love you..."
Her face turns red, and Itou's does as well.
WHY DID HE TURN IT INTO STAGE DIRECTIONS...?
UGH!
I WANT TO DRAW THIS!!!
DAN (THUD)
I WANT TO PUT IN MOVEMENT!
I WANT TO MAKE THIS SCENE REALLY FLASHY!!!
WHY...? WHY IS EVERYONE CONFESSING THEIR FEELINGS OVER TEXT...!!?
HE'S REJECTING THE VERY PREMISE!!!

A TEARFUL PRODUCTION

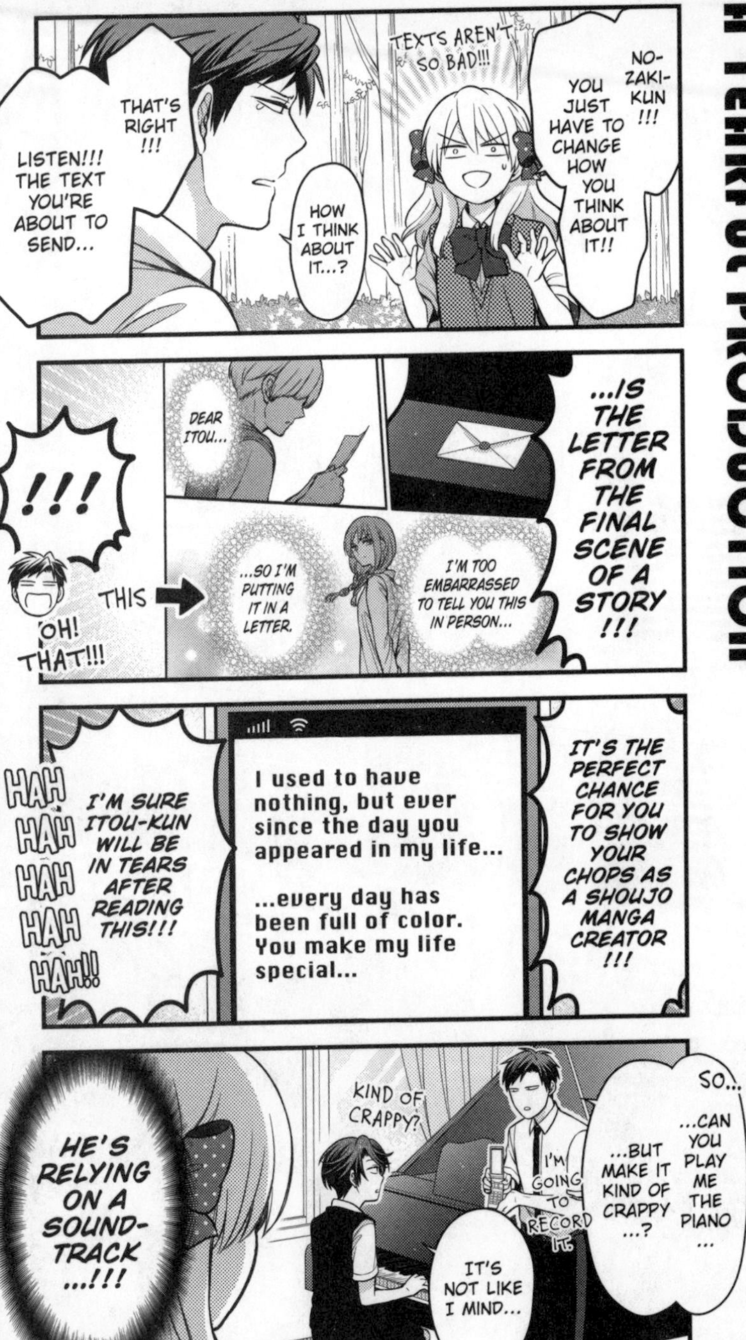
NO-ZAKI-KUN!!!
YOU JUST HAVE TO CHANGE HOW YOU THINK ABOUT IT!!
TEXTS AREN'T SO BAD!!!
HOW I THINK ABOUT IT...?
THAT'S RIGHT!!!
LISTEN!!! THE TEXT YOU'RE ABOUT TO SEND...
...IS THE LETTER FROM THE FINAL SCENE OF A STORY!!!
DEAR ITOU...
I'M TOO EMBARRASSED TO TELL YOU THIS IN PERSON...
...SO I'M PUTTING IT IN A LETTER.
THIS
!!!
OH! THAT!!!
IT'S THE PERFECT CHANCE FOR YOU TO SHOW YOUR CHOPS AS A SHOUJO MANGA CREATOR!!!
I used to have nothing, but ever since the day you appeared in my life...
...every day has been full of color. You make my life special...
I'M SURE ITOU-KUN WILL BE IN TEARS AFTER READING THIS!!!
HAH HAH HAH HAH HAH!!
SO...
...CAN YOU PLAY ME THE PIANO...
...BUT MAKE IT KIND OF CRAPPY...?
I'M GOING TO RECORD IT.
KIND OF CRAPPY?
IT'S NOT LIKE I MIND...
HE'S RELYING ON A SOUND-TRACK...!!!

THE LOOK OF SOMEONE WHO KNOWS THE TRUTH

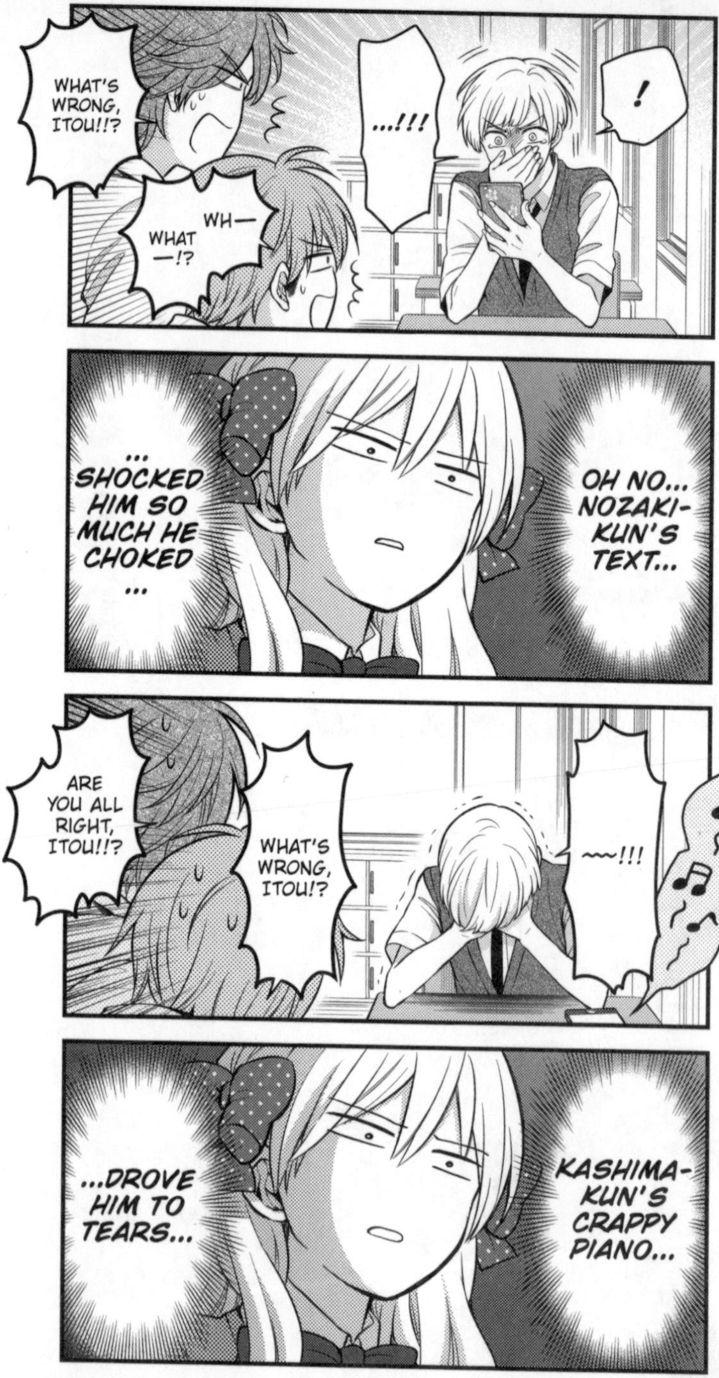
!
...!!!
WHAT'S WRONG, ITOU!!?
WH— WHAT —!?
OH NO... NOZAKI-KUN'S TEXT...
...SHOCKED HIM SO MUCH HE CHOKED...
~~!!!
WHAT'S WRONG, ITOU!?
ARE YOU ALL RIGHT, ITOU!!?
KASHIMA-KUN'S CRAPPY PIANO...
...DROVE HIM TO TEARS...

LET'S CHANGE THINGS UP

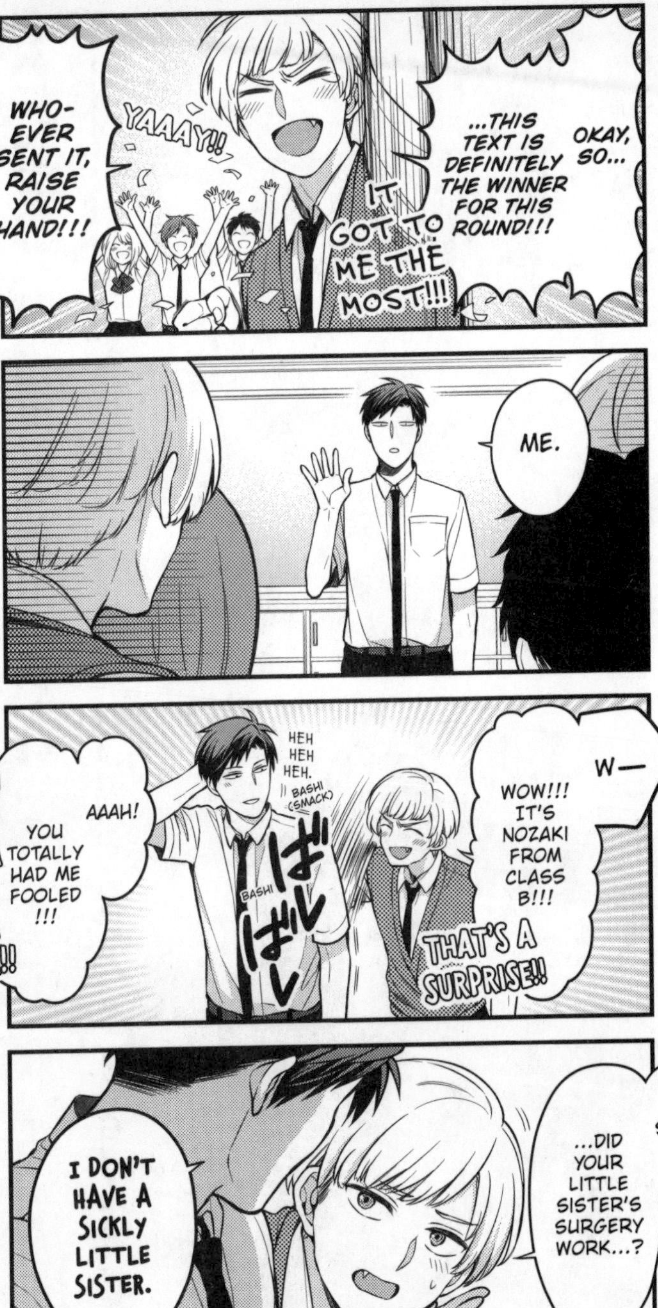
OKAY, SO...
...THIS TEXT IS DEFINITELY THE WINNER FOR THIS ROUND!!!
IT GOT TO ME THE MOST!!!
YAAAY!!
WHO-EVER SENT IT, RAISE YOUR HAND!!!
ME.
W—
WOW!!! IT'S NOZAKI FROM CLASS B!!!
THAT'S A SURPRISE!!
HEH HEH HEH.
BASHI (SMACK)
ばしばし
BASHI
AAAH!
YOU TOTALLY HAD ME FOOLED!!!
AH HA HA HA HA HA!!
SO...
...DID YOUR LITTLE SISTER'S SURGERY WORK...?
I DON'T HAVE A SICKLY LITTLE SISTER.

HER CLASSMATE AFTER THAT

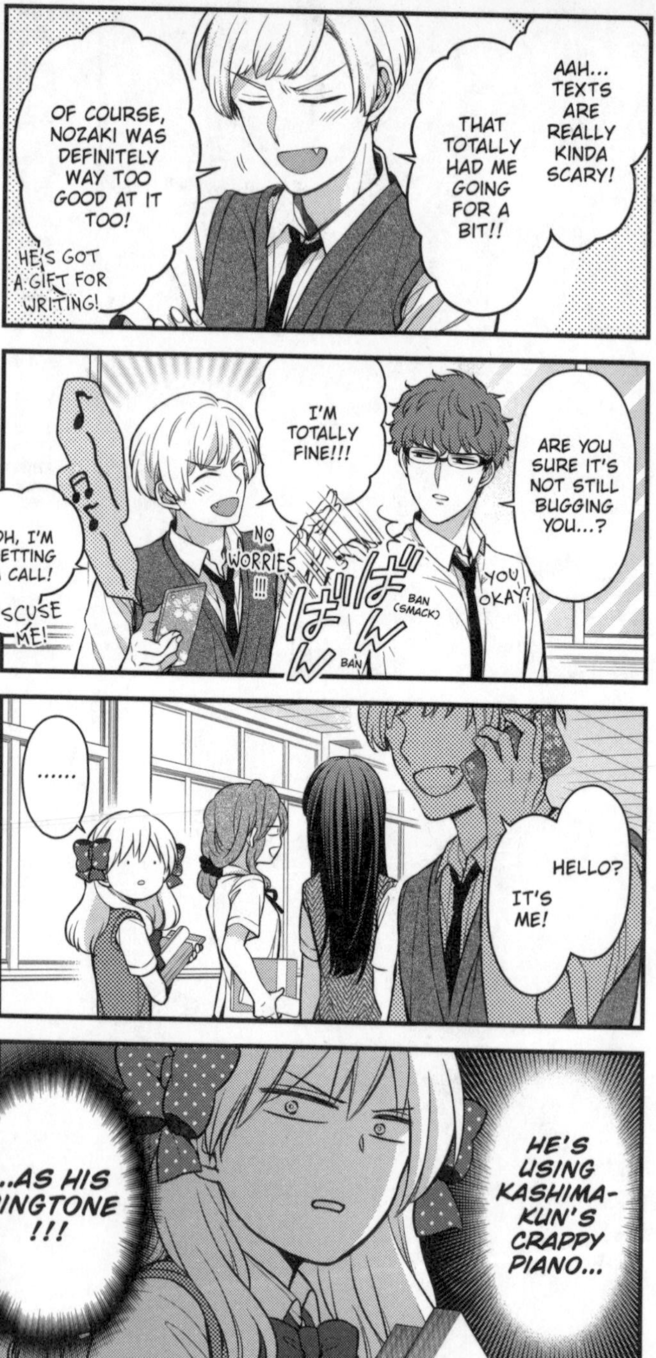

AAH... TEXTS ARE REALLY KINDA SCARY!
THAT TOTALLY HAD ME GOING FOR A BIT!!
OF COURSE, NOZAKI WAS DEFINITELY WAY TOO GOOD AT IT TOO!
HE'S GOT A GIFT FOR WRITING!
ARE YOU SURE IT'S NOT STILL BUGGING YOU...?
YOU OKAY?
I'M TOTALLY FINE!!!
BAN (SMACK)
BAN
NO WORRIES!!!
OH, I'M GETTING A CALL!
'SCUSE ME!
HELLO?
IT'S ME!
......
HE'S USING KASHIMA-KUN'S CRAPPY PIANO...
...AS HIS RINGTONE!!!

TRANSLATION NOTES

COMMON HONORIFICS

no honorific: Indicates familiarity or closeness; if used without permission or reason, addressing someone in this manner would constitute an insult.

-san: The Japanese equivalent of Mr./Mrs./Miss. If a situation calls for politeness, this is the fail-safe honorific.

-sama: Conveys great respect; may also indicate that the social status of the speaker is lower than that of the addressee.

-kun: Used most often when referring to boys, this indicates affection or familiarity. Occasionally used by older men among their peers, but it may also be used by anyone referring to a person of lower standing.

-chan: An affectionate honorific indicating familiarity used mostly in reference to girls; also used in reference to cute persons or animals regardless of gender.

-sensei: A term of respect commonly used for teachers but can also refer to doctors, writers, and artists.

-senpai: Used to address upperclassmen or more experienced coworkers.

-kouhai: Used to address underclassmen or less experienced coworkers.

PAGE 16
Japan uses the metric system to measure height and shoe size. Since 1 cm = 2.54 inches, Nozaki is approximately 6'3" inches tall. His shoe size is roughly a US men's size 11.

PAGE 22
Shounen is usually used to refer to boys, while **seinen** is used for young men or adults in general. Magazines often use the two words to distinguish the target audience of the magazine.

PAGE 32
Tanuki, or "raccoon dogs," are a mammal native to Japan that are seen as both tricksters and bringers of wealth.

MONTHLY GIRLS' ✕ NOZAKI-KUN

[Extra]

HE BIT

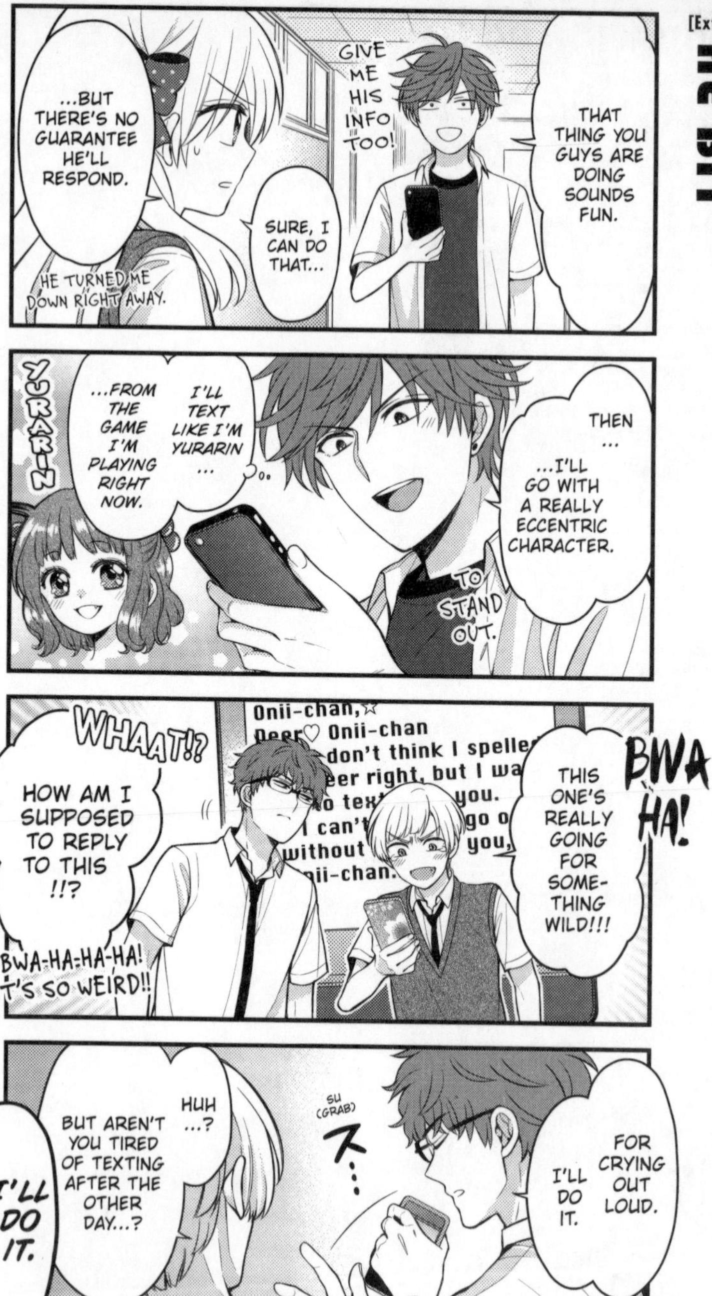
THAT THING YOU GUYS ARE DOING SOUNDS FUN.
GIVE ME HIS INFO TOO!
SURE, I CAN DO THAT...
...BUT THERE'S NO GUARANTEE HE'LL RESPOND.
HE TURNED ME DOWN RIGHT AWAY.
THEN... ...I'LL GO WITH A REALLY ECCENTRIC CHARACTER.
TO STAND OUT.
I'LL TEXT LIKE I'M YURARIN...
...FROM THE GAME I'M PLAYING RIGHT NOW.
YURARIN
BWA HA!
THIS ONE'S REALLY GOING FOR SOME-THING WILD!!!
Onii-chan,☆
Deer♡ Onii-chan
WHAAT!?
HOW AM I SUPPOSED TO REPLY TO THIS!!?
BWA-HA-HA-HA! IT'S SO WEIRD!!
FOR CRYING OUT LOUD.
I'LL DO IT.
SU (GRAB)
ス...
HUH...?
BUT AREN'T YOU TIRED OF TEXTING AFTER THE OTHER DAY...?
I'LL DO IT.

[Extra]

THAT'S WEIRD

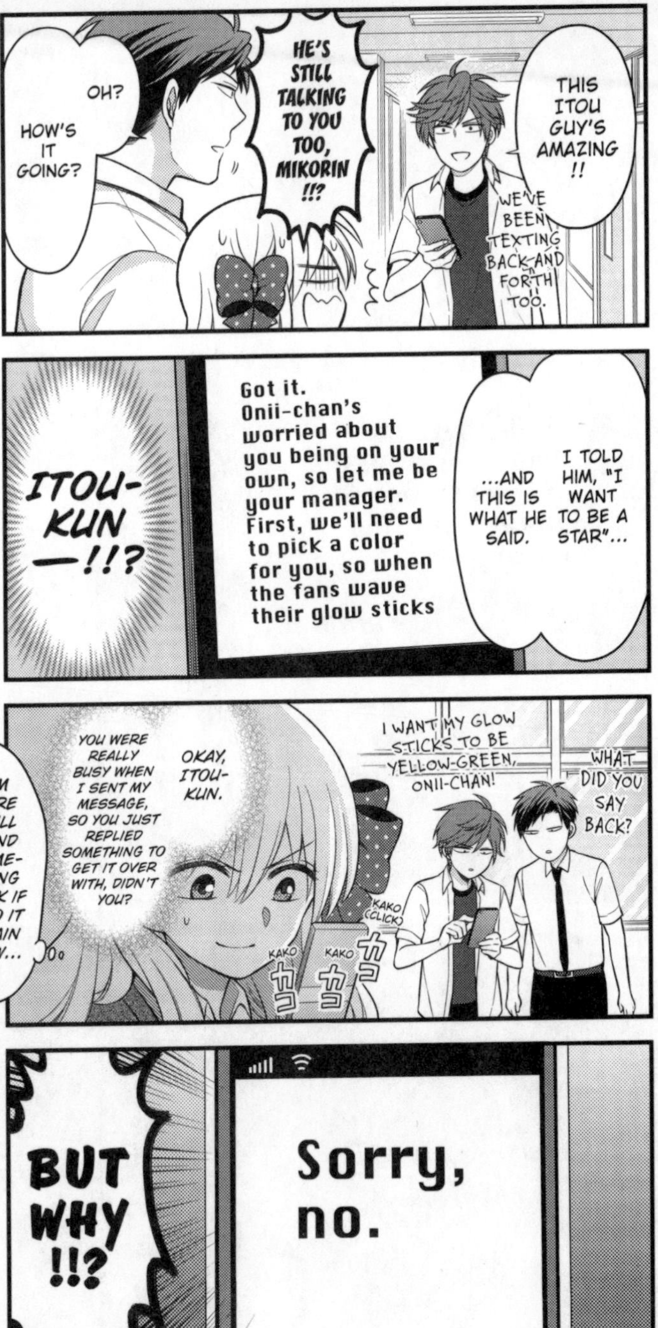

THIS ITOU GUY'S AMAZING!!
WE'VE BEEN TEXTING BACK AND FORTH TOO.
HE'S STILL TALKING TO YOU TOO, MIKORIN!!?
OH?
HOW'S IT GOING?
I TOLD HIM, "I WANT TO BE A STAR"...
...AND THIS IS WHAT HE SAID.
Got it. Onii-chan's worried about you being on your own, so let me be your manager. First, we'll need to pick a color for you, so when the fans wave their glow sticks
ITOU-KUN—!!?
WHAT DID YOU SAY BACK?
I WANT MY GLOW STICKS TO BE YELLOW-GREEN, ONII-CHAN!
KAKO (CLICK)
KAKO
KAKO
OKAY, ITOU-KUN.
YOU WERE REALLY BUSY WHEN I SENT MY MESSAGE, SO YOU JUST REPLIED SOMETHING TO GET IT OVER WITH, DIDN'T YOU?
I'M SURE HE'LL SEND SOMETHING BACK IF I DO IT AGAIN NOW...
Sorry, no.
BUT WHY!!?

[Extra]

FACE REALITY

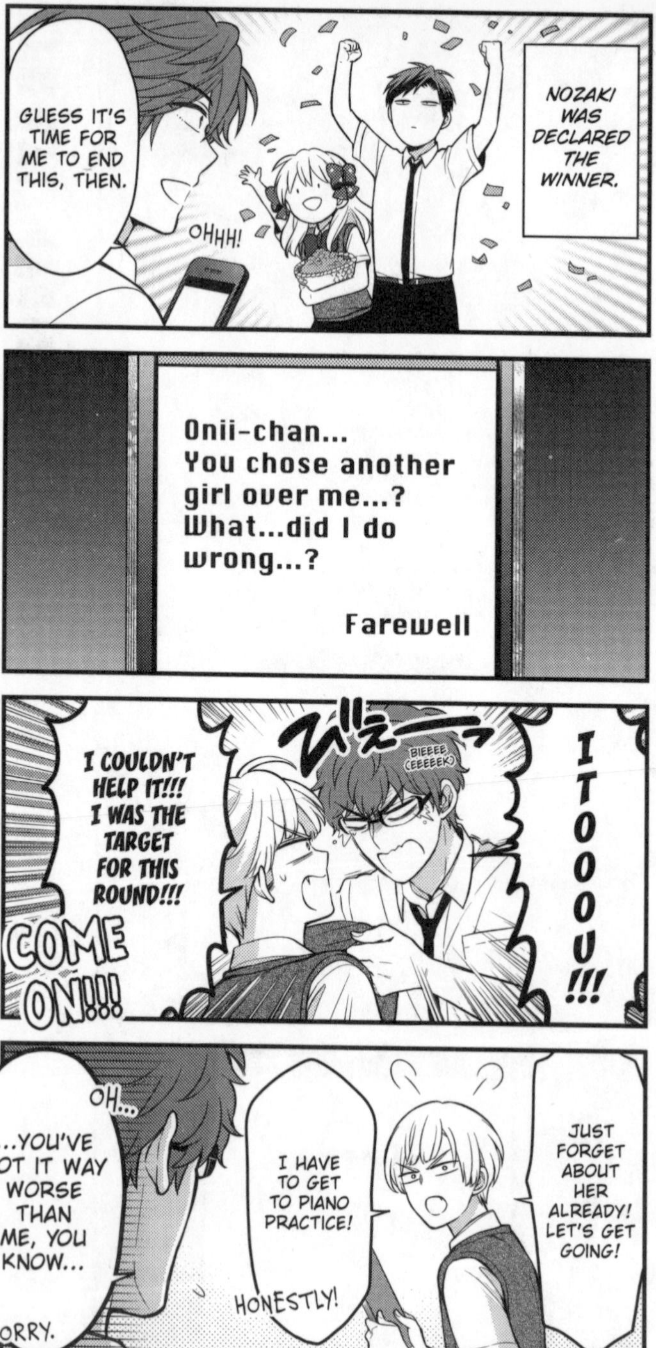
NOZAKI WAS DECLARED THE WINNER.
OHHH!
GUESS IT'S TIME FOR ME TO END THIS, THEN.
Onii-chan...
You chose another girl over me...?
What...did I do wrong...?
Farewell
ITOOOOU!!!
BIEEEE (EEEEEK)
I COULDN'T HELP IT!!! I WAS THE TARGET FOR THIS ROUND!!!
COME ON!!!
JUST FORGET ABOUT HER ALREADY! LET'S GET GOING!
I HAVE TO GET TO PIANO PRACTICE!
HONESTLY!
OH...
...YOU'VE GOT IT WAY WORSE THAN ME, YOU KNOW...
SORRY.

[Extra]

HAPPY END

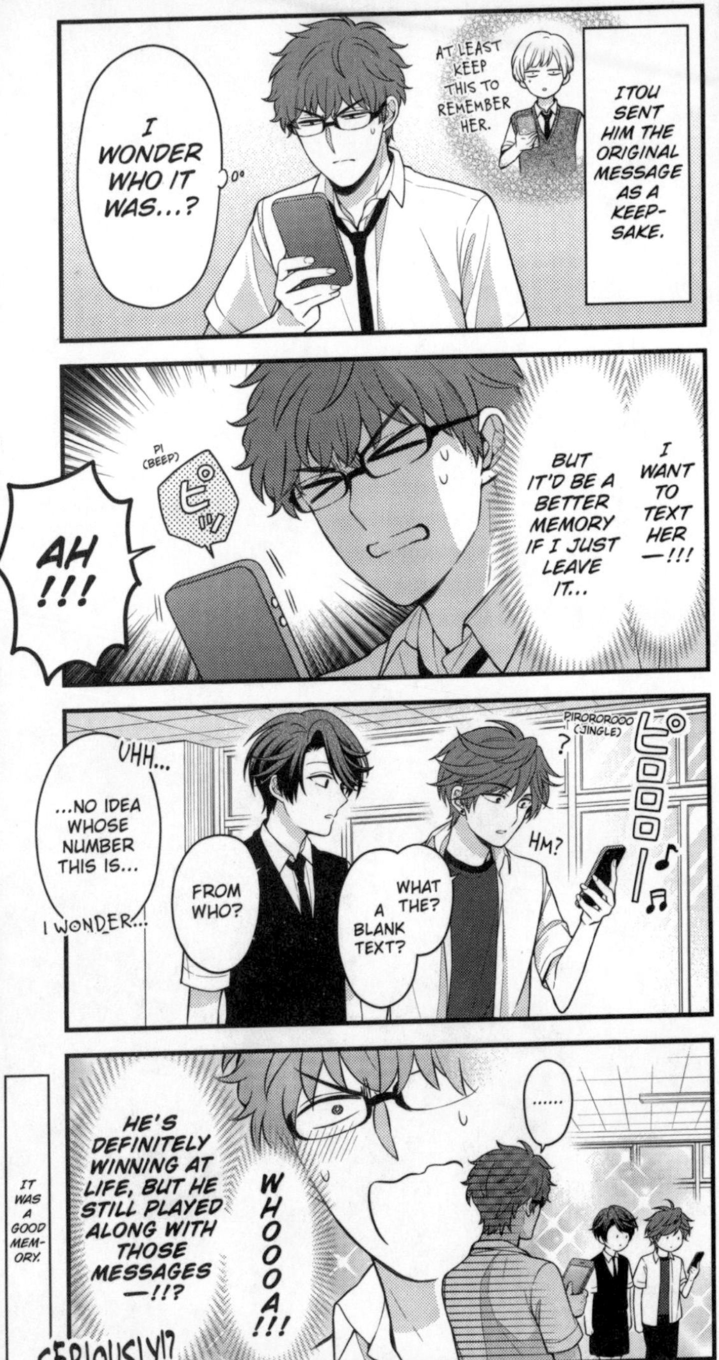
ITOU SENT HIM THE ORIGINAL MESSAGE AS A KEEP-SAKE.
AT LEAST KEEP THIS TO REMEMBER HER.
I WONDER WHO IT WAS...?
I WANT TO TEXT HER—!!!
BUT IT'D BE A BETTER MEMORY IF I JUST LEAVE IT...
PI (BEEP)
ピッ
AH!!!
ピロロロー
PIROROROOO (JINGLE)
?
HM?
WHAT THE? A BLANK TEXT?
FROM WHO?
UHH...
...NO IDEA WHOSE NUMBER THIS IS...
I WONDER...
......
WHOOOOA!!!
HE'S DEFINITELY WINNING AT LIFE, BUT HE STILL PLAYED ALONG WITH THOSE MESSAGES—!!?
IT WAS A GOOD MEM-ORY.
SERIOUSLY!?

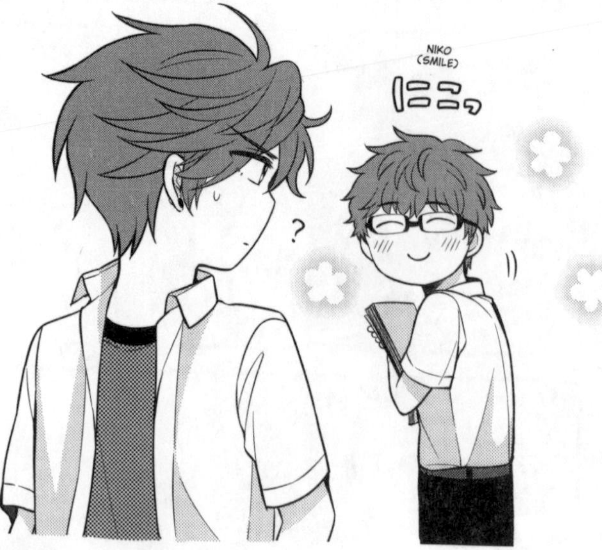
NIKO
(SMILE)
?

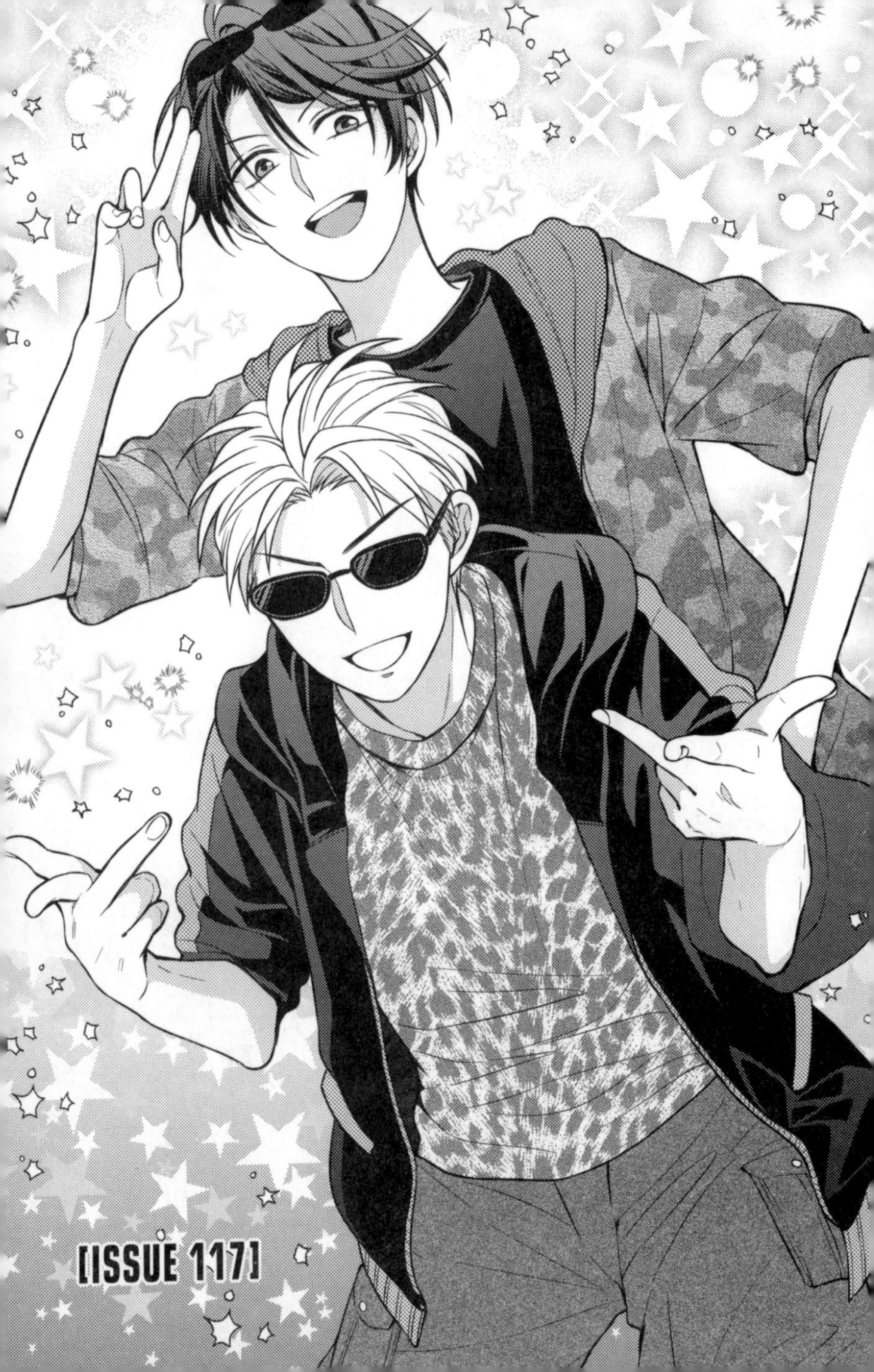
[ISSUE 117]

FAR AWAY WITH TOO MUCH TIME ON HER HANDS

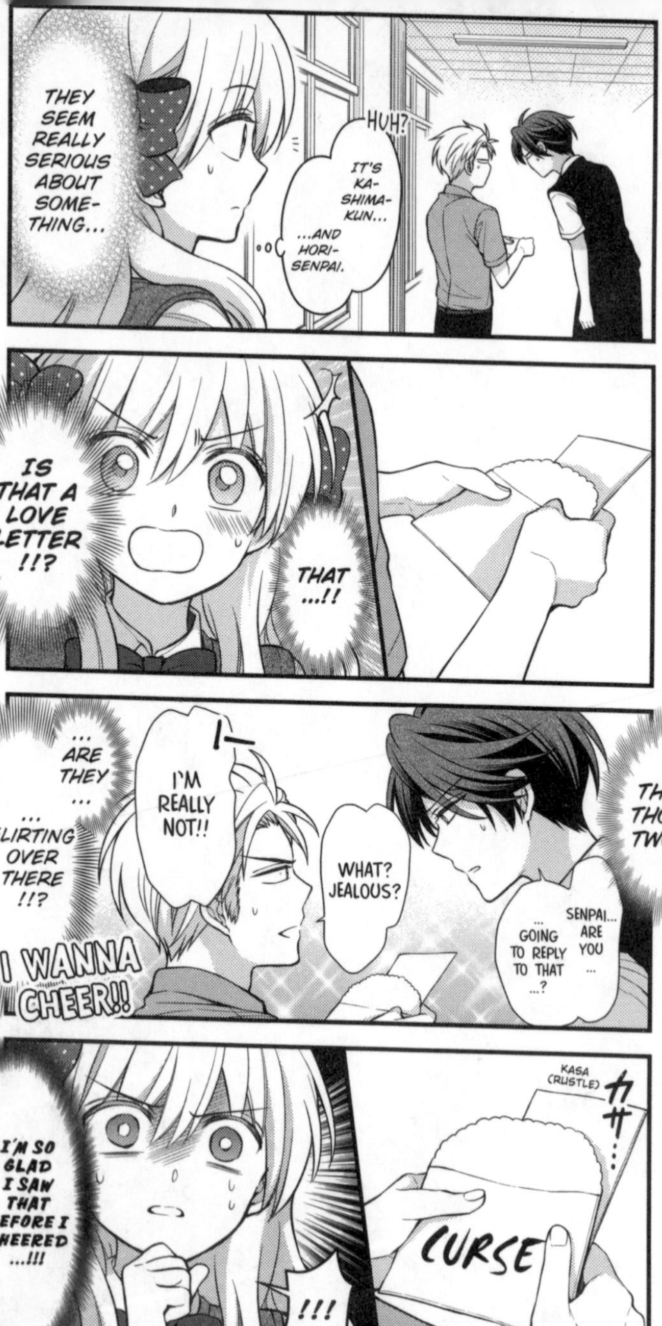
HUH?
IT'S KASHIMA-KUN... ...AND HORI-SENPAI.
THEY SEEM REALLY SERIOUS ABOUT SOMETHING...
THAT...!!
IS THAT A LOVE LETTER!!?
THEN THOSE TWO...
SENPAI... ARE YOU ... GOING TO REPLY TO THAT...?
WHAT? JEALOUS?
I'M REALLY NOT!!
... ARE THEY ... ... FLIRTING OVER THERE!!?
I WANNA CHEER!!
KASA (RUSTLE)
カサ…
CURSE
!!!
I'M SO GLAD I SAW THAT BEFORE I CHEERED...!!!

THE EFFECT OF THE CURSE

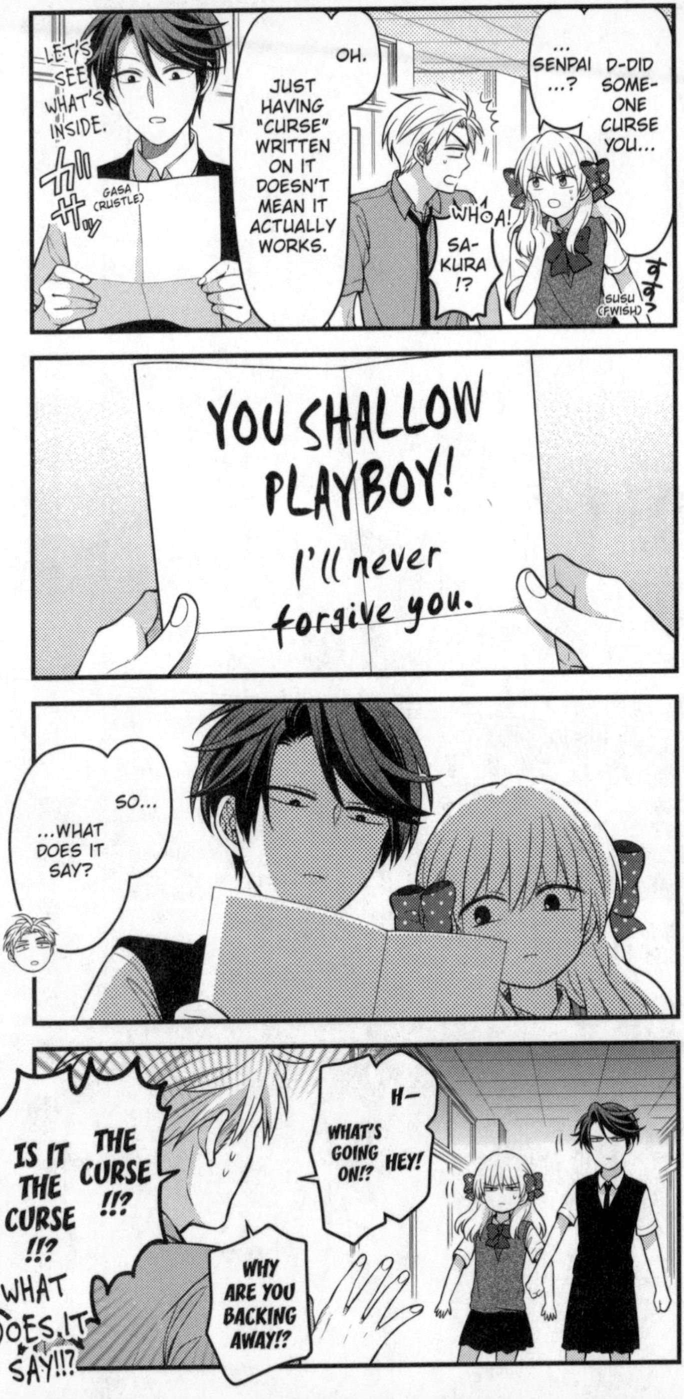
...SENPAI...? D-DID SOME-ONE CURSE YOU...
SUSU (FWISH)
WHOA! SAKURA!?
OH. JUST HAVING "CURSE" WRITTEN ON IT DOESN'T MEAN IT ACTUALLY WORKS.
LET'S SEE WHAT'S INSIDE.
GASA (RUSTLE)
YOU SHALLOW PLAYBOY! I'll never forgive you.
SO... ...WHAT DOES IT SAY?
H— HEY! WHAT'S GOING ON!?
WHY ARE YOU BACKING AWAY!?
THE CURSE!!?
IS IT THE CURSE!!? WHAT DOES IT SAY!!?

NOTHING BUT ENEMIES

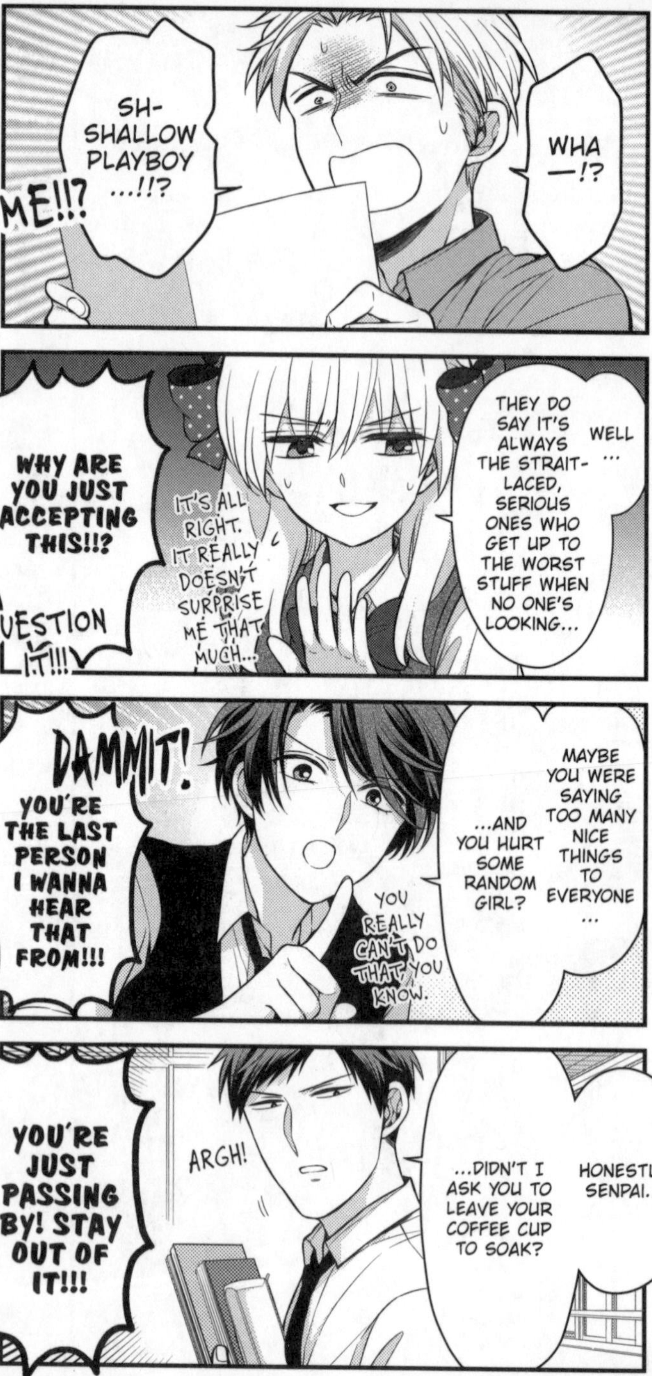
WHA—!?
SH-SHALLOW PLAYBOY ...!!?
ME!!?
WELL ...
THEY DO SAY IT'S ALWAYS THE STRAIT-LACED, SERIOUS ONES WHO GET UP TO THE WORST STUFF WHEN NO ONE'S LOOKING...
IT'S ALL RIGHT. IT REALLY DOESN'T SURPRISE ME THAT MUCH...
WHY ARE YOU JUST ACCEPTING THIS!!?
QUESTION IT!!!
MAYBE YOU WERE SAYING TOO MANY NICE THINGS TO EVERYONE ...
...AND YOU HURT SOME RANDOM GIRL?
YOU REALLY CAN'T DO THAT, YOU KNOW.
DAMMIT!
YOU'RE THE LAST PERSON I WANNA HEAR THAT FROM!!!
HONESTLY, SENPAI...
...DIDN'T I ASK YOU TO LEAVE YOUR COFFEE CUP TO SOAK?
ARGH!
YOU'RE JUST PASSING BY! STAY OUT OF IT!!!

HIS NIGHTTIME SIDE

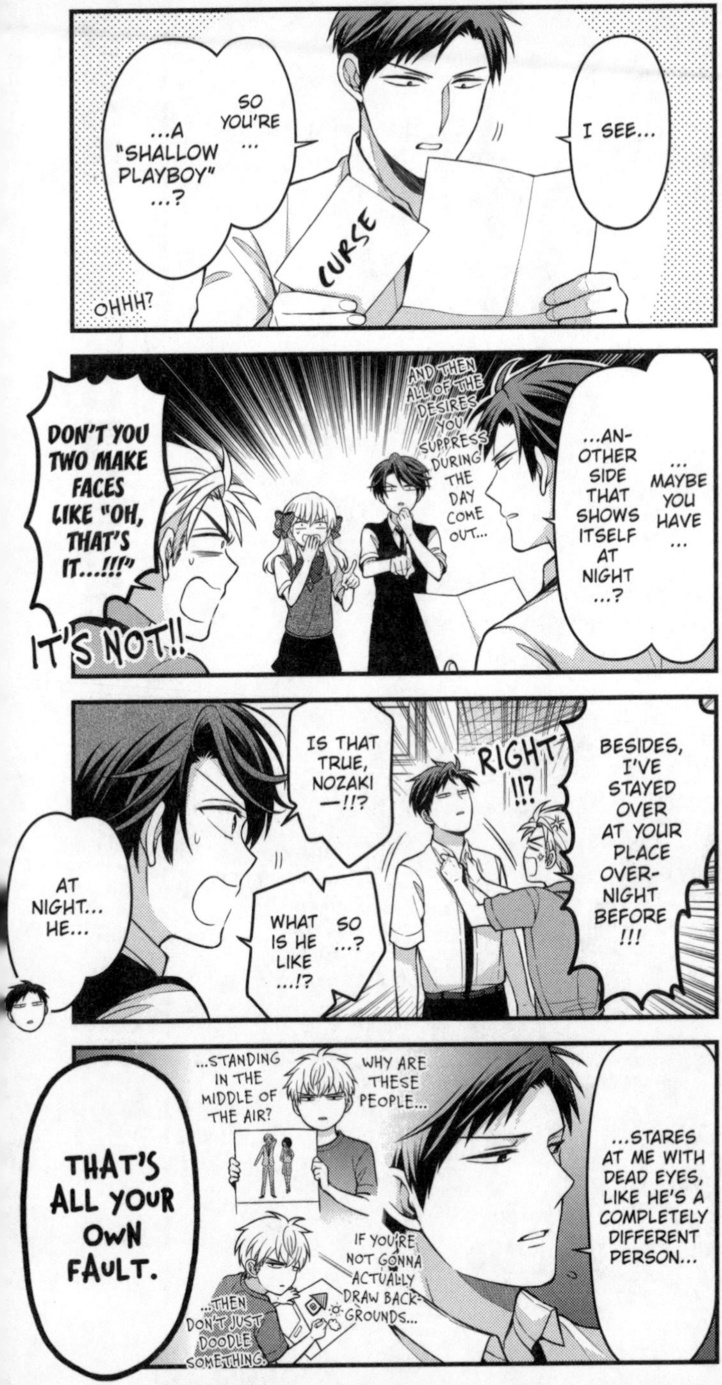
I SEE...
SO YOU'RE ...
...A "SHALLOW PLAYBOY" ...?
CURSE
OHHH?
... MAYBE YOU HAVE ...
...AN-OTHER SIDE THAT SHOWS ITSELF AT NIGHT ...?
AND THEN ALL OF THE DESIRES YOU SUPPRESS DURING THE DAY COME OUT...
DON'T YOU TWO MAKE FACES LIKE "OH, THAT'S IT...!!!"
IT'S NOT!!
BESIDES, I'VE STAYED OVER AT YOUR PLACE OVER-NIGHT BEFORE !!!
RIGHT !!?
IS THAT TRUE, NOZAKI—!!?
SO ...?
WHAT IS HE LIKE ...!?
AT NIGHT... HE...
...STARES AT ME WITH DEAD EYES, LIKE HE'S A COMPLETELY DIFFERENT PERSON...
WHY ARE THESE PEOPLE...
...STANDING IN THE MIDDLE OF THE AIR?
IF YOU'RE NOT GONNA ACTUALLY DRAW BACK-GROUNDS...
...THEN DON'T JUST DOODLE SOMETHING.
THAT'S ALL YOUR OWN FAULT.

SENPAI THE WOMANIZER

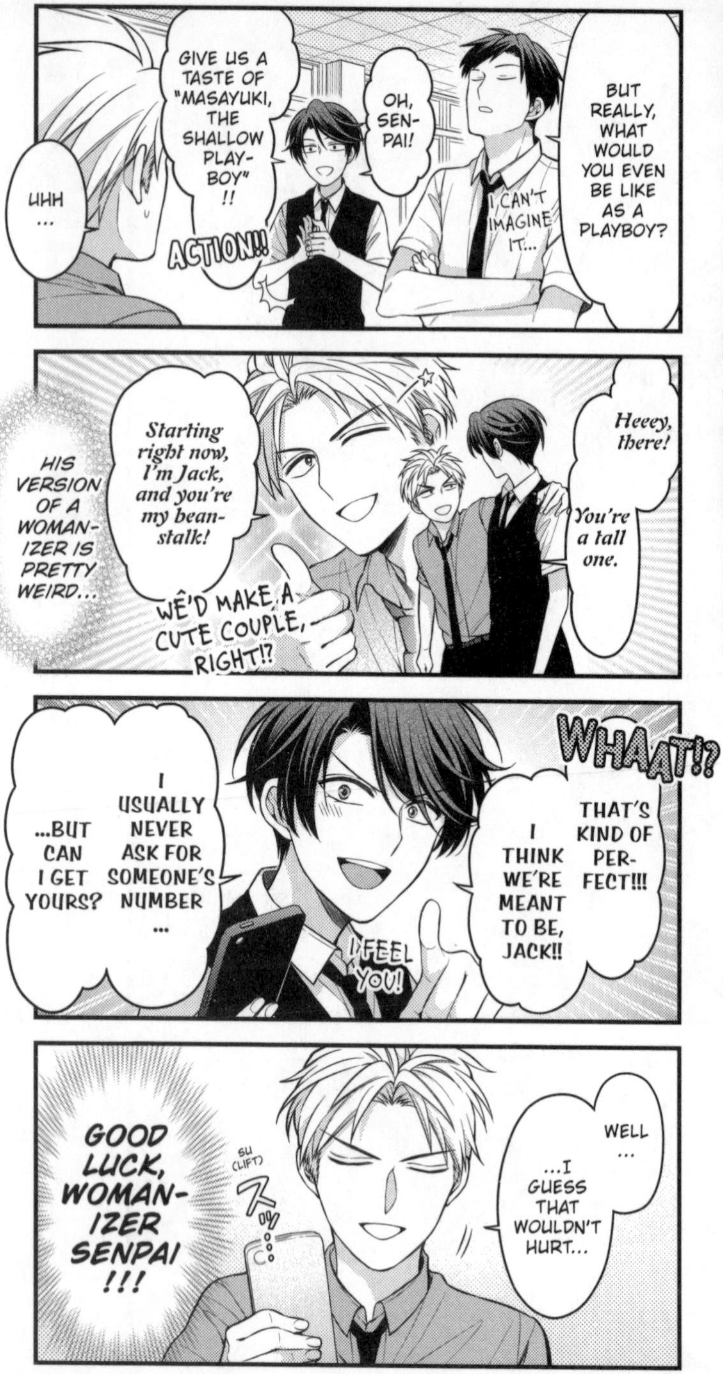
BUT REALLY, WHAT WOULD YOU EVEN BE LIKE AS A PLAYBOY?
I CAN'T IMAGINE IT...
OH, SEN-PAI!
GIVE US A TASTE OF "MASAYUKI, THE SHALLOW PLAY-BOY"!!
ACTION!!
UHH...
Heeey, there!
You're a tall one.
Starting right now, I'm Jack, and you're my bean-stalk!
WE'D MAKE A CUTE COUPLE, RIGHT!?
HIS VERSION OF A WOMAN-IZER IS PRETTY WEIRD...
WHAAT!?
THAT'S KIND OF PER-FECT!!!
I THINK WE'RE MEANT TO BE, JACK!!
I FEEL YOU!
I USUALLY NEVER ASK FOR SOMEONE'S NUMBER...
...BUT CAN I GET YOURS?
WELL...
...I GUESS THAT WOULDN'T HURT...
SU (LIFT)
GOOD LUCK, WOMAN-IZER SENPAI!!!

AN ADAPTABLE MAN

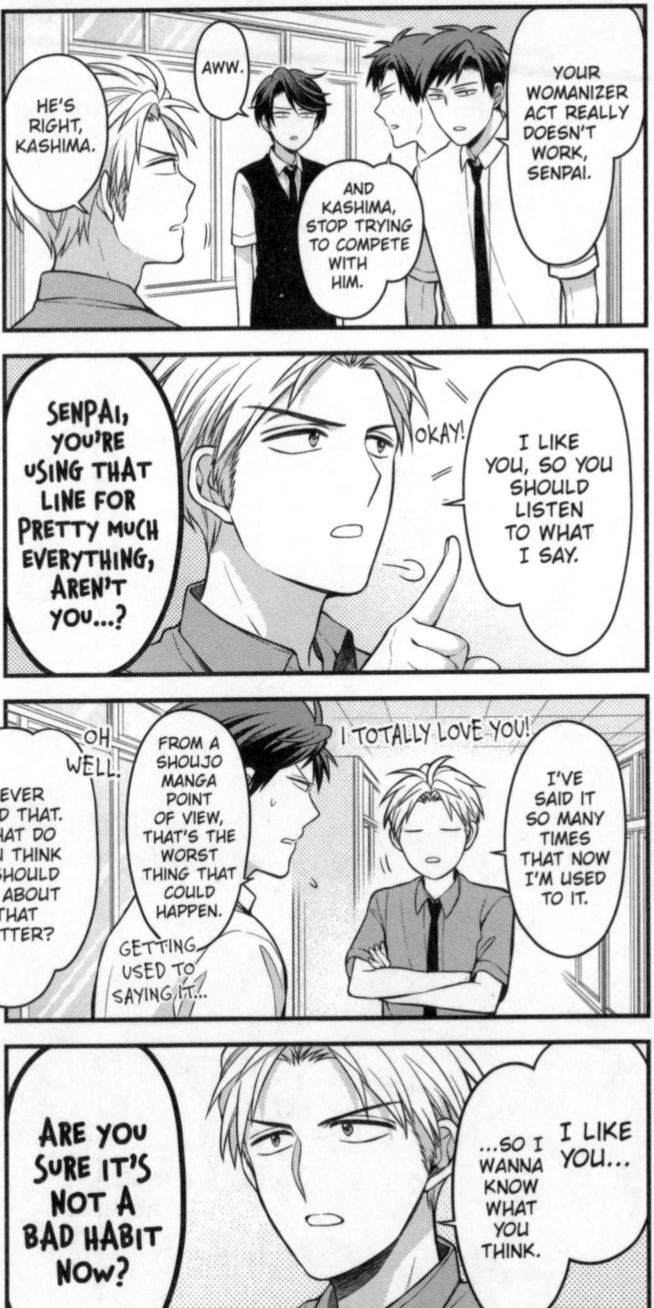
YOUR WOMANIZER ACT REALLY DOESN'T WORK, SENPAI.
AND KASHIMA, STOP TRYING TO COMPETE WITH HIM.
AWW.
HE'S RIGHT, KASHIMA.
I LIKE YOU, SO YOU SHOULD LISTEN TO WHAT I SAY.
OKAY!
SENPAI, YOU'RE USING THAT LINE FOR PRETTY MUCH EVERYTHING, AREN'T YOU...?
I TOTALLY LOVE YOU!
I'VE SAID IT SO MANY TIMES THAT NOW I'M USED TO IT.
FROM A SHOUJO MANGA POINT OF VIEW, THAT'S THE WORST THING THAT COULD HAPPEN.
GETTING USED TO SAYING IT...
OH WELL.
NEVER MIND THAT. WHAT DO YOU THINK I SHOULD DO ABOUT THAT LETTER?
I LIKE YOU...
...SO I WANNA KNOW WHAT YOU THINK.
ARE YOU SURE IT'S NOT A BAD HABIT NOW?

IF IT'S JUST THE WORDS

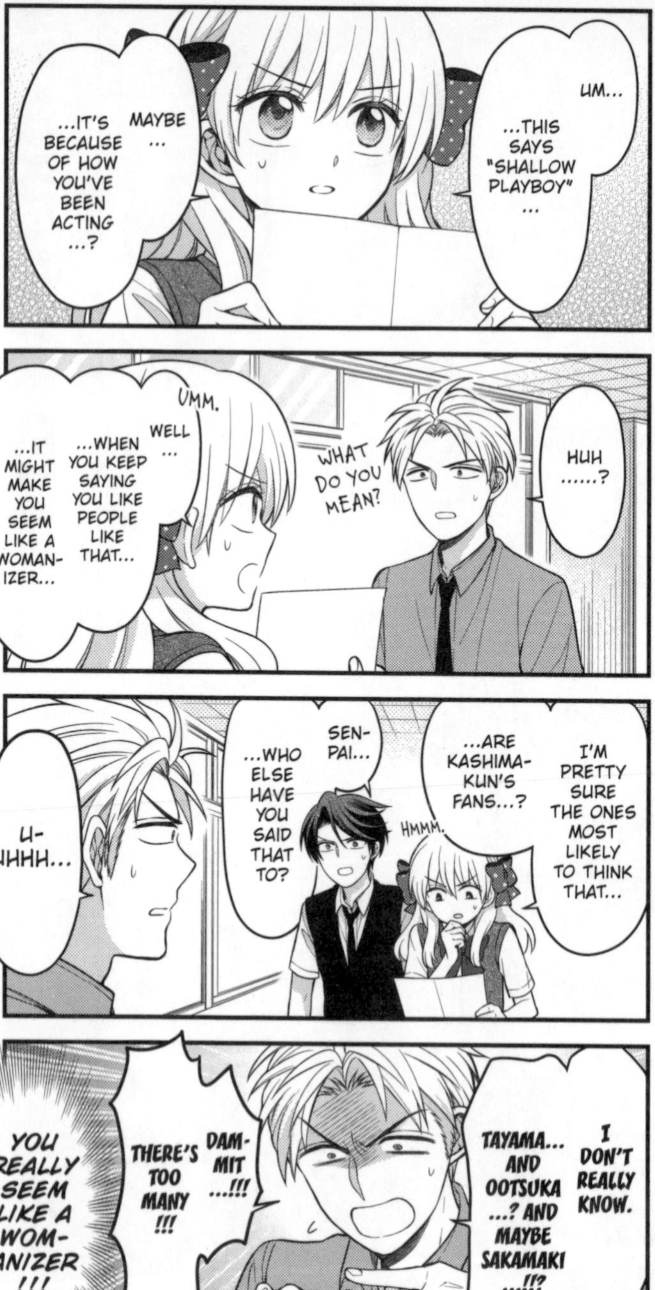
UM... ...THIS SAYS "SHALLOW PLAYBOY" ...
MAYBE ... ...IT'S BECAUSE OF HOW YOU'VE BEEN ACTING ...?
HUH ......?
WHAT DO YOU MEAN?
UMM. WELL ... ...WHEN YOU KEEP SAYING YOU LIKE PEOPLE LIKE THAT... ...IT MIGHT MAKE YOU SEEM LIKE A WOMAN-IZER...
I'M PRETTY SURE THE ONES MOST LIKELY TO THINK THAT... ...ARE KASHIMA-KUN'S FANS...?
HMMM.
SEN-PAI... ...WHO ELSE HAVE YOU SAID THAT TO?
U-UHHH...
I DON'T REALLY KNOW. TAYAMA... AND OOTSUKA ...? AND MAYBE SAKAMAKI ...!!?
DAM-MIT ...!!! THERE'S TOO MANY !!!
YOU REALLY SEEM LIKE A WOM-ANIZER !!!

HOW AM I SUPPOSED TO REMEMBER ALL THAT!?

NOZAKI-KUN'S EXPERT DEDUCTION

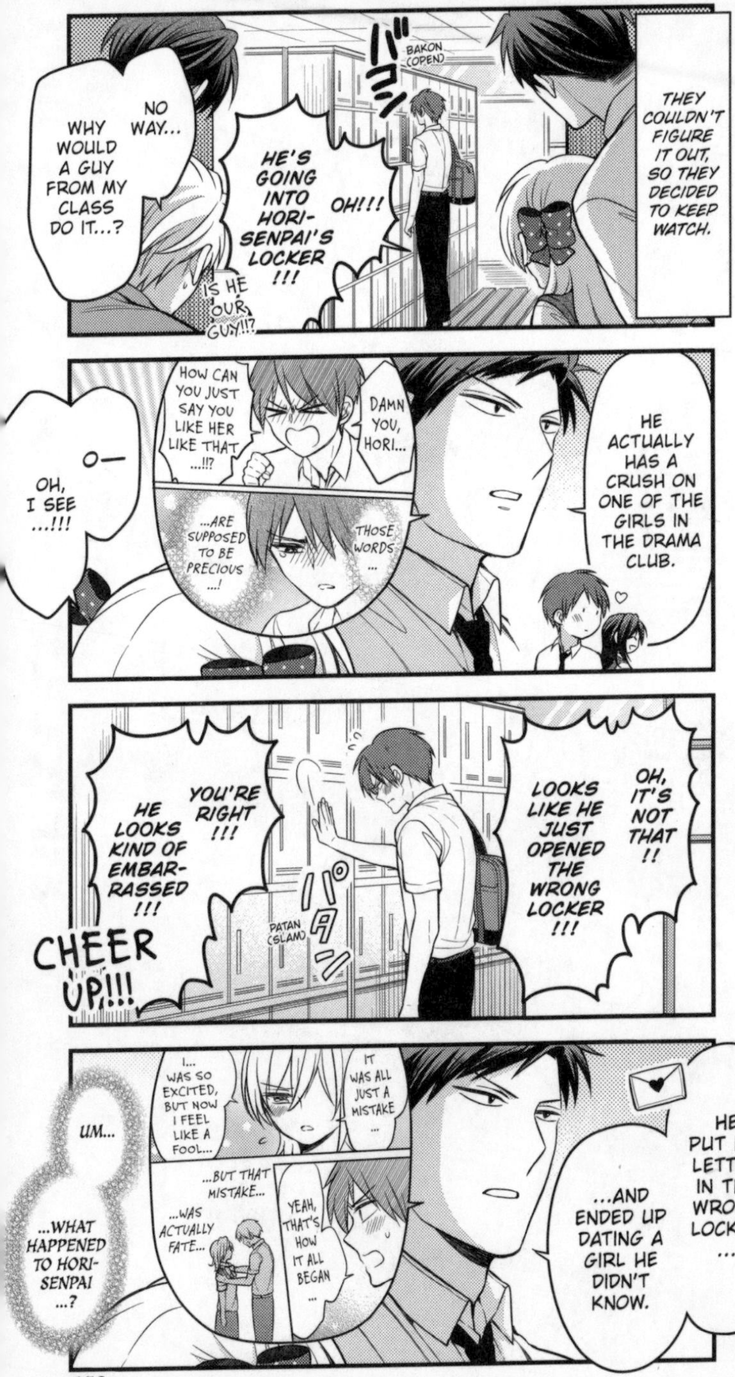
THEY COULDN'T FIGURE IT OUT, SO THEY DECIDED TO KEEP WATCH.
BAKON (OPEN)
OH!!! HE'S GOING INTO HORI-SENPAI'S LOCKER!!!
IS HE OUR GUY!!?
NO WAY... WHY WOULD A GUY FROM MY CLASS DO IT...?
HE ACTUALLY HAS A CRUSH ON ONE OF THE GIRLS IN THE DRAMA CLUB.
DAMN YOU, HORI...
HOW CAN YOU JUST SAY YOU LIKE HER LIKE THAT...!!?
THOSE WORDS...
...ARE SUPPOSED TO BE PRECIOUS...!
O— OH, I SEE...!!!
OH, IT'S NOT THAT!! LOOKS LIKE HE JUST OPENED THE WRONG LOCKER!!!
PATAN (SLAM)
YOU'RE RIGHT!!! HE LOOKS KIND OF EMBARRASSED!!!
CHEER UP!!!
HE PUT HIS LETTER IN THE WRONG LOCKER...
...AND ENDED UP DATING A GIRL HE DIDN'T KNOW.
IT WAS ALL JUST A MISTAKE...
I... WAS SO EXCITED, BUT NOW I FEEL LIKE A FOOL...
YEAH, THAT'S HOW IT ALL BEGAN...
...BUT THAT MISTAKE...
...WAS ACTUALLY FATE...
UM... ...WHAT HAPPENED TO HORI-SENPAI...?

THAT'S ONE THING, THIS IS ANOTHER

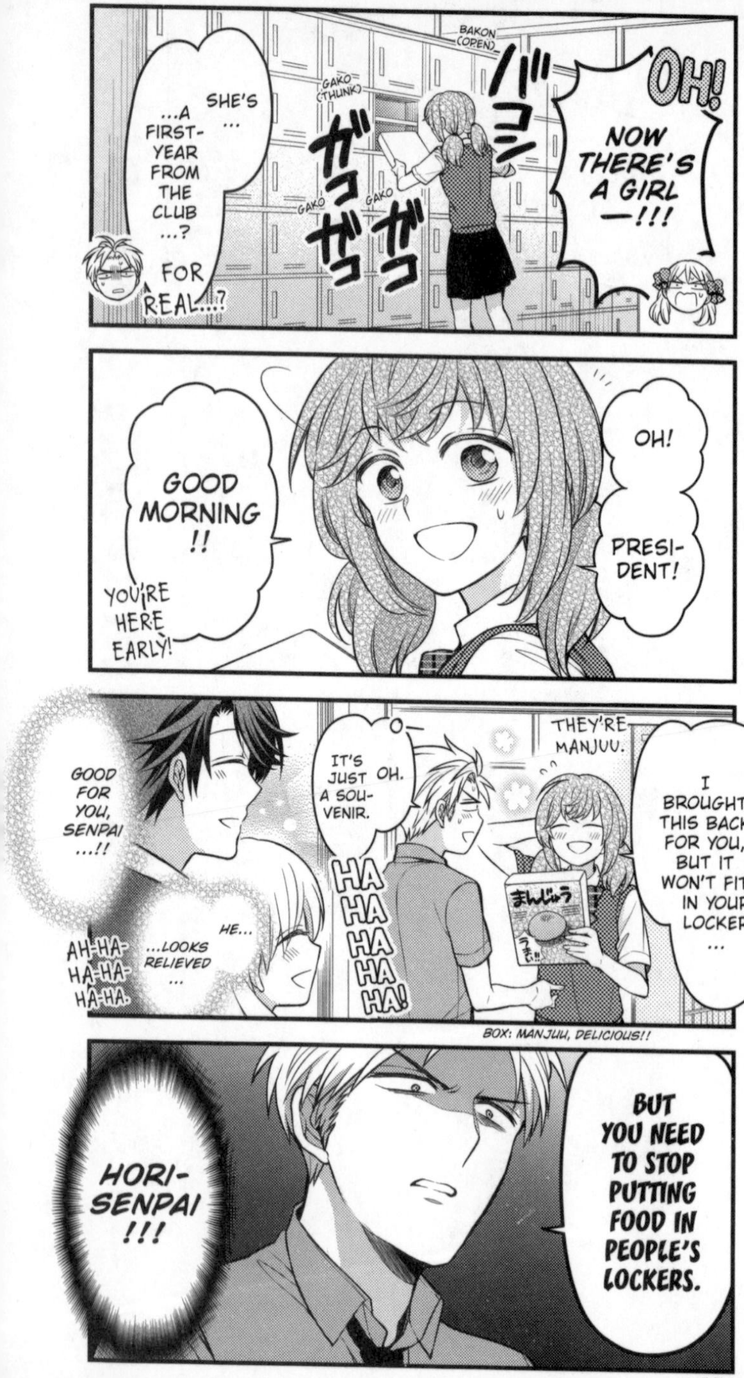

OH!
NOW THERE'S A GIRL—!!!
バコン
BAKON (OPEN)
ガコ
GAKO (THUNK)
ガコ ガコ
GAKO GAKO
SHE'S...
...A FIRST-YEAR FROM THE CLUB...?
FOR REAL...?
OH!
PRESIDENT!
GOOD MORNING!!
YOU'RE HERE EARLY!
UM...
SORRY!
I BROUGHT THIS BACK FOR YOU, BUT IT WON'T FIT IN YOUR LOCKER...
THEY'RE MANJUU.
O—
OH.
IT'S JUST A SOUVENIR.
まんじゅう
うまい!!
HAHAHAHAHA!
HE...
...LOOKS RELIEVED...
GOOD FOR YOU, SENPAI...!!
AH-HA-HA-HA-HA-HA.
BOX: MANJUU, DELICIOUS!!
BUT YOU NEED TO STOP PUTTING FOOD IN PEOPLE'S LOCKERS.
HORI-SENPAI!!!

HE DID SAY THAT

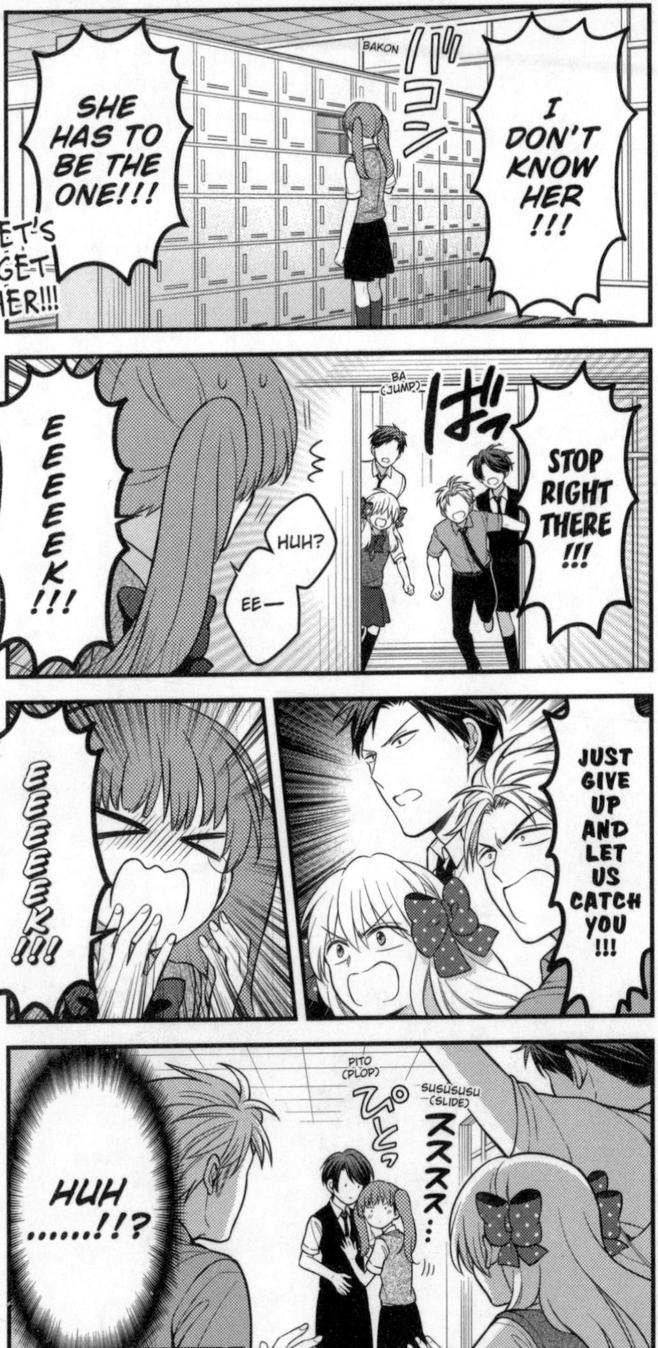

I DON'T KNOW HER!!!
BAKON
バコン
SHE HAS TO BE THE ONE!!!
LET'S GET HER!!!
STOP RIGHT THERE!!!
BA (JUMP)
ばっ
HUH?
EE—
EEEEEEK!!!
JUST GIVE UP AND LET US CATCH YOU!!!
EEEEEEEK!!!
SUSUSUSU (SLIDE)
ススス...
PITO (PLOP)
ぴとっ
HUH......!!?
HER HANDS HAD NOWHERE ELSE TO GO.

WHEN IT COMES TO HER CONFESSION...

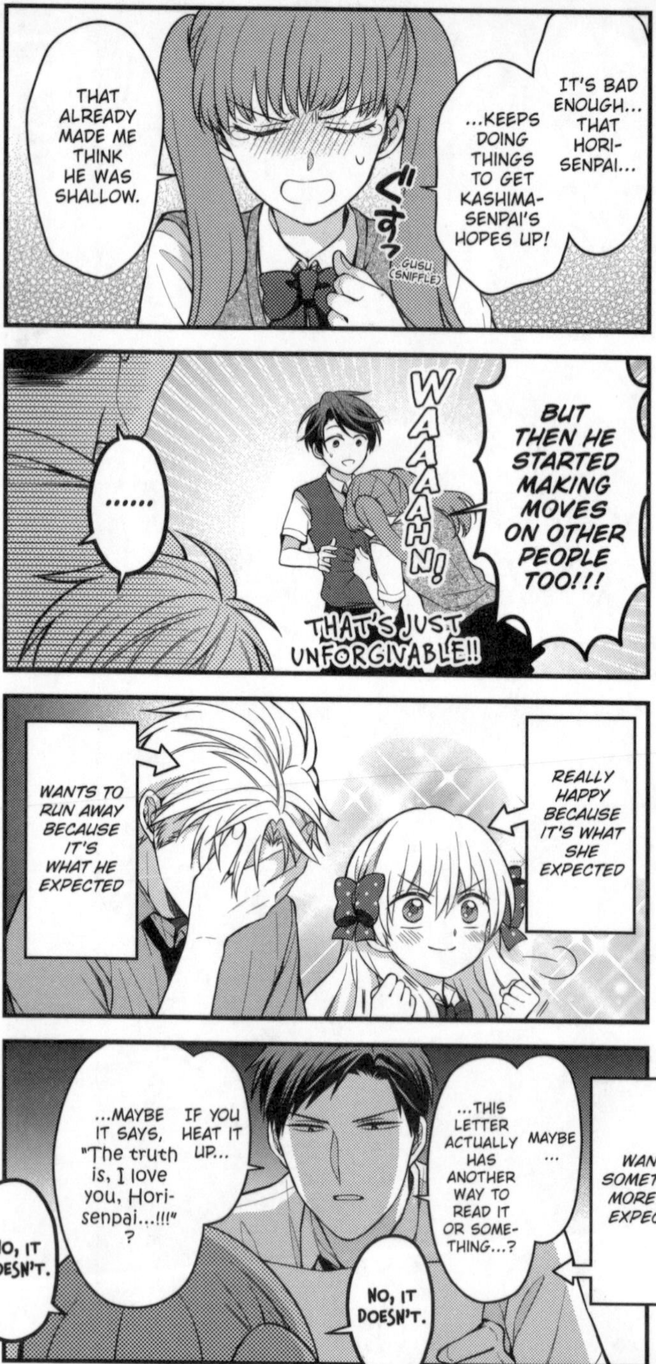

IT'S BAD ENOUGH... THAT HORI-SENPAI...
...KEEPS DOING THINGS TO GET KASHIMA-SENPAI'S HOPES UP!
ぐすっ
GUSU (SNIFFLE)
THAT ALREADY MADE ME THINK HE WAS SHALLOW.
BUT THEN HE STARTED MAKING MOVES ON OTHER PEOPLE TOO!!!
WAAAAAHN!
THAT'S JUST UNFORGIVABLE!!
......
REALLY HAPPY BECAUSE IT'S WHAT SHE EXPECTED
WANTS TO RUN AWAY BECAUSE IT'S WHAT HE EXPECTED
WANTS SOMETHING MORE UN-EXPECTED
MAYBE...
...THIS LETTER ACTUALLY HAS ANOTHER WAY TO READ IT OR SOME-THING...?
IF YOU HEAT IT UP...
...MAYBE IT SAYS, "The truth is, I love you, Hori-senpai...!!!"?
NO, IT DOESN'T.
NO, IT DOESN'T.

HE'S WORKING ON IT

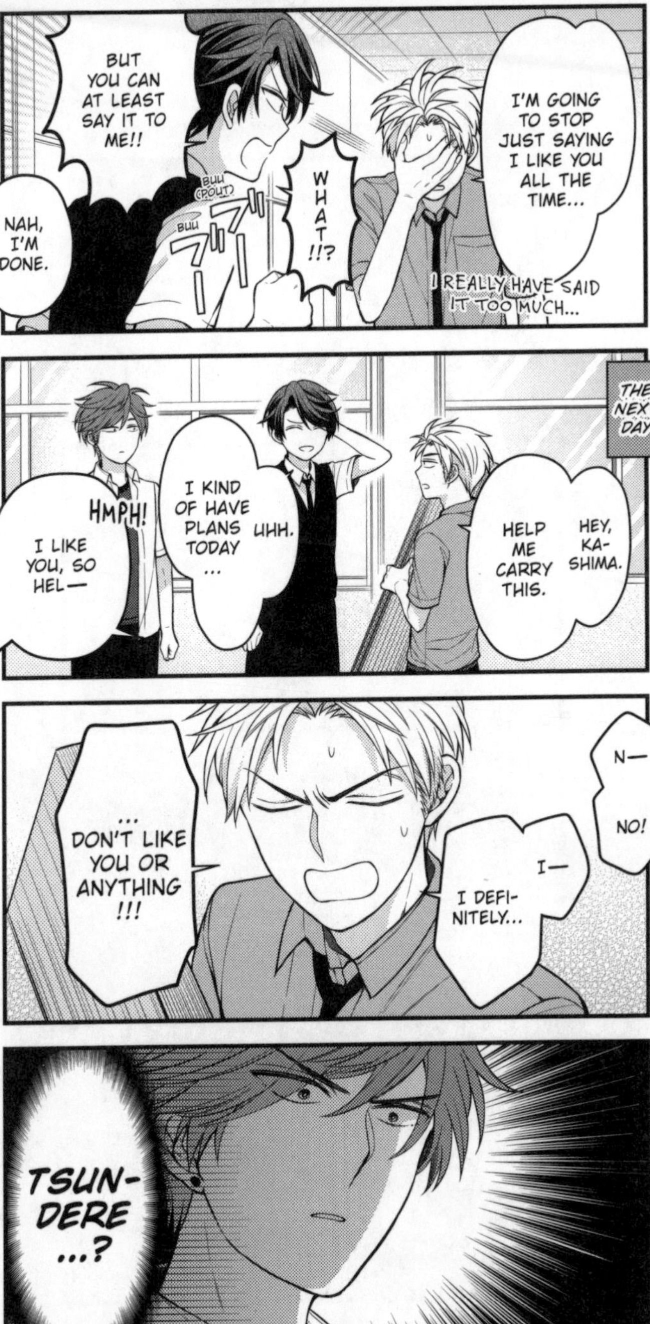

I'M GOING TO STOP JUST SAYING I LIKE YOU ALL THE TIME...
I REALLY HAVE SAID IT TOO MUCH...
WHAT!!?
BUU (POUT) BUU
BUT YOU CAN AT LEAST SAY IT TO ME!!
NAH, I'M DONE.
THE NEXT DAY
HEY, KA-SHIMA. HELP ME CARRY THIS.
UHH.
I KIND OF HAVE PLANS TODAY...
HMPH!
I LIKE YOU, SO HEL—
OH!
N— NO!
I— I DEFINITELY...
...DON'T LIKE YOU OR ANYTHING!!!
TSUN-DERE...?

SHE'LL TURN ANYTHING INTO AN OPPORTUNITY

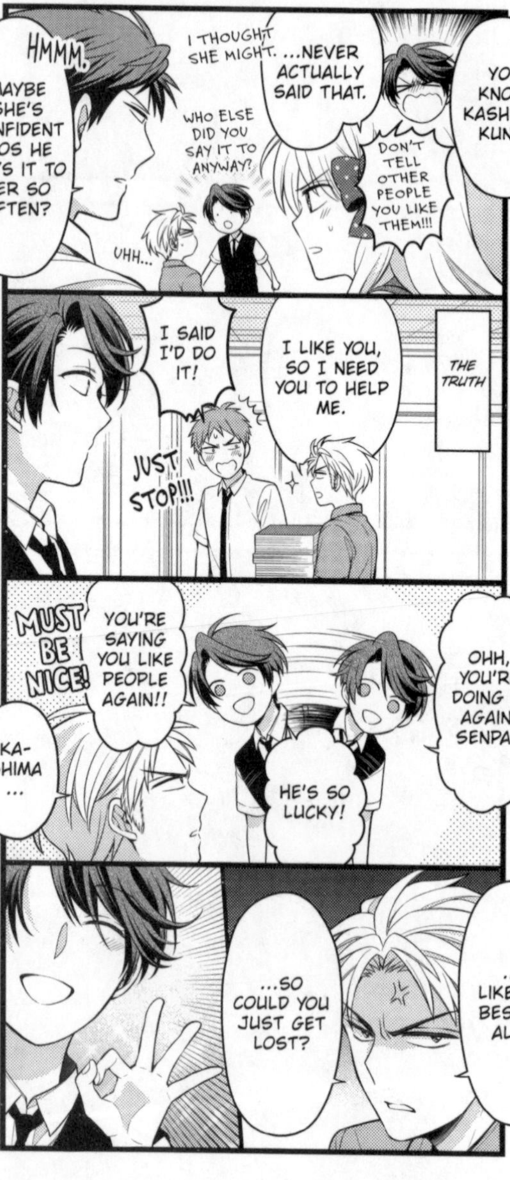

YOU KNOW, KASHIMA-KUN...
DON'T TELL OTHER PEOPLE YOU LIKE THEM!!!
...NEVER ACTUALLY SAID THAT.
I THOUGHT SHE MIGHT.
WHO ELSE DID YOU SAY IT TO ANYWAY?
HMMM.
MAYBE SHE'S CONFIDENT 'COS HE SAYS IT TO HER SO OFTEN?
UHH...
THE TRUTH
I LIKE YOU, SO I NEED YOU TO HELP ME.
I SAID I'D DO IT!
JUST STOP!!!
OHH, YOU'RE DOING IT AGAIN, SENPAI!
HE'S SO LUCKY!
YOU'RE SAYING YOU LIKE PEOPLE AGAIN!!
MUST BE NICE!
KA-SHIMA...
...I LIKE YOU BEST OF ALL...
...SO COULD YOU JUST GET LOST?

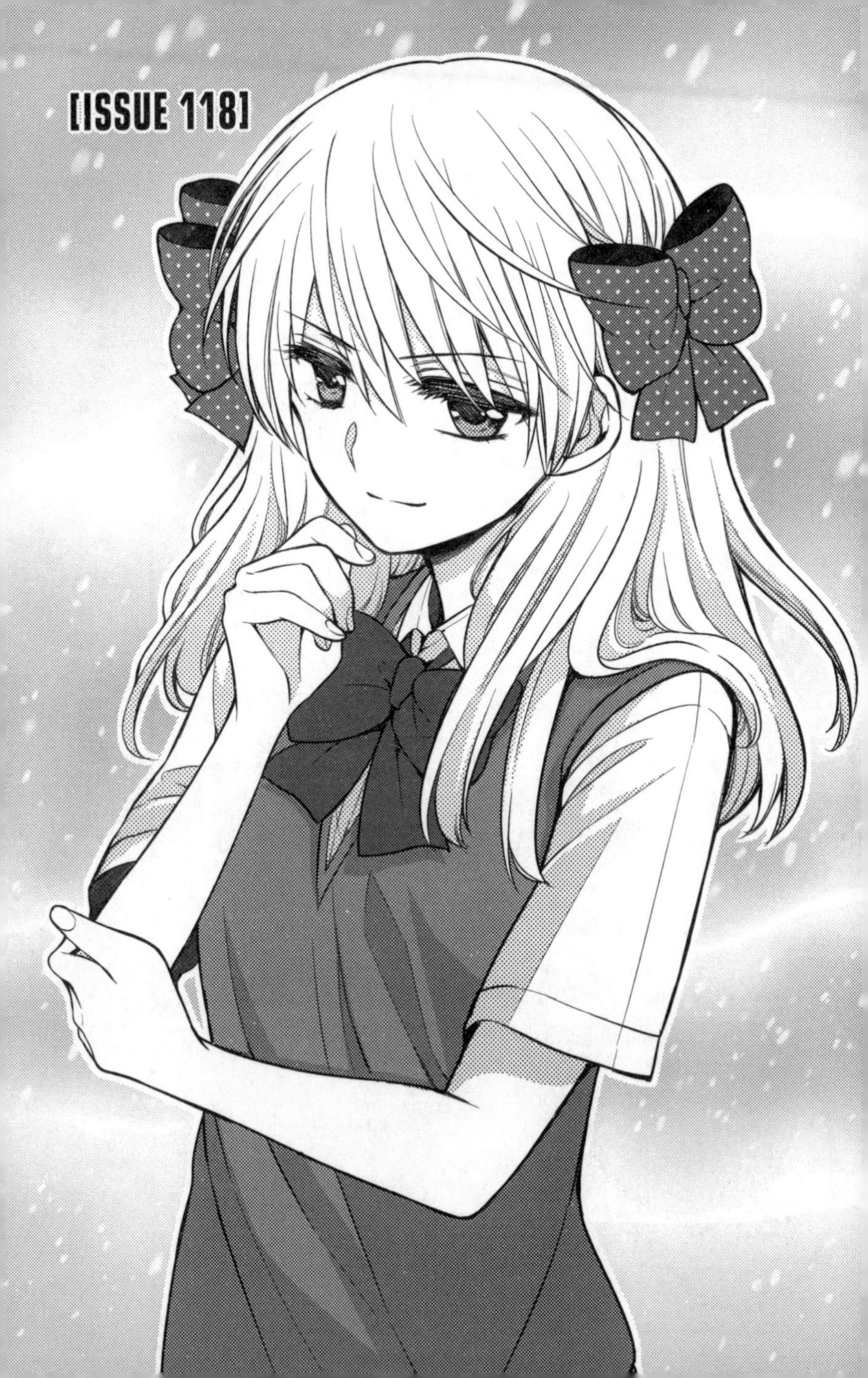
[ISSUE 118]

THE PROTAGONIST'S FEELINGS

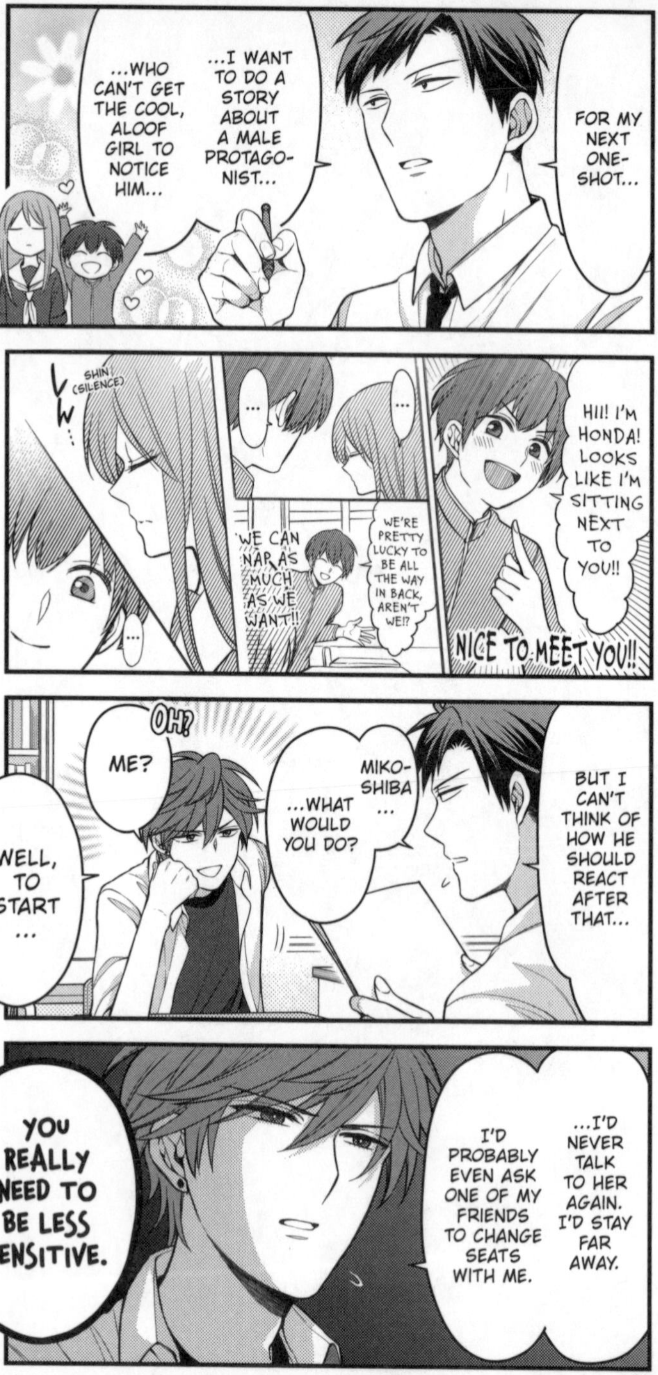

FOR MY NEXT ONE-SHOT...
...I WANT TO DO A STORY ABOUT A MALE PROTAGONIST...
...WHO CAN'T GET THE COOL, ALOOF GIRL TO NOTICE HIM...
HI!! I'M HONDA! LOOKS LIKE I'M SITTING NEXT TO YOU!!
NICE TO MEET YOU!!
...
...
WE'RE PRETTY LUCKY TO BE ALL THE WAY IN BACK, AREN'T WE!?
WE CAN NAP AS MUCH AS WE WANT!!
SHIN (SILENCE)
...
BUT I CAN'T THINK OF HOW HE SHOULD REACT AFTER THAT...
MIKOSHIBA...
...WHAT WOULD YOU DO?
OH?
ME?
WELL, TO START...
...I'D NEVER TALK TO HER AGAIN. I'D STAY FAR AWAY.
I'D PROBABLY EVEN ASK ONE OF MY FRIENDS TO CHANGE SEATS WITH ME.
YOU REALLY NEED TO BE LESS SENSITIVE.

ACTUAL EXPERIENCE

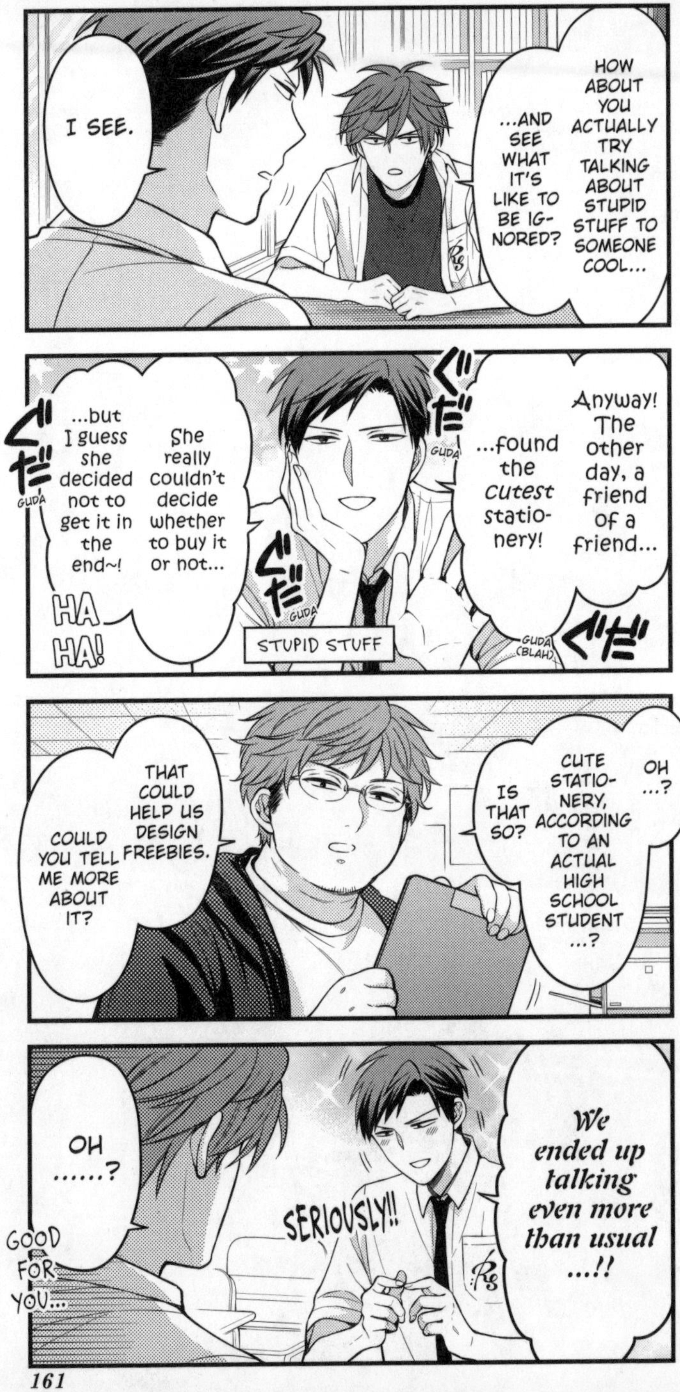

HOW ABOUT YOU ACTUALLY TRY TALKING ABOUT STUPID STUFF TO SOMEONE COOL...
...AND SEE WHAT IT'S LIKE TO BE IG-NORED?
I SEE.
Anyway! The other day, a friend of a friend...
GUDA (BLAH)
...found the cutest statio-nery!
GUDA
She really couldn't decide whether to buy it or not...
...but I guess she decided not to get it in the end~!
GUDA
GUDA
STUPID STUFF
HA HA!
OH ...?
CUTE STATIO-NERY, ACCORDING TO AN ACTUAL HIGH SCHOOL STUDENT ...?
IS THAT SO?
THAT COULD HELP US DESIGN FREEBIES.
COULD YOU TELL ME MORE ABOUT IT?
We ended up talking even more than usual ...!!
SERIOUSLY!!
OH ......?
GOOD FOR YOU...

MY DEAR FRIEND

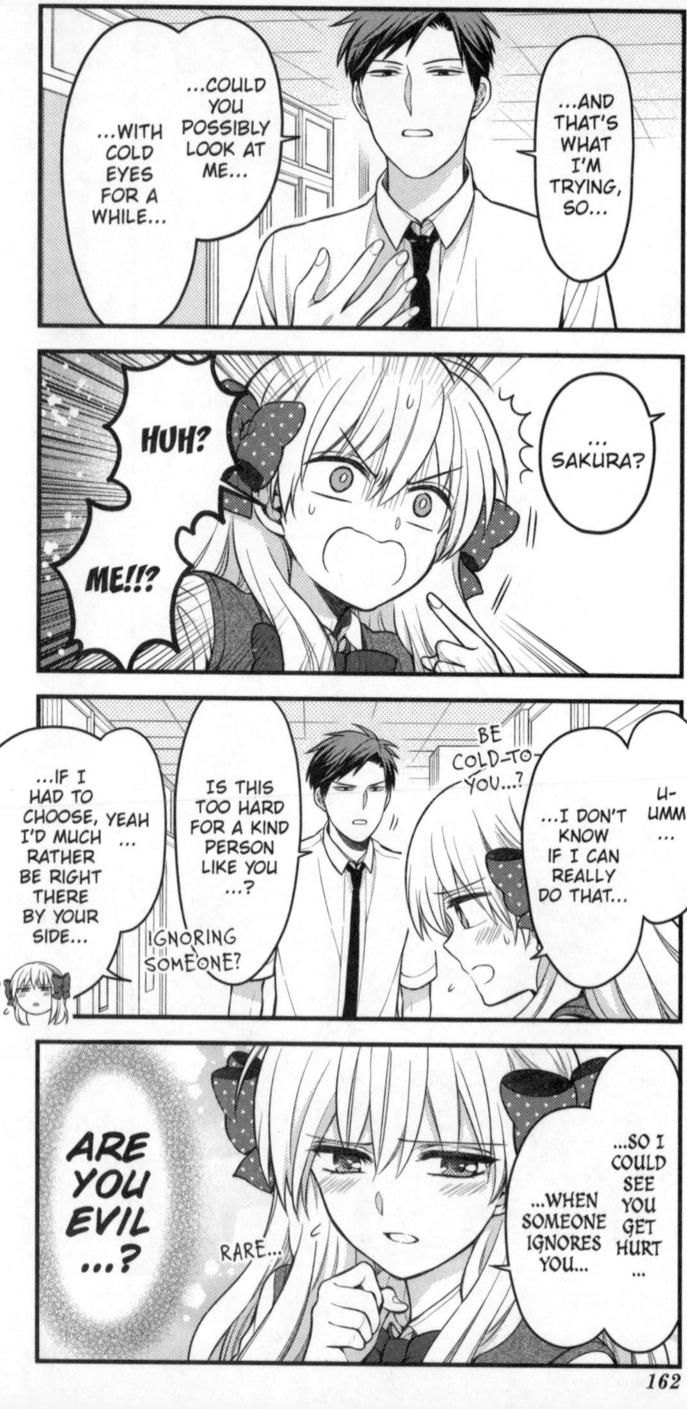

...AND THAT'S WHAT I'M TRYING, SO...
...COULD YOU POSSIBLY LOOK AT ME...
...WITH COLD EYES FOR A WHILE...
... SAKURA?
HUH?
ME!!?
U-UMM ...
...I DON'T KNOW IF I CAN REALLY DO THAT...
BE COLD TO YOU...?
IS THIS TOO HARD FOR A KIND PERSON LIKE YOU ...?
IGNORING SOMEONE?
YEAH ...
...IF I HAD TO CHOOSE, I'D MUCH RATHER BE RIGHT THERE BY YOUR SIDE...
...SO I COULD SEE YOU GET HURT ...
...WHEN SOMEONE IGNORES YOU...
RARE...
ARE YOU EVIL ...?

COOL SAKURA ①

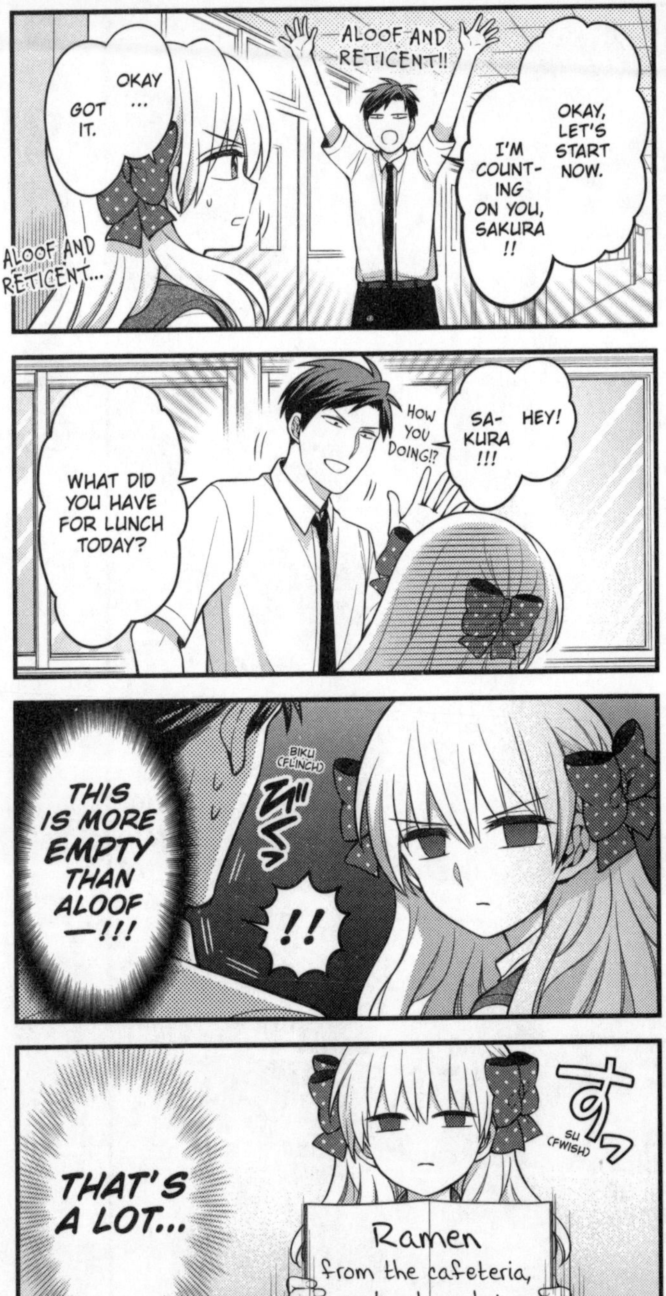
OKAY, LET'S START NOW.
I'M COUNTING ON YOU, SAKURA!!
ALOOF AND RETICENT!!
OKAY... GOT IT.
ALOOF AND RETICENT...
HEY! SAKURA!!!
HOW YOU DOING!?
WHAT DID YOU HAVE FOR LUNCH TODAY?
BIKU (FLINCH)
!!
THIS IS MORE EMPTY THAN ALOOF—!!!
すっ
SU (FWISH)
Ramen from the cafeteria, melon bread & a chocolate bun
THAT'S A LOT...

COOL SAKURA ②

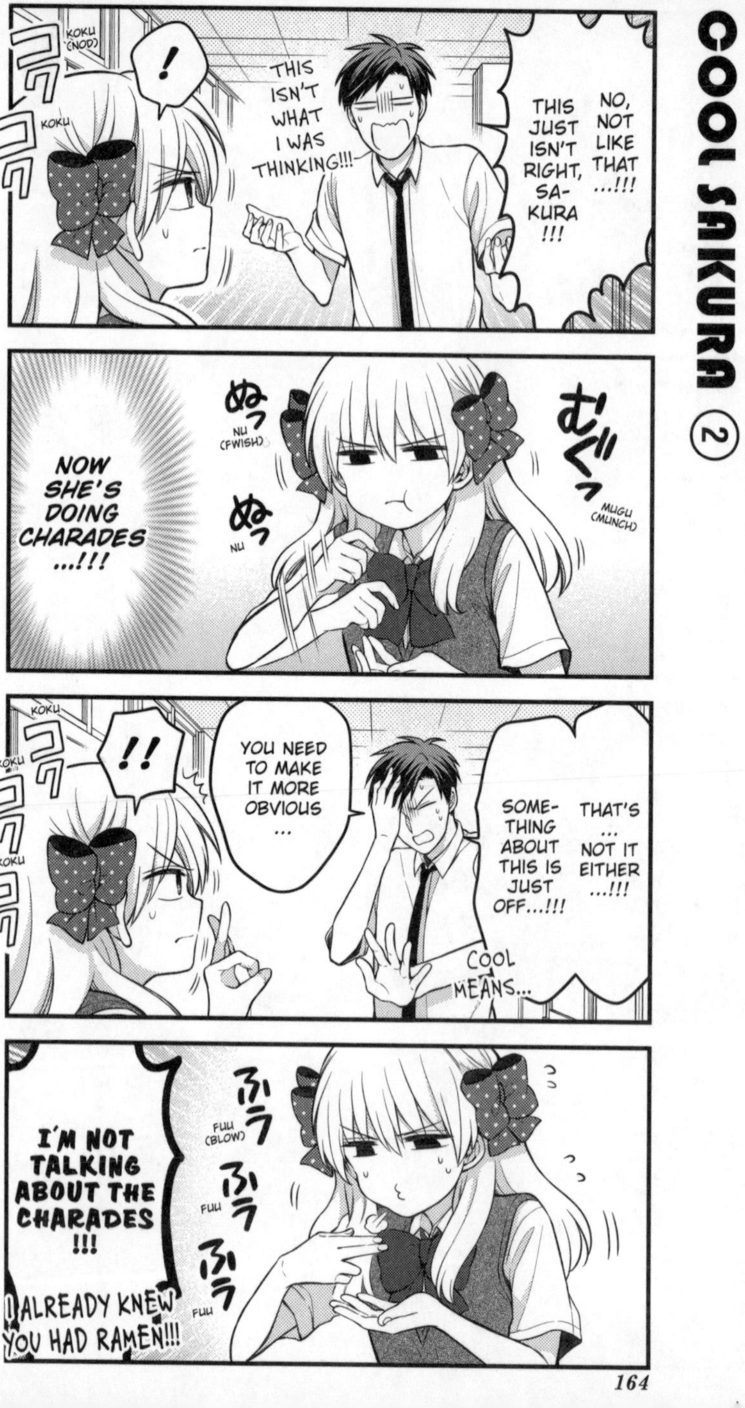
NO, NOT LIKE THAT ...!!!
THIS JUST ISN'T RIGHT, SA-KURA !!!
THIS ISN'T WHAT I WAS THINKING!!!
!
KOKU (NOD)
KOKU
MUGU (MUNCH)
NU (FWISH)
NU
NOW SHE'S DOING CHARADES ...!!!
THAT'S ... NOT IT EITHER ...!!!
SOME-THING ABOUT THIS IS JUST OFF...!!!
COOL MEANS...
YOU NEED TO MAKE IT MORE OBVIOUS ...
!!
KOKU
KOKU
KOKU
FUU (BLOW)
FUU
FUU
I'M NOT TALKING ABOUT THE CHARADES !!!
I ALREADY KNEW YOU HAD RAMEN!!!

YOUR PRESENCE LOOMS

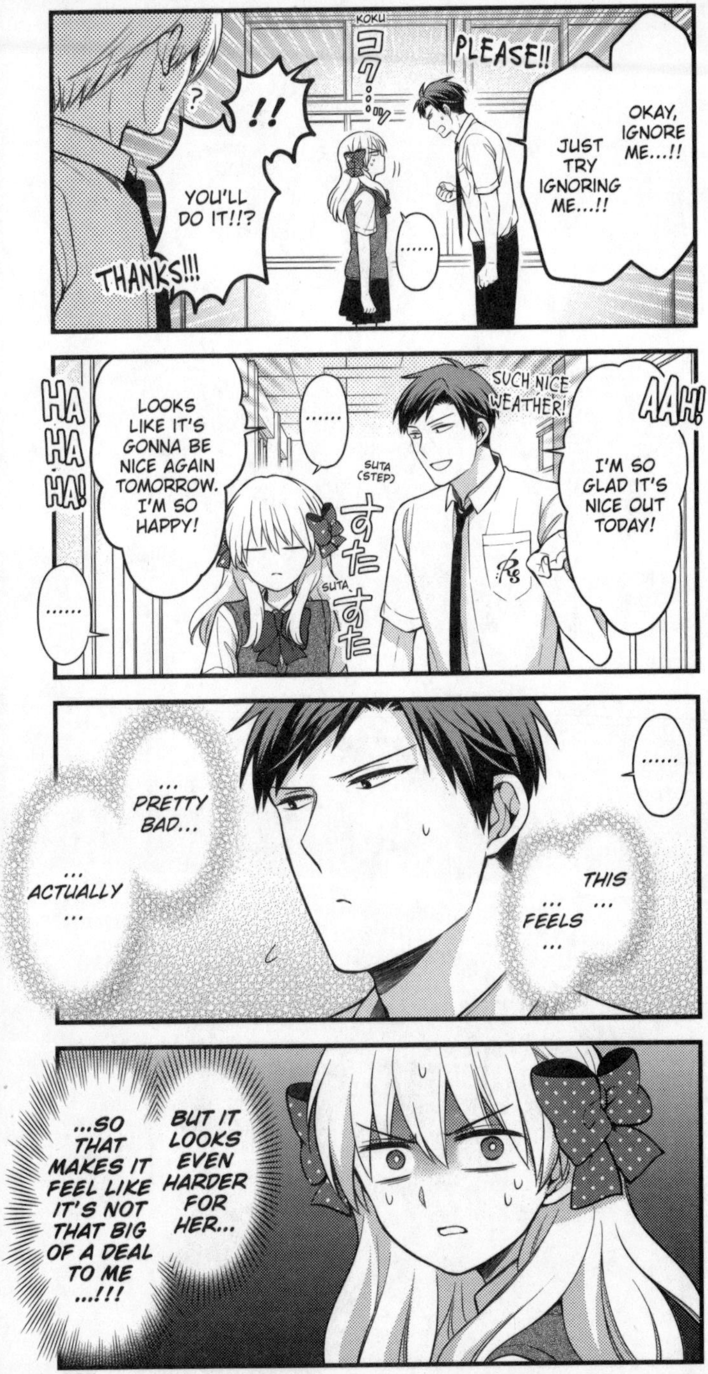
OKAY, IGNORE ME...!!
JUST TRY IGNORING ME...!!
PLEASE!!
KOKU
コク...ッ
......
!!
?
YOU'LL DO IT!!?
THANKS!!!
AAH!
I'M SO GLAD IT'S NICE OUT TODAY!
SUCH NICE WEATHER!
SUTA (STEP)
すた
SUTA
すた
......
LOOKS LIKE IT'S GONNA BE NICE AGAIN TOMORROW. I'M SO HAPPY!
HA HA HA!
......
......
THIS ... FEELS ...
... ACTUALLY ...
... PRETTY BAD...
BUT IT LOOKS EVEN HARDER FOR HER...
...SO THAT MAKES IT FEEL LIKE IT'S NOT THAT BIG OF A DEAL TO ME ...!!!

THE COOL GIRL

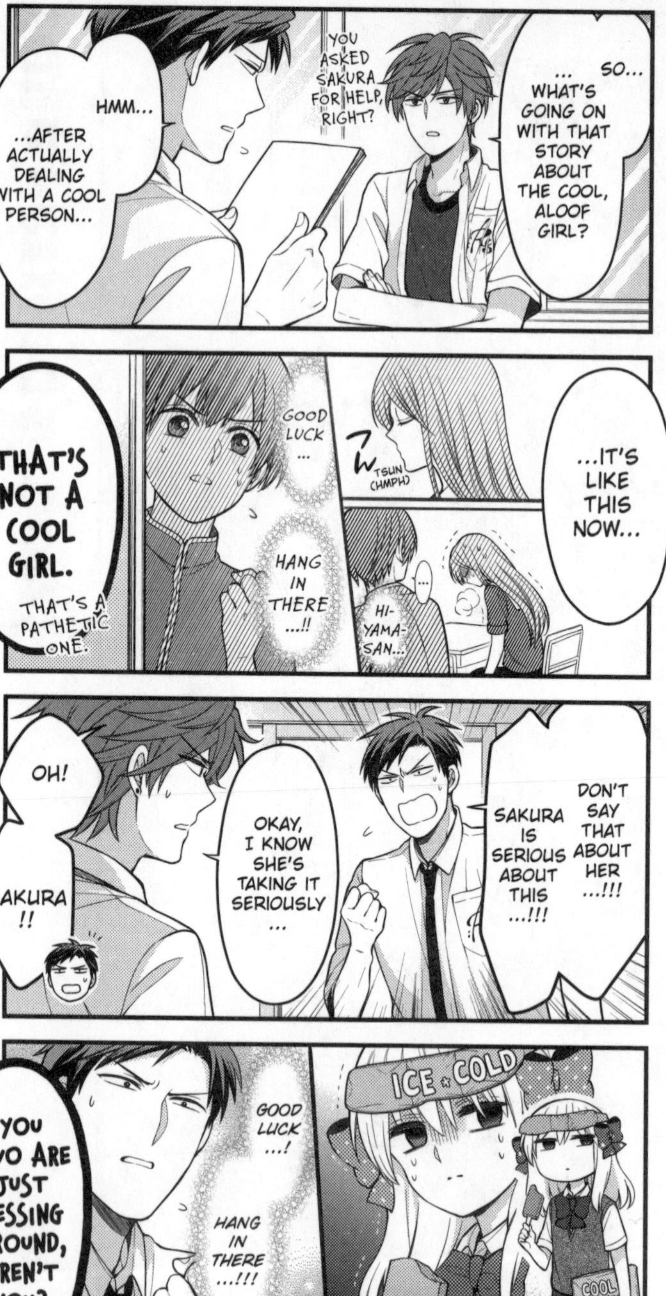

SO... ...WHAT'S GOING ON WITH THAT STORY ABOUT THE COOL, ALOOF GIRL?
YOU ASKED SAKURA FOR HELP, RIGHT?
HMM... ...AFTER ACTUALLY DEALING WITH A COOL PERSON...
...IT'S LIKE THIS NOW...
TSUN (HMPH)
GOOD LUCK ...
HANG IN THERE ...!!
...
HI-YAMA-SAN...
THAT'S NOT A COOL GIRL.
THAT'S A PATHETIC ONE.
DON'T SAY THAT ABOUT HER ...!!!
SAKURA IS SERIOUS ABOUT THIS ...!!!
OKAY, I KNOW SHE'S TAKING IT SERIOUSLY ...
OH!
SAKURA !!
ICE ☆ COLD
COOL PILLOW
GOOD LUCK ...!
HANG IN THERE ...!!!
YOU TWO ARE JUST MESSING AROUND, AREN'T YOU?

SERIOUS SAKURA

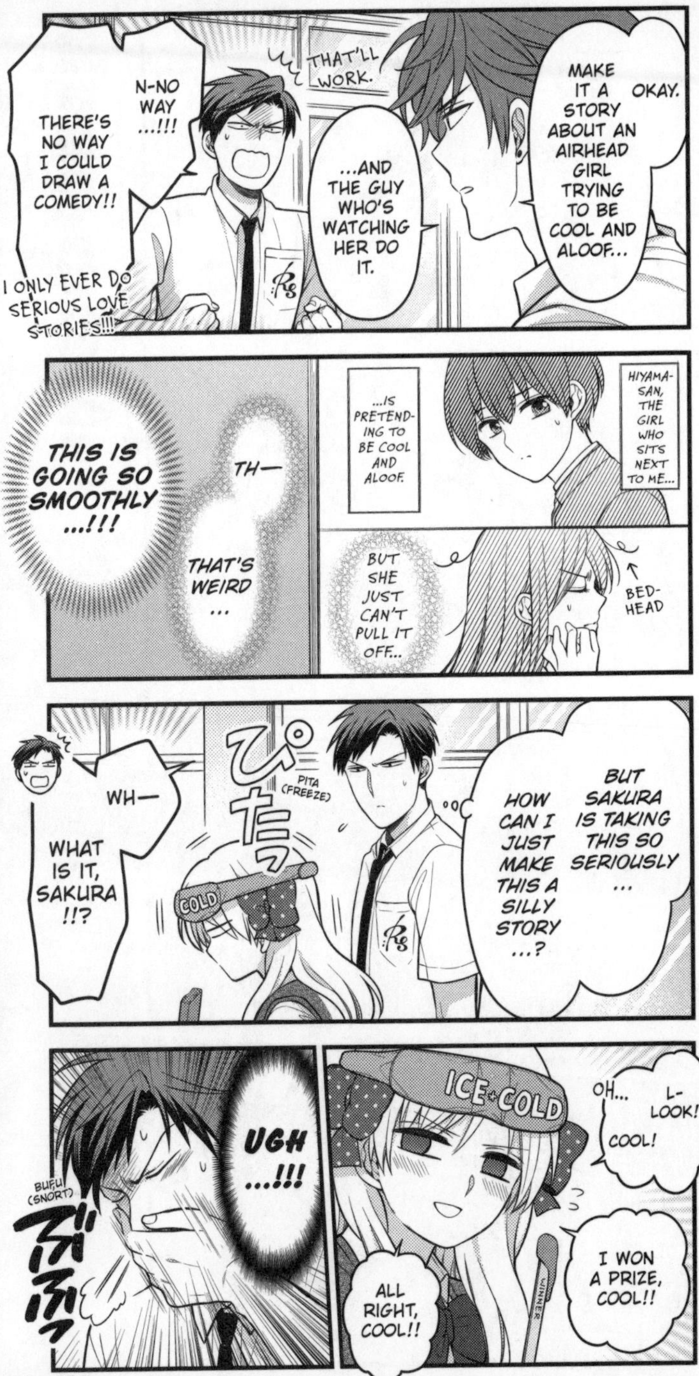
OKAY.
MAKE IT A STORY ABOUT AN AIRHEAD GIRL TRYING TO BE COOL AND ALOOF...
...AND THE GUY WHO'S WATCHING HER DO IT.
THAT'LL WORK.
N-NO WAY ...!!!
THERE'S NO WAY I COULD DRAW A COMEDY!!
I ONLY EVER DO SERIOUS LOVE STORIES!!!
HIYAMA-SAN, THE GIRL WHO SITS NEXT TO ME...
...IS PRETENDING TO BE COOL AND ALOOF.
BED-HEAD
BUT SHE JUST CAN'T PULL IT OFF...
TH—
THAT'S WEIRD...
THIS IS GOING SO SMOOTHLY...!!!
BUT SAKURA IS TAKING THIS SO SERIOUSLY...
HOW CAN I JUST MAKE THIS A SILLY STORY...?
PITA (FREEZE)
COLD
WH—
WHAT IS IT, SAKURA!!?
OH... L-LOOK! COOL!
ICE☆COLD
I WON A PRIZE, COOL!!
WINNER
ALL RIGHT, COOL!!
UGH...!!!
BUFU (SNORT)

HER REPERTOIRE

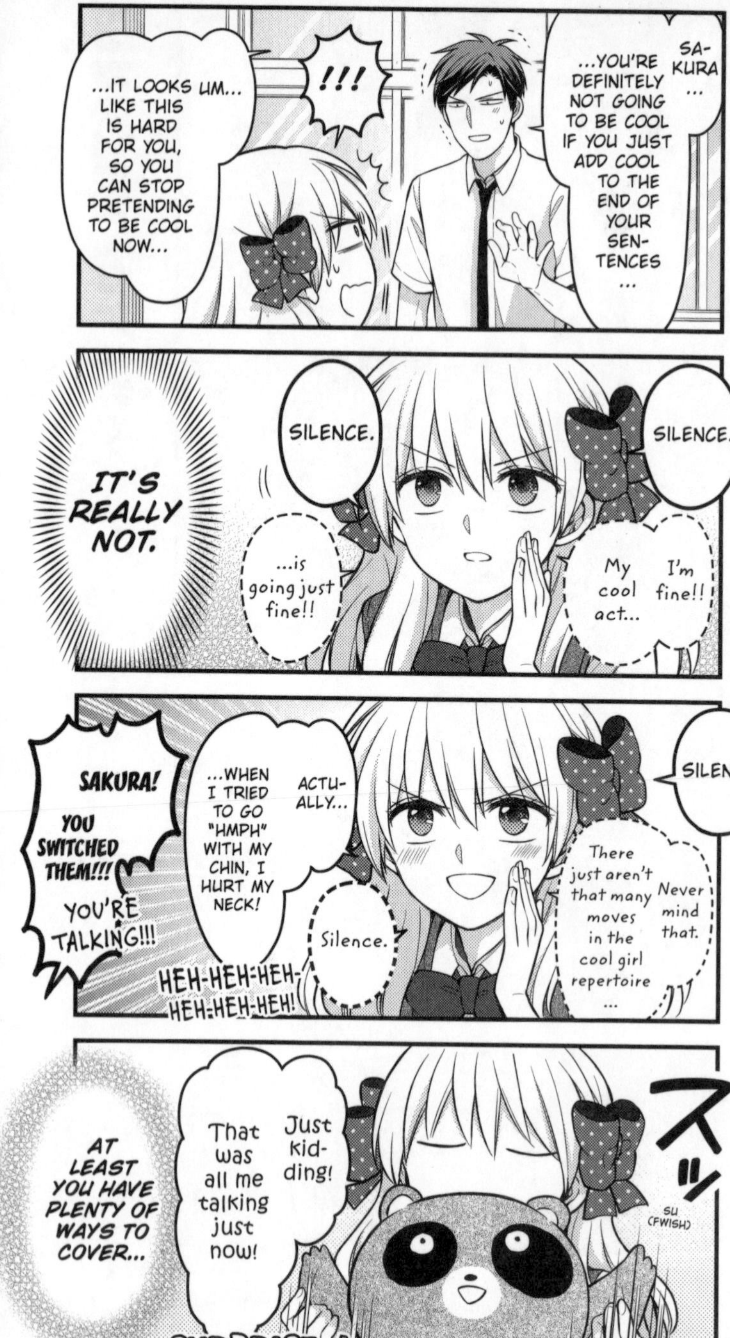

SA-KURA...
...YOU'RE DEFINITELY NOT GOING TO BE COOL IF YOU JUST ADD COOL TO THE END OF YOUR SEN-TENCES...
!!!
UM...
...IT LOOKS LIKE THIS IS HARD FOR YOU, SO YOU CAN STOP PRETENDING TO BE COOL NOW...
SILENCE.
I'm fine!!
My cool act...
SILENCE.
...is going just fine!!
IT'S REALLY NOT.
SILENCE.
Never mind that.
There just aren't that many moves in the cool girl repertoire...
ACTU-ALLY...
...WHEN I TRIED TO GO "HMPH" WITH MY CHIN, I HURT MY NECK!
Silence.
HEH-HEH-HEH-HEH-HEH-HEH!
SAKURA!
YOU SWITCHED THEM!!!
YOU'RE TALKING!!!
スッ
SU (FWISH)
Just kid-ding!
That was all me talking just now!
SURPRISE~!
AT LEAST YOU HAVE PLENTY OF WAYS TO COVER...

IRRATIONAL

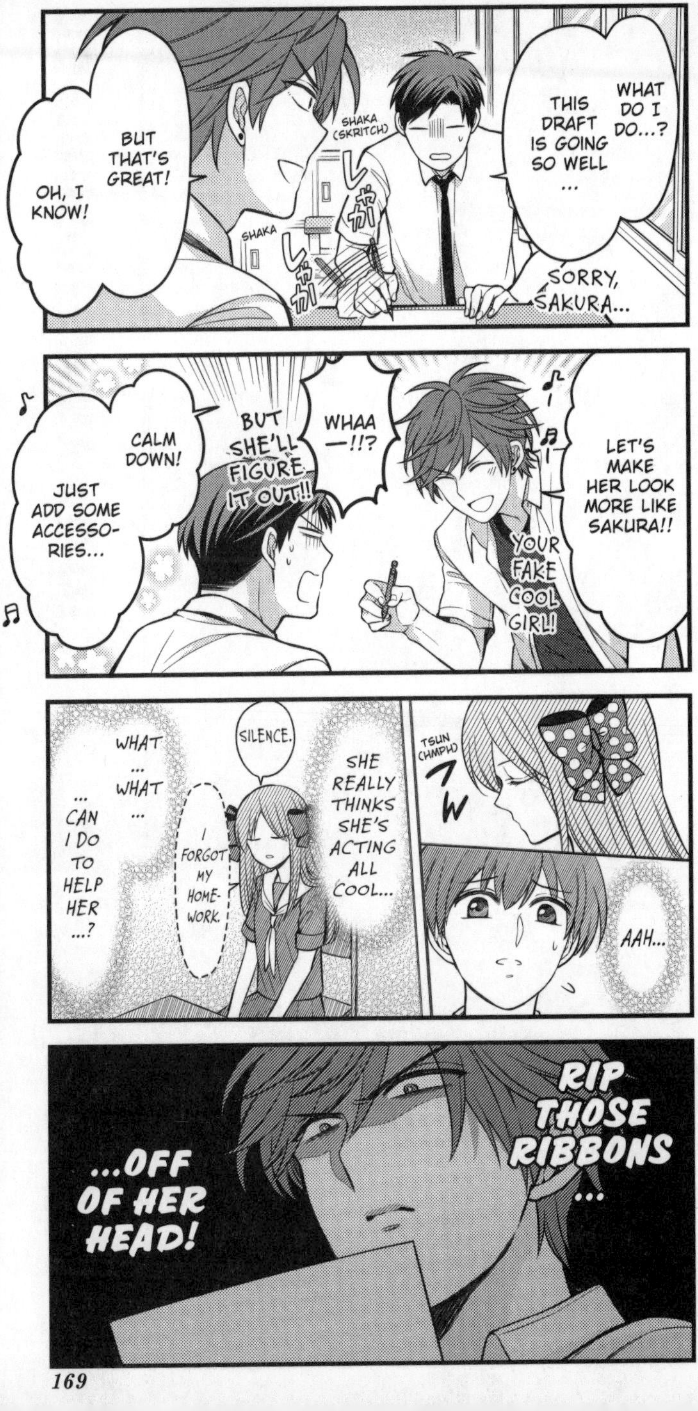
WHAT DO I DO...?
THIS DRAFT IS GOING SO WELL ...
SORRY, SAKURA...
SHAKA (SKRITCH)
SHAKA
BUT THAT'S GREAT!
OH, I KNOW!
LET'S MAKE HER LOOK MORE LIKE SAKURA!!
YOUR FAKE COOL GIRL!
WHAA—!!?
BUT SHE'LL FIGURE IT OUT!!
CALM DOWN!
JUST ADD SOME ACCESSO-RIES...
TSUN (HMPH)
AAH...
SHE REALLY THINKS SHE'S ACTING ALL COOL...
SILENCE.
I FORGOT MY HOME-WORK.
WHAT ... WHAT ...
... CAN I DO TO HELP HER ...?
RIP THOSE RIBBONS ...
...OFF OF HER HEAD!

AN UNNECESSARY ADDITION

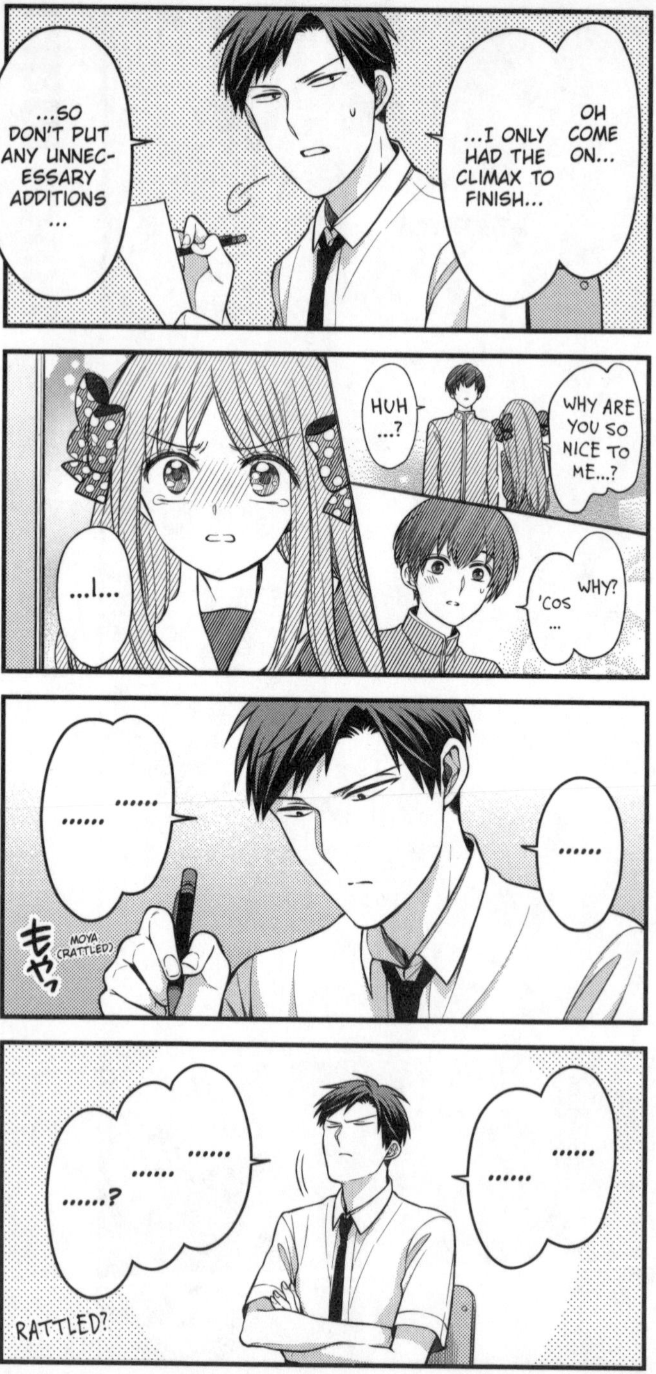

OH COME ON...
...I ONLY HAD THE CLIMAX TO FINISH...
...SO DON'T PUT ANY UNNEC-ESSARY ADDITIONS ...
WHY ARE YOU SO NICE TO ME...?
HUH ...?
WHY? 'COS ...
...I...
......
....
もやっ
MOYA (RATTLED)
....
....?
RATTLED?

I CAN'T SHOW ANYONE

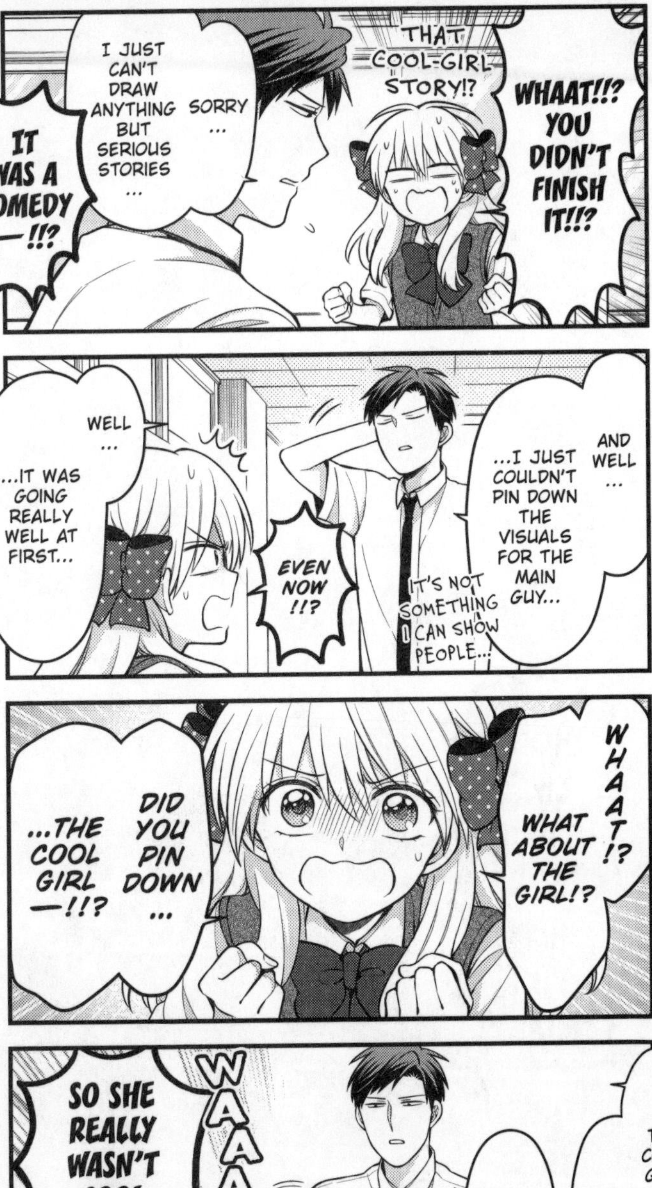
WHAAT!!? YOU DIDN'T FINISH IT!!?
THAT COOL-GIRL STORY!?
SORRY...
I JUST CAN'T DRAW ANYTHING BUT SERIOUS STORIES...
IT WAS A COMEDY—!!?
AND WELL...
...I JUST COULDN'T PIN DOWN THE VISUALS FOR THE MAIN GUY...
IT'S NOT SOMETHING I CAN SHOW PEOPLE...
EVEN NOW!!?
WELL...
...IT WAS GOING REALLY WELL AT FIRST...
WHAAT!?
WHAT ABOUT THE GIRL!?
DID YOU PIN DOWN...
...THE COOL GIRL—!!?
THE COOL GIRL...
WELL... YEAH.
SHE WAS ADORABLE.
YEP.
WAAAAAHN!!
SO SHE REALLY WASN'T COOL AFTER ALL!!!
I HAD THE FEELING SHE WASN'T!!!

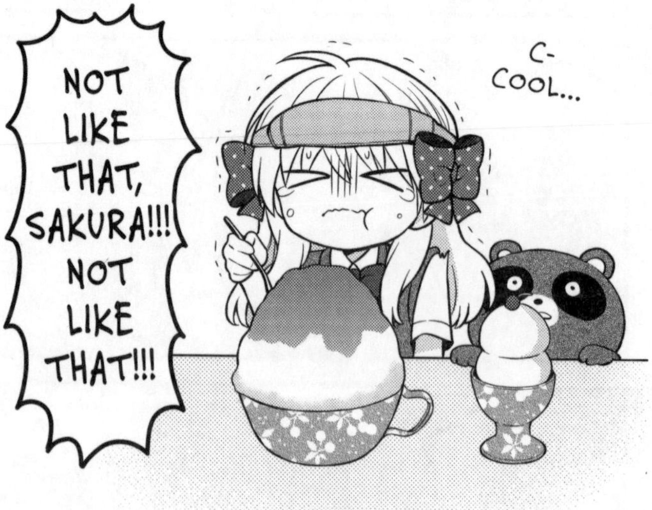
C-COOL...
NOT LIKE THAT, SAKURA!!! NOT LIKE THAT!!!

[Extra]

A SERIOUS DEVELOPMENT?

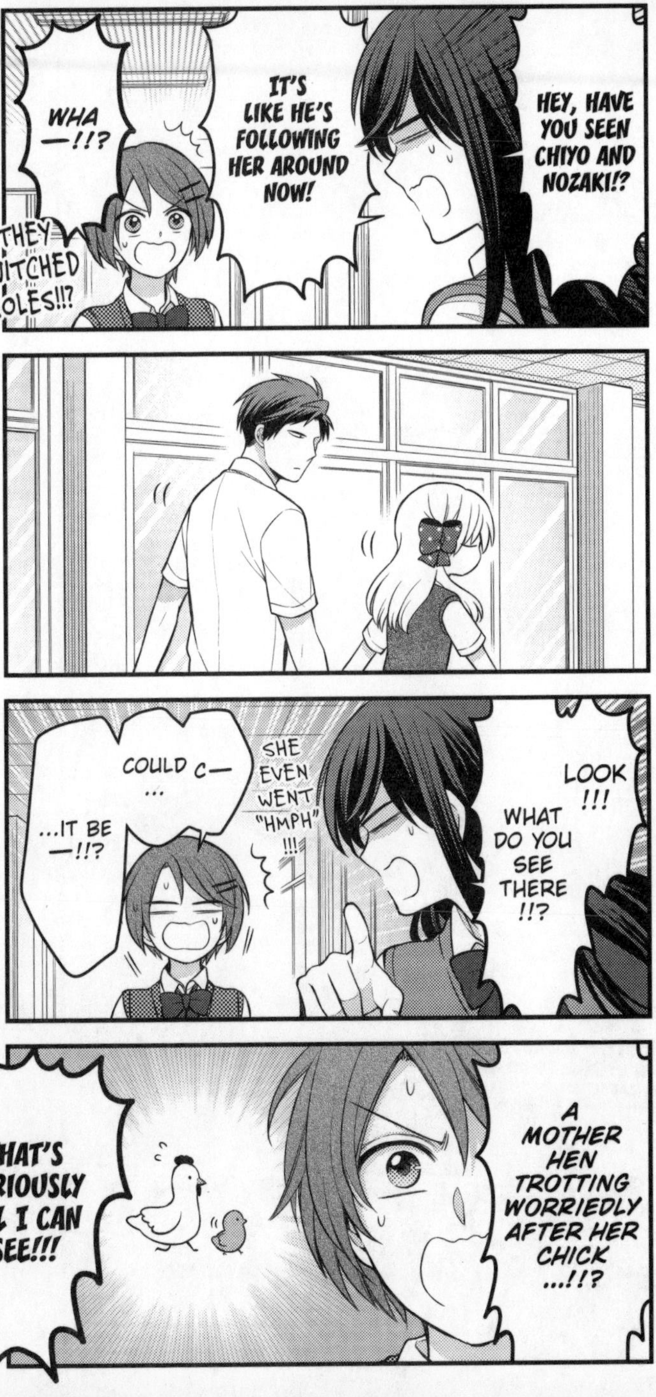
HEY, HAVE YOU SEEN CHIYO AND NOZAKI!?
IT'S LIKE HE'S FOLLOWING HER AROUND NOW!
WHA—!!?
THEY SWITCHED ROLES!!?
LOOK!!!
WHAT DO YOU SEE THERE!!?
SHE EVEN WENT "HMPH"!!!
COULD C—...
...IT BE—!!?
A MOTHER HEN TROTTING WORRIEDLY AFTER HER CHICK...!!?
THAT'S SERIOUSLY ALL I CAN SEE!!!

[Extra]

ANOTHER COOL TRY!

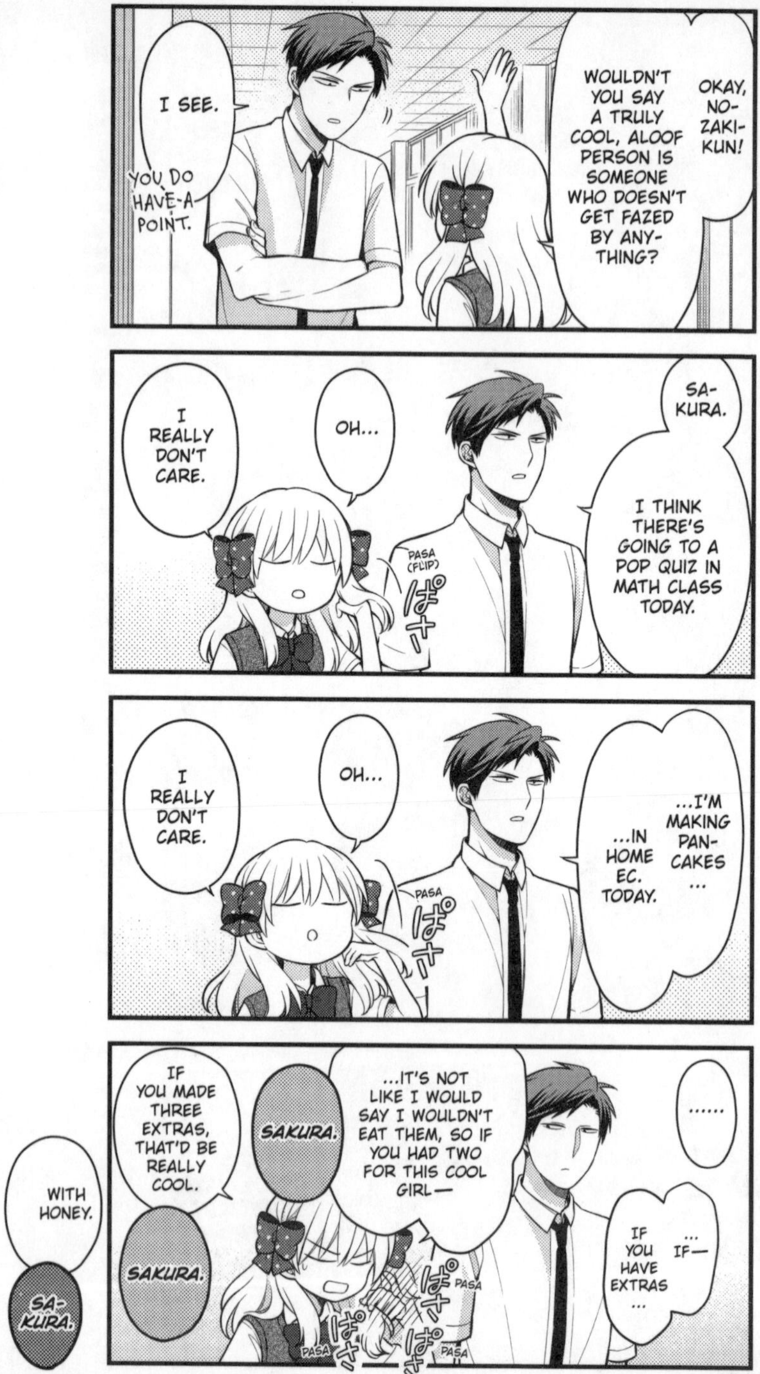
OKAY, NO-ZAKI-KUN!
WOULDN'T YOU SAY A TRULY COOL, ALOOF PERSON IS SOMEONE WHO DOESN'T GET FAZED BY ANY-THING?
I SEE.
YOU DO HAVE A POINT.
SA-KURA.
I THINK THERE'S GOING TO A POP QUIZ IN MATH CLASS TODAY.
PASA (FLIP)
ぱさ
OH...
I REALLY DON'T CARE.
...I'M MAKING PAN-CAKES ...
...IN HOME EC. TODAY.
PASA
ぱさ
OH...
I REALLY DON'T CARE.
......
... IF—
IF YOU HAVE EXTRAS ...
...IT'S NOT LIKE I WOULD SAY I WOULDN'T EAT THEM, SO IF YOU HAD TWO FOR THIS COOL GIRL—
SAKURA.
IF YOU MADE THREE EXTRAS, THAT'D BE REALLY COOL.
SAKURA.
WITH HONEY.
SA-KURA.
PASA
PASA
PASA

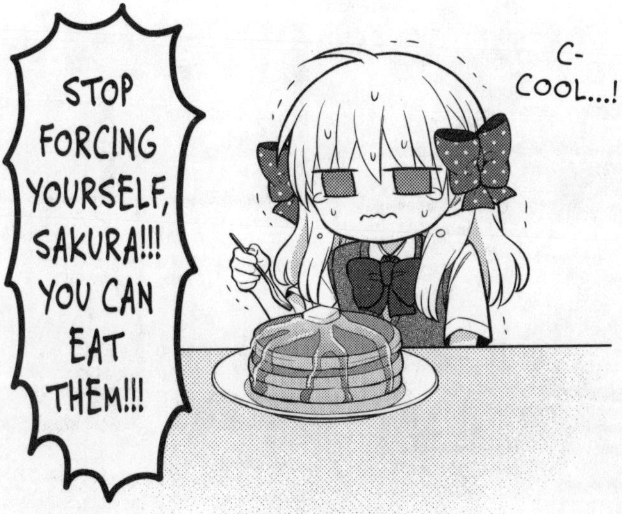
C-COOL...!
STOP FORCING YOURSELF, SAKURA!!! YOU CAN EAT THEM!!!

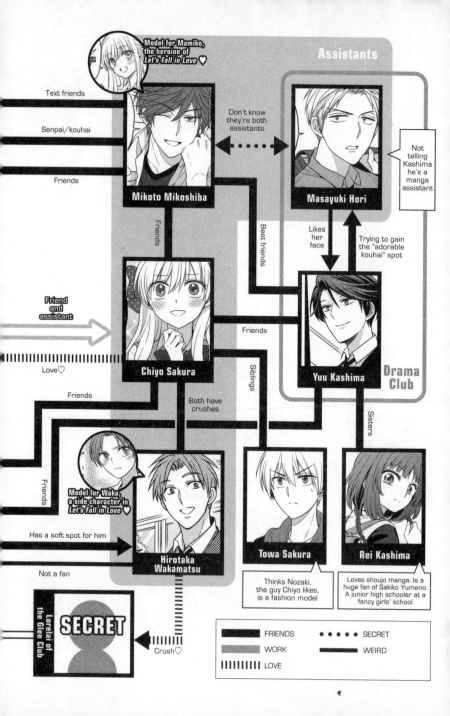

Model for Mamiko, the heroine of *Let's Fall in Love* ♡

Assistants

Text friends

Senpai/kouhai

Friends

Mikoto Mikoshiba

Don't know they're both assistants

Masayuki Hori

Not telling Kashima he's a manga assistant

Friends

Best friends

Likes her face

Trying to gain the "adorable kouhai" spot

Friend and assistant

Love♡

Chiyo Sakura

Friends

Yuu Kashima

Drama Club

Friends

Siblings

Both have crushes

Sisters

Friends

Model for Waka, a side character in *Let's Fall in Love* ♡

Has a soft spot for him

Hirotaka Wakamatsu

Towa Sakura

Rei Kashima

Not a fan

Thinks Nozaki, the guy Chiyo likes, is a fashion model

Loves shoujo manga. Is a huge fan of Sakiko Yumeno. A junior high schooler at a fancy girls' school

SECRET

Lorelai of the Glee Club

Crush♡

	FRIENDS	•••• SECRET
	WORK	— WEIRD
‖‖‖‖‖ LOVE		

Relationship Chart

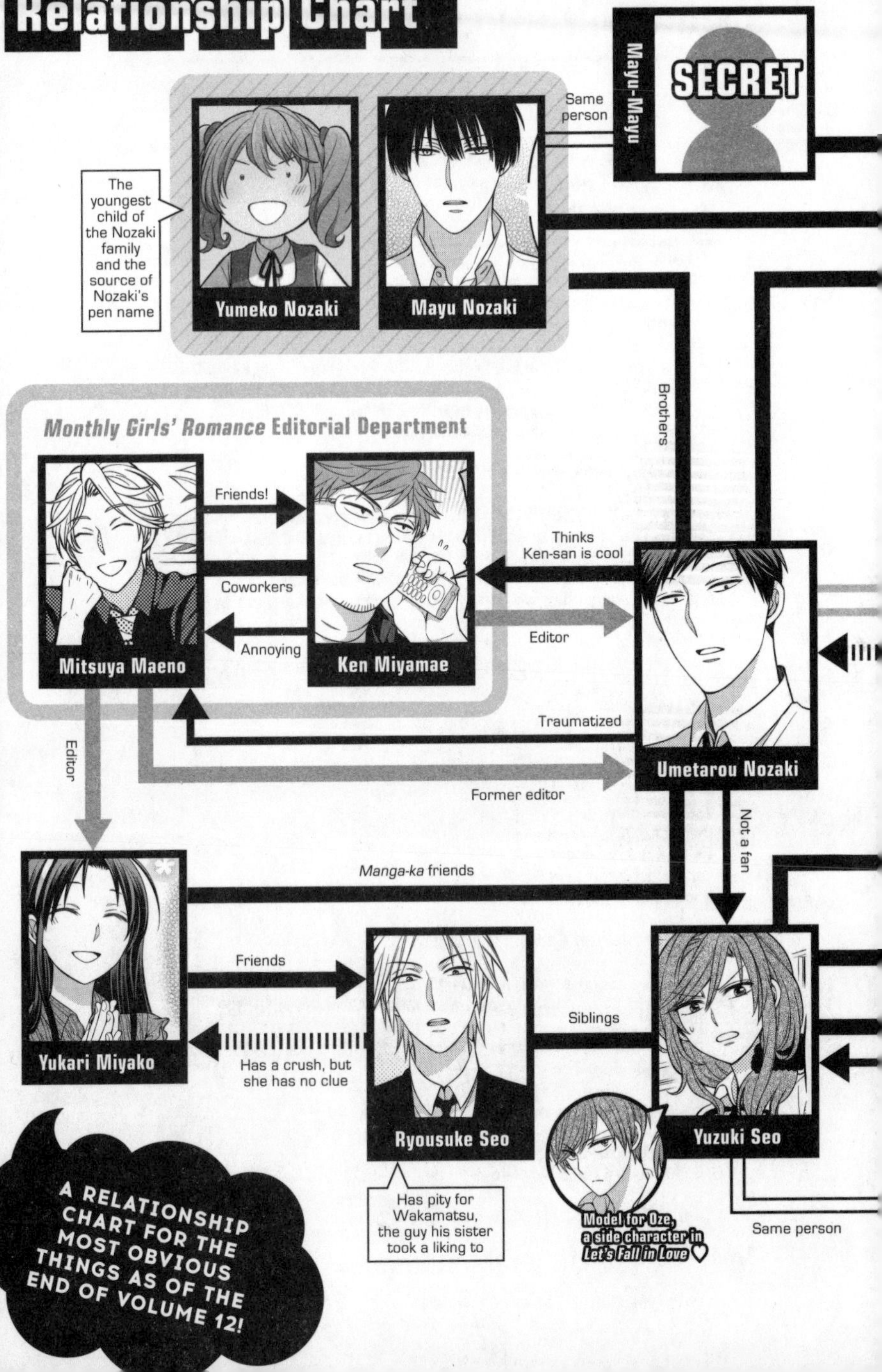
Mayu-Mayu
SECRET
Same person
The youngest child of the Nozaki family and the source of Nozaki's pen name
Yumeko Nozaki
Mayu Nozaki
Brothers
Monthly Girls' Romance Editorial Department
Friends!
Coworkers
Annoying
Mitsuya Maeno
Ken Miyamae
Thinks Ken-san is cool
Editor
Traumatized
Umetarou Nozaki
Editor
Former editor
Not a fan
Manga-ka friends
Friends
Siblings
Yukari Miyako
Has a crush, but she has no clue
Ryousuke Seo
Yuzuki Seo
Has pity for Wakamatsu, the guy his sister took a liking to
Model for Oze, a side character in Let's Fall in Love♡
Same person
A RELATIONSHIP CHART FOR THE MOST OBVIOUS THINGS AS OF THE END OF VOLUME 12!

MONTHLY GIRLS' NOZAKI-KUN 12

Izumi Tsubaki

Translation: Leighann Harvey
Lettering: Lys Blakeslee

GEKKAN SHOJO NOZAKI KUN Volume 12 © 2020 Izumi Tsubaki / SQUARE ENIX CO., LTD. First published in Japan in 2020 by SQUARE ENIX CO., LTD. English translation rights arranged with SQUARE ENIX CO., LTD. and Yen Press, LLC through Tuttle-Mori Agency, Inc.

English translation © 2021 by SQUARE ENIX CO., LTD.

Yen Press
150 West 30th Street, 19th Floor
New York, NY 10001

Visit us!
📖 yenpress.com
📖 facebook.com/yenpress
📖 twitter.com/yenpress
📖 yenpress.tumblr.com
📖 instagram.com/yenpress

First Yen Press Print Edition: May 2021

Yen Press is an imprint of Yen Press, LLC.
The Yen Press name and logo are trademarks of Yen Press, LLC.

Library of Congress Control Number: 2015952610

ISBN: 978-1-9753-2336-3 (paperback)
      978-1-9753-2337-0 (ebook)

10 9 8 7 6 5 4 3 2 1

WOR

Printed in the United States of America